THE ENCYCLOPEDIA OF
WEAPONRY

THE ENCYCLOPEDIA OF
WEAPONRY

IAN V HOGG

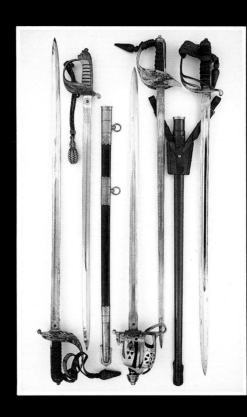

GUINNESS PUBLISHING

A QUARTO BOOK

Published in Great Britain by
Guinness Publishing Ltd.,
33 London Road, Enfield, Middlesex

"Guinness" is a registered trademark of
Guinness Publishing Ltd.

First published 1992
Copyright © 1992 by Quarto Publishing plc

ISBN 0-85112-521-2

A catalogue record for this book is available from the British Library.

This book was designed and produced by
Quarto Publishing plc
The Old Brewery, 6 Blundell Street
London N7 9BH

Senior Editor: Cathy Meeus
Copy Editors: Adrian Gilbert, Michael March, Fred Milson
Senior Art Editor: Philip Gilderdale
Designer: Hugh Schermuly
Art Assistant: Kerry Davies
Picture Managers: Rebecca Horsewood, Sarah Risley
Picture Researcher: Anne-Marie Ehrlich
Illustrator: Guy Smith
Art Director: Moira Clinch
Publishing Director: Janet Slingsby

With special thanks to Dave Kemp, Teddy Neville, Jane Parker and Katie Preston.

Typeset in Great Britain by Typestyles (London) Ltd., Harlow.

Manufactured in Hong Kong by Regent Publishing Services Ltd.

Printed in Hong Kong by Leefung Asco Printers Ltd.

CONTENTS

INTRODUCTION

From the first clubs and spears of early humanity to the "smart" bombs and laser technology of today, human history has been inextricably bound up with the twin stories of war and the weaponry used to wage it. Sometimes, the weaponry has been produced as a response to the demands of conflict; sometimes, the invention and development of new offensive weapons has been the catalyst that has led to war. Whichever the case, the unfortunate fact is that, since pre-historic times, warfare has been an endemic part of the human condition.

This encyclopedia makes no attempt to list every weapon ever developed – such a listing would be an arid catalogue and, in the end, not that informative. What it does is to chart the chronological story of weaponry, from the first weapons up to the present, looking at groups of weapons as a whole and then examining key developments in detail. As often as not, these are linked to the ways in which weapons were and are used as much as to the weapons themselves. Take gunpowder, for instance. Most people would agree that its invention was a vital milestone in weapons technology – but there is far more to the story than that. In fact, it took a long time for battlefield tactics to change in response to the birth of firearms. Early guns were primitive devices, the technology of the times being capable of developing and refining them only very slowly. Until this happened, battlefield tactics remained unchanged; it was not considered worth developing new ones to replace the tactics that had served so well for centuries.

This example leads to two further considerations – the innate conservatism of the military mind and the impact of general technological development on that of weaponry and vice versa. As far as the first is concerned, we only have to look at the stubborn survival of the belief that cavalry could retain a decisive military role on the battlefields of the First World War; it was the British commander-in-chief, not a callow junior officer, who, dismissing the call for more machine-guns, stated firmly that "bullets had no real stopping power against a horse", while, at about the same time, it was the French commander-in-chief who threatened to "remove from the promotion list" the name of any officer who wrote a book! So, it was often the case that new, improved weapons were imposed on the men who were going to fight with them, rather than the other way about.

We can see the truth of this if we look slightly further back to the days of the Industrial Revolution. This is generally considered to have had a dramatic effect on the pace of weapons development because it provided the machines to make them more quickly, but, though this is true, it is not the whole story. For the Industrial Revolution also produced a new breed of skilled, pragmatic civilian engineers, who looked at weapons with fresh eyes and saw better, quicker methods of making not just existing weapons, but of inventing entirely new ones. Military men with considerable knowledge of contemporary guns, for instance, had laboured for many years to make a repeating gun; however, it was Hiram Maxim, a man originally trained as an electrical engineer, who made the first automatic machine gun.

Maxim once said "the most important part of my knowledge is my knowledge of what won't work" and he approached his task accordingly. He did not waste time on trying to make existing weapons work better; he simply took an engineer's view of energy and mechanisms and devised something totally new. He and his contemporaries advanced weapons technology further in the last half of the 19th century than it had advanced over the previous 500 years. Indeed, the origins of many of the wonder weapons of today can be traced back to dusty patents from the 1870s and 1880s, when engineers with vision saw the technical solutions to various problems. What again was lacking was the practical engineering technology to realize them; it needed advances in metallurgy, chemistry, physics and electricity before the same ideas could be re-invented many years later. What is interesting is that many of these self-same advances were sparked off by the demands of the two world wars, so, once again, the wheel turned full circle. It is these interactions and developments we have attempted to portray in the pages that follow – not so much the nuts, bolts and microchips that go to make up weapons themselves, but rather the principles and ideas that led humanity forward stage by stage from clubs and spears to proximity fuzes and laser beams.

Many years ago, a Professor of Fortification at the Royal Military Academy, Sandhurst, observed that "the origin and rise of fortification is undoubtedly due to the degeneracy of mankind." He could well have substituted the word "weapons" for "fortification". But, leaving degeneracy aside, one can only wonder at the inventive spirit and the degree of technological effort that has gone into the business of developing tools that kill.

In the closing years of the 20th century, when new weapons seemingly appear every week, it is a sobering thought that for several millennia the basic form of weapons scarcely changed. Primitive humans armed themselves with clubs — perhaps from branches from nearby trees — and although other weapons evolved, the club still serves as a weapon today. Why did primitive weapons remain in use for so long? There are two main reasons: first, they continued to be effective; second, while early humans might have dreamed of a weapon that would cause a rock to fly through the air and smite the enemy far away, they lacked the scientific and technical knowledge to make such a device.

Technology in the primitive world developed very slowly. The principles of mechanics had to be discovered before they could be applied. The transition from weapons consisting of stones that were picked up at random to weapons such as daggers and clubs that were carved out of stone was long and gradual. With the Bronze Age, beginning in about 4000 BC, came the possibility of more effective weapons. However, unlike stone, no useful metal exists in nature in a form ready for practical use; some processing is necessary before tin, copper, or iron can be used, and a certain amount of luck, as well as trial and error, had to be present before the alloy of tin and copper that we know as bronze could make its appearance. Smelting and annealing had to be discovered before metal could be fashioned into weapons, armour, or other artifacts capable of withstanding daily use, and it took many centuries before metal weapons such as knives, swords, and spears became common. From then on, they began to be fashioned with a degree of ornamentation and grace not found in the utilitarian weapons of today.

Once the simple mechanics of how weapons functioned had been mastered, the demand for more powerful weapons was met by the development of various types of siege engine. These all employed principles already perfected in hand weapons — the sling and the bow — but displayed considerable ingenuity in scaling them up to produce greater power. They were, for their day, the ultimate weapon.

CHAPTER ONE

THE FIRST
WEAPONS

CLUBS AND MACES

THE FIRST fabricated weapon was probably the club. Cave paintings seem to indicate its use in the Paleolithic era (2 million to 40,000 years ago). Early clubs were simply branches of wood that were picked up when needed. Often it was difficult to find the right-shaped piece of wood, so soon primitive man began taking pieces of wood and shaping them, or breaking away branches that appeared to have a useful shape and forming them into weapons.

The principle of a club is simple: a weight at the end of a stick provides additional momentum by effectively lengthening the striking arm. The most efficient natural club is either one which tapers from head to handle or one cut so as to have a naturally heavy tip. The Irish *shillelagh* is the paradigm of this type, cut from a blackthorn in such a way as to have the junction of a heavier branch as the head.

Simple clubs have been made from many natural materials –

The nulla nulla
A Polynesian war club or nulla nulla formed from a single piece of wood. The handle is carved to provide a secure grip and ends in a boss to prevent the club slipping from the hand in the heat of battle.

The mace in battle
A Persian painting of Genghis Khan in battle, 1201 AD, showing the vigorous use of the mace as a weapon. Many different weapons are in use but the mace appears to be confined to superior chieftains, reflecting their position as well as providing their armament.

A Peruvian club
A Peruvian pottery jar representing a mythical warrior with the head of a deer and carrying a club. From the Mochica (pre-Inca) culture, probably c. 800 AD.

African clubs
An 18th-century bronze hand altar of King Edo Ikegobo of Benin, Africa. The figure of the king holds two ceremonial maces, while a figure representing an important court functionary, on the front of the altar, holds a large mace and a smaller sceptre as symbols of his authority.

All-metal maces
Three metal maces; left, an Italian "morning star" mace from Milan, c.1560. Made of iron and chemically browned to prevent corrosion, it has been decorated with inlaid gold. Centre, a German iron mace c. 1530; right an Italian flanged mace c. 1580, also of iron with inlaid gold decoration.

wood, bone, ivory, jade, and stone, for example – and shaped in numerous ways to provide a convenient grip and a heavy head. Compound clubs usually comprise a wooden handle with a stone or metal head attached, though they can be more complex. For example, the Polynesian club was formed from a wooden shaft with sharks' teeth bound to it, thereby making a series of cutting edges. In a similar manner, many war clubs of various origins have spikes and other lethal protuberances attached to or forming part of the head.

Flexible clubs, first appearing in western Europe during the 14th century, had the weight attached to the shaft by a chain or cord in order to extend the radius of action and increase the momentum of the head. It seems probable that this type evolved from the threshing flail commonly used by farmers from the earliest days of cereal agriculture, since many have more than one thong and weight.

All-metal (usually iron) clubs — generally called maces — were developed for use against armoured knights. Wielded with sufficient energy, such a club could severely damage metal armour and injure the wearer. Some maces had spikes and pointed tips which were capable of penetrating thin armour or the joints of thicker armour.

MODERN CLUBS

As with other types of weapon, the club took on symbolic significance and some were highly decorated. The symbolic club lives on in the ceremonial mace carried by civic dignitaries and drum-majors, the field-marshal's baton, and the chief constable's decorated truncheon.

Meanwhile the club continues to be an effective weapon; it is the standard weapon of all police forces, whether or not they carry firearms, and it is widely used by riot control forces. Modern technology has been applied to the club, and telescoping clubs, which can be carried concealed in holsters and extended by the flick of the wrist, are common among police and security forces. Some clubs incorporate a high-voltage generator so that as the victim is struck, a low-power, high-voltage shock is delivered that can stun or temporarily paralyse.

TYPES OF CLUB

1 *The simple club, derived from a natural branch, of wood or stone or other natural material.*
2 *The composite club, composed of more than one piece; here a stone lashed to a wooden shaft.*
3 *The articulated club, two pieces, one of which is hinged to the other; in this case a ball and chain attached to the handle.*
4 *The metal club, or mace, originally a war weapon but which soon acquired ornamentation and became a symbol of rank or office.*

DAGGERS AND KNIVES

A DAGGER IS defined as a "short, edged, stabbing weapon", a knife as "a metal blade with a long sharpened edge, fixed in a handle and used as a cutting instrument or weapon". As in the case of swords (see page 18), the distinction between cut and thrust tends to become blurred.

The dagger is undoubtedly one of the oldest weapons. Flint daggers dating from about 20,000 BC are well known. In their earliest form these were no more than elliptical or wedge-shaped pieces of flint, carefully chipped to form a point and a cutting edge, and left blunt at the rear end to provide a grip. Over time the grip became more pronounced and was shaped to fit the hand. Some of the late flint knives have quite symmetrical and even ornate handles. Daggers were also made from any material which offered a sharp point — wood, bone, and horn were common. Knives and daggers of semi-precious materials such as agate and jade are also known, but these were invariably for ceremonial use and were not weapons of war (though those used by the Aztecs, among others, for human sacrifice were certainly capable of killing and maiming).

The adoption of metal allowed the maker more scope in the matter of shape, as well as providing a material more suitable for cutting and more amenable to ornamentation. The first metal to be used was copper; in general this is too soft to be useful for weapons, but it was eventually discovered that hammering could "work-harden" the metal sufficiently for it to be given a reasonably sharp edge and point. It was usually necessary to make the blade broad, almost triangular, to obtain the desired stiffness.

By about 2000 BC pure copper began to give way to bronze, an alloy of copper and tin developed by the Sumerian smiths of Mesopotamia. Bronze knives began with shapes similar to those of the copper knives they replaced, but as the superior hardness of bronze began to be appreciated, the knife became more slender and more ornate. More significantly, bronze was capable of taking a reasonable cutting edge — a great advantage on the battlefield. Another feature of bronze was that it could be cast, and this, in turn, led to the development of cast handles riveted to forged blades as well as more utilitarian knives cast in one piece.

Between 1000 and 500 BC bronze gradually yielded its place to iron, but this, though easier and perhaps cheaper to work than bronze, was less rigid. It was not until the discovery of "steeling" — repeatedly hammering spongy iron — that a really satisfactory blade could be produced. This "blister steel" remained the common material for weapons until about the 12th century, when the technique of hammering several strips of blister steel to form "shear steel" finally provided a metal with all the desirable attributes of rigidity and the ability to take and hold a good cutting edge.

CURVED BLADES

The shape of the knife or dagger was, to some extent, dictated by the material and form of construction. The straight pointed blade was adequate for stabbing, whatever material it was made of, but for cutting or slashing purposes copper and early bronze were less satisfactory. To compensate, the blade was shaped so as to aid the cutting motion and as a result the curved blade came to be the

A bronze dagger
This bronze dagger, tentatively dated as from 1600-1500 BC, was discovered in a burial mound in Wiltshire, England. The remains of rivets at the shoulder indicate that a cast handle was once affixed around the tang, most of which has corroded away.

A decorated scabbard
This bronze dagger, dating from the 6th century BC and discovered in Italy, has the hilt carefully shaped to give an excellent grip, with pommel and return to prevent the weapon sliding out of the hand. The scabbard has been decorated with animals and fish, as well as a geometric pattern, embossed into the bronze.

A Japanese dagger
Japanese daggers (or tanto*) are virtually miniature versions of Japanese swords, having the same gentle curve and oblique-cut tip.*

cutter, the straight blade the thruster. The curvature took many different forms, depending upon the makers and users. Some forms have become identified with particular places; for example, the wavy-edged *kris* of Malaysia, also characterized by an asymmetrical spur beneath the handle; or the broad-bladed "katar" of India, provided with a transverse grip which enabled the user to punch it into his opponent. Curved blades became popular in the Middle East and India, an area which also introduced a pointed dagger with a T-section blade capable of piercing the joints of various types of armour. Double-bladed daggers, allowing an upward or downward thrust, were known, as well as daggers with slotted blades with which an astute fighter could trap his opponent's blade and break or bend it.

Knives and daggers still find a place in warfare; commandos and other special forces carry them for close-quarter fighting, and utility knives capable of anything from combat to chopping down small trees are still popular with soldiers, even if they are not officially issued with them.

The Scottish dirk
The earliest dirks were generally made from broken sword blades, and thereafter they were frequently made to recall their origin, by having the blade single-edged but with a short false edge for the first few inches from the tip. By the 18th century they had become articles of dress rather than serious weapons and hence took on considerable amounts of ornamentation.

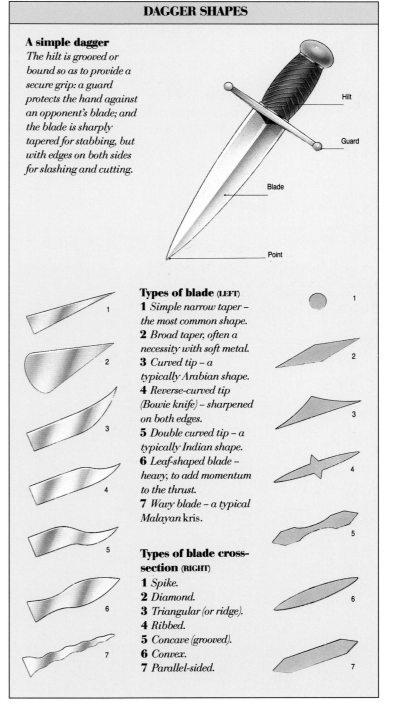

DAGGER SHAPES

A simple dagger
The hilt is grooved or bound so as to provide a secure grip; a guard protects the hand against an opponent's blade; and the blade is sharply tapered for stabbing, but with edges on both sides for slashing and cutting.

Hilt

Guard

Blade

Point

Types of blade (LEFT)
1 *Simple narrow taper – the most common shape.*
2 *Broad taper, often a necessity with soft metal.*
3 *Curved tip – a typically Arabian shape.*
4 *Reverse-curved tip (Bowie knife) – sharpened on both edges.*
5 *Double curved tip – a typically Indian shape.*
6 *Leaf-shaped blade – heavy, to add momentum to the thrust.*
7 *Wavy blade – a typical Malayan* kris.

Types of blade cross-section (RIGHT)
1 *Spike.*
2 *Diamond.*
3 *Triangular (or ridge).*
4 *Ribbed.*
5 *Concave (grooved).*
6 *Convex.*
7 *Parallel-sided.*

SLINGS AND THROWN MISSILES

AS A weapon a stone thrown by hand has its limitations, namely poor velocity, momentum, and range. Not surprisingly steps were taken to try to improve its performance by increasing the leverage of the human arm, or increasing the velocity of the launched missile, or both.

Perhaps the most successful stone-throwing weapon is the sling, a weapon of great antiquity that demands a fair degree of skill to use it effectively. The sling consists of a leather pouch to which two cords are attached. One cord is looped around the thrower's wrist, a stone placed in the pouch, and the other cord is held in the fingers. The sling is then whirled around to pick up speed and at the optimum point on its rotation the string in the fingers is released. This allows the pouch to open and the stone is ejected at high speed. The art in slinging lies in the correct judgement of when to let the string go and release the stone, since the direction and range of the stone depend on this.

Sling designs vary with their origin: African tribesmen still use slings of one piece of leather, cut to form the pouch and strings in one piece; early Middle Eastern slings were woven entirely from cord, while slings found in the Pacific Islands have been made from braided cord. The projectiles, while generally smooth stones of a convenient size, have also been cast using lead, from as early as the 2nd century BC.

> " *Then David took his staff and his sling, and he chose five smooth stones from the brook. When Goliath saw David he disdained him. "Am I a dog," he said, "that you come to me with sticks?" "I come to you in the name of the Lord of Hosts," said David. Then he put his hand in his bag and took out a stone, and slung it, and struck the Philistine on the forehead. The stone sank in and Goliath fell to the ground. David ran and stood over him and took Goliath's sword from its sheath and killed him, and cut off his head.* "

Samuel 1:17

Assyrian slingers
An Assyrian relief from the Palace at Nineveh, c.650 BC, showing soldier with slings. One end of the sling is looped around the thumb and the other grasped in the fingers, to be released at the highest point of the swing, so delivering the stone with the highest velocity.

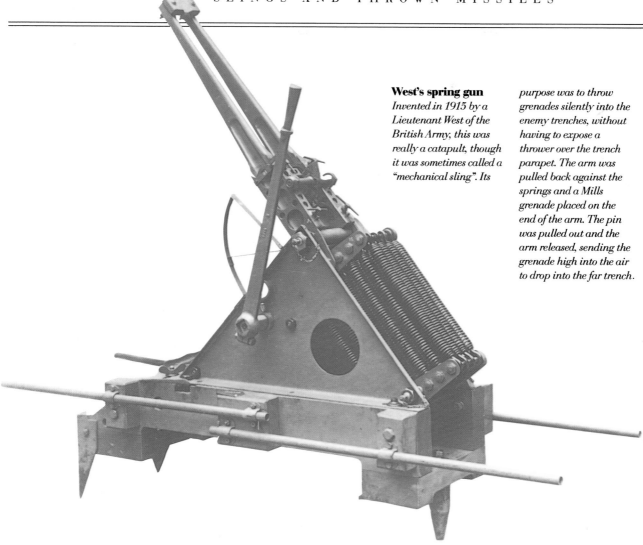

West's spring gun
Invented in 1915 by a Lieutenant West of the British Army, this was really a catapult, though it was sometimes called a "mechanical sling". Its purpose was to throw grenades silently into the enemy trenches, without having to expose a thrower over the trench parapet. The arm was pulled back against the springs and a Mills grenade placed on the end of the arm. The pin was pulled out and the arm released, sending the grenade high into the air to drop into the far trench.

An interesting but uncommon variant of the sling was the *fustibal*, a sling attached to the end of a stick. The origins of this weapon are unknown, but there is evidence that the Romans were using it early in the 3rd century BC. The *fustibal* extended the thrower's arm, and thus the radius of the sling's travel, and improved velocity and range, but it required even more skill to time the release of the sling accurately. It did, however, have a slight advantage in that it could be used in a body of men by simply swinging the stick overhead, and did not need a wide surrounding space in which to whirl the sling at shoulder level.

BIGGER PROJECTILES

While the sling offered improved range and velocity, it could only be used with relatively small stones. There were attractions in the possibility of throwing heavier, and more damaging missiles, but there were limits to the size of stone a man could conveniently handle and throw. The answer to this was to develop specialized missiles for throwing.

Clubs were a commonplace weapon, and by making the head heavy and the shaft (or helve) light, the club could be thrown with considerable accuracy for a useful distance. Moreover the club could still be used as a hand-held weapon. Various shapes have been adopted for throwing clubs, but the basic heavy head and light, stabilizing helve are common to them all. The principal drawback, of course, was that once thrown the club could rarely be regained in time to be of further use in that particular affray.

Axes developed into throwing weapons, as did knives. However, for best results the shapes had to be modified to improve the weapon's flight. Once modification began, it continued in order to improve the lethality of the weapon as well. Frankish warriors in the 5th century AD used a curved-blade axe (which the Romans called the *francisca*) for throwing. The majority of edged throwing weapons came from outside Europe. Native Americans of the eastern woodlands developed the tomahawk, whose fairly simple shape permitted it to be used both as a weapon and as a tool. Several African tribes made weapons midway between axes and knives which were purely for throwing. Often they had multiple blades so that there was no need for a specific part of the weapon to strike the target. These multiple-edged weapons could spin as they flew and strike as they chanced, as any one of several edges could cause damage.

One of the more remarkable thrown missiles was the Sikh *chakram* or throwing quoit, a simple circle of metal with a sharp outer circumference, which could be spun and then released with considerable velocity and accuracy.

Throwing, as a means of delivering missiles, had died out in Europe by the 14th century, although — interestingly — it returned in the 20th century with the hand grenade (see page 114). A combination of throwing and the medieval engine (see page 30) appeared in 1916 with West's spring gun, a form of portable catapult developed by the British for throwing grenades a greater distance than could be achieved by arm power alone.

BLOWPIPES AND AIR WEAPONS

T HE BLOWPIPE is generally associated with the natives of Borneo, Malaya, and various parts of South America, though probably it was also used in many other places. Blowpipes propel a dart by the use of human lung power, and their principal advantage is that they can be manipulated relatively quietly and discreetly — without the prominent arm movements demanded by the use of spears and bows — so that the intended target, human or animal, is not alerted. This is an important factor, since the accurate range of a blowpipe is no more than 50–60 yards and the attacker must therefore approach close to his target.

The length of the blowpipe can vary. The Filipinos used one about 3 feet long, the Borneo Dyaks a pipe about 6 feet long, and the Paraguayans one of up to 15 feet in length. The darts, too, vary from 3 inches to 18 inches in length, the most common being approximately 10 inches long. The pipe can be made from a hollow reed, or from a solid piece of wood bored out by hot irons. It takes a lot of skill to bore a hole 6–9 long feet with the accuracy needed to guarantee hitting the target.

The airgun is a logical mechanization of the blowpipe principle and its attraction is, again, the relatively silent discharge which has advantages in sporting and military use. The first airguns were produced in the early 17th century and were of two kinds, the air reservoir and the spring/air types.

DEVELOPMENT OF THE AIRGUN

An air reservoir gun is attributed to a French maker, Martin le Bourgeoys, around 1610, although no specimen has survived. The

> " *The vital weakness of a pneumatic gun, constructed on this principle, disqualifies it from ever becoming a naval arm, for its range falls far short of the range of the rifled cannon now in use by the navies of the world, and a cruiser mounting pneumatic guns would inevitably be destroyed before she could get within striking distance. Another great drawback is the necessity for much costly and unwieldy machinery for working the steam air compressor.* "
>
> The Pneumatic Dynamite Cannon:
> *Lieutenant J.C. Wray, RHA;*
> *Proceedings of the Royal Artillery Institution, Vol XVI, 1989.*

An air rifle
An air rifle made by George Wallis, an English gunsmith, in about 1770. Below the rifle is the air pump. The spherical air reservoir was screwed to the pump, then charged with air and replaced on the gun. It had a spring valve that was opened by the gun mechanism to release air for each shot.

THE ZALINSKI DYNAMITE GUN

THIS, THE ultimate air weapon, was developed in the 1880s by D.M. Mefford, an American, and perfected by Lieutenant Zalinski of the US Army. The object was to fire a shell filled with dynamite, an explosive too sensitive to be fired from a conventional gun due to the sudden shock of discharge. The inventors hoped that a "pneumatic cannon" would be less violent.

Mefford's first gun, a 30-foot tube of 2-inch bore connected to an air tank by a simple valve, fired a 5-lb shot to half a mile from 300-lbs pressure of air. Zalinski then took over the development and eventually produced a 60-foot, 8-inch calibre gun firing a 145-lb projectile, but this could only reach

to 1,600 yards, a poor performance in comparison with conventional cannon of the time. As a result, the tactical function was changed from shooting projectiles at a target to launching explosive mines into harbours, where they could form a hazard for attacking warships. A demonstration in 1887 effectively destroyed a ship target at 2,000 yards range, and the US Army planned to install batteries of these guns to defend various seaports on the eastern and western coasts of the USA. The Government of Victoria, Australia (then responsible for its own defence), also expressed interest in the design.

A number of 15-inch calibre Zalinski guns were installed in the USA, protecting

New York, Boston, and San Francisco, and the gun for Australia was brought to England for testing in 1890. But during the development of the "pneumatic cannon" much work had gone into perfecting explosives that could be fired from conventional guns, and by the time the Zalinski guns were ready for installation their performance was far outstripped by ordinary guns. Furthermore the installation of each gun demanded enormous air-compression and storage facilities, making it much more expensive than a conventional gun. By 1900 the Zalinski gun had become obsolete.

An air pistol
This rare air pistol is one of a pair ascribed to Durs Egg, a famous gunsmith of the late 18th century.

earliest known examples date from 1644 and were made by Hans Koehler of Kitzing, near Würzburg, Germany. The air reservoir consisted of a spherical flask with a valve held closed by the air pressure; it was removed from the gun and filled with compressed air using a simple pump. As there was no gauge fitted, the quantity of air was judged by the number of strokes of the pump, and burst reservoirs were not unknown. The flask was screwed back into the gun and a lead ball muzzle-loaded; on pressing the trigger, a needle was forced down to open the air valve and permit a short burst of air to propel the ball from the gun.

The spring/air weapon used a cylinder and piston; the piston was pulled back against a spring and then released to compress the air in the piston, which was directed into the barrel to discharge the ball. The spring/air gun was not a success, but the air reservoir type, with either a spherical flask beneath the action or a screw-on butt which contained the air flask, was quite popular throughout the 18th century for sporting purposes and one design, the Girardoni, was used by some light infantry regiments of the Austrian army between 1790 and 1805. With the

advent of the percussion principle (see Percussion firearms, page 76), the air weapon fell into disuse.

The idea was revived in the 19th century and the spring/air system was perfected — using better technology — to develop a wide range of cheap airguns for sporting purposes. The air reservoir type was also revived, but with a reservoir and pump incorporated in the weapon so that each shot was preceded by pumping up the necessary pressure. In about 1860 the idea of a rechargeable gas source was conceived, using liquefied carbon dioxide which could be injected into a reservoir in the weapon, the trigger releasing the stored energy. This system was moderately successful but it was not taken up commercially until the late 1940s following the adoption of sealed carbon-dioxide cartridges (as developed for soda-water machines), which were automatically pierced on loading and the contents retained by a trigger-operated valve.

Air-operated underwater guns, firing either bullets or harpoons, have also been successfully developed, using a small cylinder of compressed air as the propulsive power. Most of these have been for sporting and fishing purposes, though it is believed that various air weapons have been devised for use by special forces in underwater operations.

EARLY SWORDS

IT WAS not until metalworking became possible that the sword became a practical weapon. Bronze and iron were the first sword metals, though both had their defects. Bronze is an alloy of copper and tin, and the proportions can be changed so that the resulting bronze can be of varying strength. Early iron was of relatively poor quality, as is shown by descriptions of the battle of Aquae Sextiae in 102 BC, when the Romans fought the Teutones and Ambrones; their swords needed to be straightened beneath the swordsman's foot at intervals during the battle. Gradually, as metalworking and the tempering of metals were better understood, the sword became a reliable and capable weapon.

In the first bronze swords — of perhaps 1500 BC — the hilt and blade were like the knives of the period, two separate pieces riveted together. This made the sword adequate for thrusting but

Viking weapons
A group of Viking weapons probably from the 9th century, showing the typical hilt construction on two swords and a rather unusual method of retaining the grips on the leaf-shaped sword.

Byzantine swords
A sculpture (LEFT) from Byzantium showing typical Eastern swords of the 4th century AD, with angled grips and pommels shaped into bird's heads.

meant that it was relatively brittle and could easily snap in battle. By the 2nd century AD the Frankish smiths had developed a technique known as pattern-welding which involved layering hard and soft iron rods and twisting and hammering them into a homogeneous mass. Hardened rods were then laid along the edges and hammer-welded to the mass to provide the hard cutting edge, the blade being more resilient and thus less liable to break. The whole was then heated and plunged into water, reheated, and allowed to cool naturally before being shaped and sharpened.

Pattern-welding remained the preferred method of sword-making until about the 10th century, by which time the sword had generally assumed a slightly tapered blade in place of the earlier leaf-shape. During the same period the sword had become more than just a weapon; it had attained a certain mystical quality — which was doubtless due to the very high cost of a really first-class sword. Swords were handed down in families and some were given individual names. The Vikings, for example, regarded their swords as having magical properties and each warrior would give his weapon a suitable epithet, such as *Hvati* (keen) or *Langhrass* (long and sharp).

liable to come apart if used too enthusiastically as a slashing weapon. By about 1000 BC the technique of forging the blade and hilt in one piece had been developed, and with it a characteristic Bronze Age shape had arrived. The tang — the metal portion which formed the support for the hilt — broadened as it met the blade, which narrowed and then gradually increased in breadth to about two-thirds of the way down its length, after which it smoothly swept in to form a point. This was a practical shape for either thrusting or cutting. The whole blade is generally described as "leaf-shaped". The tang would be enclosed in pieces of wood or bone, riveted in place and shaped to provide a firm grip.

When iron came into use, the design of swords followed the pattern set by bronze. Indeed, for some time the use of bronze and iron overlapped. There are examples of swords with bronze hilts attached to iron blades, where the iron tang is the foundation and the hilt is built up on it, and everything has been secured by hammering the tip of the tang in rivet fashion. The blade was made either in one piece, hammered on the edges to give a harder finish, or built up by hammer-welding several layers of iron.

Having mastered the basic construction of swords, smiths now began to experiment with shape and form to arrive at various designs that suited the preferences of their customers. The original simple pointed and edged blade and the leaf-shaped blade were retained, but curved blades, which were more adapted to a slashing blow, became common, particularly in the Middle East. The Roman legionaries, on the other hand, adopted a short, wide sword which could be worn on the right side and drawn with the right hand — an asset in close combat.

PATTERN-WELDING

The principal technological difficulty in sword-making was that forging a piece of iron hard enough to serve as a sword often

An Egyptian sword
Dating from the period of the New Kingdom (c.1300 BC), this broad-bladed sword with its highly decorated gold hilt was unlikely to have been intended for use in battle. It was probably a symbolic weapon for ceremonial occasions.

A SIMPLE
WEAPON GAINS
SYMBOLIC
FORCE

AXES AND HAMMERS

ALTHOUGH THE axe is always mentally pictured as a handle with a blade on the end, the family had its beginnings in the hand-axe, a simple, shaped piece of flint or stone with a cutting edge at one end and with the other rounded so as to provide something to grip. Such implements were developed independently in every region where suitable stone was available and are probably among the first artefacts to be made. Specimens from the Paleolithic era (12,000 BC and earlier) have been found in Africa and Europe. At some time the additional power to be gained from the use of a shaft was discovered; it is likely that at first the hand-axe was simply lashed to a suitable stick, but certainly towards the end of the Neolithic period (8000-3000 BC) axe heads with holes for the handle were being made. At the same time more care was taken over the manufacture, and grinding and polishing to a relatively high degree of finish became common. With this skill came that of shaping the axe head to incorporate a more efficient blade, and by 2000 BC there were curved and double-bladed heads in use.

By this time bronze had made its appearance, and the technique of shaping stone axes was soon applied to working in metal. Early bronze axes were more or less the same shape as those of stone, but the adaptability of metal led to the development of other shapes as axe-makers attempted to produce

Bronze Age axes
Axe heads from the early Bronze Age (1800-1400 BC).

The war axe in use
This painted limestone stele of the 19th Dynasty of Egypt depicts Merneptah holding a prisoner by his hair and apparently threatening him with a typical stone-headed axe of the period.

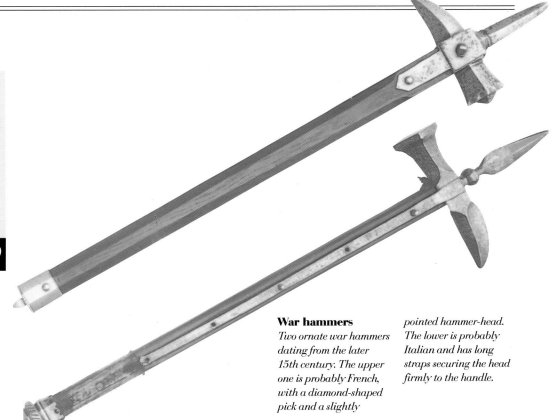

War hammers
Two ornate war hammers dating from the later 15th century. The upper one is probably French, with a diamond-shaped pick and a slightly pointed hammer-head. The lower is probably Italian and has long straps securing the head firmly to the handle.

axes more particularly adapted to either domestic or martial roles. Moreover, the more artistic manufacturers began to add decoration, either in the form of patterns worked into the metal or by adding cast or worked decorative bosses.

The attachment of the head to the handle went through several stages; the early metal axe heads were wrought, rather than cast, and it was some time before the casting of a head with a socket for the handle was mastered. In the interim, the head was formed with a splayed back and tied to the handle; or with a spiked lower end which could be driven into the handle; or formed with holes in the blind edge, alongside the handle,

A broad axe
This Bronze Age broad-bladed axe is of interest in displaying well-engineered riveting to attach it to the handle as well as a useful hammer-head at the opposite edge.

through which bindings could be tied; or formed with a central groove which could be inserted into the split end of the handle and then secured by lashing. Eventually, however, the socket became the universal method of attachment and has remained so ever since. An exception can be found in some Indian and Persian axes in which blade, head, and handle are forged as one piece.

WEAPONS AS SYMBOLS

As well as being a utilitarian weapon, the battle axe also took on a symbolic role which became reflected in its appearance. Kings, princes, and nobility required axes that made their owner's status apparent. This was done by decoration, by size, or by being of a stylized shape which showed that the bearer, while of the military caste, had no need to do his own fighting.

A more simple, and perhaps more brutal, weapon was the war-hammer. Although called a hammer (implying a blunt head), in fact it usually had a pointed head which was more in the nature of a pick. Such weapons were developed by many primitive tribes and were comparable to stone or metal axes but with a pointed shape. They were adopted in Europe during the 14th century when chain mail and other forms of armour protection (see Armour from 1100, page 38) were in vogue. The pointed head of a war-hammer proved to be an effective method of defeating mail, provided that the point and head were thin enough, and it could also be used to penetrate the joints of plate armour. With a pointed head on one side of the weapon and a blunt head on the other, the war-hammer became a twofold weapon in so far as the blunt head could be used to stun the opponent or unhorse him, after which the pick could be used to defeat his armour and give the finishing blow. The war-hammer saw considerable use in Europe during the 15th and 16th centuries, but its use declined as the armoured knight disappeared from the battlefield. As with axes, decorated war-hammers were also used as symbols of rank

LONGBOWS

T HE BOW is simply a spring by which a missile — an arrow — can be launched with far greater speed than can be accomplished by the unaided arm, so increasing range and velocity. It also allows greater accuracy to be attained, and sufficient power to give the arrow a degree of penetrative ability.

The bow appears to have originated in North Africa in the Paleolithic era, and from there it spread throughout the Mediterranean area and into Europe and Asia. It also seems to have been discovered independently in the Americas, Australia, and Tasmania. Whatever the origin, it was in use throughout the world by at least 8000 years BC and has appeared in an enormous number of forms.

Simple bows are made from a stave of springy wood, to one end of which a strong cord is permanently attached; the other end of the cord is formed into a loop, and when not required for use the bow is carried in this form. To use the bow, the stave is bent into a curve and the looped end of the cord slipped over the other end into a prepared notch. Staves have been made of virtually every sort of strong wood, though some woods have shown themselves to be more suitable by virtue of their resilience. The English longbow, for example, was made of yew, though elm was sometimes used where yew was not available.

The arrow could be fashioned from almost any straight piece of wood, though the stiffness of the arrow has a considerable influence upon its accuracy. The arrow was prepared with a notch — or "nock" — at the rear end, into which the bowstring fitted, and a head at the other end which could be anything from the tip of the wood (fire-hardened) to complex and ornate shapes of stone, bone, petrified wood, ivory, jade, or metal. Stability in flight was provided by "fletching" the arrow, fitting stabilizing "flights" at the tail end. These were usually feathers, two, three, or four arranged symmetrically around the shaft and attached by gluing or binding. Some arrows, notably those used by Bushmen and other indigenous peoples, are without flights, but these can only be used with accuracy at short ranges. For the maximum range

The asymmetric bow
Minamoto Yoritomo, later to be a famous Japanese general, is here shown at the age of 13 in his first battle. He is carrying a sword and the peculiar Japanese asymmetric bow, which took advantage of the rider's distance from the ground to increase the strength of the bow without unduly encumbering the bowman.

Bronze Age arrowheads
These early Bronze Age arrowheads (ABOVE) dating from c.1800 BC bear witness to the use of flint for arrowheads even after the discovery of metal. The skilled crafting of the barbs ensured the head stayed in the wound.

The hunting bow
(LEFT) This detail from a Hittite relief from Karkemish, c.1000 BC, shows a hunter pursuing game from a chariot, armed with a bow and accompanied by his hound.

> " *In the hands of the English the bow had become, in the form of the longbow, the most deadly and formidable weapon of its time. Every English boy was trained to use it and was taught to bring every muscle of his body to bear upon it... The result was that arrows were discharged with great rapidity and accuracy and with such strength that they were effective in the matter of penetration at astonishingly long range.* "

J.W. Fortescue, Military History

Bows at Agincourt
This depiction of the Battle of Agincourt (1415) from Froissart's "Chronicles" portrays a somewhat idealized account, suggesting that the forces were equal, whereas the French army was approximately three times larger than the English. It does, however, record the importance of the longbow in that battle.

TYPES OF BOW

Bow shapes
Many bow shapes evolved at different times and in different countries. A selection of shapes is shown here.

1 *Uncommon triangular bow.*
2 *Straight grip – constructed from several pieces.*
3 *Simple curved bow.*
4 *Recurved bow.*
5 *Double-curved bow.*
6 *Asymmetric bow – the hand grip is placed low to prevent the bow striking the ground.*
7 *Be-curved bow.*
8 *Quadruple-curved bow.*

Bow parts
The basic bow mechanism does not vary significantly between bow types. The illustration (RIGHT) shows the standard parts of a bow.

1 *Bowstring.*
2 *Notch for string loop.*
3 *Grip.*
4 *Belly – side to archer.*
5 *Back – side to target.*

flights are essential, giving a degree of aerodynamic lift to the arrow as well as ensuring that it flies straight.

Where suitable wood was not readily available, compound bows were developed, usually consisting of a wooden stave as the supporting structure to which were added other materials to provide the desired springiness. One simple system, widely used by Eskimo archers, was the attachment of a number of strings of sinew to the back of the stave to provide the desired tension. Other systems included the use of horn or sinew as a laminate, or both on opposite sides of the bowstave. One result of these constructions was to change the simple shape of the bow from a plain curve into a double reverse curve, a shape particularly common among Turkic nomads and indigenous Americans.

ASYMMETRICAL BOWS

Not all bows are symmetrical, with the grip in the centre of the span. Japanese and Burmese bows are frequently asymmetrical, with far more bow above the shooter's hand than below it. This odd shape allows the use of a large bow without it fouling the ground; this was particularly useful for mounted archers, enabling them to fire a longbow from horseback. The shorter section at the bottom is of a convenient size, while the longer section, at the top, provides more power than could be obtained from a symmetrical bow of similar dimensions.

The longbow can be fired with accuracy to about 200 yards, with a maximum range of perhaps 250 yards. Laminate bows are even more powerful, and ranges twice that of a conventional longbow have been recorded. Bows can also be fired very rapidly; a skilled bowman can loose about six aimed shots in a minute, double that number if precise aiming is not necessary. It was this rapidity of fire which allowed men with bows to overcome men armed with early firearms. A bowman could get off a dozen or more arrows while the musketeer was loading and priming his muzzle-loader.

CROSSBOWS

THE CROSSBOW appeared in China around 500 BC. How it arrived in Europe is a matter of some conjecture, the Byzantines, Saracens, and Huns all possibly responsible for its westward migration. In any case, its military impact was minimal until the end of the 11th century AD. William of Normandy had *ballistantes* in his army that invaded England in 1066 and these, it is suggested, were crossbow men, though there is no illustration of a crossbow in the Bayeux Tapestry. Nevertheless there is ample evidence of the crossbow in France by 1100, and the Second Lateran Council, in 1139, among its other business laid under anathema any person using such a godless

instrument against fellow Christians. The edict appears to have had little force since it had to be repeated half a century later by Pope Innocent III. Neither of these decrees had much effect, and the crossbow became a popular weapon throughout Europe.

The crossbow is, at its simplest, a conventional bow mounted upon a shoulder-stock; but the mechanizing of the bow produced an exceptionally powerful weapon. Instead of the simple wood bow, crossbows soon evolved into using compound bows of horn, sinew, and wood which were so strong as to demand mechanical aid in drawing. Once drawn, the string was retained by a catch, and the projectile, generally known as a bolt or "quarrel" (from the French *carreau* — the square section of the tip) was laid in a groove in the stock. Pressing a trigger released the string, and the strength of the compound bow propelled the quarrel at high velocity, sufficient to pierce chain mail at 100 yards distance.

The matter of drawing the bow caused problems. The simplest way was to fit a stirrup to the forward end of the stock, place this on the ground and put one foot into it, then seize the string with both hands and draw it up until it could be lodged in its catch.

An early crossbow
An incident from the Hundred Years War depicted in Froissart's Chronicle, one of the earliest depictions of a crossbow, in the hands of *a French soldier defending a bridge against an English attack. The affair is unidentified but must be in the latter years of the 14th century.*

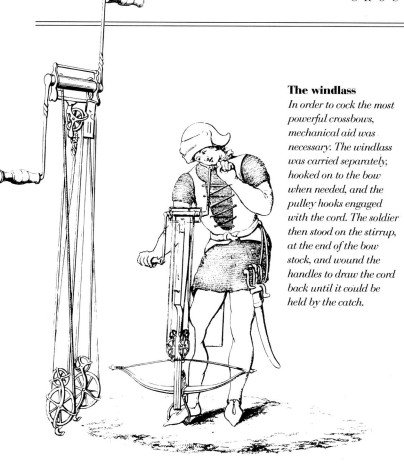

Then came the "claw", a simple hook attached to the man's belt; he stood on the stirrup, bent forward and hooked the claw onto the string, then straightened up and so drew the bow. Another method was the "goats-foot" lever, a claw-like contrivance which hooked onto pivots on the sides of the stock and, by means of a hinged hook, levered the bowstring back.

MORE POWERFUL CROSSBOWS

The really powerful bows used a mechanical aid; a small windlass was fitted at the butt end, with two crank handles. This carried a cord and hook which could be attached to the bowstring, and the windlass was then operated to draw the bowstring back. Another mechanical aid was the "cranequin", a ratchet mounted on top of the stock, though this was an extremely slow device and favoured only by hunters.

A powerful crossbow could send its bolt to a maximum range of about 350 yards, comfortably outranging the contemporary longbow. Its principal defect was its slow rate of fire; a heavy crossbow with windlass cocking could fire only about one shot per minute, in which time a longbow could have fired six well-aimed shots or as many as twelve hasty shots. The lighter crossbows, cocked by hand by using the belt claw, could fire perhaps four shots in one minute. In medieval warfare, where the target was generally massed ranks of men, rate of fire counted for more than precise accuracy. And even if the crossbow had superior penetrative power, the armour-piercing "bodkin" arrowhead fired from a longbow was still sufficient to inflict mortal injuries.

Nonetheless the crossbow survived in Europe well into the age of firearms; an English army is said to have used them as late as 1627. Elsewhere they lasted much longer; some African tribes were using primitive versions as recently as the early 20th century.

Target practice
Target shooting with crossbows, c. 1520. Hunting and target-shooting crossbows were lighter and more ornate than those used for war, though the nearer bowman has a crank handle, obviously part of some mechanical cocking device, slung around his waist.

16th-century weapons
Soldiers of the French army of the 16th century with a variety of weapons. In the upper picture the artillerymen are preparing cannon and, on the right, firing by means of a long "linstock" carrying a burning match. In the lower picture foot soldiers carry various pole-arms and a mounted man carries a crossbow.

SIMPLE POINTS

OR COMPLEX

AXE-HEADS,

ALL ON

A POLE

SPEARS AND POLEARMS

THE SPEAR began simply as a wooden shaft with a sharpened tip. It then became a dagger attached to the end of a wooden shaft so as to give the owner a greater radius of action, but from there it diversified into a variety of weapons generally classed as polearms. Because of this line of descent, in many respects it followed the same course as the knife, beginning with spear heads made from flint, through those made of bronze and iron to steel.

The pure spear divides into two groups: those for thrusting and those for throwing. As a thrusting weapon it brings advantages of weight and reach. As a throwing weapon it increases the reach; the concentrated weight of the shaft acts as a stabilizer, keeping the weapon point foremost in flight, and as a source of kinetic energy to carry the point into the target.

The spear in the form of the long pike retained its place in battle as a weapon for hand-to-hand fighting until well into the firearms' era, when it was used as a defensive screen against cavalry, behind which the musketeer could reload his weapon. In Africa and the Far East it was used against firearms until the late 19th century.

As a throwing weapon the spear's effectiveness could be increased by the use of slings or throwing sticks (see Slings and thrown weapons, page 14), which added leverage to the thrower's arm and thus gave greater range and force. The Aborigines of Australia use the throwing stick to this day.

Once the idea of a shafted weapon was accepted, variations in the form of the head began to appear. The fork and the trident made the simple spear more deadly by multiplying the points; the "partisan" spear had wing-like cutting edges below the head so as to cause more serious wounds. The pole-axe, as the name implies, was an axe mounted on a longer than normal shaft; the glaive was a long, single-edged, knife-like blade attached to the pole, with a point; the halberd was an axe blade formed beneath the spear head. These weapons gave the user the choice of thrusting or cutting, while the hook on the reverse of the axe could be used to pull a man from a horse or to trip an opponent.

A Peruvian pole-axe
An Inca warrior holding a pole-axe, the head resting on the ground. Depicted on a wooden vase, possibly c. 1200 AD.

The pole-axe
A French pole-axe, c. 1470. The head has a straight blade on the principal face and a serrated blade on the reverse. It is attached to the shaft by iron straps on four sides, and has a disc hand-guard about half-way down the shaft.

Roman spears
(RIGHT) Roman soldiers under review by their Emperor display their basic armament, the "pilum" or spear and the "gladius" or short sword. Each soldier carried several spears which he threw during his advance, then drew his sword for the final melée.

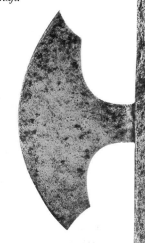

A hammer axe
A French pole-axe of the early 15th century which combines a curved blade with a spiked hammer on the opposite face. The head and upper shaft is forged from one piece of metal, socketed and strapped to the wooden shaft.

The Battle of Nantes
Above: *An illustration from the* Memoires de Phillipe de Comines *showing the 15th-century*

Battle of Nantes outside the castle of the Duke of Brittany. A variety of polearms are in evidence.

The general use of polearms died away as firearms became more common, but in many places they lingered as ceremonial weapons or as badges of rank which could be easily seen and identified in battle. British non-commissioned officers carried halberds as a symbol of rank well into the 19th century, and British Army cavalry farrier-sergeants still carry a symbolic pole-axe.

THE LANCE

When the spear was carried by a horseman it became the lance, which, at first, was wielded two-handed by the rider. The introduction of the stirrup into Europe between the 6th and 8th centuries AD made a considerable difference: it allowed the rider to brace himself and hold his lance underarm and charge, so delivering the blow with the full force of his mounted momentum rather than merely with the strength of his arm. Consequently the shape of the lance head changed from a broad spear-head to a simple pointed ferrule on a shaft which gradually thickened towards the butt, thinned to form a grip, and then thickened again to give counterbalance to the length. The war lance was a lighter and more handy weapon than the heavier and more ornate lance used for jousting and training.

With the decline of the armoured horseman, the lance became less important. However, a light and simple form remained in use in Eastern Europe, notably by the Poles in their battles against Frederick the Great (1712-86). It was later taken up by Napoleon's armies, and its use spread throughout the remainder of Europe. It was part of a cavalry regiment's equipment until the First World War (1914-18). The Polish Army continued to employ a war lance — a 9-foot long steel shaft armed with a four-edged spear-head — as late as the 1939 campaign against the Germans.

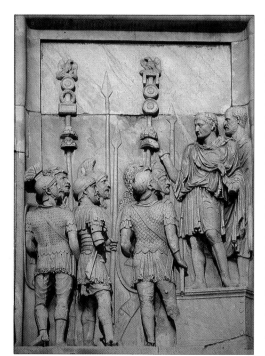

EARLY ARMOUR

EVERY WEAPON eventually generates a method of defence against it. In modern times this defence may be active and highly technical — such as an anti-missile missile — but in earlier times it was entirely passive and relied simply upon placing some obstacle in the way of the weapon. Moreover the development of a defensive measure often leads to changes in the design or tactical use of weapons. The defensive system which had been in use for some six thousand years was armour to protect the individual.

It can be assumed that some prehistoric man developed a primitive shield which he could use with one hand while with the other he wielded a spear or club. Such a shield would have had a framework of pliable wood, covered with hide, which was soaked and dried so as to harden it. Evidence of the use of the shield first appears in Egyptian paintings of 4000 BC, and a specimen found in Tutankhamun's tomb (dating from about 1300 BC) proved to be of wood covered in antelope skin.

In about 2500 BC soldiers are depicted wearing helmets, though with insufficient detail to identify the material. It is likely that these were of leather, though bronze cannot entirely be ruled out.

From about 1500 BC scale armour begins to make its appearance in the Middle East. Scale armour, as the name suggests, was constructed of numerous small metal plates attached to a cloth garment in the manner of fish scales. It was simple to make, since the armourer merely had to produce a quantity of plates two or three inches square and punch holes in them to allow them to be tied or riveted to the basic garment, but it must have been a slow process. A defect of this type of armour is the near-impossibility of covering the entire body; certain areas, notably the armpit, are virtually impossible to protect and thus a vulnerable area was left, which an astute enemy could exploit. Nevertheless, it became the standard form of armour for men who

The Battersea shield
A late 1st-century AD British shield, recovered from the River Thames. It is of high quality, beaten from bronze with the edge carefully reinforced with ornate enamelled decoration.

Thoracomachus
A 9th-century AD depiction of the Thoracomachus, *the foundation garments Roman legionaries wore beneath their armour, including undershirts, leggings, and a special shock-absorbing cap to fit beneath the helmet.*

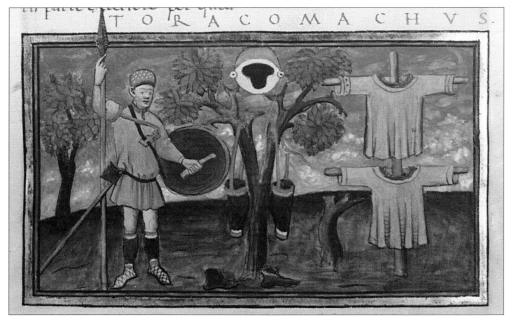

were particularly vulnerable, like chariot drivers, and the more senior soldiers; it was far too expensive to be lavished upon the common foot troops.

CHAIN MAIL

A more flexible protection was provided by "mail" — a fabric made from interlinked metal rings, the name coming from the Latin *macula* for a net, via the French *maille*. This seems to have been developed by Celts in the 3rd century BC and was certainly used by Roman troops (who called it the *lorica hamata*) by that time. Originally in the form of a shirt, it was later also fashioned into short trousers or aprons or stockings to give as much protection to the body as possible.

The Roman legionary was also equipped with plate armour, of a kind. This, the *lorica segmentata* which armoured Roman legionaries from the 1st century AD, was formed from linked and overlapping strips of metal. The complete unit was made of several sections which were laced together with leather thongs to make a complete outer shirt with additional protection at the shoulders, the whole being as flexible as could be expected and with the vulnerable areas given protection by the undershirt of mail. The legionary also wore a helmet of bronze or iron with a double peak and hinged ear flaps which were tied under the chin by a leather thong.

Even more heavily armoured than the Romans were the forces of Byzantium, the major power in the eastern Mediterranean from the fall of Rome in the 5th century AD to the sack of Constantinople in 1204. Although chain mail was used, the Byzantines seem to have preferred lamellar armour, consisting of small strips of iron or toughened leather laced together to form a continuous flexible sheet. The Byzantine heavy cavalry, known as cataphracts, wore full body armour and gave protection to their horses with quilts made from lamellar armour.

Phoenician armour
This splendid bronze plate and belt forms part of a set of Phoenician armour of the 8th century BC.

EVOLUTION OF MEDIEVAL ARMOUR

11th century
The Norman knight wore a mail hauberk over a long padded tunic, a helmet with nose-guard and mail gauntlets.

14th century
The hauberk became shorter, the helmet was augmented by a mail collar, and protection was given to the thighs and knees.

15th century
Plate armour completely covered the body, with hinged joints to permit movement but prevent the entry of swords or pikes.

In western Europe after the fall of Rome, armour was a scarce item, but gradually mail came back into use, and the Franks devised a helmet of their own which was fabricated from an iron framework, the spaces being filled with iron or leather plates and with a short mail neck-curtain at the back.

By the 11th century, the general form of armour worn in western Europe had settled into a long coat of mail — the hauberk — and a helmet derived from the Frankish type but with the addition of a "nasal", a strip of metal running down the man's nose to protect his face from a slashing attack. The hauberk was adapted for horsemen, being knee-length and with a split skirt to permit mounting and riding, and it was supplemented by a tall kite-shaped shield which protected the rider's left side. Leggings of mail completed the protection.

Until the advent of the mounted warrior knight, the emphasis of protection was on the upper body; this was probably because until that period the foot soldiers were the principal arm of warfare and while they needed some protection, their ability to march and fight on foot was the most important factor, one which could not be jeopardized by totally encasing them in metal.

POWERED

MACHINES

INCREASE THE

SCALE OF WAR

ENGINES

THE SIMPLEST form of engine is the battering ram, which was probably also the first. Indeed it has been suggested that the story of the Trojan Horse is a metaphor for a battering ram, and that the ram's horns that felled the walls of Jericho are a reference to the ornamental horns on a battering ram. The ram's first recorded use was by the Assyrians, against the cities of Judah in the 7th century BC. The first rams were probably no more than trimmed tree-trunks carried by however many men could be mustered around them. As time went on the ram became more ornate and powerful. The head was bound with iron, to prevent the wood splintering, and then became a cast or forged shoe ending in a sharp point. There is no evidence for "engineer" thinking before the Hellenistic Age (323–31 BC). Medieval rams were given their own overhead protection, generally a water-soaked fire-proof hide, to prevent the defenders assaulting the ram's crew. This covering was carried on a wheeled frame, which was also adapted to support the weight of the ram itself. The operators could then concentrate on just swinging the ram back and forth.

The next device to appear was the ballista or scorpion, an enlarged bow-and-arrow, which was also sometimes on a wheeled carriage. It began as an enlarged version of the ordinary bow, but later it was realized that the bow was not the only way of firing an arrow. Doing away with the cumbersome bow meant a more compact machine. Soon, devices began to appear in which the arrow (or arrows) were held in a rack and propelled by a spring.

MECHANICAL PRINCIPLES

Engines fall into three mechanical groups: those powered by spring force (such as the ballista); those powered by torsion; and those powered by counterweights. The spring ballista could fire a heavy

A primitive catapult
An illustration from De Machinis Bellis *by Mariano Taccola of Venice, written in 1449. This may well illustrate the general principle of the catapult, but such a device would not, in real life, generate sufficient velocity to throw a stone very far. A practical catapult would have the arm disposed so as to give considerable leverage, and the motive power would be a heavy weight or torsion rope more powerful than one man pulling on a rope.*

> **"** *By the which engine [the Turks] threw on us the Greek Fire, which was the most horrible thing I ever saw in my life. It made such a noise in its coming as if it were a thunderbolt falling from heaven. Thrice during that night did they cast the said fire from the said engine, and four times from the catapult of the tower.* **"**

Joinville; Histoire de Saint Louys, *quoted in* Military Architecture *by E.E. Viollet-le-Duc, 1860*

arrow more than 200 yards range, but it was not powerful enough to fire larger missiles to any worthwhile distance. This was because the springs, which were no more than strips of wood or horn (or both) were relatively weak. By contrast, counterweight engines, which could be built as large as the available materials and skills permitted, could increase their power simply by using bigger weights. But at the same time, preparing the machine became a strenuous business.

The torsion machine offered advantages over both the other types. In this system a loop of rope or hair or hide was twisted, stretching the material, and used to power a throwing arm. A solid framework was needed for stretching the loop across, and the bottom end of the throwing arm was passed through the loop. A windlass at each end then applied torsion to the loop, twisting the material, while the throwing arm was locked in position. Once the torsion had been applied, a missile was placed on the throwing arm and the arm released. The only other requirement was a robust stop to arrest the throwing arm in the best position.

The amount of torsion that could be applied by a band of strong men on the windlass meant that the engine could propel sizeable stones — 45-55 lbs — at good velocities and with reasonable accuracy to a useful range. This type of engine could batter at the walls of a town with some realistic hope of making a breach. The Romans called it the "onager" or wild ass, a reference to the violent kick of the rear end of the machine when the throwing arm came against its stop.

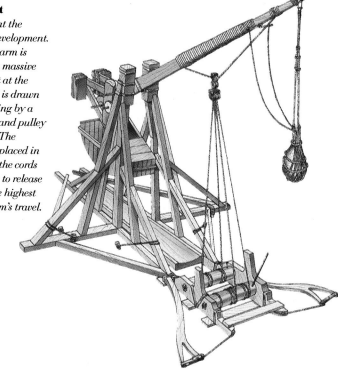

The catapult
The catapult at the height of its development. The throwing arm is propelled by a massive counterweight at the front end, and is drawn down for loading by a double winch and pulley arrangement. The projectile was placed in the sling, and the cords arranged so as to release the sling at the highest point of the arm's travel.

Roman war engines
Illustrations from Notitia Dignitatum, *a copy of a Carolingian manuscript of 1436. On the left is the* ballista quadrirotis, *a four-wheeled device for throwing spears, drawn by two horses. Below is the* ballista fulminalis, *another spear-throwing engine which appears to be statically emplaced.*

The torsion system could also be applied to discharge arrows. By using two vertical loops to hold side-arms connected by a cord, the action of a powerful bow could be reproduced without having the cumbersome width of a scaled-up bow.

The counterbalance machine — commonly known as the trebuchet — was the last of the engines to appear. The rise of well-defended stone castles in the 12th century brought the need for an extremely powerful machine to batter their walls and also to pitch missiles high enough and far enough to pass over the walls and damage the interior structures.

The basics of the trebuchet were two A-frames securely fixed to a timber base. Between the tips of the A-frames a long throwing arm was pivoted so that about one-eighth of its length was in front of the pivot and the remainder behind. A large counterweight — a box filled with heavy stones — was hung on the short end of the throwing arm. Attached to the other end was a rope-and-pulley arrangement to allow the end of the throwing arm to be pulled down, usually by windlass power, lifting the counterweight into the air. Sometimes the end of the throwing arm was shaped like a spoon, to hold a missile. More often the principle of the sling was applied, with the tip of the arm shaped so as to release one end of the sling as the arm approached the vertical. Using a sling allowed missiles of considerable size to be projected; there are records of dead horses, corpses, and other nuisance-value projectiles being slung for considerable distances into besieged castles and towns.

The drawback of the trebuchet was its sheer size and immobility. It could not be moved as it stood, but had to be brought in pieces to the scene of the action and assembled there. Putting it together took time and considerable effort and — most importantly — had to be done within range of the enemy's engines. For this reason trebuchets were used only at major sieges, and probably there were never many of them.

By the end of the 1st millennium AD metal-working was well understood and a wide array of weapons had been developed. Then, the natural order of things was overturned by the first major innovation in warfare, the discovery of gunpowder. Even so, swords and armour continued in use for several centuries.

The inventor of gunpowder or of the first gun will probably never be known, nor its place of origin. The mystery arises because, in the eyes of the Church, knowledge of the gun and its powder was dangerous, and those admitting to it risked punishment. But once such knowledge had become widespread, guns and gunpowder soon became militarily indispensable, and development moved rapidly.

The early cannon appear to have been more valuable for the effect they had upon the enemy's morale than for their lethality. The flash, noise, and smoke struck terror into the simple soldier of the 14th century, irrespective of what physical damage the projectile caused. In fact, early guns were primitive and, having no sights, were inaccurate; anyone struck by a ball could count himself unfortunate.

Early artillery was relatively static; the wheeled carriage was not invented until much later, and the first guns were carried into the field in carts to be fired from a timber bed. If the tide of battle suddenly turned they were easily lost to the enemy. They tended to be the weapon of the defender, who could place them into position before the battle, or of the besieger who had time to bring them up to the target. The use of artillery in day-to-day fighting was infrequent since it could not keep up with other forces in mobile battles.

From artillery sprang the handgun, and although this was slow to develop it soon became the universal leveller, capable of defeating the armoured knight who could now be brought down by any serf with a gun. This did not commend the gun to everyone; the mercenaries of the 14th and 15th centuries went into battle with the aim of showing a profit. A dead enemy was only worth whatever his arms and armour would fetch, but a live captive was a source of ransom money. Improved weapons did not, therefore, necessarily mean greater slaughter.

CHAPTER TWO

MEDIEVAL DEVELOPMENTS

LATER SWORDS

T HE GROWTH of personal armour in the 13th and 14th centuries (see Armour from 1100, page 38) led to a change in the sword. Since armour was more or less proof against a single-handed slash, the sword took a more slender and pointed form, so as to penetrate the armour joints wherever possible. It also grew in size, from between 32 and 38 inches in length to 50 or 60 inches, and with a longer hilt to allow a two-handed grip. Such a large and heavy sword, swung two-handed, gave a better chance of delivering a damaging blow to an armoured man, unbalancing him if nothing better and thus leaving him open to other forms of attack.

Up to this time the general form of the hilt and the quillons — the protecting wings below the hilt — were fairly simple: the quillons were usually straight, but sometimes curved down, and the hilt was simply a handle, though decorated to some degree. But in the 15th and 16th centuries armour fell into disuse and the swordsman's hand was no longer protected by a gauntlet; as a result the hilt and quillons became more complex to protect the

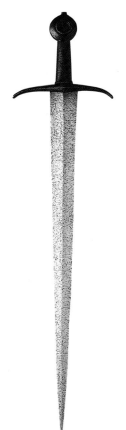

An early rapier
A French sword of the late 14th century; the blade being tapered for thrusting rather than slashing. This perhaps foreshadows the later development of the rapier, a pure thrusting weapon.

Swords and scimitars
This Persian illustration (RIGHT) dates from 1548 and depicts the invading forces of Shriaz Timur, battling their way into India. Note the characteristic curved swords, or scimitars.

" *It was in the first charge I took the eagle from the enemy; he and I had a very hard contest for it. He thrust for my groin; I turned it off and cut him through the head; after which I was attacked by one of their lancers, who threw his lance at me, but missed the mark by my throwing it off with my sword by my right side; then I cut him from the chin upwards, which went through his teeth. Next I was attacked by a foot soldier, who after firing at me charged me with his bayonet, but he very soon lost the combat for I parried it and cut him down through the head; so that finished the combat for the eagle.* "

Sgt. Ewart, Scots Greys, Waterloo
1815

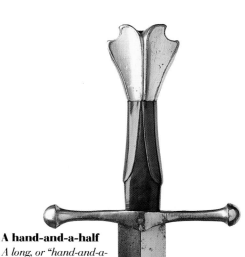

A hand-and-a-half
A long, or "hand-and-a-half" sword c. 1460, with brass and black iron pommel and hilt. This type of sword was generally used when dismounted, since it demanded the use of both hands to develop the necessary force of blow.

SWORD STYLES

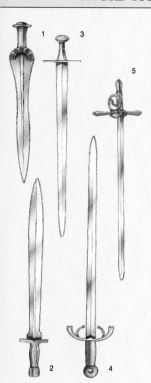

Swords developed over the centuries, though changes in shape often came about simply as a result of changes in fashion, rather than in response to specific military needs. The chief change was in the metals used, with bronze being replaced by iron and eventually by steel.

1 *Bronze Nordic short sword (c.1350BC).*
2 *Iron sword, used by Greek hoplites (c.6th century BC).*
3 *German two-edged sword (c.AD1150-1200).*
4 *Spanish sword with two finger-guards (late 15th century).*
5 *German hand-and-a-half sword (c.1540).*

The cup-hilt
A Spanish cup-hilted rapier, c. 1650. The hilt has the usual straight quillons, with a knuckle-guard and cup-shaped counter-guard. The hilt is bound, to give a firm grip, and has a heavy pommel to improve balance. Thrusting swords of this type soon led to the "school of fence" and the formalized art of the duel.

hand. This was particularly so when the art of fencing began to develop, and the hilt was often brought round upon itself so as to form a knuckle-guard, while the quillons were extended and shaped to protect the fingers and to entrap the opponent's blade. The rapier, a fine-pointed sword solely for thrusting, made its appearance and swordsmiths in Italy, Spain (particularly Toledo), and Germany (particularly Solingen) became famous.

From a single knuckle-guard it was a fairly logical step to include two or more bars sweeping from the quillons to the pommel (the end of the hilt). This process continued until the 17th century, when the basket-hilted sword became popular. A variation was the "cup hilt" in which a cup-shaped protection was placed around the blade; this was particularly common on rapiers, where the cup prevented a thrust striking the hand. In duelling, the thrust was the scoring stroke and there was little danger of having knuckles being damaged by a slashing blow.

THE ARRIVAL OF FIREARMS

By this time the firearm had established its place on the battlefield and the sword was gradually falling into disuse as an infantry weapon. It was, however, retained by cavalry since the firearms of the period were not well suited to cavalry use — they could be fired from horseback but were virtually impossible to reload — and the lance and sword remained the cavalry's chosen weapons. At the same time the sword had become a fairly commonplace article of dress for civilians, not a heavy battle sword, merely something for self-defence that was also elegant and decorative. This led to the "small sword" which gradually replaced the rapier. It was rather like a short rapier, with a simplified cup guard and somewhat wider blade, and with an elegant and discreetly decorated hilt. The small sword more or less laid down the form of decorative swords thereafter. There was very little difference between a 17th-century small sword and a 19th-century naval officer's sword, for example, since in both cases the likelihood of having to use it as a weapon was slender.

But, for the working soldier the sword remained a heavy and utilitarian article. The cavalry sword changed from a straight blade to the slightly curved sabre introduced to western Europe from Hungary by the hussar light cavalry. With minor variations, the sabre remained the cavalryman's standard weapon so long as cavalry lasted. For the foot soldier the "short sword" became a mass-produced weapon — more generally called a "hanger" — though the variations were enormous; non-commissioned officers wore different swords from those worn by the rank and file; musicians, pioneers, and artillerymen all demanded different swords, and frequently commanding officers designed swords simply to distinguish their regiment from the rest of the army. Even as late as 1914 a forward-looking officer like George Patton designed a new cavalry sabre for the US Army and could find something new to say about this ancient weapon in his book *Manual of the Saber.*

The Japanese sword
A katana of Japan, dating from the middle of the 17th century. The hilt is long, allowing a two-handed grip, and the single-edged blade and short quillons reflect the slashing mode of use preferred by the Samurai warriors.

EARLY CANNON

THE EARLIEST authentic record of a firearm is in an English manuscript *De Officiis Regnum (On the Duties of Kings)* written in 1326. This contains a picture of a man firing a small cannon; though it is not accompanied by an explanatory text, study of the picture reveals several interesting details. The gun has a bulbous rear section, tapering to a flared muzzle, indicating an early appreciation of the need for greater strength in the area where the explosion would take place. The gunner appears to be igniting the charge through a vent by means of a hot iron, which we know to have been the common ignition system of the earliest guns, and the projectile emerging from the muzzle is an arrow.

Also in 1326 the cannon is actually mentioned for the first time, in a Florentine document authorizing the making of brass cannon and iron balls for the defence of Florence; and in 1338 comes the first English reference in the form of a contract to deliver "ij [2] canons de ferr" and "un canon de fer ove II chambers un autre de bras ove un chamber" to the Keeper of the King's Ships. In the same year a French document details the fitting-out of a fleet at Harfleur to attack the English and refers to an iron cannon provided with 48 bolts, made of iron and feathered, together with saltpetre and sulphur for making the powder.

A further significant point about the 1326 illustration referred to above is the method of mounting the cannon: it appears to be simply laid upon some form of trestle table, although there may be an element of artist's licence here — firing such a gun from a table-top would result in it flying off the table and doubtless

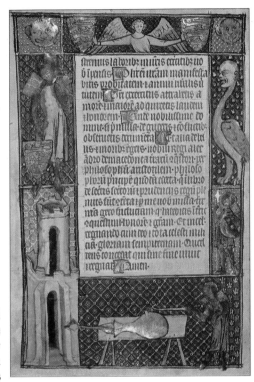

Vase-shaped cannon
The earliest depiction of a firearm; the Millimete Manuscript De Officiis Regnum *of 1326 showing the vase-shaped cannon being fired by use of a red-hot iron. The projectile is obviously an arrow, and the colouring suggests that the weapon was cast from bronze.*

Firing the cannon
An illustration from the Belli Fortis *by Conrad Leiser of Eichstatt, dated about 1400, showing the operation of an early cannon. The iron barrel is supported by a wooden pole and a simple crutch, and the soldier fires it by applying a hot iron to the vent.*

Siege cannon

The capture of a French town during the Hundred Years War. A cannon has been brought up to threaten the gate, but the actual conquest appears still to rely upon swords and bowmen. The cannon does not appear to have done much damage to the town.

Two-barrelled cannon

"The Earl of Haynault besieges and destroys Aubenton", another incident in the Hundred Years War from Froissart's Chronicles. It is of interest in showing a two-barrelled cannon mounted on a cart and carrying an overhead screen to protect the gunners from arrows while operating the gun. Again, there is little sign of damage to the town.

injuring the gunner. But the basic point is that the earliest guns were simply laid upon baulks of timber, pointed in the general direction of the enemy, and fired. Such refinements as wheeled carriages (see Artillery and mobility, page 68) and sights came much later; in the earliest days it was sufficient that the device worked at all, and the effect of the explosion on morale counted for as much as the material effect of the projectile. One account of the Battle of Crécy (1346), by Mezeray, claims that King Edward "struck terror into the French Army with five or six pieces of cannon, it being the first time they had seen such thundering machines." This earliest cannon of 1326, it seems, was cast from bronze or bell-metal, and was of the type generally known as "pots-de-fer" or "vasi" or "sclopi", but the type did not last long. The primitive casting methods and the expense of bell-metal did not encourage attempts to make larger cannon — the average pot-de-fer appears to have been about a yard in length with a bore of about 2 inches diameter — and a simpler and cheaper method was soon found.

THE GUN BARREL

The similarity of form between a hollow cannon and a hollow barrel doubtless led to adoption of the cooper's methods for gun construction. By the latter part of the 14th century the standard method was to build up the weapon by laying strips of iron lengthwise and then hammering so as to weld them together. The whole was then strengthened by iron hoops, and this led to the adoption of the word "barrel" for the resulting product. Often this iron barrel was bound with hides and rope to add more strength and to delay the onset of rust in the iron.

This system of manufacture allowed guns to be built much bigger than the early casting method could achieve. By 1377 there are records of built-up cannon throwing 200-lb stone balls and of the construction, for the Duke of Burgundy, of a cannon firing a 440-lb shot, which roughly equates to a bore of 20 inches.

From the earliest days there were attempts to develop breech-loading weapons; the "canon de fer ove II chambers" is an example. These weapons consisted of a barrel open at both ends,

fixed to a wooden bed. The chamber was a separate short piece, open at the front end, which was charged with powder and shot. It was then laid on the bed behind the barrel and secured by driving wedges between the rear of the chamber and an upstanding block of wood which formed the rear end of the bed. By preparing a number of chambers beforehand, several shots could be fired in fairly rapid succession by simply removing the empty chamber and replacing it with a loaded one.

The *petrarae* represented an improvement on this idea. It had a barrel formed with metal arms or a trough at the rear end into which the separate chamber could be dropped and wedged. This system was stronger than the separate bed method and also allowed the complete gun to be moved more easily. But in spite of these advantages, the primitive methods of construction meant that the joint between the chamber and the barrel was far from gas-tight, so that much of the explosive power leaked out. This reduced the power behind the shot and endangered the gunners.

ARMOUR FROM 1100

F ROM THE time of the First Crusade (1095–9) the Norman knight, in his knee-length chain-mail hauberk, (see Early armour, page 28) encountered the armoured horsemen of Byzantium and the Arabic Middle East. On the battlefields of Sicily, the Balkans, Asia Minor, and Palestine, two styles of warfare — eastern and western — clashed. The Normans relied on the mighty Frankish-style cavalry charge. The Byzantines and Arabs used lightly-equipped, bow-armed cavalry, supported by heavily armoured horses and riders who charged with their short spears and lances. This style of fighting was ancient: it dated back to the Persians who fought Alexander the Great in the 4th century BC. Like the eastern heavy cavalry, they too wore scale, mail, and lamellar armour.

Despite all this protective armour, the Norman knights' charge was very effective. In the words of one contemporary historian, it

The Battle of Najera, 1367

Fought during a civil war in Castile, in which both the English and French intervened, this minor battle gives an example of the type of armour used in the later 14th century.

"could make a hole in the walls of Babylon". There are stories of Arabs in the early 12th century delightedly adopting the armour captured from their western enemies.

Over the next three centuries, the knight became more and more heavily armoured, as smiths grew increasingly adept at fashioning the studs that made the rings of mail (see Early armour, page 28), and at producing steel plate in larger and larger pieces. The knights of the Third Crusade (1189–92) wore mail "trousers", carried smaller shields, and had rounded helmets — better for warding off

Chain mail

*An English iron mail shirt of the 14th century (**RIGHT**), a period which began to see the demise of mail in favour of plate armour as the armourers perfected their skills. This shirt is directly derived from the Norman "hauberk", though with somewhat longer sleeves. Like the hauberk, it would have required a fairly substantial cloth shirt to be worn underneath to prevent the metal chafing the*

skin, and would probably have had a surcoat on top to keep the iron dry in bad weather and also to carry the wearer's blazon or coat of arms. The skirt is divided in the front to allow the wearer to ride on horse and retain some protection to his thighs; this would probably have been supplemented by mail leggings retained in place by a waist-belt. Rather unusually for this period there is no sign of a hood or neck protection.

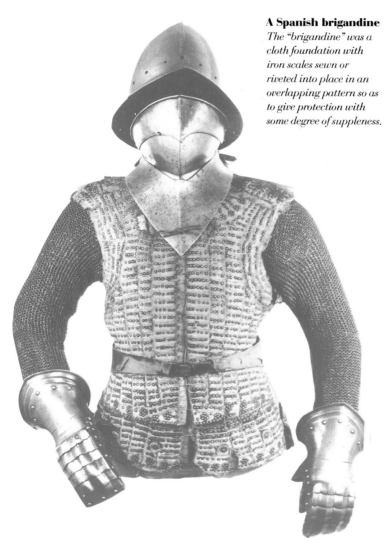

A Spanish brigandine
The "brigandine" was a cloth foundation with iron scales sewn or riveted into place in an overlapping pattern so as to give protection with some degree of suppleness.

charge by fully-armoured cavalry was made at Pavia in 1525. However, helmets and cuirasses were still worn by cavalry until the end of the 19th century.

THE ARMOURED INFANTRYMAN

Mobility was as important to the foot soldier as it was to the cavalryman. He therefore wore lighter armour than the mounted soldier. A succession of snapshots of a medieval infantryman would show, as in the case of the knight, the gradual development of more thorough protection. Initially, non-metallic materials were worn, in the form of a quilted linen tunic stuffed with cotton or old rags. Known to the Arabs as *al-Qutun* (the word for "cotton"), the westerners called it an Akheton or Gambeson. Gradually, the linen outer cover was replaced by leather, and small metal plates or scales were substituted for the cotton stuffing. This was called the "coat of plates" or "brigandine". A third form of protection, one also worn by knights, was a treated leather known as *cuir-bolli*. The leather was boiled and beaten into shape, then allowed to dry. The richest foot soldiers could afford mail shirts, and by the end of the 14th century even plate cuirasses and plate armour for the arms and legs.

During the 16th and 17th centuries armour was discarded. However, it never disappeared entirely, as the gorget of the 18th-century non-commissioned officer or — more recently — the flak jackets and helmets of the Second World War (1939–45) have shown. In fact, since the Second World War, it has undergone something of a revival, in the shape of lightweight body armour — the bullet-proof vest — made from materials such as Kevlar.

The armour of the present
A trooper of the British Special Air Service wearing modern body armour. The basic garment is made of about 24 layers of woven Kevlar, an aramid fibre with immense resistance to bullets.

blows — with nose guards. By the time of the Fall of Acre (1292) a well-equipped knight would have had an all-metal helmet that covered his entire head, with just a couple of slits for the eyes. The shield had become smaller still and was triangular rather than kite-shaped. Small plate reinforcements protected the knee.

At the battle of Nicopolis in 1396, the knights' helmets had visors to see through, which could be raised up or down to cover or uncover the face. The knights also wore gauntlets on their hands, a cuirass on the chest and back, and frontal leg and foot protection, all of which were made of steel plate. A hundred years later, during the French invasion of Italy in 1494, the knights were covered in steel plate from head to foot, were virtually invulnerable in single combat, and could often dispense with the shield altogether.

Yet while all this development was taking place, the knight's role on the battlefield was becoming less and less significant. During the 14th and 15th centuries, the foot soldier equipped with long bow, hand gun (see Handguns, page 40), or halberd triumphed repeatedly over the mounted knight, who increasingly found himself obliged to fight on foot, after his horse had been felled. (Protection for the horse could never be made as comprehensive as protection for the rider.) The last great mounted

EARLY HANDGUNS

THE "HAND GONNE" was the transitional stage between the cannon and the family of weapons which we collectively call "small arms". In the past, theories have been put forward that hand-held weapons must have preceded cannon, since it is customary to make things small at first and then enlarge them. However, in this case the custom was reversed, and for good reason: in experimenting with a substance as dangerous as gunpowder (see Powder and shot, page 46) it was obviously better to make something heavy and strong and fire it at arm's length in order to gain some understanding of the effects before reducing it and bringing it closer to the human body.

The first handguns were simply reduced cannon, though because of their smaller size it was possible to cast them rather than build them up from strips of metal (see Early cannon, page 36). The earliest known specimen is the "Tannenberg gun", so-called from its discovery in a well at the ruins of the castle of Tannenberg (not the Tannenberg in former East Prussia, but a small castle in Hesse). Since this castle was destroyed in 1399, the weapon must date from before that, and the existence of hand guns in the 14th century is borne out by the English Privy Wardrobe accounts for 1388 which record "III [3] canones parvos vocatos handgunnes". The Tannenberg gun is cast of bronze, octagonal in section, weighing about 2½ lbs, and 12½ inches long with a ¾-inch bore. A bronze gun of similar date and hexagonal in shape was recovered from the sea off Morko in Sweden. Some guns were made of iron. One of the earliest known specimens was found at Vedelspang in Schleswig, Germany. This was another castle, which records show was destroyed in 1426.

EARLY "HOOK GUNS"

Both the Morko gun and the Vedelspang gun have a large hook or lug beneath the barrel; in the former it is a forged lug with a loop shrunk onto the barrel, and in the latter it had been formed as part of the barrel. Its purpose was to anchor the gun against recoil by placing this hook over a wall or perhaps the side of a wagon, allowing the firer to direct the gun without danger from recoil

The Loshult gun

This bronze gun was found in Loshult, Sweden; it bears no marks, nor any indication of how it was mounted, but the reinforced muzzle suggests that it was an improved model based upon previous designs which had split at the muzzle, and therefore probably dates from the latter part of the 14th century.

A small calibre handgun
A cast barrel attached to the remains of its stock by an iron strap (above). This weapon is of interest since it shows a reduction in calibre from the original hand guns, doubtless to make it more controllable in use. Tentatively dated as early 15th century it also shows the beginnings of ornamentation around the barrel and muzzle.

when it was fired. The Morko gun, like most others, had the barrel attached, usually by metal bands, to a long wooden stock which could be used to direct the gun. The Vedelspang gun had the barrel extended to form a long iron stock with a knob at the end, which was probably a convenient hand grip for the gunner.

Contemporary drawings show these "hook guns" in use in the early years of the 15th century. The drawings suggest that the use of the hook allowed the gunner to take a rudimentary aim by looking along the barrel. Yet already by 1411, some thought had been given to the mechanics of directing fire; a German engraving of that year shows a handgun with a "serpentine matchlock", an S-shaped piece of metal pivoted at its centre to the side of the stock. The forward end held a piece of burning slow-match, which, when the rear end was raised by the touch of a finger, came into contact with the touch-hole and fired the gun. This allowed the gunner to use both hands to hold and fire the gun, rather than trying to wedge it under his arm while at the same time having to manipulate a length of burning cord.

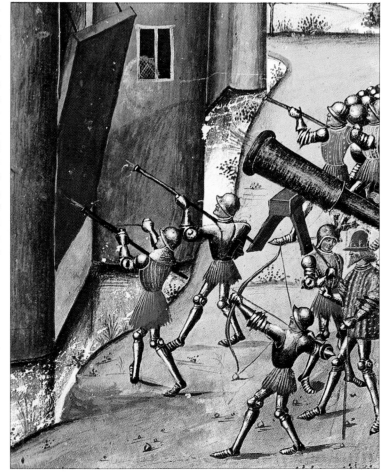

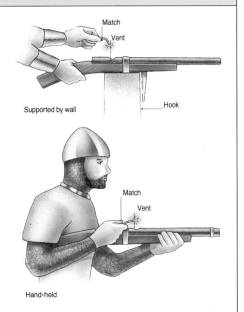

An early siege
Soldiers with hand guns, accompanied by archers and artillery, lay siege to a castle in this illumination from a manuscript of Quinte Curce, completed in 1468. *Note that the cannon is merely supported on a trestle. The hand-gunners appear to be taking a rudimentary aim and igniting their pieces with hot irons.*

FIRING THE HANDGUN

Handguns could be fired in various ways, depending upon how big they were and how experienced the user might be. Perhaps the safest method was to construct the stock so that it could be hooked over a wall or other support when fired. More often it was tucked beneath the arm and supported by one hand while he directed the match to the vent with the other. The need to watch the match and vent meant that aiming was tentative at best.

Match
Vent
Supported by wall
Hook

Match
Vent
Hand-held

A Japanese handgun
This is small enough to be used in one hand and appears to be ignited by a match. The muzzle, appearing from the mouth of a dragon, is a common Eastern decoration.

From the middle of the 15th century the firearm improved in reliability and accuracy. Hot-iron ignition gave way to the matchlock, which was followed by the intricacy of the wheel-lock, though the cheapness of the matchlock ensured its retention even though a better technical system existed. In this period too, gunmakers began to develop their skills and produce elegantly proportioned and decorated weapons for private owners, and it was in this manner that the wheel-lock gained ground. The wheel-lock also could be carried already cocked and primed, and this, in turn, led to weapons that could be carried concealed and used in one hand, and hence the pistol.

A one-hand weapon was ideal for the cavalryman, who had to control his horse with the other hand. By 1549 men-at-arms in the French army carried a pair of pistols on their saddles, and from then onwards the pistol remained the most popular cavalry arm.

Cannon also began to improve. The wheeled carriage appeared, making the artillery more mobile, though it remained slow as the gunners still had to walk alongside. The gunners began to experiment with different projectiles, moving from stone to iron balls, then to balls linked with chain, and hollow balls filled with incendiary mixtures and even gunpowder, though the problem of how to explode the shell effectively took a great deal of solving. Moreover, the science of explosives remained imperfectly understood. One problem that taxed gunsmiths was that the immense force produced when a cannon ball was suddenly set in motion tended to generate friction between the grains of gunpowder, exploding the shell before it left the cannon barrel.

The cannon was also used at sea, though in the early days this was probably more for show than for effect. Shooting at a moving target from a moving platform is not easy even today, and doing it without sights and with an erratic smoothbore cannon must have caused naval gunners much frustration.

CHAPTER THREE

THE AGE OF GUNPOWDER

POWDER AND SHOT

The Royal Laboratory
A painting, c. 1750, showing the manufacture of gunpowder in the Royal Laboratory, the ammunition department of Woolwich Arsenal. It is interesting to note the protective clothing, and the generally clean appearance of the room, evidence that by that time the hazards of powder manufacture were well understood.

> *The said Master of the Ordnance, his office is, that if there be any Captain that lacketh ammunition for his soldiers, the said captain shall come to the Master of the Ordnance and he must command the clerk to deliver such ammunition as he lacketh; providing always that the clerk do take a bill of the captain's hand for the said ammunition, and at the pay day the clerk shall deliver the said bills unto the treasurer, that he may stay so much moneys as shall answer to the Queen for the ammunition so delivered.*

Grose: Military Antiquities, *quoting a manuscript dated 1578.*

THE ORIGINS of black powder or gunpowder are far from clear. The first written record in the West is in an anagram concealed in a scientific treatise written by Roger Bacon in 1242. The first open record is in another Bacon treatise, written in 1266, in which he refers to "the powder, known in divers places, composed of saltpetre, charcoal and sulphur." This implies that it was generally known by that time, but the context suggests that it was simply a scientific oddity, something to startle and amaze people, which had no specific use. It was not until the gun was developed that the powder was found to have a practical application. But Bacon never revealed the origin of the powder and over the years there have been several other claimants to its invention. Exhaustive research has not produced any definite result, but it is now generally accepted that it was probably developed by the Arabs and then found its way into Europe. The frequently stated belief that it originated in China seems to have little foundation.

The formula given by Bacon in his 1242 manuscript called for 41.2 per cent saltpetre, 29.3 per cent sulphur and 29.5 per cent charcoal; it is doubtful if the materials of the day were very pure, and this, together with the stated proportions, leads to the conclusion that the powder was relatively weak. It was made by grinding the individual ingredients in a dry state, and then mixing them by hand to produce a fine powder. When the powder was poured into a gun, it settled into a dense body. This made ignition

Making gunpowder in 1630
The manufacture of gunpowder in the 17th century shown in a contemporary engraving. One man mixes the dry powder in a mortar, and his companion then passes it through a sieve in order to obtain a final product of regular size.

difficult as the flame could not penetrate the fine mass very quickly. It led to erratic action and inconsistent performance.

This weakness, however, was a blessing in disguise as the early guns could not have withstood a more effective and powerful powder. Stone shot was commonly used because it weighed less than an equivalent iron ball, so that when the powder was ignited the stone shot moved off quickly and prevented a build-up of high pressure behind it. Firing an iron ball of large calibre would probably have burst the gun before the shot left the muzzle.

The earliest guns used arrows (see page 40). The arrow was a missile that was accepted and understood, and by binding the shaft with leather until it fitted into the gun bore, it could be launched with some degree of accuracy. But arrows of a size and strength to withstand firing were difficult to make and expensive, and therefore the iron ball was developed. However, once the drawbacks outlined above made themselves known, the stone ball was widely adopted instead. It was cheap and effective; it could batter down light structures; it could kill and injure unprotected men, and if it struck a hard surface it would shatter, showering the area with dangerous fragments.

GUNPOWDER

The first gunpowder, known as "serpentine powder", had another defect. When it was carried in barrels and subjected to jolting, the heavy saltpetre and sulphur tended to settle to the bottom of the barrel, leaving the lighter charcoal on top, so that the gunner had to remix the powder before he could use it. The first ammunition improvement came in the early 15th century and is believed to have originated in France. This was the manufacture of "corned powder" in which the three ingredients were first ground, and then well wetted and mixed together. The resulting "cake" was dried and broken up before being passed through a sieve to obtain a consistent size of grains. When these were loaded into the gun, they did not pack so tightly as serpentine powder and thus the ignition flame could pass between them and ignite the whole charge almost instantaneously. The result was that for a given weight, corned powder was about three times as powerful as serpentine. It was also less susceptible to damp, unaffected by shaking or jolting, and was easier to handle, and it left less residue after firing. The only drawback was that it was too powerful for the built-up guns of the period, and therefore its adoption had to wait until cast guns became a possibility.

With cast guns and corned powder the iron ball came back into favour as the standard projectile. Iron was relatively cheap and a simple mould allowed balls to be cast very easily, whereas stone balls had to be laboriously hand-shaped. The loss of the shattering effect of stone on impact was more than balanced by the greater force which the improved powder, stronger guns, and iron balls could deliver.

The only real drawback to the ball was its limited effect against personnel: fired into a mass of men it would only damage those on its trajectory, leaving their companions to either side unharmed. To compensate for this many ingenious arrangements of balls linked with chains or iron bars were invented, so that they would swing in flight and thus carve a wider path of destruction.

PROJECTILES FOR EARLY GUNS

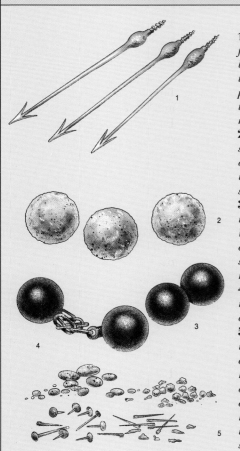

1 *The very first cannon fired arrows, simply because the arrow was the most familiar projectile. The shaft had to be bound with rags to make it fit the gun barrel.*
2 *Later came stone shot, since stone was freely available, easily worked into shape and did not strain the gun.*
3 *Stronger guns allowed the use of metal shot. While this meant casting and more expense, spent shot could sometimes be retrieved and re-used.*
4 *Chaining two shot together was an effective anti-personnel weapon.*
5 *Langridge was the term used to describe the collection of scrap metal, horse-shoe nails, gravel and anything else calculated to wound, loaded into the gun over a wad and fired like a shotgun.*

HACKBUT AND ARQUEBUS

BY THE early part of the 15th century the handgun began to change its form. It was realized that the large-calibre weapons were difficult to fire while the serpentine matchlock (see Early handguns, page 40) made control slightly easier. Moreover the match had been moved to the side of the weapon, making it feasible to take some sort of aim across the top of the barrel. However, the long stock or tiller, tucked beneath the arm, made this impossible.

The handgun with the hook beneath the barrel (see Early

Hand cannon
A Swiss hackenbusche (below) with wooden stock, dating from about 1400. Note that this carries a hook beneath the barrel which can be anchored on a wall to resist the recoil force and make the gun more controllable.

handguns, page 40), adapted for firing over walls or using some other solid rest to absorb recoil, now became the "hagbut" or "hackbut", a corruption of the German *hackenbusche* — "hook gun". In the past this has frequently been confused with the "arquebus", but the distinction between hackbut and arquebus (which often appears as harquebus) is apparent from a French document of 1527. It records the pay of "arquebusiers" and "hacbuttiers", noting that the latter were paid 10 times as much as the former, which suggests that the hackbut was somewhat more efficient than the arquebus. However, as the arquebus was improved it overtook the hackbut in general utility and by the latter half of the 16th century the hackbut was fast disappearing.

As the hackbut became lighter the need for the hook was reduced, since a man could support the recoil. The bore of the gun decreased, as did the size of the bullet and powder charge: the barrel was made lighter, longer, and more slender, giving better direction to the ball. All that remained was to make the gun controllable, and this was achieved by developing the first full stock, generally called the Landsknecht stock, after the German

An arquebusier of 1607
From Jacques de Gheyn's Manual of Arms, the picture (left) shows a typical arquebusier with his matchlock weapon and its firing rest. Note that he has the loose match gathered in his free hand, and that the match is lit at both ends; should the end in the cock be extinguished, it can be quickly re-lit from the free end.

The matchlock in use
An engraving by Theodore de Bry, dated 1594, showing Spanish Conquistadors herding prisoners (right). The matchlock is well in evidence, with typically Spanish curved stocks and simple hand-grip triggers. The men with firearms have retained their swords for close-quarter fighting.

FIRING THE LONGARM

*Firing the longarm was simply a step forward from firing the hand gun. Early Longarms were fired by tucking the staff under one arm while applying the match (**1**). As the barrel grew longer (and more accurate) it was found better to support it on a fork, still tucking the end of the stock under the arm (**2**). Eventually the stock became shorter and broader and could be placed against the shoulder.*

1

2

mercenaries who devised it. It consisted of a length of wood with a step in it so that the rear end of the barrel butted against the step while the whole barrel was supported by the wood and retained in place by iron straps. The rear end was shaped roughly to fit against the man's shoulder, and the usual type of serpentine lock was retained. Occasionally the wood was shaped to provide a better grip for the firer's hands.

Soon craftsmen began assembling the elements into more graceful shapes, carving the butt and stock, decorating it, and, at the same time, developing the serpentine lock into a more compact and reliable form — the snapping matchlock. This improvement to the handgun led to the arquebus, a long arm capable of being fired from the shoulder, though in practice it was common to use a forked rest to support the weight of the barrel.

With the weapon at his shoulder the soldier could now line up the barrel on his target with some degree of accuracy. To achieve greater accuracy rudimentary sights became more common. As early as 1450 there are examples of guns fitted with a simple blade foresight and an upright block with a notch for a rearsight. By 1500 a rearsight made by fixing two metal plates parallel to the barrel and filling the space between them with lead, then filing a groove in the lead, was in use. The earliest guns were so inaccurate that they could dispense with sights, but as the accuracy improved, owing to better and more careful manufacture, the desire to hit the target led to gradual acceptance of sighting devices. By the middle of the 16th century competitive shooting, which would be virtually impossible without sights, was relatively common in Europe. Not only were there contests between firearms, but contemporary engravings show that contests between firearms and crossbows were frequently held, and that the honours were fairly evenly divided.

MATCHLOCK AND WHEEL-LOCK

THE FIRST attempt at mechanically firing a handgun was the serpentine (see Early handguns, page 40), a curved piece of metal with a lighted match at one end that could be brought into contact with the touch-hole of the cannon. To make this idea effective it was necessary to enlarge the mouth of the touch-hole into a pan, into which powder could be sprinkled, thus giving a larger ignition area and decreasing the need for an accurate and therefore difficult connection with the match.

The next step was to make the serpentine less cumbersome, and thus the "snapping matchlock" evolved. In this system, which appeared in about 1500, the burning match was held at the tip of a curved arm which was hinged to the stock of the weapon. A short lever bore against this arm, keeping it away from the touch-

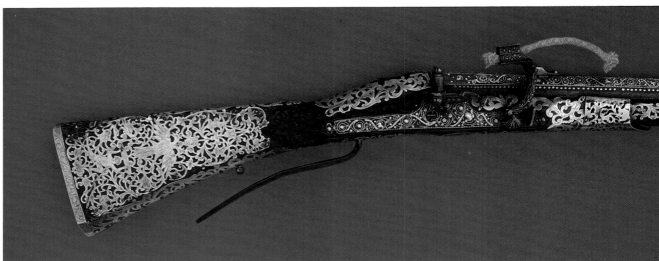

Matchlock

A richly decorated Italian 17th-century matchlock gun, with the match cord carried in its holder. The lever-shaped trigger brought the burning match into contact with the priming powder in the pan. The stock is inlaid with pierced brass work and the barrel decorated with silver.

Ramming the ball

A German soldier of the early 17th century armed with a matchlock musket. He carries a powder flask over his shoulder and is busy ramming the ball on top of the powder charge. After removing the rammer he will pull the match back to a safe position and then charge the pan with powder. Note that he also carries a sword in case he is surprised during the act of loading.

hole, and a rod, through the stock, was attached to this lever so that pressure on the rod by the firer's thumb or finger would disengage the lever and allow the curved arm to fall by its own weight and so bring the match into contact with the powder.

The match referred to was a length of tow, twisted from hemp, flax, or cotton and then soaked in a strong solution of saltpetre and allowed to dry. When ignited it burned at about one inch per minute, and a suitable length could be clamped into the end of the curved arm and ignited before battle commenced. An even slower rate of burning could be achieved by varying the strength of the saltpetre solution.

The snapping matchlock was only in use for a relatively brief period during the 16th century, although a number of them eventually found their way to Japan and the system was adopted there and remained in use until the middle of the 19th century. In Europe the snapping matchlock was replaced first by a primitive trigger mechanism, derived from that used on the crossbow (see Crossbows, page 24), and then by a neater trigger and sear mechanism concealed within a lock mechanism inserted into the stock. The curved arm was given a notch into which a metal strut fitted, and a spring to propel it forward. The strut was controlled by the trigger, so that pressure on the trigger removed the strut

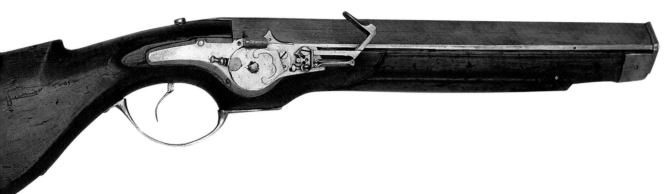

Wheel-lock
A German wheel-lock carbine dating from about 1620. The squared end of the wheel axle, upon which the spanner fits, can be seen, the wheel being concealed within the lock casing. The cock, holding the pyrites, is folded forward in the "safe" position and the pan cover is closed.

and allowed the match arm to be driven forward by the spring to make contact with the powder in the touch-hole. In this form the matchlock survived as a military system until the latter part of the 18th century, largely because of its cheapness and simplicity.

Carrying around a weapon with a smouldering match was inconvenient, however, for hunters and sportsmen, and even for a soldier there was always the danger of misjudging the length of the match and finding it extinguished at a critical moment.

THE WHEEL-LOCK

By 1530 — from the evidence of a dated pistol in the Royal Armoury of Madrid — the wheel-lock had been invented, introducing the first self-contained ignition system. Although it appears to have originated in Italy, the wheel-lock seems to have attained its greatest perfection in Germany, and many elegant German specimens have survived.

The wheel, from which the lock derives its name, has a serrated edge and revolves immediately behind, and partially into, the powder pan leading to the touch-hole and barrel. A short chain is attached to the axle of the wheel and to a powerful leaf spring; the axle has an exposed square end to enable a spanner to turn the wheel backwards against the pressure of the spring. When the wheel is turned back sufficiently far, a peg enters a hole or recess in the wheel and is retained there by the trigger mechanism. A "dog" or "cock" — a hinged arm — carries a piece of iron pyrites clamped in its jaw and is also under spring pressure and retained by a catch linked to the trigger. Pressing the trigger then releases the dog which swings over and strikes the circumference of the wheel, which has also been released and is spinning forward. The serrated edge strikes sparks from the pyrites, and the sparks fall into the pan and fire the weapon.

A variety of methods to achieve this mechanical end were developed over the two centuries during which the wheel-lock prospered. A pan cover was soon adopted, keeping the powder dry and in place, linked to either the wheel or cock so that it opened automatically as the sparks were struck. Some mechanisms used gearing to make spinning the wheel easier, or to make it rotate longer, while others used the movement of pulling the cock forward — "cocking" the weapon — to wind up the wheel spring and thus perform both actions at once. Less common were locks that used merely a segment of the wheel (the "sector lock") or even a flat piece of metal with teeth (the "rasp lock").

The development of the wheel-lock was a major step in the evolution of firearms, since it meant that a weapon could be carried cocked — ready to fire — at any time, without the need for a cumbersome burning match. The weapon could thus be drawn and fired with one hand, making possible a one-handed weapon, the pistol. This concept was welcomed by the cavalry, who were now able to carry a firearm into action. However, a pistol could be concealed, and by the middle of the 16th century several European countries had passed laws restricting the ownership and use of wheel-lock weapons to those classes deemed less likely to commit crimes.

MATCHLOCK AND WHEEL-LOCK MECHANISMS

Operating the matchlock
Once loaded, the cock was pulled back and the pan filled with powder. The match was then clamped into the jaws of the cock. Pressing the trigger then released the cock to fly forward and bring the match into contact with the powder, so igniting the charge.

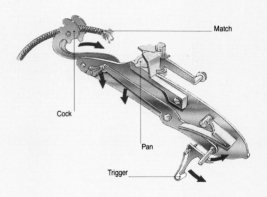

Operating the wheel-lock
The cock was pulled forward to the full cock position, the pan loaded with powder and the cover closed. The striking wheel was then wound up. On pulling the trigger the pan cover slid away, the wheel spun, the cock fell and brought the pyrites into contact with the serrated edge, and the sparks flew into the pan to ignite the charge.

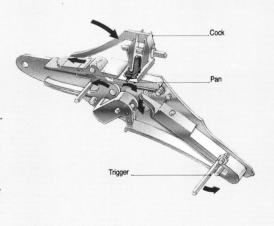

LATER CANNON

I N THE early part of the 15th century the improvement in gunpowder brought about by the introduction of corned powder (see Powder and shot, page 46) meant that the built-up gun was incapable of taking advantage of the new explosive. It became necessary to perfect a method of casting larger, stronger guns. Fortunately the skills acquired in the casting of bells were available, and by the middle of the century the casting of cannon in bronze was routine — so routine that the Turks, besieging Constantinople in 1451 and Rhodes in 1480, actually sat down under the city walls and cast the artillery they needed on the spot. And these were guns 18 feet long and of a 25-inch calibre firing huge stone balls.

Bronze was expensive, iron cheaper, and by the 16th century the casting of iron guns was under way. The first English iron guns were cast in 1543. By 1574 there was a surprising variety of ordnance available, from the robinet of 1½-inch calibre firing a 1-lb shot to the cannon of 8-inch calibre firing a 60-lb shot, by way of such weapons as the falconet, minion, saker, demi-culverin, and extra cannon.

By this time the gun had acquired wheels and could be hauled along behind a cart by a team of horses or oxen. But while these guns were movable they were scarcely mobile, and it was not until the reign of Gustavus Adolphus of Sweden (1594-1632) that artillery became portable enough to manœuvre in battle (see Mobile artillery, page 68). Gustavus split his artillery into two branches, field and siege, classing everything above the 12-

Proving cannon
An engraving showing a method of proving cannon used in the 17th century. Rather than risk disaster by firing, the cannon was first attacked by strong men with sledge-hammers to detect any flawed metal in the casting. Only if the cannon survived this test was it loaded and fired — from a distance, by using a length of slow match.

Firing from platforms
"Assault on a strong town in Africa"; a 15th-century French picture showing early cannons on wooden platforms firing at the walls and gate of the town while crossbowmen keep the enemy's head down. Firing still appears to be done by means of red-hot irons.

The Siege of Malta
An assault during the Siege of Malta in July 1565. Note that the use of hand arms and cannon is now common. The attacking Turks have a battery of cannon buried in the earth on the right, while cannon on wheeled carriages are in use by the defending forces.

pounder as siege. The field guns were mounted on light carriages. He also devised the famous "leather guns", built from light copper barrels bound with rope and leather reinforcement. These were more mobile than anything previously seen and, combined with cavalry, allowed him to develop simple fire-and-movement tactics.

After Gustavus's death, his ideas were largely ignored and artillery went through a period of quiescence until the War of the Spanish Succession (1702–13), when the Duke of Marlborough (1650–1722) revealed an innate tactical ability and a gift for the decisive handling of artillery that won many battles. He again saw the need for mobility, and used it, but, when he fell from grace with the politicians in Britain, his artillery theories went with him.

THE FIRST PERMANENT ARTILLERY

One of the difficulties of the time was that artillery was expensive, principally because it needed teams of horses and skilled gunners, both costly to maintain in peacetime. As a result, horses and their drivers were hired at the start of a campaign and dismissed when it was over. Frequently they dismissed themselves as soon as they heard gunfire, avowing that they were hired to lead horses, not to get shot, and many guns and gunners were often stranded by the sudden departure of their transport. Eventually it was accepted that the cost of a permanent artillery force had to be borne, and in 1716 came the first properly organized artillery unit, Britain's Royal Artillery, complete with all the requisite animals, wagons, and specialists.

The aiming of the gun had also improved. At first it was simply a question of lining up the barrel with the target, elevating it, and firing; the gunner put in more powder or less to reach his target.

But by 1500 the "gunner's quadrant" was in use, a simple angular scale inserted into the muzzle, with a plumb-bob and line to indicate the amount of elevation required, provided by knocking a wedge beneath the breech end. In about 1578 the method of elevating the gun by means of a screw passing through a lug at the breech end was developed, giving finer control. Aiming for line, however, was still no more than a matter of looking across the top of the barrel, sometimes aided by a notch cut into the muzzle.

Unusual cannon
Two unusual designs of cannon depicted by Valturio in his De Re Militari *of the 16th century. One is a form of mortar, designed to drop its projectiles over a defending wall, while the other is provided with a prow-shaped screen to act as a carriage and also protect the gunners from enemy fire.*

NAVAL WARFARE TO 1500

S EAFARING THROUGHOUT the eastern Mediterranean was a commonplace activity by the 2nd millennium BC. The establishment of maritime trade links was followed by the development of warships, as seagoing raiding became a profitable activity. The expansion of the Persian empire in the 5th century BC led to conflict with the Greek cities off the coast of Asia Minor. This led to the first large-scale naval actions for which substantial written records exist.

Salamis (479 BC) was a battle between two fleets of oar-propelled ships — the Athenians against Phoenicians, Egyptians, and the Greek subjects of Persia. Most of the vessels that took part were probably triremes — oared ships with about 150 rowers. At the bow of the trireme, just at the waterline, was a bronze three-pronged ram, designed to smash the hull of the adversary's vessel. Thus, the whole ship served as a missile. The Athenians, who were the victors at Salamis, became very skilled in the use of ramming tactics. A well-handled trireme could rake the oars off one side of an enemy vessel using its bow, and then return later to sink the now-helpless victim at its leisure.

In the 4th century BC warships got bigger. The standard vessel was the quinquereme, which was possibly an enlarged trireme, but it is not known for certain how the quinquereme was built. Battle tactics remained much the same. Following the collapse of Athenian military and naval power at the hands of the Macedonians in the Lamian War (323–1 BC), the Carthaginians became the Mediterranean's supreme masters of sea warfare. They too were known for their mastery at sea manoeuvres.

ROMAN DEVELOPMENTS

However, in the First Punic War (264–59 BC), the Romans captured a beached Carthaginian quinquereme, and used it as a model to build a fleet of their own. Cleverly, they chose to negate the Carthaginians' skill by developing the *corvus*, a weapon that could lock an enemy ship alongside. The *corvus* was basically a large plank with a spike or

15th-century warship
An illustration (RIGHT) from Valturio's Del'Arte Militare of 1483, showing a stylized view of a contemporary galley. The central "castle" was intended to give command over an enemy ship and permit arrows and handguns to be fired down on to the decks. The assorted armament of cannon, handguns, crossbows and polearms suggests either an invading force or a powerful boarding party.

Roman galley
A depiction of a Roman galley, from a mosaic in Sousse, Tunisia. The barbed ram forms an extension to the bow. With sails and oars working together, this ram was the most formidable weapon the galley had.

grappling hook at the end. When an enemy ship came close enough, as it would have to do in order to rake off the oars, the *corvus* was dropped and hooked into the opponent's deck. Soldiers (or marines) could then run across the plank and engage the enemy in hand-to-hand combat, at which the Romans excelled. The *corvus* helped to end Carthaginian naval mastery, and to bring about a successful end to the war for the Romans.

There are records of some larger ancient naval vessels mounting catapults, ballista, and similar engines (see Engines, page 30). However, the chances of scoring a hit on a moving galley — from a moving galley — with a weapon as ponderous as a catapult would have been relatively slight. The engines may have served to bombard the enemy with heavy missiles — perhaps burning ones — just before the impact of *corvus* or ram.

From the end of the First Punic War until the 14th century, naval warfare often consisted of little more than laying one ship against another so that the two crews could fight it out hand-to-hand. Admirals were effectively generals whose army fought the enemy from a self-contained fortress that moved by oars or at the behest of the changeable winds. Even the development of cannon (see Early cannon, page 36) during the 14th century did little to change this.

CANNON

The Venetians were probably the first to employ cannon in a warship. In 1378 a fleet of Venetian war galleys armed with "bombards" attacked the Dalmatian port of Zara and later captured Cataro. Other records show cannon being used at the battle of Sluys (1346) between the English and the French, and in a sea fight between the Moors of Tunis and those of Seville in 1350, but the evidence is not completely reliable.

The bombard developed into the galley's main armament: the fitting of a bombard — mounted to fire over the bow — became standard in the Venetian fleet. It was mounted in a very simple manner, lashed to a block of timber that was laid on the deck. There was no way of elevating the gun, and it was left to the gunner's skill, as the ship rolled, to fire at the right moment for the shot to reach the required distance.

Early cannon were of small calibre. The ships of the 14th and 15th centuries were not large enough to withstand the recoil of heavy artillery, so weapons were principally anti-personnel devices. Essentially sea fighting remained the same; the introduction of firearms merely made it more bloody.

Unlike the soldier on the battlefield, the sailor firing at a boarding party just yards away needed to be able to reload quickly. For this reason the "serpentines" — as the smaller-calibre shipboard guns were known — were often breech-loaders of the *petraera* type, complete with a separate chamber. A supply of loaded chambers could be kept handy and rapidly changed for the empty chamber after firing. The method of mounting the guns aided this system. The wooden block had a solid upturned end, and the chamber was placed in front of this and then forced against the barrel by a wedge. To reload, all you had to do was knock out the wedge, pull out the empty chamber, drop in the loaded chamber, drive the wedge back in, and you were ready to fire again. The gas seal at the breech was poor, but the speed of firing was considered to be more important.

The corvus

The Roman corvus *(LEFT) was an ingenious device for securing an enemy ship alongside and providing a means of entry for the boarding party. Hinged to one side of the galley, when not in use, it could be hauled up against the mast out of the way. When the galley came alongside an enemy ship, the* corvus *was released, falling on to the victim's deck where it was secured by the large spike. Once locked in place, it formed a bridge for the boarding party.*

MORTARS AND SIEGECRAFT

A MORTAR IS defined as an artillery piece that fires only at angles of elevation greater than 45 degrees. A gun fires at angles less than 45 degrees, and a howitzer can fire at any angle above or below this figure. The attraction of firing "high angle" or "in the upper register" lies in the ability of the projectile to pass over intervening obstacles and descend on the target; there is also an advantage in that gravity improves the velocity on the downward leg of the trajectory, giving the mortar projectile considerable smashing power. It was this feature which led to the invention of the mortar, ascribed to Mohammed II at the Siege of Constantinople in 1451. His object was to drop stone shot onto enemy ships anchoring a chain boom across the harbour entrance, thereby allowing a seaborne attack by his Turkish forces. The siege lasted so long that the Turks had time to set up a gun foundry outside the city and to build a mortar that succeeded in destroying the Byzantine ships with stone shot.

It is probable that the same idea occurred in Germany at about the same time, since mortars are recorded there in the mid-15th century. With them came the explosive projectile, a hollow ball filled with a charge of gunpowder, ignited by a simple fuze (see Ammunition, page 70). This led to a somewhat hazardous technique being developed, that of "double fire": the gunner had to manipulate his match very rapidly so as to light the shell fuze first and then ignite the propelling charge immediately afterwards, discharging the bomb on a high trajectory over the wall of the target, so that it burst in the air and scattered fragments below. The danger lay in the likelihood of the mortar failing to fire; before the gunner could do much to rectify matters the shell would explode in the mortar. For this reason the early mortars were not entirely popular, and it was not until the mid-16th century that the technique of allowing the flash of the exploding propellant powder to ignite the shell fuze was

The siege mortar
A Portuguese drawing of the early 17th century depicting a mortar in use. The perfectly vertical position of the barrel can be taken as artist's licence; some angle of elevation would be needed to throw the ball the requisite distance. The drawing also depicts the bursting of the ball, suggesting that either a powder-filled shell or an incendiary "carcass" was familiar to the artist.

The tower
An illustration from De Machinis Bellicis (Machines of War) by Mariano Taccola, 1449, showing a tower or "beffroy" in use. The structure is in stages, and the top stage contains archers who will engage the defences as the tower is pushed towards the wall. Once closed with the wall, the men below will rush up the ladders to the top stage and then over the wall.

The Siege of Sebastopol
British mortars in action at the Siege of Sebastopol, 1854. It can be seen that the mortars in use at this late date were little changed from the 17th-century weapon shown opposite. The elevation angle was constant at 45 degrees, and the range was varied by using more or less powder behind the shell.

The Siege of Constantinople
It is believed that the siege of Constantinople by the Turks in 1451 saw the first use of the mortar. Afterwards these guns were left where they stood and remained for centuries; some were later used to bombard ships passing through the Bosporus until the early 19th century.

discovered and became standard. With that, use of the mortar became more common.

So far as siege warfare was concerned, the mortar was an ideal weapon, since at that time the effect of direct fire against thick walls was not decisive because of the weakness of the guns and powder. Throwing a bomb over the fortified wall was more destructive since it attacked the target and not the protection; it also placed the inhabitants of the place in considerable danger. This was thought to be a useful morale-breaker, particularly during that early period when guns were still a mystery to most.

MORTARS AND GUNS IN UNISON

As guns increased in power, they were applied to the task of breaching the walls of the place under siege. While the guns battered the wall, the mortars wreaked destruction inside the wall, and between the two the resistance of the defenders was gradually worn down. Eventually the guns would cause a section of wall to collapse, whereupon the foot soldiers stormed the gap.

In the late 17th century soldiers began to bring some formality into the process of a siege. It became necessary to employ several batteries of guns to threaten several points, so that the defenders were in doubt as to where the final assault would come from. Trenches, known as saps, ran in zigzag fashion from the lines of encirclement towards the walls, and periodically these would be linked by an encircling trench line, so that gradually the besieged place was enclosed by a tighter and tighter loop of entrenchment. Eventually, under cover of darkness, one trench would reach the encircling ditch as the artillery made its final bombardment to breach the selected wall. The wall debris falling into the ditch, together with timber and earth thrown there from the sap, allowed the attacking party to pass down the sap, across the ditch and storm the breach as soon as it was made. Indeed, the conduct of sieges became so formalized that it was customary, as soon as a "practicable breach" was made in a wall, to cease fire and call for a surrender — a demand that was usually successful.

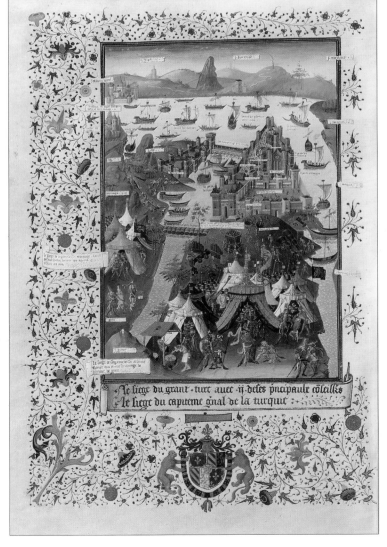

This period, broadly covering the 17th and 18th centuries, might be called the "flowering of the primitive" with major improvements in both muzzle-loading small arms and artillery. The flintlock became the standard method of ignition for small arms, though not to the total exclusion of the earlier systems, for match- and wheel-locks lingered on in many parts of the world. The flint system was also tried as a method of ignition for cannon, though never very successfully, being too delicate and expensive in heavy weapons. But the gunmaker's art progressed and some of the most beautiful pistols and muskets ever made come from this era.

As the science of weapons advanced, so did the art of warfare. Arming the soldier with a flintlock instead of the erratic matchlock allowed the development of volley firing, the disciplined use of mass firepower, and with this came the evolution of various military tactics designed to deliver a body of men to the correct place and in the correct alignment to discharge this deadly salute. Similar measures were introduced for cannon, leading to the formation of mobile artillery units, capable of moving rapidly on the battlefield to take up tactical positions, firing, and then quickly moving to a new position. How best to move the guns and gunners in a body took many years to perfect, and the age-old system of impressing farm labourers to act as drivers and waggoners gave way to the formation of complete units of artillery that could be relied upon to remain together under fire and retained in peacetime ready to be called on when needed.

Naval warfare developed in a similar way, from haphazard engagements between individual ships to the disciplined and ordered movements of fleets under a single command, manoeuvring so as to place themselves in the best position to deliver the broadside calculated to reduce the enemy to matchwood at the first blast. However, so long as the movement of the ships depended on wind and currents, seamanship remained rather more important than gunnery in deciding the outcome of a sea battle.

CHAPTER FOUR

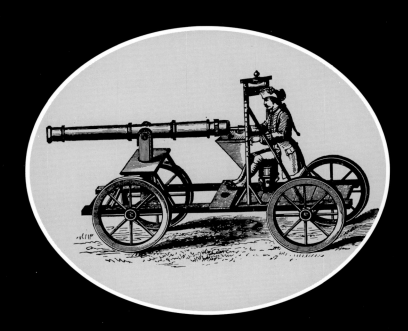

MOBILE WARFARE

CHEAP AND RELIABLE GUNS FOR ENTIRE ARMIES

FLINTLOCKS

PEOPLE HAD used flint to strike sparks for many thousands of years, so it was not surprising that this system should be applied to firearms; the only problem lay in how to achieve it. The flintlock appeared in the 16th century, though the exact origin of its birthplace is in some doubt.

Very likely, the first was the Spanish lock or "miquelet", of which there is record as early as 1547. It was probably developed by Simon Marquette, the son of an Italian gunmaker who had

Snaphance

An unusual Scottish snaphance gun in which the "furniture" — the stock and butt — are of richly decorated brass instead of the more customary wood. Such weapons, while robust,

would be too heavy for constant carrying as a military arm, but acceptable as a sporting weapon. The weight would reduce the recoil and probably improve the accuracy.

Brown Bess

Brown Bess (**ABOVE**) *was the flintlock musket that armed British soldiers for 200 years. Here, the lock is in the fired position; the cock has gone forward and knocked the frizzen so as to strike sparks and reveal the pan with the priming powder. Note the maker's name, "Grice 1759", and the Royal monogram indicating a military weapon.*

settled in Spain. It consisted of a cock with jaws, which gripped a piece of flint, and a frizzen, an angled steel plate which covered the priming pan and also intercepted the fall of the spring-driven cock when the trigger was pulled. After the weapon was loaded with powder and ball, the cock was pulled back until a cross-bolt, or sear, moved across the lock frame to hold it back. The frizzen was then hinged forward to expose the pan, powder sprinkled into the pan, and the frizzen pulled back to cover the pan and hold the powder in place. On pulling the trigger the cross-bolt sear was withdrawn, the cock sprang forward, and the flint struck the flat rear face of the frizzen. This struck sparks from the flint, and the impact also knocked the frizzen forward, exposing the powder in the pan to the falling sparks.

At much the same time as the "miquelet" the Dutch "snaphaunce" lock appeared. This used the same elements as the Spanish lock but was different in some important respects. The mainspring pulled the cock rather than pushing it, and the frizzen acted only to strike sparks. The pan cover was a separate, sliding component with a rod to link it to the cock, so that as the cock moved forward it pushed the pan cover open. Another significant difference was that the Spanish lock carried its spring on the outside, where it could be easily repaired, while the Dutch lock carried it inside, where it was better protected against damage.

Once these two locks had been introduced, variations followed.

Musket drill

This drawing by Thomas Rowlandson shows a soldier priming the pan of his musket after loading. His next move will be to close the

pan cover and pull back the cock to the "full cock" position, before lowering the musket to the ground and awaiting the next order, "Present and Fire".

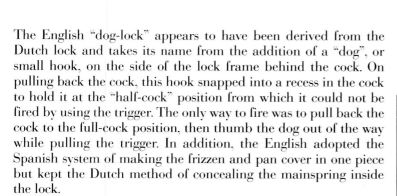

The English "dog-lock" appears to have been derived from the Dutch lock and takes its name from the addition of a "dog", or small hook, on the side of the lock frame behind the cock. On pulling back the cock, this hook snapped into a recess in the cock to hold it at the "half-cock" position from which it could not be fired by using the trigger. The only way to fire was to pull back the cock to the full-cock position, then thumb the dog out of the way while pulling the trigger. In addition, the English adopted the Spanish system of making the frizzen and pan cover in one piece but kept the Dutch method of concealing the mainspring inside the lock.

The Swedish lock used a long and slender cock which appears to have been influenced by the matchlock, giving this lock a distinctive appearance. The separate frizzen and concealed spring of the Dutch lock was used, but the pan cover was not connected to the cock and had to be opened before pulling the trigger.

THE FRENCH FLINTLOCK

After studying these variations, the French perfected the mechanism into the final flintlock design, the French lock. Their first attempt resembled the Dutch design, but without the interconnected pan cover. Their principal innovation was the "tumbler", a shaped cam inside the lock on the rotating shaft which carried the cock. The tumbler had notches which engaged with the trigger to give full- and half-cock positions and also a notch for the mainspring to provide the driving force for the cock.

This was soon superseded by the perfected French model which eventually became the accepted standard. For this the French went back to the Spanish lock and the one-piece frizzen and pan cover, shaping it more carefully to ensure certain ignition and opening. Together with the tumbler, the new frizzen made the French lock as foolproof and reliable as possible, and from its appearance in about 1635 to the end of the flintlock era some 200 years later there was very little improvement in the design. The flintlock had several advantages over the older, wheel-lock (see Matchlocks and wheel-locks, page 50): first, its reliability of action; second, its ease of maintenance, especially since flint was more readily obtainable and much more durable than the pyrites demanded by the wheel system; and third, its cheapness, since it was much simpler and easier to make than the complicated wheel-lock. Adoption of the flintlock was a cheap method of equipping whole armies with reliable firearms using mechanical ignition. While a master gunsmith could make a flintlock that was a thing of beauty and grace, a blacksmith could make a less graceful but just as effective and reliable one. The development of the flintlock was instrumental in lowering the price of firearms and spreading their ownership and use.

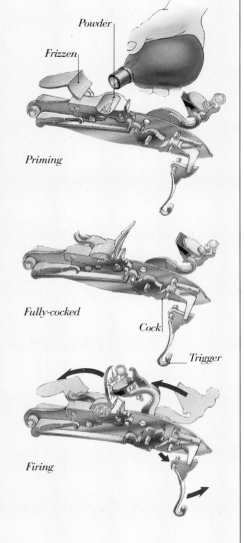

OPERATING THE FLINTLOCK

The powder and shot could be loaded before or after priming the pan. The usual military practice was to prime the pan before loading the barrel. To prime, the cock was drawn back, usually to the half-cock position, the frizzen opened (top), and fine powder sprinkled into the pan from a powder-flask. The frizzen was then snapped shut and the cock drawn back to the full-cock position.

On the order "Present!" the weapon was raised and pointed at the target; on "Fire!" the trigger was pulled, releasing the cock to fly forward and strike the frizzen. This generated sparks, and the blow of the cock threw the frizzen forward, exposing the powder in the pan to the falling sparks, so igniting the charge in the barrel.

Powder

Frizzen

Priming

Fully-cocked

Cock

Trigger

Firing

MULTI-SHOT LONG-ARMS AND PISTOLS

T HE AGE of the military flintlock lasted from about 1660 until the middle of the 18th century. There was little change in its design until the end of the 18th century, when the adoption of quicker-burning gunpowder enabled the barrel to be made shorter. The older, slower, gunpowder needed a long barrel to discharge its power, but improvements in the quality of the powder meant that combustion could take place in a shorter barrel. This development led to weapons that were easier to make and simpler to use.

Gunsmiths of the period tried to find ways of increasing the firepower of portable weapons, since a single-shot muzzle loader was not so effective when the user was faced by more than one enemy. One solution, adopted by guards and ship's officers in the last quarter of the 18th century, was the "duck's-foot pistol". This consisted of four splayed barrels attached to a common chamber. A single charge of powder was loaded through any barrel, and then all four barrels were loaded with a ball. Firing the pistol produced four bullets that spread the shot. The weapon proved useful in dealing with a mutinous crew on board ship.

One of the most famous of the multi-shot weapons was Nock's Volley Gun, invented by James Wilson in 1779 and named after the

Nock's Volley Gun
The volley gun's seven barrels were brazed together, the outer six having their breeches plugged. The central barrel screwed on to a hollow spigot which formed the chamber and was connected to the vent. This chamber fired through smaller vents to ignite the charges in the outer barrels. At first the barrels were all rifled, but this led to loading difficulty and most were later made smooth-bored, which improved rate of fire but reduced range and accuracy.

gunsmith Henry Nock. Nock was contracted to manufacture the gun, and 635 examples were sold to the Royal Navy. The gun consisted of six barrels arranged around a central seventh barrel and connected to it by ports. A flintlock mechanism fired through a vent that led to the chamber of the central barrel. When all seven barrels were loaded, firing caused ignition in the central barrel, and the resulting flash passed through and ignited the other six barrels, so that all seven fired more or less simultaneously.

Originally, the Volley Gun was intended for the fighting tops of warships, to fire down on the deck of an enemy vessel as it closed

The turn-off pistol
A turn-off pistol with the barrel removed; this pistol was originally made as a flintlock by John Waters of Birmingham (d. 1788) and later converted to the percussion system. With this class of pistol the ball could be made slightly larger than the bore, so forcing it to engrave in the rifling and make a better seal than would be possible by muzzle-loading. This improved the velocity and accuracy. The system was probably developed in Europe in the mid 17th century, an example dating from 1650 being known.

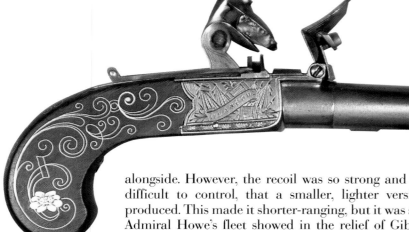

The muff pistol
One of a pair of "muff pistols", so-called from their being small enough to be concealed within a hand-warming muff and quickly produced for protection against highwaymen. No more than five inches long overall, the pistol is a flintlock, the lock mechanism concealed inside the body (hence known as a "box lock") and with the trigger also concealed by being folded up into the body until released by cocking the pistol. Thus there was little danger of inadvertent discharge while it was concealed.

The blunderbuss
This 18th-century flintlock blunderbuss is typical, with a short but heavy barrel which increases in calibre from chamber to muzzle, and a bell-mouthed muzzle. In fact the bell mouth does not help spread shot, but in the hands of a mail-coach guard, it must have been a daunting sight for any highway robber. The standard loading was "as many pistol balls or buckshot as can be chambered easily."

alongside. However, the recoil was so strong and the weapon so difficult to control, that a smaller, lighter version had to be produced. This made it shorter-ranging, but it was still effective, as Admiral Howe's fleet showed in the relief of Gibraltar in 1782. According to some reports, it was nevertheless unpopular because of the danger of a ship's sails and rigging catching fire from the muzzle blast.

Another way to improve firepower was by quicker reloading. In the latter part of the 17th century the "turn-off" pistol, developed in Central Europe, became popular, especially in England. This was a standard flintlock but with the barrel screwed into the breech-piece, which was firmly attached to the stock. The barrel could be quickly unscrewed by hand, loaded from the breech end, and screwed back onto the breech. After priming the lock, the pistol was ready to fire. The system had the added advantage of allowing the ball to fit snugly in the barrel so that the chamber could be bored to take a heavier charge. The turn-off pistol offered higher velocity, longer range, and better accuracy than its predecessors.

THE BLUNDERBUSS

Another weapon of this period which attained notoriety was the blunderbuss, a name derived from the German for "thunder gun". This was a short-barrelled, large-calibre weapon loaded with small shot, which was popular with stagecoach guards and on ships. Originally it was commonly made with a wide bell mouth. Many purchasers of weapons believed that this would spread the shot at close range. Good gunsmiths knew very well that this didn't happen, but the image of the bell-mouthed blunderbuss became firmly fixed in the public's mind. The gun continued to be made in this way, though some of the more astute gunsmiths made them with a parallel bore and added a moulding at the muzzle which made it look like a bell mouth. As an extra for close-quarter combat, some blunderbusses were fitted with bayonets that were hinged beneath the muzzle and activated by a spring.

One of the best-known firearms from the 18th century is the duelling pistol, though undoubtedly many more were made than were ever used in anger. Duelling pistols, which usually came in matched pairs, were small-calibre weapons for their day (usually about ·57-inch) and had barrels about 10 inches long. The first models, made in the early 1770s, were full-stocked to the muzzle, but from 1775 the wooden stock was shortened to leave about half the barrel exposed. Barrels could be round, octagonal, or half-and-half — that is round for the front half, octagonal to the breech. Common features of duelling pistols were their graceful shape and excellent balance.

**THE SPEAR
ADAPTED
TO AN
INDUSTRIAL
AGE**

BAYONETS

THE BAYONET stems directly from the various forms of polearm (see Spears and polearms, page 26); it was obviously inappropriate to have a firearm-bearing soldier encumbered by a pike, yet there was need for a polearm to stand off cavalry and for hand-to-hand encounters when ammunition was gone or when there was no time to go through the complicated process of reloading.

The original "bayonnette" — the name came from the town of its supposed origin, Bayonne in France — was introduced into the French Army in 1647. It was a plug bayonet, a spear-like blade to which was attached a long conical steel plug inserted directly into the muzzle of the soldier's musket, a collar lodging against the barrel to prevent it sliding too far in. This was serviceable enough, but had certain defects; the musket obviously could not be fired once the bayonet was fitted, and during the act of fitting the soldier was virtually unarmed. Misfortune overtook an English army at Killiecrankie in 1689, when a sudden rush of Scottish Highlanders overwhelmed them as they were fixing bayonets.

As a result of these defects, the socket bayonet was developed;

Plug bayonet
An English plug bayonet of 1688. The wooden handle was pushed into the muzzle of the musket to convert the weapon into a rudimentary pike. Once fitted, the musket could not be fired, so the bayonet tended to be a weapon of last resort.

this had the blade cranked and attached to a hollow sleeve which slipped over the muzzle of the musket. The blade lay below the axis of the barrel and left sufficient clearance to permit the weapon to be loaded and fired while the bayonet was fixed. The bayonet was firmly secured by a slot in the socket engaging with a stud on the barrel, requiring a half-turn to fix or unfix it.

Although generally considered as the infantryman's assault weapon, the bayonet was originally a defensive instrument. Steady infantry standing two or three deep and adopting a "square" formation could defend their position against a sudden rush of

The square
The 28th of Foot (The Gloucestershire Regiment) form a square at Waterloo to resist a French cavalry attack. The front ranks kneel and brace their muskets against the ground, the blades angled up to disembowel any horse getting close.

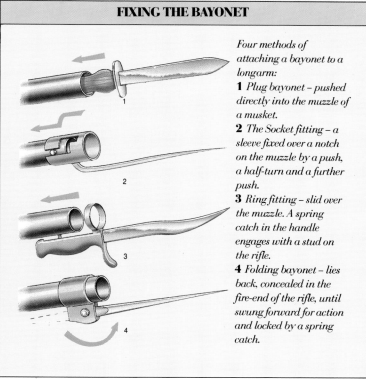

Four methods of attaching a bayonet to a longarm:
1 *Plug bayonet – pushed directly into the muzzle of a musket.*
2 *The Socket fitting – a sleeve fixed over a notch on the muzzle by a push, a half-turn and a further push.*
3 *Ring fitting – slid over the muzzle. A spring catch in the handle engages with a stud on the rifle.*
4 *Folding bayonet – lies back, concealed in the fire-end of the rifle, until swung forward for action and locked by a spring catch.*

The glorious bayonet
A French Marine impales a German soldier on his bayonet during the Siege of Paris in this typical morale-raising drawing of the period.

cavalry; the combined length of the musket and bayonet was sufficient to permit a standing soldier to reach a man mounted upon a horse. It was this employment which led to the standard form of blade, a triangular reed-shaped section, which remained in use until the 19th century.

A CHANGE OF ROLE

The idea of using a short sword as a bayonet was tried from time to time but the first regular users of the sword-type blade appear to have been the British rifle regiments in the early 1800s. However, the advent of breech-loading (see Breech-loading small arms, page 86), and then magazine arms (see Magazine rifles, page 88), provided infantry with a firepower capable of beating off cavalry, at which time the bayonet turned from being primarily defensive to being a personal offensive weapon. For this a knife-like blade was of more use than a spike blade, and so from the middle of the 19th century the knife or sword blade became common, though a few armies still retained spike blades.

The difficulties of fixing bayonets in the heat of the battle led some armies to adopt permanently-attached bayonets which folded above or below the barrel of the weapon and could be released and locked into place very quickly when required. A singularity of the Imperial Russian Army, which carried over into the Soviet Army, was the permanently fixed bayonet; no scabbards were issued, and the bayonet remained on the rifle muzzle at all times.

With the adoption of modern short assault rifles the utility of the bayonet as a weapon was placed in doubt; the combination is not well suited to bayonet fighting. Indeed, one would be hard-pressed to demonstrate that more than a token number of men have been seriously wounded or killed by a bayonet since 1918.

> All nations boast of their prowess with the bayonet, but few men really enjoy a hand-to-hand fight with the bayonet. English and French both talk much of the bayonet but in Egypt in 1801 they threw stones at each other when their ammunition was exhausted and one English sergeant was killed by a stone. At Inkerman again the British threw stones at the Russians, not without effect; and I am told upon good authority that the Russians and Japanese, both of whom profess to love the bayonet, threw stones at each other rather than close, even in this twentieth-century.

J.W. Fortescue, Military History

THE QUEST
FOR
ACCURATE
HEAVY
GUNS

EARLY ARTILLERY

The Gunner's Tools
A German engraving of the 16th century showing the gun chamber, rammer and powder scoop marked in numbered sections, suggesting that this illustration originally appeared in a gunnery manual in order to show how the range could be regulated by varying the amount of powder and the position of the ball when rammed. Early guns had a limited amount of elevation and varying the charge gave greater flexibility.

Emplacing a mortar
A detachment of the 1850s with a mortar on its transporting carriage. By raising the carriage shafts the wheels can be removed and the mortar, on its bed, can be lowered to the ground. It could then be aimed for direction by slewing the bed around, and for range by varying the powder charge, since the angle of elevation was fixed at 45 degrees.

A RTILLERY DEVELOPED slowly, as mistakes could be disastrous, and experimentation took place with the greatest caution.

The gun carriage (or block trail carriage) which comprised two wheels joined by an axle with a heavy wooden trail to support the weight and the shock of firing, had generally replaced the gun cart by the end of the 15th century. At about the same time came the first gunnery instrument, the gunner's quadrant. Reputedly the invention of the Holy Roman Emperor Maximilian I, this was simply a 90-degree quadrant with one edge extended for resting the gun barrel, and with a plumb-line hanging from it so that the elevation of the gun barrel could be measured. (When the gun was horizontal the plumb-line fell against the blank end of the scale, hence the expression "point-blank" for firing at short range.)

Having a scale of elevations was of little use unless these were equated with ranges. The gunner had to find these out for himself, since every gun had its own special ballistic character and one

gunner's scoop of powder was not the same as another's. So the gunner fired his gun at various elevations to discover how far it could shoot. To elevate the gun it was heaved up with levers beneath the breech end and held in position by driving in wedges. Later, in about 1574, an English Master Gunner called John Skinner invented an elevation screw to give fine control. Some early guns used an arc perforated with holes alongside the breech; the gun was elevated until a pin could be pushed through a set of holes to support the breech at approximately the correct angle, but this was only suitable for lighter guns. However, there was still no way of aiming other than by looking over the top of the barrel.

Artillery development remained static until Benjamin Robins, a mathematician and experimenter, published his *New Principles of Gunnery* in 1742. His main innovation was the ballistic pendulum. This was a block of wood slung on a pivot which, when hit by a cannon ball, swung through an arc. By knowing the weight of the block and measuring the swing of the arc, it was possible to calculate the power of the gun and to test how various types of powder, shot, and cannon performed. Robins also calculated the loss of velocity as range increased, and derived a formula for the motion of the projectile which took account of both gravity and air resistance. He also understood the significance of rifling (see Rifling, page 72), though technology was somewhat behind him in this area.

Once Robins had shown that gunnery was susceptible to measurement and calculation, other experimenters were able to devise machines that measured the speed of the projectile. By the end of the 18th century, gunnery had ceased to be a "black art". It had become a scientific pursuit.

SHRAPNEL

Now that performance could be quantified, advances were made in other aspects of gunnery. During the siege of Gibraltar by the Spanish (1779–83), the British fired mortar shells, filled with gunpowder, from a 24-pounder gun, using a powder-burning fuze to burst the shell on the air so as to spread fragments on Spanish boats beneath (see From case shot to cartridges, page 70). Lieutenant Henry Shrapnel, who was stationed in Gibraltar in 1787, carried out some trials and devised a method of filling a shell with musket balls and a small charge of powder, adding a powder fuze. He showed that, with the fuze accurately measured and cut, he could burst the shell close above the target, releasing the musket balls to devastate a 30-foot circle beneath. After many more years of trials and tests the spherical case shot was introduced in 1803. It lived on for another century and a half as the shrapnel shell.

There were also tactical innovations, particularly during the Peninsular War (1808–14). For instance, during the siege of San Sebastian in 1813, British artillery fired over the heads of their own advancing infantry, and only ceased firing as they closed in for their final assault. This was the first application of what was later to develop into the barrage, and the first use of a "fire plan" related to the movement of the infantry. Up till then, the artillery simply conducted a duel with the guns of the enemy or shot at whatever target presented itself on the battlefield. Another novelty from this period was the use of mountain artillery, a force which carried light guns, stripped to their component parts, on the backs of mules. By this means, guns could be taken into places otherwise inaccessible to artillery. These forces played a considerable part in the fighting in the mountains of Spain.

The Crimean War
An 18-pounder field gun in an emplacement outside Sebastopol during the Crimean War (1854-6). The rammer, sponge, handspike and other implements, are ready around the gun.

The Napoleon
The French 12-pounder gun, familiarly known as the "Napoleon", was France's principal armament during the Napoleonic Wars and after. It was also adopted by the Americans in the early 19th century.

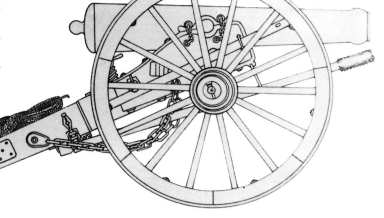

SEAGOING
CANNON AND
SPECIALIZED
WARSHIPS

NAVAL WARFARE: THE AGE OF SAIL

THE ADOPTION of cannon (see Cannon, page 50) at sea was a slow process. For a long time sea battles were largely a matter of two ships grappling together while the crews fought it out hand to hand. The cannon was confined to short-range work, and was loaded with a mixture of scrap metal and stones to repel the boarders. It was not until the latter part of the 15th century that firing cannon across the water to damage the enemy from a distance became a standard tactic. One problem had been the size and weight of the long-ranging gun. Only after the general adoption of cast-iron guns and corned powder were cannons useful on a ship.

THE SHIP'S GUN

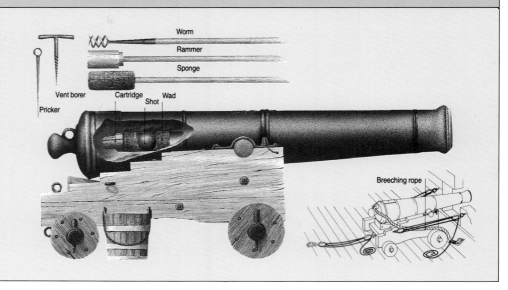

A typical naval cannon and its accessories. The smoothbore gun can be seen loaded with cartridge, wad, shot, and second wad to hold the ball in place against the rolling of the ship. The gun is mounted on a truck carriage. The sponge was dipped into the bucket of water and used to remove any smouldering remains of shot; the rammer rammed down the cartridge, wads, and shot; and the worm was used if the gun had to be unloaded without firing — its screw hooks would bite into the wads and cartridge. The vent borer was for clearing the vent of powder residue, and the pricker for punching a hole in the cartridge to ensure it ignited. The smaller drawing shows the breeching rope which restricted recoil, and the tackle with which it was hauled back to the firing position after recoil and loading.

By the mid-16th century the seagoing cannon was an accepted weapon, and its advance paralleled that of land guns. The principal difference between the two weapon types was in the mounting. The first naval guns were simply barrels laid in wooden beds. The bed was fixed to the ship and the barrel recoiled within it, restrained by ropes and chains. Then it was realized that increasing the mass of the recoiling parts would reduce the amount of recoil, so the gun was secured to the bed and the whole assembly permitted to recoil, checked by ropes. Later, small wheels, or trucks, were added to the bed, and from this the truck carriage evolved.

The truck carriage consisted of two stout side-pieces, shaped at the top to carry the trunnions (stub axles) of the gun so that it could be elevated and depressed. The side pieces were connected together by wooden transoms (cross-pieces). The gun rode on four trucks and was permitted to recoil across the deck, until checked by a breeching rope which passed through the cascable, the iron loop cast on the breech end of the gun. Once it had recoiled into the ship, the gun was reloaded and then, by hauling on the breeching rope, it was run out again ready to fire. The truck carriage was a cumbersome device, and sailors had to take care to avoid being struck as it recoiled. But it was robust and, most important, could easily be repaired by the ship's carpenter if it was damaged.

EVOLUTION OF THE WARSHIP

Until the 16th century the fighting ship was, with few exceptions, a made-over merchant ship. Anyone who sailed any distance on the oceans expected to have to fight sooner or later, and it took little adjustment to adapt the ship to a warship when necessary. Moreover this saved the State the cost of a standing navy. But gradually it was realized that whereas the merchant ship had to be beamy to pack in as much cargo as possible, a warship needed to be lean and agile, and so the specialist naval vessel came into being. As this increasingly became a fighting machine, so the armaments proliferated and became more specialized. Long culverins and demi-culverins could reach out to strike the upper parts and rigging of an enemy vessel before it came close. Should the enemy survive this and come closer then the smaller and fast-firing minions, sakers, and falconets would sweep their decks.

Not everyone followed this trend, but the experience of the Spanish Armada in 1588 proved the point. The Spaniards scorned the gun and relied upon having hundreds of soldiers aboard the ships to deal with the hand-to-hand fighting. The English fleet sailed with few soldiers but large numbers of long cannon, and relied upon seamanship to circle and harass the Spaniards. Their ships were sunk or damaged before they could come close enough to use their mass of soldiers.

Although such tactics worked for the most part, the light guns of the day could not sink ships; they could damage rigging and kill the crew, but they were incapable of sending a ball through three or four feet of oak below the waterline. To do that, heavier guns were needed, which called, in turn, for bigger ships. This move did away with the mixture of ordnance and eased problems of ammunition supply. Until then, ships had carried whatever cannon they could lay hands on, but warships of the mid-17th century were built with ranks of guns of one calibre on each deck, cutting down on the various types of shot required. This also produced a formidable feature of naval warfare — the broadside — as an entire row of guns on one side of the ship could fire at once, wreaking havoc on an enemy. The English King Charles I's great *Sovereign of the Seas*, launched in 1637, carried 20 cannon-drakes on the lowest tier, 30 culverins above, and 30 demi-culverins on the open deck. The effect of all those guns being fired at once is hard to imagine.

These developments led to a change in tactics. Instead of firing at long range to keep the enemy away, it now became the fashion to close to point-blank (see Early artillery, page 64) range and let off the entire broadside. From that distance — 250 yards or so — the shot could easily smash the timber of the target ship and seriously injure the crew with the flying splinters. Not uncommonly two enemy ships some 200 yards apart would blast away at each other until one sustained so much damage that the

fighting ended.

In 1747 Benjamin Robins (see Early artillery, page 64) proposed a new type of gun for the Royal Navy, which would be of the same weight as existing types but would be of a larger calibre and throw a heavier ball. He said this could be achieved by a "better distribution of the metal" in the gun, that is, by making the gun walls thinner. The matter was referred to a committee, and forgotten. But in 1778 a private firm, the Carron Ironworks, developed a short, light, large-calibre gun for arming their private merchant fleet. The carronade was of 8-inch bore and fired a 68-lb ball from a short barrel. Within a short time Carron were selling their guns to private owners as fast as the firm could make them. The Navy realized what they were missing, and by 1781 had equipped 429 of their ships with carronades.

Another idea to improve naval firepower originated in France. To even the score with the pirates of Algiers, in 1682 the French had invented the bomb ketch. This was a light craft with reinforced decks mounting mortars, with which they bombarded Algiers to good effect. The idea was taken up by other navies, albeit slowly, and in 1788 the Russian fleet won a significant victory over the Turks by using explosive shells (see From case shot to cartridges, page 70) and incendiary missiles fired from mortars and light cannon. In 1795 the French adopted explosive shells and settled upon a principal armament of 36-pounder guns firing explosive and incendiary projectiles. But this had its drawbacks. Although it did damage to the enemy, any shot striking a French ship was likely to start a huge fire if the magazines were hit. Nevertheless, the French persevered, and by the mid-19th century they had begun to look at a rationalization of calibres, combined with explosive ammunition and steam propulsion — developments that promised an "unbeatable navy".

The carronade

(BELOW) *The carronade was designed to fire the standard long gun 68-pounder shot at low velocity and short range. The gun was bored to a slightly smaller diameter than the long gun, making the ball a better fit, improving the accuracy and giving it just enough velocity to smash into the timbers of a ship.*

Le Redoubtable

(RIGHT) *The French first-rate* Le Redoubtable *reduced to a dismasted hulk by close range fire at the Battle of Trafalgar, 21 October 1805. This exemplifies the English short-range broadside tactic and Nelson's dictum "Only numbers can annihilate".*

68

**LIGHTER
GUNS FOR
RAPID
ATTACK**

MOBILE ARTILLERY

A LTHOUGH ARTILLERY had adopted wheeled gun carriages in the 15th century (see Early artillery, page 64), this had done little to improve the speed of manoeuvre. The gunners walked alongside the gun and thus the gun was tied to the speed of a marching army. At the battle of Oudenard (1708) for example, little artillery was used because the movements of the two armies outstripped the pace at which the guns could be moved.

Among the first attempts to add tactical flexibility was the battalion gun introduced by Gustavus Adolphus of Sweden in the early 17th century; this was a light gun dragged by infantry. However, it posed a dilemma: if it was light enough to be pulled by infantry, it was too light to do any damage; if it was heavy enough to be effective, it slowed the infantry's rate of advance.

Frederick the Great of Prussia found a useful compromise. In 1740 Frederick succeeded his father as king and inherited a formidable army. The Prussian cavalry were trained not to manoeuvre but to halt and engage the enemy with firearms. Frederick considered mobility vital and restored the traditional swords and lances. To provide the firepower, he devised horse

The Battle of Blenheim
A painting by John Wootton that shows two pieces of artillery being virtually ignored as the movement of cavalry and infantry swirls around them, a situation typical of the period (1704).

> *The state of the artillery was so bad during the latter half of the 17th century that it is strange that it did not entirely disappear from the battlefield. Field guns were almost useless from the difficulty of moving them...But while the artillery slumbered on in an undisturbed repose, isolated and unchanging, the efficiency of cavalry and infantry advanced.*

Lieutenant Colonel Hime: *The Mobility of Artillery, Past & Present. Proceedings of the Royal Artillery Institute, Vol VII, 1871*

artillery. The difference between artillery pulled by horses and Frederick's horse artillery was that his gunners were mounted, so that the whole force was capable of moving together at speed. The guns were light yet sufficiently powerful, and the ammunition was carried on light carts, which were gradually replaced by specialist limbers (two-wheeled gun carriages) during the Seven Years War (1756–63).

Frederick's ideas were slow to make an impression on the rest of Europe. In France the Chevalier Folard had developed a very lightweight gun in 1723, but it blew up the first time it was fired. This decided the inventor that guns were useless and he proposed reverting to catapults and arrows. In Germany, at the same time, light 4-pounder and 8-pounder guns were designed to be fired without unhitching them from the horses. They were succeeded by "galloper guns" which had the trail in the form of shafts for draught horses, which were unhitched before firing.

Marshal de Saxe, in France, decided that "artillery is unlikely to move faster and could hardly move slower". He devised the *amusette*, a light, hand-drawn heavy musket that fired a half-pound ball and was pulled by one man. Nothing came of this, nor of a later idea for a one-pounder on a light four-wheeled cart which could be fired on the move.

ARTILLERY SYSTEMS

Eventually, Frederick's ideas gained acceptance and different systems of horse artillery were tried out. They included the detachment system in which all men rode horses; the off-horse system where the gunners rode on the off-horses of the guns and wagons; the limber system where seats were provided on the gun and limber; the car system where the gunners were given a special carriage; and the wagon system in which the gunners rode on the ammunition wagons. The size of the horse team decided the size of the gun, and from the early 17th to the early 20th centuries this was a prime consideration in gun design. Since six horses were a convenient team, and could gallop with 30 cwt (1,525 kg), this became the upper limit of weight for horse artillery guns.

Frederick's ideas spread in the wake of his victories in the field. In 1774 the Austrian Army formed a mobile artillery force, first on the car system, then on the limber system. In 1776 the French artillery was radically overhauled by Gribeauval, but owing to political opposition he was unable to push all his reforms through; French gunners still marched alongside their guns until 1792. The British Army formed its first horse artillery units in 1793, using the detachment system.

The remainder of an army's artillery was divided into two groups: the foot artillery and the siege train. The former was the mobile artillery for a field army, but, as before, it was restricted to the speed of the men who walked alongside. Larger guns could be used, though the size was still governed by what could be pulled by a manageable team of horses or, in some cases, oxen. The siege train comprised the heaviest weapons; these were often too heavy to be drawn in one piece; the carriage was pulled on its own wheels, and the barrel was carried on a special cart which, since it did not have to withstand firing, could be lighter than a gun carriage. Siege trains were drawn by large teams (up to 20 animals) and moved ponderously. Arriving at their scene of action they had to be assembled by ropes and tackle before they could be used.

GUN CARRIAGES

Light breech-loading artillery
A mobile breech-loading cannon proposed by M. le Bonneville, a French engineer officer, in about 1755. The gun was to weigh about 180 lbs and fire a 1-lb lead shot; it was also proposed to fire on the move.

The amusette
A design by Marechal Saxe for a light gun firing an 8-ounce ball and capable of being operated by one man. He proposed distributing these liberally in the front of the line of battle, but nothing came of the idea.

The galloper gun
The galloper could be drawn forward by a horse, but the ammunition followed on a cart and the gunners were on foot

These systems of transportation remained as standard until the closing years of the 19th century and, in the case of horse and foot artillery, much later. Much of the German and Soviet artillery in the Second World War went into action behind teams of horses.

FROM CASE SHOT TO CARTRIDGES

FOR SOME 500 years, ammunition for firearms meant powder and ball, though the "ball" frequently changed its form. In the early days cannon balls were often made of stone, which was cheaper than metal and placed less strain upon the gun (see Powder and shot, page 44). Iron shot is mentioned as early as 1350, but stone shot continued in use until well into the 17th century. Bronze and lead shot are also recorded in the 14th century, but they were expensive and their use in cannon was uncommon on account of the expense.

A single projectile was not particularly effective against personnel; and very soon the idea of multiple projectiles was adopted. The earliest system, developed during the 15th century, was to shovel iron, nails, flints, and anything else calculated to cause injury, into the gun on top of a wad and to fire it in the manner of a shotgun. The intention was to cut a swath through the enemy's ranks. This ammunition was later refined as a bag or a canister ready-filled with scrap or musket balls, which became known as case shot. Its use is recorded from the late 15th century.

Another early innovation was red-hot iron shot. This was introduced by Stefan Batory, King of Poland, in 1579, though it was to be several years before the technique was perfected. Many accidents occurred before the use of wet wads — to keep the heat of the shot from the powder — was properly understood.

SHELLS AND FUZES

The idea of a hollow projectile, filled with powder, which would burst explosively and scatter lethal fragments also originated during the 16th century, but was slow to develop. The principal problem was making the shell burst at the correct point on the

Stefan Batory
Stefan Batory (1533-88) was King of Poland and is said to have invented red-hot shot, loading it over a wad of wet rags and turf, and firing it before it had time to cool.

A Light Ball
An early (c.1750) "Light Ball" intended to give light on the battlefield and also act as an incendiary. The body was made of coiled strip metal and the gaps were filled with quickmatch fuze. The gunner thrust a light down the muzzle to ignite the fuze, then fired the gun. The fuze burned away, exposing the inflammable contents, and finally ignited them at the end of the flight.

Grape-shot
Grape-shot (ABOVE) takes its name from its supposed resemblance to a bunch of grapes. It consists of a round plate with a central stem, *around which balls of lead were assembled and then secured by a tarred canvas cover lashed with cord. This was loaded into the cannon over the gunpowder charge.*

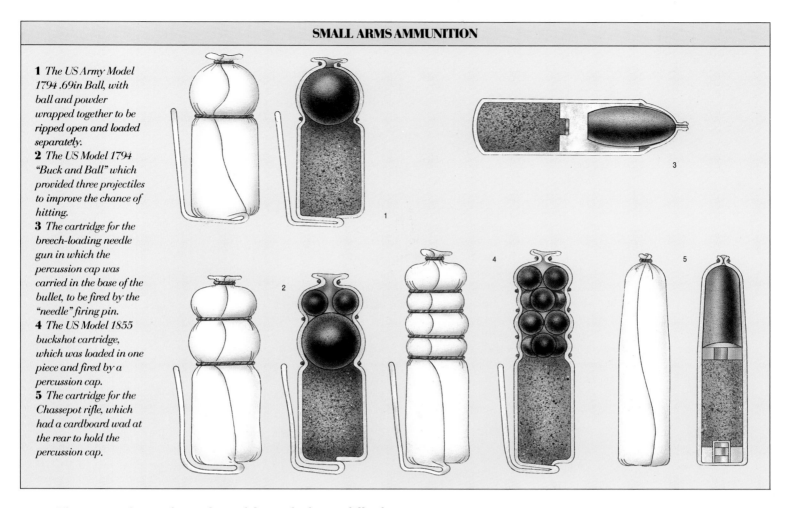

SMALL ARMS AMMUNITION

1 *The US Army Model 1794 .69in Ball, with ball and powder wrapped together to be ripped open and loaded separately.*
2 *The US Model 1794 "Buck and Ball" which provided three projectiles to improve the chance of hitting.*
3 *The cartridge for the breech-loading needle gun in which the percussion cap was carried in the base of the bullet, to be fired by the "needle" firing pin.*
4 *The US Model 1855 buckshot cartridge, which was loaded in one piece and fired by a percussion cap.*
5 *The cartridge for the Chassepot rifle, which had a cardboard wad at the rear to hold the percussion cap.*

target. This required some form of timed fuze, which was difficult because there was no ready means of measuring short intervals of time. An early example of a shell was used by the Venetians at the siege of St Boniface in Corsica in 1421. It consisted of a ball made in two halves which were filled with powder and joined together by an iron band. The fuze was a sheet-iron tube filled with powder and attached to one of the hemispheres. The use of similar shells filled with "wildfire" — pitch and resin mixed with gunpowder — was recorded later in the same century.

In 1672 the Prince Bishop of Munster, Christopher Van Galen, designed the carcass. This was a ball made from an iron frame wrapped in canvas or leather and filled with an incendiary mixture of pitch, resin, sulphur, and linseed oil. This form of carcass was gradually superseded by a hollow iron shell with three or four vents that exposed the mixture to ignition by the powder flame and allowed the blazing mass to spill out at the target. The carcass remained in use until the early years of the 19th century, partly as a fire-raising instrument and partly as a form of illumination at night.

The invention of the watch in 1674 helped solve the problem of time measurement, and by the early years of the 18th century a serviceable fuze had been developed. It took the form of a beechwood peg with an axial hole filled with a mixture of saltpetre, sulphur, and fine gunpowder. The peg was marked off in seconds and could be cut to the required length before being driven into the shell.

CARTRIDGES FOR SMALL ARMS

Small arms ammunition underwent little change. The idea of wrapping the bullet and charge in a paper package — or cartridge — was introduced in the late 16th century but no further significant advance was made for another 200 years or more. In 1812 Samuel Pauly, a Swiss gunsmith working in Paris, developed a self-contained cartridge for a breech-loading gun. This was followed by von Dreyse's invention of the "needle gun" and its self-contained cartridge in 1841 (see Needle gun and Chassepot, page 78). With breech-loading small arms now practicable, it was simply a matter of time before the metallic cartridge case appeared. In 1846 Houiller, another French gunmaker, devised a cartridge with a percussion cap (see Percussion firearms, page 76) inside, struck by a pin protruding from the side, and Casimir Lefaucheaux designed a gun to suit, in which the falling hammer struck the pin. Next came the rim-fire cartridge, made entirely of metal and with the percussion mixture distributed around the rim where it could be directly struck by the hammer. The final move, which took place in the mid-1850s, was to place a percussion cap in the centre of the cartridge base and arrange the firing mechanism to strike centrally, producing the centre-fire cartridge. Once the self-contained metallic cartridge had been made to work in small arms, it was not long before the principle was scaled up to produce metallic cartridges for artillery.

ARMIES ADOPT

PRECISION

WEAPONS

FROM THE

SPORTING

FIELD

RIFLING

AGUN'S ACCURACY is improved by rifling, that is the cutting of helical grooves inside the barrel. If the projectile can be made to expand into or otherwise grip these grooves, it will spin on its longer axis as it moves up the barrel. This will stabilize the projectile, ensuring that it remains nose-first during flight. The ball fired from a smoothbore barrel has no such stability. It will fly off in the direction opposite the last contact it makes with the barrel's interior, leading to inaccurate shooting.

Rifling first appeared towards the end of the 14th century. Gunmakers in Nuremberg are given the credit for its invention. For a long time its value was not appreciated. The lead ball of the day had to be driven down with a ramrod and mallet to engrave it into the rifling as it was loaded, and this frequently deformed it so much that it was no longer round and it flew erratically. The poor-quality gunpowder, which left hard fouling encrusted in the barrel, was another drawback to rifling. Indeed, some guns had straight grooves, largely to allow the fouling to collect in them and thus leave what was virtually a smoothbore, though clean, barrel.

At first rifles were precision weapons for sporting use, where time spent reloading was not vital. It was some two centuries before rifling was taken up by the military, and even then rifles were used only by specialist troops. Christian IV of Denmark had wheel-lock (see Matchlocks and wheel-locks, page 48) rifles made for some of

Lieutenant Colonel Patrick Ferguson

Patrick Ferguson joined the army at the age of 14. In 1774 he began designing his rifle. He demonstrated it before the king at Windsor and before officers at Woolwich, resulting in orders for 100 rifles. Ferguson supervised manufacture, trained a company of men in the use of the rifle, and sailed for America in 1777. After serving with distinction in the Battle of Brandywine, Ferguson was severely wounded and his company disbanded. He returned to duty in 1778. In 1780 he became Inspector General of Militia. He was killed, by an American rifleman, at the Battle of King's Mountain on 7 October 1780.

The Ferguson rifle

A rifle of Ferguson pattern, though not actually one of the 100 supervised by Ferguson. Although abandoned by the army after Ferguson's death, the design was taken up by gunsmiths for private customers and many beautiful guns were made. This shows the screwed breech plug in its open position, achieved by a turn of the combined lever and trigger-guard. The chamber was loaded with ball and powder through the hole in the top, after which the plug was screwed home. Ignition was by the normal flintlock method.

> **"** *Whatever state shall thoroughly comprehend the nature and advantages of rifled barrel pieces, and, having facilitated and completed their construction, shall introduce into their armies their general use, with a dexterity in the management of them; they will by this means procure a superiority which will almost equal anything that has been done at any time by the peculiar excellence of any one kind of arms.* **"**

New Principles of Gunnery;
Benjamin Robins, 1742

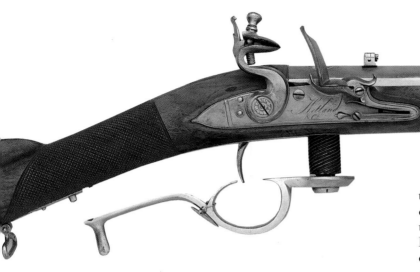

his troops in about 1600 and some French cavalry were issued with rifles by 1680.

The American War of Independence (1775–83) led to the more general acceptance of the rifle as a military weapon. The American frontiersmen with their hunting rifles showed that they could outshoot the British soldiers with their smoothbore muskets, and so the British too adopted the rifles. The most notable weapon was the Ferguson, a breech-loading rifle that used a vertical screw to close the breech. Loading from the breech avoided all the problems of muzzle loading and in this regard the well-made Ferguson rifle was ahead of its time. Colonel Patrick Ferguson, the inventor, took a company armed with his rifle to America where the rifle performed well. But when Colonel Ferguson was killed (ironically, by an American rifleman) in 1780 his company was disbanded.

The difficulty in loading muzzle-loaders was eventually overcome by Captain Gustave Delvigne of France who devised a rifle with a chamber of smaller diameter. Once the powder was loaded,

the ball (which was an easy fit in the bore) came to rest against the end of the chamber and was then expanded into the rifling by a few taps with the ramrod. A rifle of this design was adopted by the French in 1842. Delvigne continued with his experiments and discovered that the best shape for a bullet was a cylinder with a conical nose. However, it took several years before he could convince the French army to adopt his alternative to the ball.

The next advance was the pillar breech of Colonel Thouvenin, in which the chamber had a central pillar and the powder was loaded around it. The conical bullet dropped down the bore to rest on the pillar and, again, a tap or two with the ramrod caused the end of the bullet to be expanded into the grooves.

THE SELF-EXPANDING BULLET

The final step was the Minié bullet, which was self-expanding. At its base it carried a thin iron cup, which when struck by the gases from the explosion of the cartridge, forced the skirt of the bullet outwards into the rifling. By the time this was perfected in the 1850s, the French Army had decided to adopt a breech-loader (see Needle gun and Chassepot, page 78). However, the Minié bullet was used extensively during the American Civil War (1861–5) where it was the most common round used by both the rebel Confederates and the Union army.

The amount of twist in the rifling is critical to achieving the required degree of stability for the bullet. By making the rifling only just stabilize the bullet, its power to cause physical injury is increased because of its rapid destabilization on impact. On the other hand, a twist of rifling that overspins the bullet will increase its penetrative power, but reduce its capacity to wound. The size of a bullet is also important. Projectiles which are more than about eight times as long as their calibre (diameter) cannot be successfully spin-stabilized.

To put less stress on the projectile, progressive or increasing twist rifling is often used. This starts with straight grooves, or a very slow twist, so that as the projectile accelerates up the bore it takes up spin gradually. The degree of twist then increases along the bore to the optimum, which continues to the muzzle. Progressive rifling is common in artillery, which uses heavy projectiles. Under high acceleration a heavy projectile could easily shear its connection with the rifling if the speed of its rotation were increased too rapidly.

In recent years high-velocity artillery has reverted to smoothbore barrels, using fins to stabilize projectiles, in an attempt to obtain the highest possible velocities for the penetration of armour. A rifled gun wastes a proportion of the propelling energy in overcoming the friction of the rifling: the absence of this drag allows higher velocities to be achieved.

MINIE BULLET

The essential feature of the Minié bullet was its expansion. The bullet did not catch in the rifling as it was rammed down the bore during loading. When the charge exploded, the gas pressure acted on the cup in the base and forced the thinner skirt outwards to engage with the rifling, so generating spin as the bullet was driven up the bore.

Loaded

Not engaged with rifling

Firing

Engaged with rifling

The Industrial Revolution of the late 18th century took time to make itself felt in the armaments field. The invention of percussion ignition opened the door to methods of operation that had been hampered by the use of flint ignition and powder and shot as ammunition. The percussion cap led to the self-contained cartridge and hence to the breech-loading principle. The advantages of rifling were already well known, and once arms could be reliably breech-loaded it was only a matter of time before repeating weapons, in which the ammunition was carried in the gun and fed into the breech by simple operations, became practical. From loading the weapon manually, the next step was to load it mechanically by the application of manual power. This was followed closely by the weapon being used to provide the power to load itself. Within 80 years of Forsyth perfecting the percussion lock, Maxim had perfected the automatic machine gun — a rate of progress that, compared with the slow advance of firearms in the previous four centuries, is remarkable.

Similarly rapid advances can be seen in artillery, though they tend to be obscured by the constant shifts and changes as systems were tried and discarded. The percussion system made little difference to the big gun at first. More important was the development of a reliable breech-loading system allied to a system of rifling. The main problem here was the enormous pressure and high temperature in the gun, considerations that were not understood by the engineers who attempted to design new weapons. As a result, many of the early systems failed when applied to the heavy guns that were demanded to combat the ironclad warship, and many countries reverted to heavy muzzle-loading guns until better breech systems could be perfected.

The rise of the ironclad warship saw the investment of immense sums of money in the defence of harbours and naval bases. The gun, the submarine mine, and the controlled torpedo became tools of defence, though all were later to become more deadly as offensive weapons.

CHAPTER FIVE

THE AGE OF INVENTION

PERCUSSION FIREARMS

THE SEQUENCE of events in firing a flintlock weapon — the strike of sparks from the flint, the ignition of the powder in the pan, and finally the explosion of the propelling charge in the gun chamber — takes time. This did not matter so much to the military, but in game shooting it often led to the intended prey being frightened away before the ball could reach it. The flint system was also easily affected by rain — which was a more serious drawback for the military. Ingenious inventors of the time looked for ways to overcome these problems.

A first step was Edward C. Howard's discovery, in 1799, of "fulminating" materials — which would explode or ignite when struck. However, because of their extreme sensitivity to handling it was some time before any practical application was found. Eventually, the Reverend Alexander Forsyth, vicar of Belhevie in Scotland and a keen game shooter, discovered a method — the percussion lock — which he patented in 1807. This employed the mechanism of a flintlock, except that the cock did not carry a flint, but a suitably shaped hammerhead. In place of the pan and frizzen (see Flintlocks, page 58), a hollow bolt led into the gun's chamber, and revolving on the outer end of this bolt was a tubular magazine. The gun was loaded with powder and ball in the normal way, and the magazine was filled with Forsyth's "fulminating mixture", a combination of mercury fulminate and potassium chlorate. The magazine was then twisted through a half-circle to deposit a small quantity of mixture in the tube leading to the chamber. Twisting the magazine back moved the

A percussion conversion
A four-barrelled, all-steel, turnover pistol which was originally made as a flintlock in Belgium, in about 1750. It was later converted into percussion by modifying the hammers and screwing nipples into the vents.

Forsyth's sliding primer
A pair of pocket pistols, made in 1815 by Alexander Forsyth and Company, complete with accessories. These are fitted with Forsyth's patented "sliding primers". In front of the hammer is a small box containing the percussion powder. As the hammer is drawn back to cock the pistol, so the box slides back and deposits a quantity of the powder into the pan. On pulling the trigger, the hammer falls, pushing the "primer" back to its forward position, and falling so that the peg on the hammer strikes the powder in the pan and so fires the gun. This system replaced the "scent bottle" system.

mixture-carrying part out of the way so that a solid section, carrying a short movable rod, sat above the vent and the priming charge. Squeezing the trigger made the hammer fall and strike the rod, which drove down and struck the priming composition. This fired, igniting in turn the powder in the chamber.

Forsyth offered his invention to the Master-General of the Ordnance in London, who was responsible for the weapons used by the British Army. But before he could perfect his design the whole scheme was abandoned because of the prejudices of army traditionalists. Forsyth, however, promoted his idea commercially with considerable success before his death in 1843.

THE PERCUSSION CAP

In 1818, once the percussion idea was shown to work, improvements soon followed. Joe Manton, the famous English gunsmith, invented a percussion tube, a thin copper tube that was inserted into the vent of the gun and struck by the falling hammer. However, removing the spent tube could prove difficult. A better idea was the percussion cap, which had first appeared in about 1814. This resembled a small metal top hat in section, with a layer of fulminating mixture in the "crown". The gun was made with a tubular extension from the vent — called the nipple — which was shaped so that the cap could be pressed over the open end to fit snugly. When the hammer fell onto the cap, it crushed the mixture between the cap and the mouth of the tube, and the flash of the exploding mixture went through the tube and into the gun chamber to light the gunpowder. The hammer usually had a recessed head which enclosed the cap at the moment of firing, so as to prevent fragments of copper, split off by the explosion, from injuring the shooter. After firing, the shooter cocked the hammer and removed the remains of the cap from the nipple.

Although the metal percussion cap was eventually adopted almost universally, other percussion systems were tried. One was the pill lock, patented by Manton in 1816. This was an open pan that used fulmination composition pressed into small pills or tablets. When a pill was placed in the pan, the falling hammer crushed it, sending the flash into the gun. Another idea was percussion caps made from oiled paper which could be placed against a suitable vent and struck by the hammer (a system still used in children's cap pistols). In the tape primer — invented by

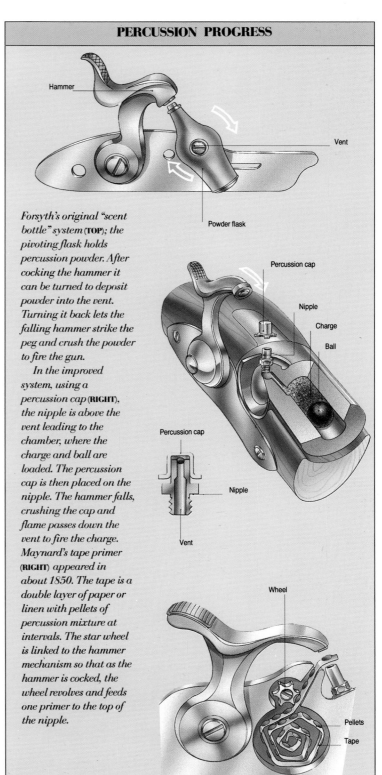

PERCUSSION PROGRESS

Forsyth's original "scent bottle" system (TOP); the pivoting flask holds percussion powder. After cocking the hammer it can be turned to deposit powder into the vent. Turning it back lets the falling hammer strike the peg and crush the powder to fire the gun.

In the improved system, using a percussion cap (RIGHT), the nipple is above the vent leading to the chamber, where the charge and ball are loaded. The percussion cap is then placed on the nipple. The hammer falls, crushing the cap and flame passes down the vent to fire the charge. Maynard's tape primer (RIGHT) appeared in about 1850. The tape is a double layer of paper or linen with pellets of percussion mixture at intervals. The star wheel is linked to the hammer mechanism so that as the hammer is cocked, the wheel revolves and feeds one primer to the top of the nipple.

Edward Maynard of the USA — a double paper tape containing pellets of fulmination composition was carried in a magazine in the lock. The action of cocking the hammer each time advanced a fresh length of tape and pellets. Numbers of Maynard tape-primed rifles were used in the American Civil War (1861–5).

NEEDLE GUN AND CHASSEPOT

THE FIRST practical breech-loading sporting gun was developed in 1812 by Samuel Pauly, a Swiss gunsmith working in Paris (see also From case shot to cartridges, page 70). With a drop-down barrel and firing a self-contained cartridge, it was the father of the shotgun, and about 50 years ahead of its time. Indeed, it was so revolutionary that no military authorities took it seriously.

The needle gun was the brainchild of Johann Nikolaus von Dreyse, a Prussian gunsmith who, after his apprenticeship, travelled around Europe gaining experience with various masters. Between 1809 and 1812 von Dreyse worked for Pauly, but by 1815 had returned to Prussia. There he began working on percussion muzzle-loaders, from which he progressed to developing a military breech-loader. In 1841 he offered his needle gun to the Prussian Army. Trials and modifications followed and the rifle was finally adopted as the infantryman's standard firearm in 1848.

BOLT ACTION

The needle gun can justly be considered the ancestor of every bolt-action rifle, since it was the first weapon to feature the bolt system of closure. The bolt, resembling a common door-bolt, moved in a frame behind the rifle chamber. With the handle vertical the bolt could slide backwards and forwards to open and close the breech. Once the breech was closed, the handle was turned down in front of a lug in the frame to lock the bolt. The front end of the bolt was carefully coned to fit into the similarly coned breech opening, forming a gas-tight seal when the bolt was closed. The cartridge was a paper cylinder containing the bullet and powder charge, and the bullet carried a percussion cap on its base. The "needle" from which the gun derived its name was a long firing pin passing through the bolt. It was pulled back manually against a spring before the bolt was opened, and held by a catch. When the bolt was closed, pressing the trigger released the catch and caused the needle to pass right through the paper cartridge, striking the percussion cap and firing the round.

The bolt seal was effective when the weapon was new but it soon wore away and leaked gas. Nevertheless, the needle gun was broadly reliable, easy to use, and a potent weapon on the battlefield. It gave the Prussian infantry a rate of fire — perhaps eight rounds per minute — never known before and astonished

The needle-gun

When the Prussian Army adopted the needle gun the details were carefully kept secret for many years. It was not until 1864 and its use against Denmark that its superiority became apparent. Nevertheless, it had two serious defects. First, the long needle-type firing pin, which passed entirely through the cartridge, was thus exposed to the explosion of the charge and corroded very quickly, leading to breakage in action. Secondly the sealing of the bolt soon deteriorated so that flame from the cartridge often burned the firer's face. Men soon learned to fire a worn needle-gun from the hip not the shoulder.

> **"** *I could see only infantry there (at about) 1,600 paces distant. But the moment the head of the Brigade was about to cross the bridge we suddenly received from Flavigny such a hail of chassepot bullets that one officer, the trumpet-major, three men and six horses were hit.* **"**
>
> Prince Kraft zu Hohenlohe
> Ingelfingen, Letters on Artillery, 1887

THE NEEDLE GUN

The father of all bolt-action rifles, the Needle Gun took its name from the long firing pin which passed through the paper cartridge to strike a cap in the base of the bullet. The explosion of the powder was confined by having the face of the bolt recessed and ground to a tight fit with the rear end of the barrel

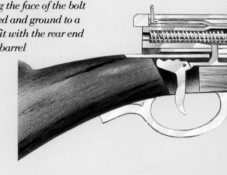

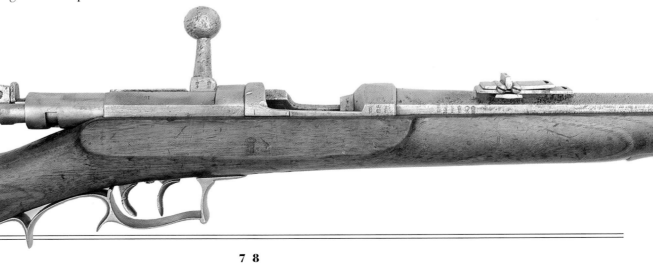

The Chassepot in use
French troops engaged in a street fight with the Prussian forces during the Franco-Prussian war of 1870. The Chassepot rifle differed from the needle gun in not driving its firing pin entirely through the cartridge, and in having a more efficient rubber breech seal. The calibre was smaller, giving longer range, but the small bore was easily fouled.

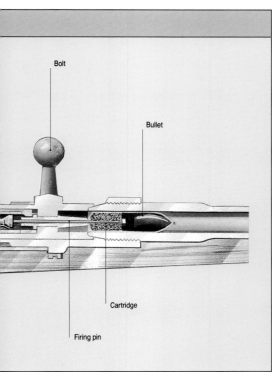

the military world when it was first used in the Danish-Prussian war of 1864 and then in the Austro-Prussian war two years later.

On learning of the Prussian needle gun, the French immediately began developing their own version, the Chassepot rifle. Named after its inventor, a gunsmith at the Chatellerault arsenal, the gun appeared in 1863. It was, in fact, another bolt-action rifle, very similar to the needle gun but with a shorter firing pin. When used in conjunction with a paper and linen cartridge that carried a percussion cap in its end, the firing pin passed only a short way into the Chassepot chamber before striking the cap and firing the round. The breech was sealed by an india-rubber ring around the head of the bolt. The pressure of the explosion pushed the bolt face back and squeezed the ring sideways to seal the chamber. However, the high temperature soon wore away the

rubber, so each soldier carried a number of spare rings and was well drilled in changing them as soon as gas leaks occurred.

The Franco-Prussian War of 1870–1 matched these two weapons against each other. During the fighting the Chassepot seemed to prove superior to the Dreyse needle gun; time and again the Prussians launched assaults on the French, only to come under such a withering fire outside the range of the needle gun that the attackers were either massacred or forced to give ground. However, subsequent tests on firing ranges have not confirmed the Chassepot's superiority.

The needle gun and the Chassepot proved conclusively that a breech-loader was better than a muzzle-loader, and signalled to the armies of the world that they should re-equip with breech-loading small arms as soon as possible.

EARLY BREECH-LOADING ARTILLERY

THE ADOPTION of breech-loading rifles by infantry gave them weapons with which they could outrange the smoothbore field artillery of the period, and by the 1850s it therefore became vital to develop breech-loading artillery.

The advantages of breech-loading and rifling (see Rifling, page 72) were well-enough known, but the long peace after Waterloo had stultified technical development in all armies. As early as 1821 a Lieutenant Croly of the British infantry had proposed a rifled breech-loader using a shell coated with lead; he could raise no interest in it. A similar system, better engineered, was proposed to the Swedish Army by Baron Wahrendorff in 1846 and he fared no better. In 1842 Colonel Treuille de Beaulieu of the French Army proposed a system of deep rifled grooves and a shell fitted with studs which was inserted into the grooves at the muzzle, while in 1845 Major Cavalli of the Sardinian Army proposed a similar system using two grooves and a shell with ribs which matched the grooves. All were briefly considered and turned down. The principal objection was the considerable expense of re-equipping armies already fitted out with serviceable smoothbore guns.

The Crimean War was the catalyst which brought all these ideas to the surface; money was suddenly available, and the advances in engineering of the 19th century produced men who were sufficiently interested in the technical challenge to set about

KRUPP'S 1000-POUNDER GUN.

The Krupp breech-loader
The Krupp 1,000-pounder breech-loading gun shown at the Paris Exhibition of 1867 and then presented to the King of Prussia. It returned to Paris in 1870 to bombard the city during the Franco-Prussian War. The shell is shown without its lead coat, revealing the ribs by which the lead was bonded to the iron shell.

developing their own ideas on artillery. One of the first was Charles William Lancaster, an English gunsmith who developed a "rifling" system which was actually an oval gun bore, with the axis of the oval twisted. The solid shot was also oval in section, and as it rode up the bore, so it spun.

THE ARMSTRONG GUN

ARMSTRONG BASED his design on the best engineering principles of the day and took no more than a passing glance at the gun as it existed in 1854. He decided on wrought iron as his material and constructed a barrel with numerous thin grooves of spiral rifling. In order to give this thin tube the desired strength he made a "hoop" of wrought iron, machined it precisely, heated it so that it expanded, then slid it over the barrel so that, as it cooled, it contracted and strengthened the barrel. He repeated this with more hoops, putting more thickness over the chamber of the gun where the greatest pressure would occur.

The rear of the barrel was formed with a vertical slot, behind which was a hole with a coarse screw-thread. A steel block, or "vent-piece" was dropped into the slot, and secured tightly against the rear of the barrel by a hollow screw that passed through the threaded hole and was tightened by a handle. The face of the vent-piece carried a copper ring which pressed tightly against the machined rear face of the barrel to seal in the explosion. A vent ran through the vent-piece to permit ignition of the charge.

The shell was coated with a layer of lead; the cartridge was a bag of gunpowder. Both were loaded into the chamber through the hollow screw, after which the vent-piece was dropped into position and the screw tightened. On firing, the lead coat of the shell bit into the fine grooves of the rifling, and the shell emerged spinning. Armstrong also designed an impact fuse which ignited the powder filling of the shell when the shell struck the target.

The heaviest Armstrong

(RIGHT) *A replica 110-pounder 7-inch Armstrong naval gun. The top of the vent piece, with its two lifting handles and central vent, can be seen.*

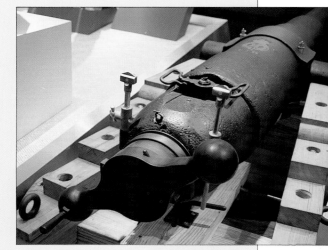

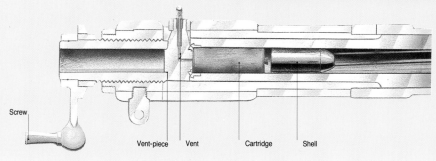

Screw · Vent-piece · Vent · Cartridge · Shell

The Whitworth gun
A 9-pounder Whitworth gun of the 1860s with two of the hexagonal projectiles standing beneath it. The breech block encloses the rear end of the gun and opens by a part turn of the weighted arms to disengage interrupted lugs. Note the open sights, the foresight on the trunnion and the rear sight to the right of the breech, and the screw-jack for elevating the piece.

LESSONS OF THE CRIMEAN WAR

Napoleon III, greatly interested in artillery, decided upon Treuille de Beaulieu's rifled muzzle-loading system, using six deep grooves. Krupp, in Germany, developed a similar design but allied it to a breech-loading system which used a sliding block of steel across the rear of the gun; a ring of copper was set into the block to seal the rear of the chamber. But the best-developed system was put forward by William Armstrong, who, though trained as a lawyer, was a mechanical genius and had set up an engineering company in Newcastle-on-Tyne to build hydraulic machinery. Reports from the Crimea convinced him that the contemporary gun was far too heavy and technically outmoded, and he straightaway designed a revolutionary weapon which, after considerable trial, was taken into service by the British Army and Navy in 1859.

Armstrong's principal competitor was Joseph Whitworth, another British engineer, who developed a system similar to that of Lancaster, using a hexagonal-bored barrel with a twist in it. His projectile was planed on six sides so as to fit the bore, the sides being obliquely cut to match the angle of the rifling. He also developed a unique breech closure which used a screwed cap that fitted outside the barrel, the only one of its kind ever perfected. The British Army, after their experience with Lancaster, were loath to trust a mechanical-fit, twisted-bore design and consistently refused the Whitworth gun, but numbers were sold to the USA during the Civil War (1861-5) and, given regular cleaning and careful loading, they appear to have performed well.

AN OLD
TECHNOLOGY
ADAPTED TO
THE NEW
INDUSTRIAL
WORLD

RIFLED MUZZLE-LOADING ARTILLERY

TTACKING THE ironclad warships demanded powerful guns. By the 1860s it was obvious that the early breech-closing systems were not strong enough to withstand the force of large charges in heavy guns. It therefore became necessary to revert to the muzzle-loading systems in order to provide artillery of sufficient power to defeat ironclad ships. Nevertheless, many of the innovations due to Armstrong (see Early breech-loading artillery, page 80), notably rifling and the process of building up a gun by a succession of hoops shrunk around the barrel, were retained.

The problem to be overcome was that of loading a projectile so that it would slide down easily from the muzzle but engage in the rifling and take up spin when it was fired. The initial solution was to adapt the de Beaulieu's deep grooves and studded shell, though the British used only three grooves instead of the French six. The charge was rammed down the barrel into the chamber, the shell was loaded base-first into the muzzle, and the gun was fired by the age-old system of a vent, though instead of loose powder a prepared quill tube was used, ignited by friction.

While the system worked and delivered the smashing power necessary to propel iron shot, it was essential to have some clearance between the shell and the barrel, otherwise the air trapped beneath

A training session c. 1880

The granite embrasure and iron shield of this British 10-inch 18-ton RML coastal defence gun are typical protection against gunfire from the target ship. France and the United States developed similar forms of protection.

Loading a 16-pounder
In this scene of British volunteers c. 1885, one man is "serving the vent" – that is, placing his thumb over the firing vent to prevent any rush of air from igniting any smouldering remains.

would prevent the shell being loaded. On firing, a great deal of the energy of the propellant gases passed through this "windage" or clearance and was wasted. Moreover, in its passage, the hot gas eroded the bore of the wrought iron guns and wore them away.

STEEL-BARRELLED GUNS

By the 1870s knowledge of the forging of steel was sufficient to be able to make moderately reliable thin cylinders and therefore the basic barrel was now forged from steel, though wrought iron was

BREECH LOADER VERSUS RML

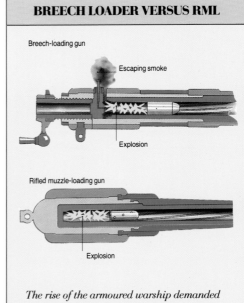

Breech-loading gun

Escaping smoke

Explosion

Rifled muzzle-loading gun

Explosion

The rise of the armoured warship demanded guns powerful enough to penetrate their defences. The breech closure of the Armstrong gun (TOP) was too weak to withstand the high pressures needed to propel shot at sufficiently high velocity. Whereas the solidly constructed rifled muzzle loader (ABOVE) could be built to the strength required for the job.

still used for the massive hoops which provided most of the strength of the gun. The hoops were too large and thick to be made from steel, since this was still a far from perfect material, and making large castings which were free from flaws was a matter of chance rather than skill.

The next step was to place a shaped copper cup on the base of the shell before loading. This was of the correct diameter to enter the barrel easily and had raised ribs to match the rifling grooves: the ignition of the charge behind it forced the sides of the cup outwards to seal against the walls of the gun barrel and thus trap almost all the propellant gas behind the shell, giving a considerable improvement in efficiency and reducing the rate of wear.

Armstrong then discovered that since the cup – or "gas-check" – was provided with lugs and rode in the rifling, if it was attached firmly to the shell it could do the rotating, and the shell no longer needed to be made with studs, so making shell manufacture easier.

Improvements in the manufacture of gunpowder paralleled those of gun development. The coarse-grained gunpowder was relatively slow to ignite in the huge quantities demanded for these large guns, and much of it was ejected from the muzzle whilst still burning. The next step was to mould the gunpowder into hexagonal prisms, with a hole down the centre, and stack these in the cartridge bag in a regular manner so that the holes were aligned, giving flash channels from one end of the charge to the other. Ignition commenced about one-third of the charge length from the rear end, at the point where the vent was bored through the top or side of the gun, and passed rapidly through the charge.

Unfortunately this brought more problems. Since muzzle-loading guns had to be drawn into their emplacements to be loaded, they needed to be short – particularly on warships. But the new large grains of powder did not have time to be fully consumed before the shell left the muzzle in short guns, and thus much of the charge was ejected without having done any useful work. It was time to think again.

THE HUNDRED-TON GUNS

THE MOST powerful rifled muzzle-loading guns ever made were 17.72 inches in calibre and weighed 102 tons – and two of them still exist.

Sir William Armstrong had perfected the design of the RML guns for the British Army and the Royal Navy and went on to sell numbers to other countries. In 1875 the company was approached by the Italian Navy to produce four 17.72-inch guns to arm the new battleship *Duillio* and to license manufacture of more guns to the Italian government for further ships of the class and for the protection of the great naval base of La Spezia on Italy's northwestern coast.

The prospect of warships armed with such guns being let loose in the Mediterranean alarmed the British government, who, in 1878, purchased four of the 17.72 inch guns from Armstrong. Unfortunately, being naval guns, there were no mountings available to permit them to be emplaced on land and it was 1880 before these were designed and built. Thereafter two guns were sent to the fortress of Malta and two to Gibraltar to protect these British bases. They were finally installed and declared operational in 1886.

The "Hundred Ton Guns" – as they came to be known – fired a 1,968lb shell at a velocity of 1,550 feet-per-second to a maximum range of 6,800 yards. At 1,000-yards range the shell could penetrate 26 inches of wrought-iron armour. Their emplacements were provided with steam-driven hoists and rammers built into shell-proof underground compartments. To load, the gun was swung to one side of the emplacement and depressed in line with the rammer; a cartridge containing 450lbs of gunpowder was brought up on a lift from the magazine and thrust into the barrel by the rammer. This was then withdrawn and a shell was hoisted and rammed. The gun had 28 rifling grooves, and the shell was fitted with a saucer-shaped copper plate on the base which, under the pressure of the propelling charge, expanded outwards and bit into the rifling to spin the shell. One shot could be fitted every four minutes.

100-ton Armstrong Gun
In this RML gun installed at the Magdala Battery, Gibraltar, the loading arrangements are protected beneath the concrete emplacement in front of the gun.

Ironically, in the very year that these guns became operational, the British Director of Artillery began purchase of the first heavy breech-loading guns. The "Hundred Ton Guns" never fired a shot in anger and were declared obsolete in 1907. Such were the problems of removing them, however, that one has remained in place in each fortress.

ADAPTING THE OLD RIFLES TO THE NEW TECHNOLOGY

SMALL ARMS CONVERSIONS

THE ADOPTION of the Needle Gun and the Chassepot (see Needle gun, page 78), by the Prussians and French respectively, made the other armies of the world think seriously about breech-loading rifles. They had to replace their old muzzle-loading rifles or be left behind, but the expense of completely re-equipping major armies was a daunting thought. The most attractive solution was to find some system which would permit their enormous stocks of muzzle-loading weapons to be converted into breech-loaders; this would give their troops a reasonably efficient weapon, after which they could take their time about finding and adopting something better. It was clear that the rate of mechanical discovery was such that whatever they adopted, something better would appear soon after.

The broad solution was to cut out a section at the rear end of the muzzle-loaded barrel and replace it with a hinged block carrying some means of ignition. The earliest such conversion was, in fact, ahead of its time: performed in 1849 by Sylvestr Krnka, a Bohemian gunsmith, it was a conversion of existing percussion muskets to use a paper cartridge. The hammer was retained, and a nipple and vent on the hinged breech block took care of ignition. The block was swung sideways to open, a paper cartridge inserted into the barrel, and the block closed. A cap was placed on the nipple and the hammer fired it, igniting the powder in the cartridge. While this worked, the Austrian Army were not much impressed and the idea was turned down.

Krnka then turned to other things, but came back in 1852 with a modified design suitable for the Lefaucheaux metal-rimmed paper cartridge. From this design he developed a number of rifle conversions for the Montenegrin (1866) and Russian (1869) armies.

THE SIDE-HINGED BREECH BLOCK

In Britain the inevitable committee was set up to examine the question, and they recommended the conversion designed by Jacob Snider Jr, a New Yorker who submitted his idea in 1864. This was a

> **"** *The 4th King's Own, the Baluchis and the Bombay Sappers, supported by the 10th Coy. R.E., advanced along the plateau, the Madras Sappers moving to the right to cut off a retreat by the valleys on that side. The Sniders quickly took effect, and some thirty bodies dotted the plateau before the regiments formed line to the left, pouring volleys into the enemy who were massed in the ravines on their flank. In spite of our superiority it cannot be denied that their resistance was that of a brave people; though driven off the plateau their advance was so well sustained that our baggage guard itself was closely engaged.* **"**

The Abyssinian Expedition:
Lieutenant E.F. Chapman, RHA; in
Proceedings of the R.A. Institution,
1870

Gurkhas and the Snider
The Snider rifle saw only two campaigns in British hands — Abyssinia in 1868 and the Ashanti War of 1873 — but remained in use with the Indian Army until the turn of the century. Original models were conversions from the Enfield muzzle-loading rifles and carbines, but in 1868-70 new weapons were made, which used steel instead of wrought iron for the barrels.

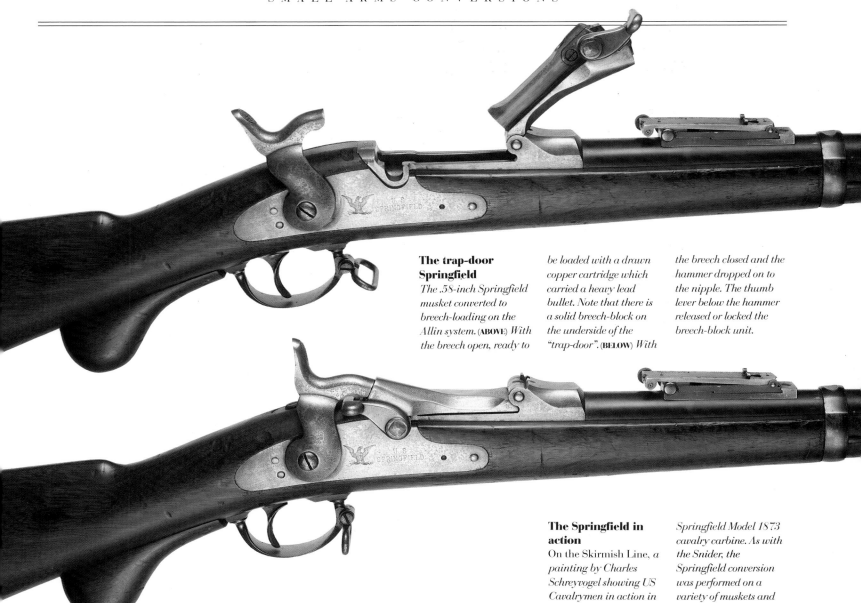

The trap-door Springfield
The .58-inch Springfield musket converted to breech-loading on the Allin system. (**ABOVE**) With the breech open, ready to be loaded with a drawn copper cartridge which carried a heavy lead bullet. Note that there is a solid breech-block on the underside of the "trap-door". (**BELOW**) With the breech closed and the hammer dropped on to the nipple. The thumb lever below the hammer released or locked the breech-block unit.

The Springfield in action
On the Skirmish Line, a painting by Charles Schreyvogel showing US Cavalrymen in action in the West, using the Springfield Model 1873 cavalry carbine. As with the Snider, the Springfield conversion was performed on a variety of muskets and carbines.

side-hinged breech block which carried a firing pin and which, once opened, could be pulled back to operate an extractor to pull out the empty cartridge case. To go with the Snider design, a cartridge with a body of wrapped sheet brass and a rimmed brass base was designed, carrying a .577 bullet and with a percussion cap in the centre of the base. The original percussion hammer of the Enfield Pattern 53 rifle musket was retained; when released by the trigger, it struck the firing pin in the breech block and then in turn the cap in the cartridge. The new rifle and cartridge were approved for service in September 1866. The Snider conversion was also taken up in Denmark, and in France the similar Tabatiere system was adopted in 1867.

The alternative to a side-hinged breech block was one hinged at the front and lifting up and forward, and this proved popular in many places. Perhaps the best known was the Springfield "Trap-Door" rifle, a conversion of the standard Springfield musket which appeared in 1870, having been designed by Erskine Allin, the Superintendent of Springfield Arsenal. Like the Snider conversion it carried its own firing pin.

Similar forward-opening conversions were adopted in Belgium (Albini-Braendlin) and Switzerland (Amsler) in 1867. These

conversion systems were economical, in so far as they managed to bring the stock of military muzzle-loaders into the breech-loading era, but similar commercial conversions for the sporting market were less successful; private owners preferred to wait until the breech-loading design question settled itself, and by the late 1860s there were plenty of commercial breech loaders available.

BREECH-LOADING SMALL ARMS

AFTER THE various armies had satisfied their immediate needs by converting their muzzle-loading rifles into breech-loaders (see Small arms conversion, page 84), the next move was to settle upon a properly designed breech-loading system, and by 1870 there was no shortage of those. Unfortunately, most of them were not robust enough for military service, and those that were had largely been designed for paper cartridges and were difficult to adapt to the new metallic cartridges.

The American Civil War (1861-5) had accelerated the introduction of breech-loading into military circles with such weapons as the Sharps, Spencer, Burnside, Joslyn, and Starr carbines and rifles. The Sharps used a vertically sliding breech block operated by a lever; the top edge was sharpened so as to slice the end off the paper cartridge as it closed, and it was fired by a hammer and percussion cap. The Starr used a linen cartridge and relied upon the force of the cap to pierce the linen and fire the powder. The Joslyn used a paper cartridge and closed the breech by a lifting flap carrying a gutta-percha seal. The Spencer and Burnside used metallic cartridges, the former a fairly ordinary rimfire, the latter a peculiar type which had to be loaded into the separate chamber base first before closing the weapon.

While these systems were adequate, none were sufficiently sound to attract interest from the major armies; the US Army, for example, settled on the Springfield conversion (see Small arms conversion, page 84) and stayed with it until 1892 – by which time some very sophisticated systems were available. European armies, however, committed themselves to finding improved breech-loading systems and examined the various options available. Three types became popular – the rolling block, the falling block, and the bolt.

THREE BREECH-LOADING SYSTEMS

The rolling block system was perfected by Remington in the USA in 1864. Designed for a rimfire cartridge, it used a hinged block to close the breech; this block had a curved undersurface and behind it was the hammer, with a curved upper surface, so that as the hammer fell this surface passed beneath the block and securely

> **❝**
> *So long as the infantry had a smooth-bore musket, and had thus no precision in action beyond 100 paces, it was little inclined to exact scientific researches. But the precision and the long range of the rifled weapon, and in particular the improvement of it due to various breech-loading systems, compelled the infantry to occupy themselves seriously with the sciences which have to do with the trajectory; in order to see how far the precision and the range could be improved and the best possible infantry arm be obtained.* **❞**

Letters on Artillery VII: *Prince Kraft zu Hohenlohe-Ingelfingen, 1887*

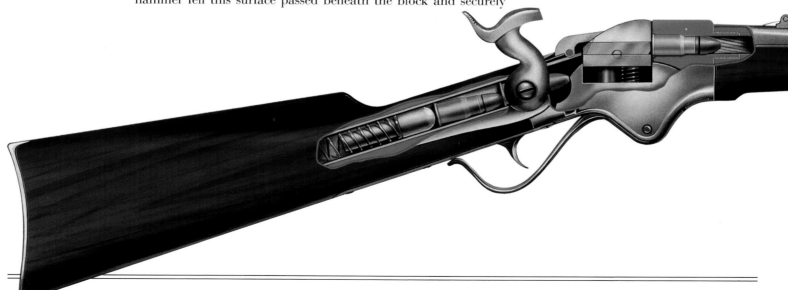

The Prince breech-loader

This design by Frederick Prince (c.1855) incorporated a system tried by several inventors. The lever beneath the barrel was turned and pushed to unlock the barrel from the fixed breech-piece and then slid forward to expose the chamber. After loading, the barrel was pulled back and turned so that the lugs on the breech-piece engaged in the chamber and locked the barrel in place. This system proved too cumbersome in action to be practical.

supported it against the explosion of the cartridge. The Remington system, in various calibres, was adopted by Sweden, Norway, Denmark, Spain, Greece, China, Egypt, and others.

The falling block was first developed by Henry Peabody of Boston in 1862. In this system the barrel was screwed into a rectangular box in which a solid breech block was pinned at its rear end. A lever beneath the weapon allowed this block to be swung down, exposing the mouth of the chamber, and a cartridge was inserted. Pulling up the lever raised the block to close the breech. The external hammer had to be cocked manually, and when released by the trigger it struck a curved firing pin in the block which in turn struck the rim of the cartridge and fired it. Peabody rifles were adopted by Canada, France, Bavaria, Mexico, and Switzerland.

In Switzerland Friedrich von Martini improved upon Peabody's idea by placing a firing pin and spring inside the breech block and arranging for it to be cocked as the opening lever was operated. This did away with the need to cock the weapon as a separate action and also allowed the use of the system with centre-fire cartridges. It was adopted by the British Army in 1871 as the "Martini-Henry" since it was combined with a barrel designed by Alexander Henry. The Martini system was also used by Turkey and Italy; Austria made some minor changes and adopted it as the Werndl rifle, and the Belgian Francotte-Martini was another of several variations.

The bolt system was developed extensively by Mauser, who set about improving the Chassepot rifle (see Needle gun, page 78) in the hope of interesting the French. His principal improvement was in adapting the idea to a cased cartridge and using a firing pin which was automatically cocked by the closing action of the bolt. The bolt had a prominent handle which was turned down in front of a lug on the receiver wall to lock the breech closed, and it was fitted at the rear with a safety catch which prevented the firing pin moving forward when applied.

The Spencer rifle

Dating from 1860 the Spencer used a tubular magazine inserted into the butt, feeding rimfire cartridges by a spring. Operating the under-lever rotated the breechblock back and picked up a cartridge from the tube; returning the lever chambered the cartridge and locked the breech. The external hammer then struck a firing pin in the breechblock.

WINCHESTER,
LEE AND
MAUSER:
THE RIFLE
GAINS ADDED
FIREPOWER

The Mauser of 1898
*This "Karabin 98k" was
to remain the standard
infantry rifle until 1945.*

MAGAZINE RIFLES

HAVING SETTLED upon a particular breech-loading system (see Breech-loading small arms, page 86), the armies of the world turned to considering the adoption of a magazine rifle, in order to give the individual soldier more firepower. There were, of course, arguments against this: given a full magazine, said the opposition, the soldier will simply fire off all the ammunition as soon as he sees an enemy a mile away. But the siege of Plevna (1877) showed that this was not necessarily so. At Plevna the Turkish defenders, each with 500 rounds, were armed with Winchester magazine carbines, and they repulsed several Russian attacks with withering, disciplined firepower. This showed that any army without a magazine rifle was at a disadvantage.

Despite its success at Plevna, the American Winchester was rarely used as a military weapon; but it introduced the tubular magazine, in which a row of ammunition was carried in a tube beneath the barrel. Individual rounds were pushed back by a spring and fed up to the chamber by working a lever that also cocked the hammer. This was satisfactory with soft-nosed bullets, but the small-calibre jacketed bullets that the military were contemplating using risked firing the cap of the next cartridge in front under the shock of recoil, and accordingly the tubular magazine was not trusted.

Nevertheless, the French adopted the tubular magazine for their 8-mm Lebel rifle (1886), as did the Germans for their Commission rifle (1888), since it provided a quick solution. The British and other nations preferred to test various options before selecting a system, and the only practical solution was the box magazine.

THE BOLT-ACTION RIFLE

James Paris Lee, a Scot who emigrated to the USA, had developed a bolt-action rifle. Beneath the bolt was a metal box, into which cartridges were placed on top of a spring. As the bolt was opened, the spring forced the cartridges up against a stop; the bolt pushed the top cartridge into the chamber as it closed. After firing, the opening of the bolt extracted the empty cartridge case, and the return stroke loaded a fresh round. The box could be detached for refilling, and the rifle was provided with a spare magazine for quick reloading in action. Lee had produced a few sporting rifles on this principle, and after severe testing, the Lee bolt and magazine were adopted by the British Army in the Lee-Metford rifle, Metford being the designer of the barrel. Another innovation was the adoption of a jacketed bullet of .303-inch calibre, a considerable reduction from the .45 calibre which was usual for military rifles of the day.

The small jacketed bullet was developed by Major Rubin of the Swiss Army. It had high velocity (giving better accuracy) and, due to its metal jacket, did not leave a coating of lead in the rifle barrel. The French took the same course, though using a solid brass bullet, with their M1886 rifle, as did the Germans with their M1888 rifle.

The Germans realized that their tubular magazine weapon had been a mistake, and applied to Mauser for something better. He adapted the box magazine idea and produced a rifle with a five-shot box magazine concealed inside the stock. The rifle's bolt action was improved, locking into the chamber of the barrel, and the Mauser rifles developed in the 1890s were to be exported throughout the world.

The short Lee-Enfield
The Lee bolt action, allied to either the Metford or Enfield barrel, armed the British Empire from 1888 to 1954, and until the 1980s as a sniping rifle. Although theoretically less accurate, due to using locking lugs at the rear end, than the Mauser, it was sufficiently accurate for combat shooting and had the advantage of far smoother and faster action than any other bolt action before or since. Sergeant Snoxall of the Small Arms School fired 38 shots in one minute in 1914, and at 300 yards' range put every shot into the inner ring of the target, a record never surpassed.

> *What no one had really fully appreciated was the potential of the rifle in really skilled hands, particularly since by then the rifle was a magazine weapon firing smokeless powder. The British on the whole shot badly. They were conditioned to the concept of pouring either swift volleys or rapid magazine fire into hordes of charging fanatics, but they were poor at long range, individual shooting and even worse at snapshooting at the mere fleeting glimpse of a head or limb. The Boers on the other hand, brought up frugally in a land where cartridges were expensive and a missed buck meant an empty belly, shot well as a matter of day-to-day necessity.*

The Soldier's Trade; F.W. Myatt,
Macdonald & Jane's, 1974.

In Austria, Count Mannlicher designed another magazine rifle, similar in some respects to the Mauser but eventually adopting a "straight-pull" bolt and a rotating magazine, still concealed inside the butt. The straight-pull bolt relied upon cam action: the bolt handle was pulled straight back, withdrawing a sleeve which drew a stud through a curved cam path in the bolt body, causing it to rotate. Some people said it was quicker than a turn-bolt, but it was generally more fragile. The Swiss adopted a straight-pull design, while the Japanese and Italians copied Mauser. Only the Scandinavians and the Americans tried something different, in the Krag-Jorgensen rifle, which had an odd side-mounted magazine fed through a trapdoor.

The Kropatschek
A French marine with a Kropatschek magazine rifle of 1878. It used a tubular magazine running beneath the barrel; operation of the bolt caused a "lifter" to bring a cartridge up in front of the bolt face.

MAGAZINE RIFLE MECHANISMS

The Lebel mechanism
The mechanism of the bolt-action Lebel rifle, showing how the ammunition lies in the tubular magazine beneath the barrel. The bolt is closed, with a round ready to be fired, and the cartridge lifter is down, ready to lift the next cartridge after it has been pushed onto the lifter by a spring.

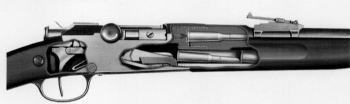

The Lee bolt mechanism
A sectioned drawing of the Lee action; the bolt has just been opened, extracting the empty case. The simple trigger mechanism, and the folded spring which forces the cartridge up in front of the bolt as it closes can be seen.

The Krag-Jorgensen rifle
Adopted by the US Army in 1892, the Krag was a Norwegian design which used a similar bolt to the Lee with the magazine laid horizontally below, being loaded by a trapdoor. Closing the door after loading drove a spring against the cartridges and pushed them under and around the bolt to arrive on the left side, to be caught and driven forward by the bolt face. The ballistics of the Krag were poor, and after exposure to the Mauser in the Spanish-American War the USA abandoned it for the Springfield, which used a bolt and magazine system licensed from Mauser and a more powerful cartridge.

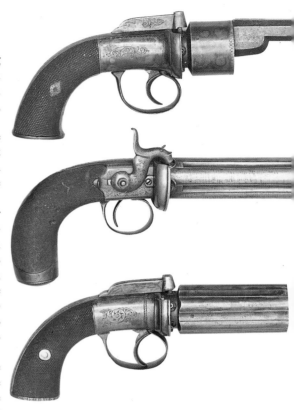

FAST, ACCURATE GUNS FOR WAR AND WILD WEST

REVOLVERS

THE REVOLVER is the oldest magazine system. Firearms using several barrels grouped in a circle first appeared in the 16th century, the barrels being revolved manually to bring each one into alignment with the firing mechanism, whether matchlock, wheel-lock, or flintlock (see Matchlock and wheel-lock, page 48 and Flintlock, page 60). As might be imagined, these weapons were cumbersome and complex and often dangerous to the user, but specialist gunmakers did produce some very elegant examples. They were of course very expensive weapons and therefore were never common and certainly never seen in general military use.

The revolver as known today owes its inception to Elisha Collier and Artemus Wheeler, both of the USA, who developed a hand-rotated flintlock revolver in 1818. The significant part of this design was the mechanical rotation of the cylinder by a spring, and its positive locking when one chamber was aligned with the barrel; hitherto this had been done manually. Another innovation was the use of a spring to force the cylinder into contact with the barrel to avoid powder gases leaking out. Several London gunmakers produced pistols, shotguns, and rifles using this system but it was not adopted by any military force.

The percussion system of ignition (see Percussion system, page 76) led to the development of the modern revolver; prior to this the complexity of making a flintlock revolver produced only expensive and delicate weapons. Samuel Colt patented his percussion revolver in 1836. He had invented nothing new, but had assimilated the best ideas into a sound design and had the forethought to take out ironclad patents which covered any mechanically-rotated revolver. His initial design was too far ahead of its time and his enterprise failed, but war in Mexico in 1846 led to a demand for pistols and he was soon back in business. Colt's revolvers were of the open-frame

---

THE COLT FRONTIER MODEL

THE COLT "Frontier" model was introduced in 1873 for the US Army, but it spread far beyond that and became the symbol of the Old West. No other weapon stayed in production so long: from 1873 to 1940, by which time 357,859 had been made. After ten years public demand was so insistent that it went back into production in 1955 and has remained in the Colt inventory ever since. The original model of 1873 was made in .45 calibre for

military service, but for commercial sale it was available in thirty different calibres from .22 to .476. Post-1955 models were available in .38, .357, .44 and .45 calibres, with a special lightweight "New Frontier" model in .22 calibre. Barrel lengths from 3 to 12 inches have been made, the latter being the "Buntline Special" which originated in a special order from "Ned Buntline", a Western novelist, in 1878. He presented five to famous Western figures, but other long-barrelled models were later made for open sale and attracted the same name.

The original Colt
(LEFT) *This original 1873 model is seen here with holster and ammunition.*

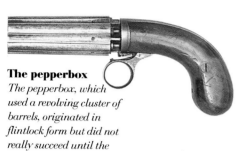

The pepperbox
The pepperbox, which used a revolving cluster of barrels, originated in flintlock form but did not really succeed until the percussion era. (CENTRE LEFT) a hand-rotated model, (BELOW LEFT) a self-cocking model with over hammer, (ABOVE) a self-cocking under-hammer model and (TOP LEFT) a "transitional" revolver, the step between the pepperbox and the revolver proper.

The Gunfighters
(RIGHT) A painting by Charles Russell (1902) depicting a difference of opinion being settled in the traditional Western manner in the 1880s by "Colonel Colt's Equalizer".

type, simple and robust, and soon acquired a high reputation – aided by his consummate salesmanship.

THE COLT REVOLVER'S RIVALS

In Britain the principal revolver design was produced by Robert Adams in 1851; this was a solid-frame weapon, inherently stronger than Colt's open frame, and the firing mechanism was self-cocking – pulling the trigger raised and then dropped the hammer. By contrast Colt's revolver employed a single action, in which the hammer had to be manually cocked and then released by the trigger. Adams's and Colt's designs competed for many years for military approval, both being adopted by various forces; the general opinion was that the Colt had the advantage in accuracy, the Adams in speed of operation.

When Colt's master patent expired in 1857 there was a rush of competitors with designs roughly based on the Colt, but these were all percussion weapons. Horace Smith and Daniel Wesson, looking to the future, patented a rimfire cartridge in 1854 and acquired another master patent covering any cylinder with chambers bored through from end to end. In 1857 they went into production with a 0.22-inch calibre rimfire-cartridge revolver and, thanks to their patent, enjoyed a virtual monopoly in the USA until 1869.

These early revolvers all suffered from the same drawback: each chamber had to be emptied of its spent case and reloaded individually, a process which took time. In an effort to speed things up, many cylinders had quick-release devices so that they could be removed and replaced with a loaded cylinder in less time than it took to reload each chamber. A further and more permanent solution was provided by the hinged-frame revolver in which the barrel and cylinder could be swung away from the frame, exposing the rear of the cylinder for reloading. Various collective ejection systems were devised, usually relying upon a star-shaped plate in the middle of the cylinder being forced out during the opening

action and catching beneath the rims of the empty cartridge cases, to eject them simultaneously.

Some manufacturers believed the hinged frame to be weak, and retained the solid frame. They solved the ejection problem by mounting the cylinder on an arm which swung sideways, carrying the cylinder out to one side of the frame, where a rod was pressed to operate the ejection plate and thrust out the empty cases.

In spite of the vast number of revolver designs since, almost all military revolvers belong to a handful of types. These include the British Webley, a strong heavy-calibre weapon which was first a solid-frame (then adapted for the hinged frame in the 1880s) and which armed British and Empire forces until the 1950s; the Colt and Smith & Wesson solid-frame types with side-opening cylinders, introduced in the 1890s and still widely used and equally widely copied; and the Belgian-designed Nagant, which armed the Russian and Soviet Armies from 1895 to the 1950s. The design of this weapon was unique; reviving Collier's original idea of forcing the cylinder and barrel into close contact to prevent gas leakage.

An unusual pattern that found considerable favour in the 1900s was the Webley-Fosbery automatic revolver, an attempt to counter the growing popularity of the automatic pistol. In this weapon the barrel and cylinder were capable of moving backwards across the butt frame; the cylinder had zigzag grooves cut in its circumference. As the barrel unit recoiled, a stud in the frame ran in these grooves and rotated the cylinder one-twelfth of a turn; the hammer was cocked during this rearward movement. A spring then returned the barrel unit to the forward position, during which time the stud and groove system rotated the cylinder another part-turn to bring a fresh cartridge into alignment with the barrel. The Webley-Fosbery was fast and accurate but the mud of the Flanders battlefields of the First World War caused it to seize-up at critical moments and its popularity waned.

BREECH-LOADING ARTILLERY 1870-1900

BY THE late 1870s the adoption of slow-burning gunpowder had demanded guns of greater length, but these were inconvenient to pull back into cover for loading at the muzzle. At the same time, the major gun-makers of Europe were exploring the many different systems of breech-loading, testing them and then submitting them for military approval. By this time the use of brass-cased small-arms ammunition was commonplace, and it was logical to "scale-up" the small-arms cartridge to artillery sizes. This solved two problems at once: it made the propelling charge a convenient mass to handle and, by virtue of the expanding of the brass case under pressure, sealed the rear end of the gun. Nevertheless, some designers did not consider this a practical solution in large calibres because the cartridge became too big to handle and impossible to attach securely to the shell. Two basic systems of operation therefore came into use.

The cartridge-case system was largely embraced by European

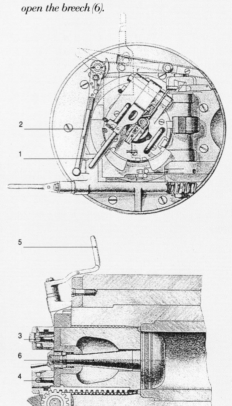

THE THREE- MOTION BREECH

A naval 9.2 inch gun of 1889 (rear and side views). The folded handle (1), assisted by the ratchet lever on the left (2), turns the screw to the breech to unlock the breech; the two grips (3, 4) allow the screw to be withdrawn on to the carrier; the crank handle (5) was then turned to rotate and open the breech (6).

The De Bange breech

Breech of a French gun (c. 1880) with the De Bange breech system. The out-folded handle is rotated to the vertical position to unlock the breech screw, after which the looped handle is pulled to withdraw the screw on to the carrier tray, which then hinges to the right to open.

designers – Krupp of Germany, Nordenfelt of Sweden and Hotchkiss of France. The bag-charge system was pioneered by Schneider of France and Armstrong of England. Broadly speaking, every artillery piece developed since 1880 can trace its existence back to one of these makers.

Once the particular system had been chosen, the next task was to devise a practical and robust method of closing the breech of the gun, one which would withstand the heaviest pressures and yet be convenient and reasonably quick to operate. It is at this point that the variations on the basic themes begin to diverge from the mainstream; the number of breech mechanisms which have been proposed over the past century are legion.

Krupp, from his earliest days, adhered to the sliding-block breech; the rear of the barrel was enclosed by a square block of steel with a slot, through which a rectangular block of steel slid sideways, controlled by various mechanisms. The rear of the block was cut

away to allow the shell and cartridge to be loaded.

THE SCREW BREECH

Hotchkiss used a similar system but slid the block vertically. Nordenfelt swung the block up and followed it up with a wedge which locked it firmly in place. He then developed an entirely new idea, the "eccentric screw", in which the rear of the gun was closed by a rotating block of steel with a U-shaped cutaway portion. When the breech was open, this cutaway lined up with the barrel and allowed the cartridge to be loaded; it was then revolved through 120 degrees so that the cutaway was replaced by a solid portion of the block which contained the firing pin. This system became famous when it was adopted for the French 75-mm gun in 1897.

The adherents of the bag-charge system adopted the screw-breech mechanism. In the first instances this was simply a cylinder of steel with a coarse screw thread which was screwed into the rear of the gun. But then it was realized that cutting away segments of the screw on the breech and inside the gun allowed the cylinder to be rapidly inserted, its screwed segments passing through the clear segments of the gun, and then given a partial turn so that the threads engaged. Sealing of the explosive gas was done by placing a metal cup on the front of the cylinder (or breech block) so that it entered into the gun chamber and was expanded by the explosion pressure. An alternative system was the Broadwell Ring (Mr Broadwell held the patent), a ring of soft copper let into the face of the block so that it pressed against the edges of the chamber, the action of the screw forcing it tightly into contact.

Both these systems had faults and were replaced by the De Bange system in which a resilient pad was attached to the front of the breech block, secured in place by a steel cap. On firing, the cap was forced back by the explosion, squeezing the pad outward to provide a gas-tight seal. With minor modifications this system has survived to the present day.

Volunteer artillery
British Volunteer Artillery on manoeuvres in 1895 (ABOVE), using the 12-pounder breech-loading gun.

Mountain artillery
French mountain gunners in Tonkin in the 1880s (BELOW), with a mule-carried breech-loading gun. This Mle 1878 gun was among the

first mountain weapons to use the De Bange breech-loading system.

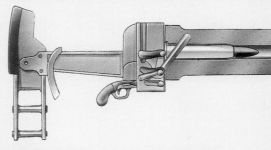

THE BREECH-LOADING SYSTEMS

The Hotchkiss Vertical Sliding Block breech
Pulling the lever caused the steel block to slide down, allowing loading; pushing it up closed the block, and the pistol grip trigger fired the cartridge.

The De Bange breech
In this sectioned view of the screw and the "mushroom head", the sealing pad fits between the screw and the mushroom so as to be compressed on firing.

NAVAL GUNNERY 1820-1870

AFTER THE Napoleonic Wars (1792–1815) the French Navy became interested in guns firing explosive shells (see From case shot to cartridges, page 70) rather than solid shot. In 1822 General H. Paixhans proposed rationalizing the armament of ships, and simplifying munitions supply by adopting guns all of one calibre. For example, heavy guns firing powerful charges and shorter guns firing lesser charges were all capable of firing shells. Paixhans advocated the shell rather than solid shot because he believed it would do far more damage to a wooden ship by its explosive power and would not demand such heavy guns or such powerful charges. It would also enable quicker reloading and thus more shells would land on target in a given time.

Traditionally, navies are reluctant to accept suggestions from soldiers. Paixhans' ideas took time to be assimilated, but in 1837 the French Navy settled on the 22-cm calibre standard and adopted shell guns throughout its fleet. The British and Russian navies followed suit, the British adopting the 6.4-inch, 32-pounder as their standard.

The French were responsible for another major innovation in 1854, during the Crimean War. To bombard Russian coastal forts, they built a number of floating batteries protected with 4 inches of armour plate. These were so successful that the French considered armouring their warships. In 1858 France built the *Gloire*, the world's first ironclad warship. Britain responded by

A 32-pounder gun
A 32-pounder smoothbore in HMS Warrior. This gun is fitted with a percussion lock, a device rarely seen on preserved guns, in which a "tube" or enlarged percussion cap, was fitted in the vent and fired by a hammer operated by a lanyard.

The Dahlgren gun
US Navy sailors manning an 11-inch Dahlgren gun during the American Civil War. The Dahlgren was cast so as to produce a very hard inner surface to the bore to resist wear.

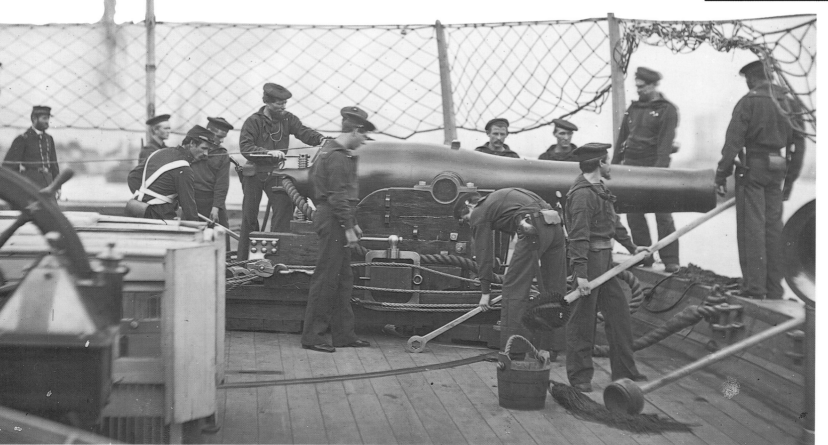

A French gun deck
Early breech-loading guns in a French armoured cruiser of about 1885. They are mounted on carriages which recoil up the inclined plane of the "slide", which in turn is fitted with wheels to permit traversing to right and left. The amount of recoil was controlled by friction clamps and a hydraulic brake between the carriage and slide. Elevation and traverse were both done by mechanical gearing. Cutlasses can be seen arranged on the walls in a convenient place; the days of repelling boarders had not yet passed.

laying down its own ironclad, the *Warrior.* The naval race was on.

The *Gloire* was a wooden ship plated with wrought iron armour nearly 5 inches thick and armed with thirty-four 16-cm shell guns. Short and beamy, the ship was designed to dash across the English Channel and catch the British fleet unawares in its bases at Plymouth, Dover, and Portsmouth. The *Warrior* was longer and finer, designed for service on the high seas. It was built completely of iron and armed with forty-eight 68-pounder guns firing shot of 8.12 inches calibre. The *Warrior* could outshoot the *Gloire*, and because Britain was more highly industrialized than France it could also build more iron ships.

The arrival of the ironclad coincided with the British adoption of the Armstrong gun (see Breech-loading artillery, page 80). However, tests soon showed that the Armstrong was not powerful enough to penetrate iron armour. Only the old 64-pounder smoothbore could do this, and then only at short ranges. The Royal Navy reverted to rifled muzzle-loading guns, (see Rifled muzzle-loaders, page 82) which could deliver armour piercing shells at sufficient velocity to defeat iron or steel plate at longer ranges. Other navies faced the same problem and took one basic route — big guns firing shells. However, many different systems were used: French rifled muzzle-loaders, Krupp breech-loaders, and the huge American Rodman 15-inch smoothbores.

Mounting these large guns became a problem, since they were far heavier than the old cannon. Moreover, they had to be protected by armour, and the form that the armour took had to be given some thought, since merely adding iron would impair the sailing qualities of the ships. *Warrior* placed the armour in the centre, leaving the bow and stern unarmoured so as to relieve the strain on the hull in high seas.

RETURN OF THE RAM

By the 1860s warships were steam-driven and therefore no longer at the mercy of the wind and the ancient idea of the ram was revived (see Naval warfare to 1500, page 52). The forefoot of the ship — the bow beneath the waterline — was formed into a reinforced and pointed ram which could be used to pierce the hull of an enemy vessel. The idea was tested at the battle of Lissa in 1866, when the steamships of the Austrian fleet charged into the Italians and sunk their flagship. The reappearance of the ram meant that a warship would henceforth be facing the enemy more often than abeam. A ship's ability to fire forward and astern as well as in broadsides was thus vital. The first idea was to have a central battery in which all the guns were clustered in an armoured citadel in the middle of the ship, reducing the amount of armour needed and concentrating the fire. An alternative was to turn the citadel into a lozenge shape, with sloped faces towards the bow and stern, allowing the guns both broadside and a degree of forward and aft fire. The solution eventually adopted, which was arrived at only after many false avenues had been explored, was the rotating turret. This had been popularized by the *Monitor* during the American Civil War (1861-5), but the *Monitor* was a poor sea-keeping ship and the design had to be modified considerably before turrets were generally accepted. The improved turret was the brainchild of Captain Cowper Coles of the Royal Navy. Unfortunately, his instructions were misinterpreted by a draughtsman and his experimental turret ship *Captain* capsized and sank, with all hands (including Coles) on board, during a gale in the Bay of Biscay. The ship's instability was caused partly by the need for a full rig. It took the development of more powerful engines and boilers to allow seagoing ships to dispense with sailing rig. Then, at the start of the 1880s, the turret became almost universal in ironclads.

SEA MINES AND TORPEDOES

I N 1776 the Americans used submerged explosive charges in an attempt to disable and sink English ships. They failed because the tactics demanded more sophisticated technology than was available at the time. Russian sailors tried to do the same in the Crimean War (1853–6), and with the same result. The problem was largely that the only known explosive was gunpowder and the ignition systems were vulnerable to damp. However, the American Civil War (1861–5) brought improvements

> *In the case of the contact mines used at Santiago de Cuba and in the channel off Key Toro in Guantanamo Bay in the Spanish-American War, it was found that after several weeks' immersion a growth of barnacles and shells had formed between the flanges on the plungers and the outside of the mine case, sufficient to prevent the plungers from acting. A periodical examination of contact mines, to ensure their effective action, is necessary.*

US Navy Textbook of Ordnance & Gunnery, 1899.

Controlled mines
Seamen testing controlled mines prior to laying, c. 1895. These mines were laid in patterns across harbour entrances and other sensitive points, to be fired electrically by an observer when an enemy ship was above them. The electrical circuit was sensitive to water, and
the insulating materials of the time of doubtful efficiency. So periodically the mines had to be hauled up and the wiring and sealing thoroughly checked and repaired if necessary, after which the mines were re-laid.

in submerged charges, and torpedoes — as they were then called — scored a number of successes. For a weaker naval force, like the Confederate navy, the mine (as it has come to be known) proved to be the ideal weapon, especially in riverine warfare at that stage of its development.

The mine of the Civil War period was simply a waterproof canister fired with gunpowder, with a percussion cap device to initiate the explosion. This could be actuated by various means. Often a stake was held by chains in the river so as to slant up towards the surface, and the explosive charge was tipped by a soft metal blister containing a firing pin and cap. A ship striking the tip of the stake would crush the blister and fire the cap and the charge. In deeper channels the canister was anchored by a weight and would be provided with several firing pin units so that a strike at any angle would set one off.

An alternative approach was the "spar torpedo", a charge attached to a long pole and carried by a small boat. The boat would be manoeuvred close to the target in darkness, and the spar driven against the target's hull. The charge was fired either by making contact or by a trigger operated by the boat's crew. The attackers' chances of surviving were minimal. An improvement was to detach the mine once contact was made, pull clear and fire the mine by a

The Whitehead torpedo
Two specimens of Whitehead torpedo, separated by some 50 years. Above is the original 1860s pattern, a slender tapering device calculated to slide
through the water under the low power of the original motor. Below is a First World War French torpedo, much heavier, with a more powerful warhead, and with a blunt head carrying the sensitive "firing pistol", a
shape which could be driven through the water by the far greater power of the improved engines of the day. Note the arms of the firing pistol, guaranteeing detonation even on a glancing blow.

The spar torpedo
A photograph taken c. 1885 showing a Royal Navy steam pinnace carrying a spar, or outrigger, torpedo. The *long wooden spar has the explosive charge at its forward end, fitted with a simple contact fuze. The operational tactic was simple; the boat was* *driven at the target at full speed so as to strike the fuze against the enemy's hull, whereupon the warhead detonated and damaged the enemy ship.*

long line. The Russians were quite successful with spar torpedoes during their war against the Turks (1877–8).

In 1869, Captain Harvey of the Royal Navy invented a towed torpedo, a fish-like container at the end of a long line that could be manipulated to strike an enemy ship. The idea was sound but putting it into practice was difficult. Few towed torpedoes were ever adopted for service.

The arrival of ironclad ships with armoured sides (see Naval gunnery, page 94) made the idea of torpedoes even more attractive, since they appeared to be the only way to strike below the armoured protection. A self-propelled torpedo was devised by an Austrian, Commander Giovanni de Lupis, in the 1860s. With the help of an English engineer, Robert Whitehead, the idea was further developed, and in 1866 the Austrians began manufacture of the Whitehead torpedo. It was propelled by a compressed-air engine, carried 18lbs of dynamite, and had a range of about 200 yards. Its most important feature was a self-regulating device which kept the torpedo at a constant preset depth.

After selling torpedoes to the Austrian and French navies, in 1868, Whitehead sold the sole rights to the Royal Navy, who further improved the design. By 1875 the torpedo's speed had been doubled to 12 knots and the range increased to over 300 yards; or by reducing the speed to 9 knots it had a range of 1,200

yards. They also improved the technique of accurately launching the torpedo from a moving ship.

To accompany the torpedo, the torpedo-boat was developed. This was a light, fast craft armed solely with torpedoes. Its role was to dash into a harbour at high speed, loose off its torpedoes at whatever targets it could find and then dash out again, relying upon its speed to preserve it from enemy fire. To counter such attacks machine-guns were adopted and, later, light quick-firing guns (see Quick-firing artillery, page 102). Moreover, a new class of fast warship was developed, called the torpedo-boat destroyer, which became known simply as the destroyer.

SHORE-BASED MINES AND TORPEDOES

Mines and torpedoes were also employed in harbour defences. Minefields were laid in and around harbours and were electrically controlled from the shore. Any hostile warship was tracked, and its position was plotted on a chart on which the location of the mines was marked. When the ship moved over a mine, the mine was electrically fired. Controlled minefields were extensively laid by all the major powers from 1868 until the start of the First World War, but were very rarely put to use.

Shore-based torpedoes were introduced into coastal defence by the British, who adopted the Brennan torpedo in 1885. This was an invention of Louis Brennan, an Australian of Irish extraction. The Brennan torpedo was a cigar-shaped device carrying two reels of fine wire. The reels were attached to drums in the shore station, which were revolved by a steam engine. Drawing the wire off the torpedo reels drove the torpedo's propeller by a differential gear system. The torpedo was launched down a rail, and steered by changing the speed of one drum, using the differential gear, which actuated the rudder. A flagstaff that protruded above the surface showed the controller the torpedo's track, and a gyroscope ensured that it remained upright. Brennan torpedo stations were installed in many coastal defence forts throughout the British Empire. The Brennan torpedo is truly the ancestor of the many wire-guided missiles that exist today.

The Brennan was made obsolete in about 1905 but the principle was retained by several nations who installed standard naval torpedo tubes in coastal defences. The last known use of such a device was in 1940, when the Norwegian fort of Oskarsborg sank the German warship *Blücher* in Oslo Fjord by a combination of gun and torpedo fire.

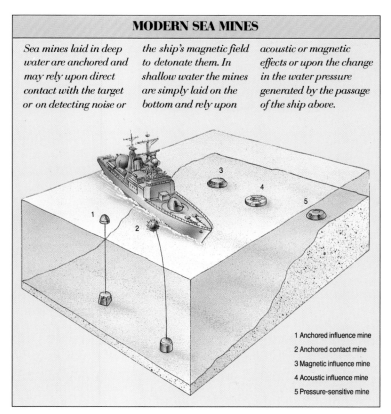

MODERN SEA MINES

Sea mines laid in deep water are anchored and may rely upon direct contact with the target or on detecting noise or *the ship's magnetic field to detonate them. In shallow water the mines are simply laid on the bottom and rely upon* *acoustic or magnetic effects or upon the change in the water pressure generated by the passage of the ship above.*

1 Anchored influence mine
2 Anchored contact mine
3 Magnetic influence mine
4 Acoustic influence mine
5 Pressure-sensitive mine

MECHANICAL MACHINE GUNS

THE PROSPECT of a weapon that would keep up a continuous stream of fire attracted inventors quite early in the development of firearms. But so long as the ammunition was powder and ball and the means of ignition a spark there was little chance of an elegant mechanical solution. Most of the attempts were simply revolvers (see Revolvers, page 90) of one sort or another, as, for example, the "Defence" made by James Puckle in 1718. Though tripod-mounted it was simply a large revolver with a cylinder behind its single barrel; the cylinder had to be unlocked and turned manually. Even so, Puckle managed to demonstrate a rate of 63 shots in seven minutes, which was impressive for the time.

With the arrival of the percussion cap came a number of volley

The Nordenfelt gun
A ten-barrel Nordenfelt machine gun (**LEFT**) on a field carriage. The vertical box contains the ten columns of .45 cartridges and the crank handle on the left is revolved to fire. The handle on the right is for opening the breeches for cleaning and for initially loading the chambers. The empty cases were ejected through the chutes seen under the barrels. A muzzle cover is fitted to keep out dirt.

The Gardner gun
A two-barrel Gardner gun operated by sailors (**ABOVE**). The feed system is a grooved strip into which the rims of a box of cartridges could be slid, after which the box was removed. Turning the handle operated a crankshaft which fired the two barrels alternately. The gun is on a ship mounting, with elevation and traverse controlled by handwheels.

RATES OF FIRE COMPARISON

Result of trials held at Woolwich, 11 August 1870
Comparison of numbers of shots and hits during two minutes' firing against targets representing 150 infantry and 90 cavalry

Type of gun	Shots	Hits
1.0-inch Gatling	316	10
0.65-inch Gatling	239	236
0.42-inch Gatling	616	369
Mitrailleuse	185	171
9-pounder muzzle-loading field gun (shrapnel)	10	208
12-pounder muzzle-loading field gun (shrapnel)	9	268
Martini-Henry rifle	141	74
Snider rifle	83	63

guns – a collection of rifle barrels mounted in a wheeled frame which, after loading, could be fired in succession. This produced an impressive volley but one that was followed by a long pause while the barrels were all reloaded.

The American Civil War (1861-5) spurred inventors on. One of the first practical weapons was Wilson Agar's "Coffee Mill" gun, so-called from the appearance of a hopper above the weapon. Into this went a number of steel tubes, each loaded with powder and ball and having a nipple with a percussion cap. Turning a crank forced a tube from the hopper into the chamber, dropped a hammer onto the cap, extracted the tube, and loaded the next one. Once the supply of loaded tubes ran out, there was a pause for reloading. Agar sold 54 of these guns to the Union forces, who used them in the defences of Washington DC.

Breech-loading allowed a return to the volley gun idea; the Billinghurst-Requa, also used by Union forces in the Civil War, was simply a wheeled frame carrying 24 rifle barrels. At the rear was an iron frame into which 24 cartridges were inserted, and a

THE GATLING GUN

THE BEST known of all mechanical machine guns is the Gatling Gun, invented in 1861 by Richard Jordan Gatling, a doctor of dentistry from North Carolina. He never practised as a dentist and devoted his life to mechanical inventions; none but his machine gun is now remembered.

The gun consists of a group of six barrels mounted in a revolving frame, with the loading and firing arrangements behind them. Operation is by a hand crank at the side of the gun, and the cartridges are placed into a feed box on top of the gun and fall into the mechanism by gravity.

When the crank is turned the six barrels revolve around a central axis; each barrel has a bolt and firing pin controlled by a cam groove in the casing around the breech end of the gun. As the unit revolves, projections on the bolts, riding in the groove, cause each

bolt to open and close in its own barrel breech. Taking one barrel as the example, at its topmost position the bolt is open and a cartridge falls in from the feed box. As the barrel continues to move round, the bolt is closed by the cam groove, and as the barrel reaches the lowest position the firing pin is released and the cartridge fired. Then, as the barrel begins moving upwards on the other side of the circle, the bolt is unlocked and opened and the empty cartridge case is extracted and ejected so that the barrel arrives back at the topmost position empty and with the bolt open ready to be reloaded.

The first models were not quite so mechanically perfect, but they were quite serviceable and General Benjamin Butler of the US Army bought 12 guns at $1,000 each and used them with success in the Civil War. As Gatling's native state was part of the Confederacy, his political allegiance was

suspect, and it was not until 1865 that his gun was officially adopted by the US Army. Worldwide sales followed, including numbers to Russia, where it became the "Gorloff" and was claimed to be of Russian invention. Indeed, the Russian guns were probably the last ever to see service, since they were used against the Japanese at Port Arthur in 1904.

Field Gatlings
Two slightly different field Gatling guns, that on the left being the .50- inch calibre US model of 1865. Feed was by a slanting strip of cartridges inserted from the left side in both models. Screw control of elevation was provided, but traverse was simply by heaving the entire carriage sideways. Although the weight of these guns demanded this type of carriage, it also led to confusion with artillery and sometimes misemployment of the weapon.

lever thrust them into the barrels. These cartridges had no means of ignition, but had a hole in the base. Once the gun was loaded a single percussion cap was placed on a nipple on the iron frame and fired by a hammer, the flash passing through the frame to ignite all 24 cartridges. The American Civil War also produced perhaps the most famous mechanical machine gun – the Gatling. Given good ammunition the Gatling was reliable and effective, so much so that the principle remains in use to this day.

THE MITRAILLEUSE

The Montigny Mitrailleuse was a Belgian design, adopted in great secrecy by the French Army in 1869. It had 25 rifle barrels in a cylindrical casing; behind was a breech block which slid back to allow a plate carrying 25 cartridges to be dropped into the weapon; then the block was closed, chambering the cartridges. Turning a crank now dropped 25 firing pins in succession, fast or

slow according to the speed of the crank. Reloading meant simply opening the breech, removing the plate with spent cases, and dropping in a freshly loaded plate. The Mitrailleuse worked well, but failed to come up to expectations during the war against Prussia (1870-1) largely because it was tactically mishandled.

The Gardner machine gun was a two-barrelled weapon operated by a crank which loaded and fired each barrel in turn, feeding from a top-mounted magazine. It was an extremely reliable weapon; in 1879 Gardner demonstrated it by firing 10,000 rounds in 27 minutes, and it was adopted by the British Army and Navy in 1880. They also adopted the Nordenfelt machine gun, which came in various configurations from two to ten barrels, each with its own magazine. Pulling back a lever opened and closed a breech block operating on all the barrels, loaded a round into each barrel, and fired it. The Nordenfelt was produced in several calibres.

AUTOMATIC MACHINE GUNS

ALTHOUGH MECHANICAL machine guns operated well enough, they left a lot to be desired, and one or two inventive minds began to explore the possibility of tapping some of the energy which was liberated when a cartridge was fired. There were the muzzle blast, the recoil force, and the gas pressure inside the barrel, all waiting to be put to work. The first man to grasp this idea and to exploit it was the American Hiram Maxim.

Maxim had an inventive mind and had applied it to such varied subjects as vacuum pumps, gas-generating plants, and electric lights. He visited the Paris Electrical Exhibition in 1881 and, so the story goes, was told by a fellow countryman that the quickest road to financial success was to "invent something that will enable these fool Europeans to kill each other quicker". Whether this is true, or whether it registered with Maxim or not, the fact remains that he settled in London and began work on an automatic machine-gun. He soon realized the amount of energy that was available, took out patents which appeared to cover just about every eventuality, and then set about perfecting a design which utilized the recoil of the gun.

In 1885 he demonstrated his first model to the British Army without result: he then retired to improve and simplify it, and by 1886 was travelling Europe to demonstrate its superiority over the mechanical weapons then in use. The Maxim Gun Company was formed and by 1890 the gun was in service with the British, Austrian, German, Italian, Swiss, and Russian armies.

The Maxim's success spurred other inventors to act: John Moses Browning, well-known in the USA, began by exploring the muzzle blast but then turned to the propelling gas as a motive force. He drilled a hole in the gun barrel to divert some of the gas behind the bullet into a cylinder to drive a piston, which performed the various tasks of extracting the cartridge case, reloading, and firing. By 1890 he had perfected a weapon and

> " *Sir Francis de Winton had the machine gun ready and, working it himself, poured a tremendous volley into the nearest tower. The bullets rained in through the portholes and between the planks, killing numbers of the enemy. The breastwork and other towers were treated in the same manner and in a few minutes it was seen that the garrison was issuing from the fort and flying for their lives. Such was the consternation created by the rapid and accurate shooting of the gun that the chief war town was evacuated, as well as other villages of the same nature, and the chiefs surrendered.* "

Report on the use of a Maxim .45 machine gun in The Gambia, 21 November 1887.
Proceedings of the RA Institution, Vol XVI.

The Vickers gun
The .303 Vickers Gun Mark I served the British Army from 1912 to 1968. It was belt-fed and water-cooled and was renowned for its reliability and accuracy. The gun shown here has its ammunition belt box and water condensing can; cooling water turned to steam from the heat of the barrel was fed to the can by the hose and there condensed back into water, to be poured back into the gun as opportunity offered.

The Maxim Squad
The Maxim detachment of the 1st Battalion, King's Royal Rifles, 1895. The gun is the Maxim .303 Mark I, and the rifles are .303 Long Lee-Enfields. The ornate gun tripod has a seat for the gunner, elevation and traverse controls, and also a machine for loading the fabric belts with cartridges.

Maxim's first attempt
The original Maxim gun of 1885; this used the recoil of the barrel to store energy in a flywheel, which then performed the actions of loading, extracting and feeding the ammunition belt.

offered it to the Colt company; it was adopted by the US Navy in 1895. The Colt machine-gun modified Browning's original idea by using an unusual piston which was driven downward, in an arc beneath the barrel, to activate the gun mechanism. This downward-swinging lever soon earned the gun its nickname "The Potato Digger", since it prevented the weapon being used too close to the ground.

EUROPEAN DESIGNS

In Europe, Austria led the field in 1888 with a simple design from the Archduke Salvator and Count Dormus, produced by the Skoda company. This relied upon the gas pressure blowing the cartridge case out of the chamber to drive the breech block back against a powerful spring; it was the first practical application of the principle later to be known as the "blowback" weapon.

Another Austrian, Captain Odkolek, approached the French firm Hotchkiss & Cie with a design using gas to drive a piston back beneath the barrel. Hotchkiss saw some merit in the idea, bought the patents outright, improved the design, and marketed it as the Hotchkiss machine gun with considerable success. The French Army were the first to adopt the gun in 1897.

These three systems – recoil, gas, and blowback – have dominated machine-gun design ever since, in spite of sundry other developments which have briefly appeared. Although the basic Maxim was used until the 1950s in the USSR, it was replaced in Britain by the Vickers and in Germany by the Parabellum by 1912. These both used the Maxim action but inverted it and adopted a lighter form of construction to save weight, but without sacrificing reliability. The Hotchkiss, used by the Japanese, and the Danish Madsen machine-gun, used by the Russians, opposed each other in the Russo–Japanese war in 1904 and opened the eyes of many to the machine gun's potential.

RATES OF FIRE COMPARISON

	Rounds per minute					
Type of gun	100	200	300	400	500	600
Skoda M1888	• • • • • • • • • •					
Colt 6mm M1895	• • • • • • • • • • • • • • • • • • • •					
Schwarzlose M1905	• • • • • • • • • • • • • • • • •					
Madsen M1900	• •					
Vickers .303 Mk 1	• •					
Browning M1917	• •					
Hotchkiss M1897	• •					
Maxim .45 Mk 1	• •					
Maxim Original	• •					

QUICK-FIRING ARTILLERY

A quick-firing howitzer

A German 15-cm field howitzer model of 1902, manufactured by Krupp. Once the quick-firing system had been mastered it was rapidly extended to larger calibres, though this 150-mm weapon, weighing just over two tons, was probably as big a QF weapon as could be comfortably managed in the field. Note the cradle beneath the barrel, containing the hydro-spring recoil mechanism.

THE DEVELOPMENT of quick-firing artillery was a response to the need to improve on mechanical machine-guns as a defence against torpedo boats. As these boats became stronger, the small machine-gun bullets could no longer do sufficient damage, so heavier-calibre weapons were required. These could not be made to operate in the same manner as machine-guns, because of the extra weight of the mechanism and ammunition, but some of the technical features were adapted to facilitate a high rate of fire.

As often happens, the same idea simultaneously arose from two sources. Hotchkiss of France and Nordenfelt of Sweden had both been trying to design a heavy-calibre machine-gun for some time. Then, in the late 1880s, both produced 47-mm and 57-mm guns, and these were widely adopted by the world's navies. The guns used rounds of ammunition that consisted of a brass cartridge case containing the propellant charge and a percussion primer (see Percussion firearms, page 76) for ignition, to which was attached the projectile, a powder-filled pointed shell (see From case shot to cartridges, page 70) carrying a simple base fuze. This ammunition, which was virtually a scaled-up rifle or machine-gun cartridge, allowed the gun to be loaded in one simple movement, using a breech mechanism that consisted of a block of steel sliding up and down behind the chamber. The breech mechanism merely had to retain the cartridge in position during firing. The breech was sealed by the expansion of the brass cartridge case, which then contracted and was ejected automatically as the breech block was opened. Both guns were identical except for size. At first, they were mounted rigidly on a steel pedestal which suffered the recoil blow. Later, the gun was carried in a "cradle" and permitted to slide back under the recoil force, its movement arrested by a hydraulic brake. A spring returned the gun to the firing position.

A round of ammunition

*A typical quick firing round (**LEFT**), for the British 6-pounder (2.244-inch calibre) coast defence and naval gun. The shell is pointed for piercing upperworks of ships and carries a powder charge and base fuze. The propelling charge is inside the brass cartridge case, with a percussion cap in the base.*

Revolving cannon

The Hotchkiss 37-mm revolver gun was intended for use against torpedo-boats. It lacked sufficient range, and the quick-firing gun soon rendered it obsolete. But the ammunition principles developed for it were carried over to the larger calibre and laid the foundation of the quick-firing system.

The 47-mm gun, in the hands of a skilled crew, could deliver about 30 shots per minute, the 57-mm about 25. This was adequate to defend warships against torpedo boats, and the same guns were then adapted for land use to defend harbours against a similar threat. Their success prompted armies to ask gunmakers for a field artillery gun with a comparable performance.

The difficulty lay with the recoil force. Field guns were more powerful than the 47-mm and 57-mm naval weapons and were not anchored to a massive ship structure to absorb recoil. Unless recoil could be controlled, the gunners would be unable to load the gun fast enough to develop the desired rate of fire.

THE "FRENCH 75"

The problem was eventually solved by the French artillery arsenal at Puteaux, where a Captain Deport developed the 75-mm gun Mle 1897, the famous "French 75". This fired a fixed round of ammunition, had a quick-acting breech mechanism, and controlled the recoil of the gun by means of a complex and highly secret hydro-pneumatic braking system. This was so effective that a coin balanced on the gun's wheel would remain in place while a shot was fired. Since the gun carriage now remained still, it was provided with a shield so that the gunners were partially protected from small-arms fire. These four features — the fixed ammunition, shield, quick-acting breech, and an on-carriage recoil system — became the hallmark of the "quick-firing (QF) gun". French artillery was now ahead of the rest of the world. All the major armies rushed to follow their example and produce their own QF guns, which they eventually did. These guns differed in matters of detail but included the four essential features of the original French QF gun.

The seventy-five

The French 75-mm quick-firing gun, model of 1897. This formed the pattern for future quick-firing field guns. It was widely adopted abroad, and was used until the 1950s in some countries.

> *The manoeuvres of 1900 saw the debut of the famous '75s', and the batteries — guarded by the police against too close examination — were the cynosure of all eyes. But it was to be some years before they were to be seen at practice, and still more before their secret was disclosed. Their design and manufacture, and the success with which their secret was kept [the precise operation of the recoil system], form perhaps the most remarkable achievement in the history of artillery armament.*

Major-General Sir John Headlam,
History of the Royal Artillery, Vol II

BIG GUNS

IN STRONG

FORTRESSES

PROTECT

AGAINST

NAVAL ATTACK

COASTAL DEFENCE

T HE DEFENCE of coastlines, from the earliest days of artillery, had simply been a matter of placing batteries of guns to cover harbour entrances. But the development of the ironclad warship made matters more complicated. Heavy guns on shore were needed to defeat the ironclad's armour, and this, in turn, meant heavier guns on board ship to duel with the shore guns. Moreover, the steam-driven ironclad required secure bases to house the extensive machine shops and dry docks necessary for its repair and maintenance. As a consequence, naval bases and dockyards were expanded, and their fortifications strengthened against bombardment by enemy fleets.

The tactics were dictated by the technology of the time. In the late 19th century the only guns that could defeat ironclads were heavy-calibre short-range weapons. Since the ships carried identical weapons, the shore installations needed as much protection as the ironclads themselves. This took the form of the casemate, consisting of arched chambers of heavy stone protection for the guns, faced with heavy armour plate with gun ports. The muzzles were poked through the ports to fire, recoiled within the

The disappearing gun

A 12-inch disappearing gun in Fort Wright, New York, firing at practice in the 1920s. Here, the gun is seen just beginning to recoil.

casemate on firing, where they were reloaded, and then run out again to fire the next round. The process was slow. The only hope of defeating a naval attack was to concentrate large numbers of guns at vulnerable points. Furthermore, there was little coordination between gunners, with each gun captain responsible for aiming his gun at whatever target he could find.

To protect the ammunition from enemy fire, the magazines were buried beneath the gun battery. Ammunition was supplied to the guns by hand-worked lifts. For proper protection granite and iron armour was needed, but this was expensive. Indeed, by the 1870s the architecture of a gun emplacement cost about three times as much as the gun itself. This situation gave rise to new ideas on coastal fortification.

The "disappearing gun" was a system developed by Captain Alexander Moncrieff of the Edinburgh Militia Artillery in the late 1860s. The gun was carried at the top of a pair of arms, and

REAL ESTATE WITH GUNS

At the turn of the century, coast defence was changing from massive and obvious forts to invisible emplacements sunk into the ground. Fort Pembroke, Malta, consists simply of two emplacements for 9.2-inch guns with an underground magazine between them, a guard house, a rest room for the gun crews and an

underground engine room to provide the hydraulic power for operating the two guns. Sited some distance from the sea, it was virtually invisible to any ship and thus an impossible target, though it had a perfect field of fire across St George's Bay and out to sea. The gun crews lived in a nearby barracks and only manned the fort

when danger threatened. Day-to-day security was performed by a small guard post. The 9.2-inch gun was the standard British heavy coast defence weapon from the 1890s until the end of coast artillery in 1956.

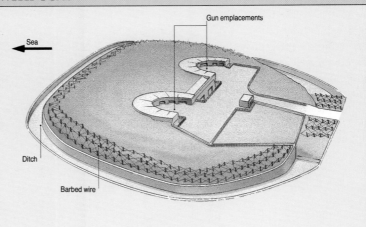

pivoted with a heavy counterweight at the foot. When the gun was fired, recoil drove it back, causing it to turn about its pivot, lifting the counterweight, and lowering the gun into the pit in which the "disappearing carriage" was placed. Once down, the gun was held by a brake and could be reloaded by the gunners in the pit, away from enemy fire. The gun brake was then released, the counterweight dropped, and the reloaded gun was pulled up, over the parapet of the pit, ready to fire again.

The simple pit was much cheaper than the granite and armoured casemate, so the Moncrieff system was enthusiastically adopted. At the same time, however, guns were increasing in power and the breech-loading gun was appearing. Experience showed that Moncrieff's simple design could not cope with guns of more than 7-inch calibre. Even so, the principle was sound and the idea was modified to use hydro-pneumatic cylinders to absorb the recoil, lower the gun, and then return it to the firing position. This adaptation could accommodate even the most powerful guns, and the system was adopted, in different forms, by most major maritime countries. In the USA, disappearing carriages were used to mount guns up to 16-inch calibre.

As a result, the traditional coastal defence fortress gradually vanished, to be replaced by gun batteries that appeared as pits in otherwise open ground. They were invisible except when the gun rose and fired, and virtually impossible for a ship to target.

Another tactic developed during the 1860s was to fire howitzers at steep angles, dropping shells onto the decks of warships, rather than attacking the ships' sides, which were stronger and better protected. The howitzers were kept behind hills and out of sight of the sea to defend points from where warships could bombard dockyards and other targets. France adopted coastal defence howitzers in the 1870s, the USA and Britain in the 1880s.

HYDRO-PNEUMATIC RECOIL

With the introduction of the quick-firing field gun in the latter 1890s (see Quick-firing artillery, page 102), the technology of hydro-pneumatic recoil became standard. Compared with the quick-firing gun the disappearing gun was slow, on account of the time taken by the gun's movement; and it lacked range because of the geometry of the mechanism, which restricted elevation. Using more conventional types of mounting and modern hydro-pneumatic recoil, the gun could fire more rounds in a given time and, with greater elevation possible, could maximize its range. Even if the gun were exposed all the time, because it was a long way away it presented a virtually impossible target to a moving warship. By the early years of the 20th century the disappearing pattern of coast gun mounting was being replaced by the now-standard barbette type, in which the gun is placed behind a concrete parapet so that only the barrel is visible over the top.

Many countries abandoned coastal defence artillery in the 1950s, because of vulnerability to attack by ballistic missiles (see Strategic missiles, page 184). Some of the Scandinavian countries still deploy coastal artillery, much of it mounted in modern armoured turrets adapted from the technology of the tank. Other countries such as China, Iraq, and Argentina have adopted missiles for coastal defence purposes. (An Exocet missile fired from a naval mounting lashed to a trailer struck HMS *Glamorgan* during the Falklands War of 1982.)

Sweden's modern defences
A turreted 120-mm coast defence gun of the Swedish army. This is the only visible portion of a massive buried installation which includes power supplies, magazines, fire control with radar and optical aids, living quarters and even NBC decontamination facilities. The water-cooled gun fires a 24-kg shell to a range of 27 km at a rate of 25 rounds a minute.

UNDERWATER DEFENCES

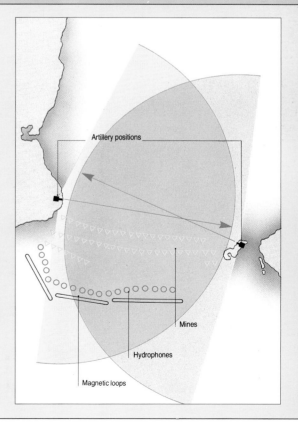

A chart showing the underwater defences guarding the entrance to Chesapeake Bay and Newport News naval base in the USA in the 1930s. Approaching from the sea, there was first a row of magnetic loops which would detect any ship passing across them; next came a row of hydrophones to detect engine and screw noises. Finally came three rows of electrically controlled mines. Alerted by the loops and hydrophones, observers could locate the approaching ship and detonate the appropriate mine on command. The water area was also covered by heavy coast artillery on both sides of the entrance, shown here by their arcs of fire.

Artillery positions

Mines

Hydrophones

Magnetic loops

ROCKETS TO 1918

The Chinese rocket
Authenticated instances of the Chinese use of rockets in ancient times are rare; this picture actually shows the use of rockets against Nanking during the Taiping Rebellion of 1860-5. Although the launching devices resemble cannon, they are actually tube launchers, and the characteristic trail of sparks behind the rocket is well portrayed. It is possible that these were Congreve rockets; records of the Ordnance Committee of the period record the transfer of Congreve rockets from Hong Kong to the Chinese Government.

S OME PEOPLE claim that the use of rockets dates back to antiquity, but the evidence is doubtful. The first fairly reliable report comes from 1232, when the Chinese are said to have employed rockets against the Tartars. Timur, the great 14th-century Turkish conqueror and lord of Samarkand, is also said to have used rockets against Delhi in 1399. A later report suggests that the fort of Bitar, in India, was destroyed in 1657 by a rocket falling in the vicinity of the magazine. Apparently, they were also used in the west, at Chioggia in 1380 during a war between Genoa and Venice. However, in the west there was little enthusiasm for them and for several centuries they were forgotten as weapons, though they remained in use as fireworks.

In 1650 Kasimir Simineowicz, a Polish artillery officer, proposed an improved rocket. The idea was to have three or four powder-filled tubes arranged so that igniting the first tube began the flight and then, as this burned out, it ignited the second and so on — the system known today as two-stage or three-stage motors. Simineowicz also suggested stabilizing the rocket's flight by the use of fins instead of a stick. However, there is no record of any of this actually being applied to a practical weapon.

In the time of Tipu, the Sultan of Mysore (1749–99), war rockets were used in India, in particular against the British who besieged Seringapatam in 1792. The British Adjutant General reported that a single rocket killed three of his men and wounded four others. Contemporary accounts suggest that these rockets

> *The Committee forward an abstract of results of practice with the 24pr rockets, manufactured in accordance with the specification furnished by Mr. Hale, with a view that if on a trial they should continue to yield the same satisfactory results as were obtained with the previous supply, manufactured by Mr. Hale himself, the consideration of that gentleman's claim for compensation should receive the early attention of Her Majesty's Government. The Committee are of opinion that this recent practice fully establishes the value of rockets constructed on Mr. Hale's principle.*

Ordnance Select Committee, Minute 15928, 29 June 1865.

weighed about 10lbs, were attached to a 10-foot stick and had an effective range of about a mile. A second engagement at Seringapatam in 1799, where more rockets were used, led the British Army to ask the Royal Laboratory for rockets, but none were available. Consequently, Sir William Congreve set about developing one. The attraction of the rocket was that it exerted no recoil force on its launcher, so it could be used in small boats and by individuals to discharge projectiles with as much power as artillery (see Early artillery, page 64).

The Congreve rocket consisted of a tubular steel casing about 2 feet long, filled with gunpowder, on the end of a 10-foot stick. The rocket was launched from a light trough supported by two legs. A piece of slow match ignited the rocket. Given the limitations of the artillery at the time, the Congreve rocket could range as far and as accurately as any field gun. Moreover, Congreve developed shrapnel (see Early artillery, page 64) and incendiary warheads which made a rocket that found its target as effectively as any gun.

In October 1806, during the Napoleonic Wars, eighteen British ships fired 2,000 rockets into Boulogne and set fire to the town; in 1807 the same thing was done at Copenhagen and at Walcheren. At the Battle of the Nations, Leipzig, in 1813 the Rocket Brigade helped turn the tide of battle in the Allies' (Prussia, Poland, Austria and Sweden) favour. Congreve rockets are even celebrated in the US national anthem, commemorating the bombardment of Fort McHenry in 1814 by the British.

The Congreve rocket was superseded in 1867 by Hale's War Rocket, developed by an American engineer. This had three vents at the rear, the jets impinging on vanes which caused the rocket to spin as it flew and so stabilized it without the need for a stick. A 24-pounder Hale Rocket had a range of almost 2,000 yards with reasonable accuracy. Like Congreve's rocket, it was filled with a gunpowder composition, rammed hard so that it burned relatively slowly and generated the necessary thrust. Hale's rocket was first used by the Americans during the Mexican War (1846–8), but after that it was dropped in favour of conventional artillery. It was taken up for a short time by the British, who deployed rockets in the Abyssinian campaign in 1867, but was little used subsequently. From about 1870 the rapid improvements in artillery soon outstripped the performance of the rocket.

FIRST WORLD WAR ROCKETS

In about 1900 Count Unge of Sweden attempted to promote an improved version of Hale's rocket, but with no success, since it could not compete with artillery in either range or accuracy. It was not until the aviators of the First World War (1914–18) demanded a destructive weapon for attacking observation balloons that the rocket returned to favour. The call was answered by Y.P.G. Le Prieur, a French naval officer. Le Prieur's rocket reverted to the casing and stick of the Congreve model, but with an incendiary warhead which was intended to ignite the hydrogen gas in balloons or Zeppelin airships. Slung beneath the wings of fighter aircraft and fired electrically, it proved highly effective against its designated targets.

Explosive versions of the rocket were also used, for attacking troops on the ground, although machine-guns and bombs were much more common for this task. The Le Prieur rocket was also tried as an anti-aircraft weapon by ground troops, who fired it at both German aircraft and observation balloons. But as soon as the war was over the rocket was once again cast aside.

Congreve's rocket
The Rocket Troop ("O" Battery, Royal Horse Artillery) training with Congreve's rocket in 1835. The launcher is a simple tube on legs; this was later replaced by a trough launcher, as it was found that a faulty rocket bursting in the tube could wreck the tube and cause injuries, whereas one bursting in a trough was generally harmless. The Rocket Troop gained this honour title for their services at the Battle of Leipzig in 1813. As with the other picture of this weapon, one is inclined to doubt whether the observers would have placed their horses quite so close to the launcher.

Practice on the Marshes, 1845
Congreve rocket practice on Plumstead Marshes, south of London. The tube launcher is still in use, but has a more substantial support, and the tube has been reinforced with rope. The sergeant at the left front holds the lanyard of what appears to be a loaded gun, perhaps to demonstrate the efficiency of the gun compared with the rocket.

AUTOMATIC PISTOLS

THE DEVELOPMENT of the automatic machine-gun raised the possibility of applying similar principles to other arms, particularly hand-guns. By the late 1880s the revolver was more or less perfected and many of its elements were protected by restrictive patents. Consequently, designers sought to develop a new form of hand arm that would both be more efficient and evade these patents. One such attempt was the mechanical repeating pistol, based on the bolt-action system then in use on magazine rifles (see Needle gun and Chassepot, page 78). Several designs were put forward in which the firer's forefinger fitted into a ring attached to an operating arm. Pushing the arm forward to open the bolt and pulling it back to close the bolt loaded a cartridge from the magazine, ready to fire the next round. But these weapons only worked when clean and perfectly lubricated and adjusted, and they proved impractical as military arms. Their failure merely accelerated the search for an alternative.

One such weapon was patented in 1892 by an Austrian named Joseph Laumann. At first, it failed to arouse interest, but he modified the design so that the explosion of the cartridge in the chamber blew back the bolt against a spring. The spring then returned the bolt, loading a new cartridge and leaving the pistol cocked and ready to fire. A handful of these pistols were made by the Steyr factory in Austria and marketed in 1892. It was the first automatic pistol ever made for sale, but it was unreliable and generally not a success.

The next design came from Hugo Borchardt, a skilled gunsmith who had worked in the USA and Europe. In the 1880s

The Mauser c/96, or "Military" model, has a unique appearance, with the magazine ahead of the trigger and the peculiar "broomhandle" grip, but it was made like a fine watch, not a single screw or pin being used in its assembly except to hold the wooden grips in place. This model has a "9" carved into the butt, indicating that it was chambered for the 9-mm German Army cartridge, one of a special batch made during the First World War. Otherwise the Mauser was always in 7.63-mm calibre.

An ungainly pioneer
The 8-mm Roth-Steyr M1908 was the first automatic pistol to be adopted by a first-class power, being used by the Austro-Hungarian Army.

he was in Hungary, where he witnessed the initial demonstrations of the Maxim machine gun (see Automatic machine-guns, page 100). Impressed by what he saw, he began developing a weapon that used the same toggle action as the Maxim to lock the breech. In about 1890 his design was accepted by the Loewe company in Berlin, and in 1893 the Borchardt pistol went on sale. About 3,000 were made. Although the pistol was somewhat cumbersome, when properly looked after it was reliable and accurate. It is regarded as the first successful automatic pistol, and it provided the basis for the more famous Parabellum pistol, designed by Georg Luger in 1898.

At about the same time, Theodor Bergmann of Berlin marketed a pistol designed by Hugo Schmeisser. This used the simple blowback system, pioneered by Laumann, in which the cartridge explosion pressure blew back the bolt and a spring returned it. This principle has remained in use ever since, though

THE ELEGANT MAUSER

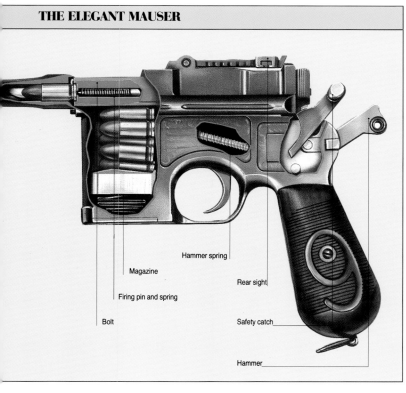

Hammer spring

Magazine

Rear sight

Firing pin and spring

Bolt

Safety catch

Hammer

confined principally to smaller calibres using low-pressure cartridges. The Bergmann pistols became popular as weapons for sport and self-defence, but were never put to military use.

MAUSER AND BROWNING

The third major development of this period was the Mauser automatic pistol, which appeared in 1896. It took the same 7.63-mm cartridge developed for the Borchardt pistol, but used a different method of locking the bolt. The Mauser magazine, like that of a rifle, was a box in front of the trigger, whereas the Borchardt pioneered the use of a magazine inserted into the butt. Like the Borchardt, the Mauser could be fitted with a wooden butt and used as a form of carbine (short rifle) with good accuracy. Although an efficient and reliable weapon that was used throughout the world, the Mauser was never adopted as an official army pistol.

In the USA John Browning almost single-handedly pioneered the modern automatic pistol, offering his designs to Colt and to the Belgian company Fabrique Nationale (FN) of Liège. Browning developed the third major breech-locking system, in which the barrel is connected to the pistol frame by a swinging link that unlocks the breech as the barrel recoils. His greatest success was the Colt .45 pistol adopted by the US forces in 1911 and only relinquished in the late 1980s. His final design, the Browning High-Power, was first produced in 1935 and is still being used worldwide.

The Government Model

John Browning began work on this pistol in 1897, and after several preliminary models it was adopted by the US Army in 1911. After experience in the First World War there were some slight changes, turning it into the M1911A1, but to the Colt company it was always "The Government Model". The breech-locking system was widely copied after Browning's patents expired and remains virtually the standard system to this day. A powerful weapon, accuracy required practice, but once mastered it was a formidable defence. The magazine held seven rounds, and an eighth in the chamber. The M1911A1 remained in service until 1985 and is still made for commercial sale.

The First World War deployed all that weapons technology had perfected during the latter years of the 19th century — quick-firing guns, explosive shells, magazine rifles, machine guns, submarines, torpedoes, and mines. It also accelerated the development of new weapons demanded by the pressure of war — the aeroplane, poison gas, the light machine-gun, and the tank. These, in turn, led to the development of counter-measures so that the aeroplane gave rise to the anti-aircraft gun, the tank to the anti-tank rifle and gun.

Warfare itself changed, from the rapidly moving pursuit of one force by another to the stalemate of the trench lines extending from the North Sea to the Swiss border. This led to the supremacy of the high explosive shell — more effective for the destruction of trenches — over the shrapnel shell — more suited to the attack of troops in the open. The trench mortar and the grenade were rediscovered and brought to new levels of lethality, and the railway gun reached the full flowering of its brief life.

The tank and the machine-gun (together with the barbed wire entanglement) are the abiding images of the First World War, even though their impact was perhaps less than is popularly supposed. The tank never gave a good account of itself until the battle of Cambrai in 1917, largely because of the impossible terrain over which it operated and its early mechanical unreliability. The machine-gun was a formidable defensive weapon and, once the portable light machine-gun appeared, played its part in the offensive as well. But the war was primarily an artillery war, with thousands of guns deployed on each side, and artillery was the prime cause of casualties.

The First World War was also notorious for the use of poison gas, though casualty figures show that it was far less lethal than is commonly supposed. The number of deaths due to gas was one-third of one per cent of the total casualties of the war. Even so, the revulsion caused by the use of gas led to a series of international agreements that ensured that gas was not used in the next war.

CHAPTER SIX

THE FIRST WORLD WAR

SHOOTING

ON AN

INDUSTRIAL

SCALE IN

TRENCH WAR

MORTARS AND MACHINE GUNS: 1914-18

WHEN THE rapid manoeuvering of the first few weeks of the First World War came to nothing, and stalemate set in on the Western Front, the two opposing armies dug lines of trenches that stretched from the Swiss border to the English Channel. Trench warfare fuelled the demand for short-range weapons as well as weapons with which to keep the enemy at bay.

MORTARS

The first requirement was a weapon that could bombard the enemy trenches. The standard artillery piece was of little use, since its long range and flat trajectory were not suited to this task, while the shorter-range howitzer was too cumbrous. The infantry needed a small weapon under their own control. Krupp, the famed German arms-maker, had developed such a weapon before the war, but, as with many weapons, the army could see no tactical role for it in open warfare. However, the Krupp trench howitzer was ideal for trench warfare, and it was immediately put into production. It was a light, short-barrelled weapon that fired a spherical bomb on the end of a stalk that fitted into the mortar. With the barrel elevated to 75 degrees or so, a small charge was enough to project the bomb almost vertically so that it dropped into a trench 300 or 400 yards away.

This idea was rapidly copied by the Allies. The French Army even scoured its museums and stores of old equipment to find muzzle-loading mortars, which were pressed into use, while gunmakers set about inventing new, short-barrelled weapons. In Britain, the engineer Wilfred Stokes developed a simple weapon consisting of a 3-inch calibre smooth-bored barrel supported on a bipod, and with the rear end resting on a baseplate. A cylindrical bomb, with a shotgun cartridge full of powder at the bottom and a simple time fuze at the nose, was dropped down the barrel. On striking the fixed firing pin, the cartridge exploded and the bomb

> *(Mortar bombs)...of all projectiles, are, I think, the most nerve-racking. The trouble is, we can see them. They are sent from trench mortars and their path therefore is at first almost a vertical one in the air, and, after reaching a great height, they descend on their target in a long curve. The moment they reach the highest point in their path, they become visible...and in their descent their course becomes very erratic and it is impossible to judge exactly where they will strike the ground.*
>
> Lieutenant Colonel A.E.C. Bredin, DSO, MC. Three Assault Landings.

The Livens Projector
The Livens Projector was a highly specialized form of mortar designed solely to launch cylinders of poison gas. A charge of guncotton was loaded from the muzzle, with an electric igniter and a length of wire. The gas cylinder, with a simple impact fuze, was loaded on top. Hundreds or more would be prepared, carefully directed at a specific area, and fired simultaneously. The result was to drench the enemy area with a sudden storm of heavily concentrated gas.

The Lewis gun
The Lewis light machine gun was a success story of the First World War. Designed in the USA and ignored there, the inventor took it to Europe just before war broke out. The BSA Company of England, began making it for export. Once war *had begun it was adopted in small numbers by the British and Belgian armies and, once its tactical place* *had been worked out, in ever-increasing numbers. The device beneath the muzzle is the anti-aircraft sight.*

was blown from the tube. Because of its shape, the bomb turned end-over-end as it flew, but it was surprisingly accurate. The Stokes mortar was put into service in August 1915.

Stokes next designed a fin-stabilized bomb that flew without tumbling. He also developed a 4-inch mortar that could fire a heavier bomb, and this became one of the principal gas delivery weapons. Meanwhile the Germans had produced the *Minenwerfer* ("bomb thrower"), a very short and portable howitzer that fired a muzzle-loaded shell. Several calibres — 76-mm, 170-mm, 180-mm, 240-mm, and 250-mm — appeared in due course, and by the end of the war there were some 17,000 of them in use. They were heavier and more complex than the Stokes mortar, and had recoil systems and wheels. They were harder to move about and had a slower rate of firing.

In answer to these heavy German weapons, the British developed the Newton 6-inch mortar firing a 48-lb bomb, and the French a 240-mm device firing a 190-lb bomb. The British and French Armies were supplied with each other's mortars, the French 240-mm being called the 9.45-inch in British service.

MACHINE GUNS

The question of a rapid-fire weapon to deal with massed infantry attacks was equally pressing. The machine gun was the obvious answer, and the Maxim and Vickers guns already in use were mass-produced. But they, and similar weapons, were heavy and required a supply of cooling water. As such, they were adequate defence, but a lighter weapon that could both be used for defence and as support in attack was soon in demand. The German Army simply took their standard Maxim off its tripod, fitted a small bipod and a shoulder-stock, and called it a light machine-gun. They did the same with other water-cooled guns — the Dreyse and Bergmann — and made them lighter by replacing the water-jacket with a perforated steel tube around the barrel which allowed a degree of air cooling.

Winning the VC
Lieutenant Thomas Wilkinson of the Royal North Lancaster Regiment won the Victoria Cross in France in 1916 by stopping a German advance with a Vickers machine gun. The reliability of the Vickers was legendary, and battalions of them were used as fire support during attacks. In the attack on High Wood in August 1916 ten guns fired almost one million rounds in 12 hours, one gun firing over 120,000 rounds without a stoppage. The Vickers' maximum range was 4,500 yards, though at this range it was far from accurate and was simply an "area weapon".

Britain adopted the Lewis Gun for the light support task. This was an American design that was made in Belgium and mass-produced in Britain. It was air-cooled and used a 47-round drum magazine instead of the canvas belts found on heavier weapons. The Lewis Gun was reasonably light, reliable, and a useful addition to the infantry's firepower.

The French developed the Chauchat light machine-gun, which was not a success. It used an operating system known as "long recoil" in which the whole barrel and breech ran back and forth with each shot. This action soon wore out the barrel bearings, contributing to the weapon's inaccuracy and gross unreliability. The Chauchat fired from a semi-circular box magazine beneath the weapon. In spite of its defects, it was manufactured in tens of thousands. It was also issued to the American Expeditionary Force, to their disgust.

A far better weapon was the Browning Automatic Rifle, developed in the USA for use as an assault weapon. It was slung from the shoulder to give "marching fire". The ammunition was fed from a 20-round box magazine. Reliable, robust, and accurate, it remained the US Army's light-machine gun until the 1950s.

As the faults of the Chauchat became apparent, France turned to the maker of their heavy machine-gun, Hotchkiss, who produced a light, air-cooled version that appeared in 1916. Ammunition feed was by means of a metal tray of cartridges, pushed in at one side of the gun and ejected, empty, at the other. This was later modified into a form of metal link belt which was more convenient to use. The Hotchkiss was also adopted by the British Army and remained in use for many years after the war.

BALANCING THE

USER'S SAFETY

AND THE

WEAPON'S

LETHAL

EFFECT

EARLY GRENADES

GRENADES — SMALL bombs thrown by hand — have been in use since the 16th century. They were originally hollow iron balls filled with gunpowder and ignited by a length of slow match. To be effective, the soldiers who threw them had to be tall and strong. They became known as "grenadiers". In open warfare grenades were not often used. They were mainly used by

The grenadier
An early 18th-century print of French soldiers, among them a grenadier. He holds a length of burning slow-match, from which to light the fuze of the grenade, and will then throw the lit grenade at the enemy. Grenadiers were invariably tall men, capable of throwing heavy grenades to a good distance. Note also that he has no other weapon, but a pikeman is at his side for his protection.

The Mills bomb
A Mills hand grenade open. In the central tube is a striker, pulled upwards against a spring and retained by the tip of a lever engaging in a notch in the end of the striker rod. A safety pin holds the lever in place. Beneath the tip of the striker is a percussion cap attached to a length of fuze which curls up into the side tube. The remaining space is packed with explosive, ignited by a detonator at the end of the fuze.

the defenders in sieges, who threw them into the surrounding ditch when they were under assault. The fuze was notoriously unreliable, and as late as the 1860s the official manuals cautioned against holding the grenade too long after igniting the fuze.

The use of grenades almost died out by the end of the 19th century but it was revived during the Russo-Japanese War of 1904–5. The troops in the trenches surrounding Port Arthur made various improvised devices before they were equipped with factory-made grenades. Foreign observers of the war who reported their use revived interest in the development of grenades. However, effective grenades were, for the most part, found wanting when war came in 1914. When, for example, the British Grenade No 1 — a cast-iron canister on an 18-inch stick, with a contact fuze — was used in the confines of the Flanders trenches, it frequently struck the rear wall of the trench and killed the thrower.

Scores of different grenades were fielded by the various combatants, but only a few designs achieved a workable balance between safety for the user and lethality to the enemy. Three

Storm troops, 1918
A German storm-trooper in 1918 throws a "potato-masher" grenade. Like the 18th-century grenadier, he carries no other weapon and is protected by a rifleman who also carries extra grenades. A drawback of the grenade is that the thrower must expose himself to fire in order to throw. As a result, grenades were more used in close-quarter combat when clearing trenches and dug-outs than in open warfare.

The stick grenade
The German stick grenade was developed in the First World War and continued in use with very little change until 1945. The head is of thin steel, with a high capacity for explosive; the handle of wood. The screw cap at the end covers a string which is pulled to ignite the fuze inside the head. The head unscrews to allow the detonator to be inserted; like all grenades it is transported without its detonator.

models were found to stand the test of battle — the British Mills bomb, the French "pineapple" and the German "potato-masher".

William Mills was a Birmingham engineer who devised an ovoid cast-iron bomb, with a central spring-loaded firing pin and a spring-loaded lever locked by a pin. When the grenade went off, the cast-iron casing shattered, producing a shower of incapacitating metal fragments. The fingers were held over the lever, the pin was removed and the grenade was then thrown. Once the grenade was in the air, the lever flew up and released the striker, which ignited a four-second time fuze, allowing the thrower to take cover before the grenade exploded. Originally issued as Grenade No 5 for hand use, it was later modified to accept a screwed-in rod so that it could be fired from a rifle, and was redesignated the No 23. Later still, a disc was fitted to the bottom which enabled it to be fired from a cup discharger, whereupon it became the No 36 and remained in British service until the 1960s.

The French "pineapple" was similar in shape but used a slightly different method of ignition, though it was still controlled by a lever and pin. The German "potato-masher", or stick grenade, had a wooden handle about 10 inches long carrying a metal canister at its head. Pulling a string inside the wooden handle lit a friction igniter and time fuze. Most grenades were explosive, anti-personnel weapons, but others were designed to emit smoke or gas.

THE RIFLE GRENADE

The maximum range of a hand grenade depends upon the strength and skill of the thrower, but is rarely more than 120 feet. Thus they were principally used in the final stages of an assault. To bombard an opposing enemy trench required more range, so the rifle grenade was developed. This idea had been first mooted before 1914 but met with little enthusiasm. Now, however, as with hand grenades, the demands of trench warfare rekindled interest in the rifle grenade. The original patterns were all based upon the prewar designs of Martin Hale, an English engineer. He developed a cylindrical iron grenade mounted upon a thin steel rod and

fitted with a simple impact fuze. The rifle was loaded with a blank cartridge and the grenade rod inserted into the barrel. On firing, the gas released from the cartridge threw the grenade a distance of 600 feet.

The drawback to this system was that prolonged use could cause bulging in the rifle barrel and rendered it unfit for ordinary shooting. Consequently, the British developed a cup that fitted onto the muzzle of the rifle, which could hold a standard Mills bomb.

Firing a blank cartridge produced gases which blew the grenade a considerable distance — in some cases more than 650 feet. Remarkable accuracy could be attained by a skilful user.

France and Germany also adopted muzzle cups but approached the launch problem differently. The French rifle grenade was the "Vivien Bessière", named after its inventor. It was fired from a cup but had a hole running axially through it so that instead of a blank cartridge, an ordinary bulleted cartridge could be used. As the bullet travelled up the central tube, it tripped a trigger which started a time fuze. The momentary blockage of the tube was sufficient to allow the propelling gas behind the bullet to launch the grenade. The Germans adopted the same idea but simplified the detonation process by placing a percussion cap in the central tube so that the bullet struck it and directly lit the time fuze train. Both these grenades had a range of about 450 feet.

EARLY FIGHTING AIRCRAFT

BEFORE 1914 aircraft — whether heavier-than-air aeroplanes or lighter-than-air airships — were seen almost entirely as having a reconnaissance role. One or two prophets suggested that these machines might, on occasion, meet and therefore ought to carry some light weapons, and there were a few experiments in arming aircraft. But these largely consisted of taking up a rifle or machine-gun to see if a weapon could be fired without causing the aircraft to crash. Very little thought was given to aerial tactics.

The British had, by 1914, a few aircraft purpose-built for military use, among which the BE2 was one of the most advanced. This biplane, designed by de Havilland and Green in 1911, was intended for reconnaissance and bombing, but carried no guns. Another British war-plane, the FB-5, was designed by Vickers in response to an Admiralty request in 1912 for an aircraft that could carry a machine-gun. The French and Germans, on the other hand, relied entirely upon commandeered civil aircraft at the start of the war. The German *Taube* was extensively used for scouting on the Eastern front, and one flew from the Marne to Paris and dropped a few hand grenades (see Early grenades, page 114). This was the first bombing attack on a major city. The French used Blériot monoplanes as scouting aircraft.

Once their initial advance was over, the Germans began to use aircraft for artillery spotting, and could soon direct their guns to burst shrapnel over British troops. To counter this, on 22 August, 1914, two British Royal Flying Corps pilots, Lieutenants Penn-Gaskell and Strange, took to the air with a Lewis machine-gun and loosed off some shots to drive off a German spotter plane. But although successful, this was considered too dangerous to repeat.

Although pilots began carrying pistols, rifles, and even shotguns, and took pot-shots at the enemy, these were little more than gestures, since the aircraft were slow and ponderous. All the intended victim had to do was turn away and the fight was ended.

When the French began bombing raids on targets behind German lines, the Germans quickly countered by arming scout aircraft with machine-guns. Generally these were two-seater aeroplanes with the observer acting as a gunner. In the case of "pusher" aircraft, in which the engine was at the back of the crew nacelle, the gunner rode in the front seat and had a wide field of fire ahead of the machine. By contrast, the "tractor" machine, which had the engine in the nose, had the observer in the rear seat, firing to the rear and sides. Gradually the tractor became the

The Bristol Fighter
The Bristol Fighter first flew in September 1916, and first saw action in the following April. It could fly at 125mph and could stay up for three hours on patrol. The pilot had one synchronized Vickers machine gun mounted above the engine and the observer had one or two free Lewis machine guns on a ring mounting. The "Brisfit", as it became known, was as manoeuvrable as a single-seat fighter. It could withstand enormous damage and still manage to fly home. In addition to its role as a fighter it could carry a dozen 20-lb Cooper bombs beneath the wings for ground attack purposes.

The nose gunner
A photograph taken before the outbreak of war in 1914 shows two French Army officers testing a Hotchkiss machine gun in a Henri Farman biplane. Many early aircraft were of the "pusher" type with the propeller behind the short fuselage, allowing the observer to occupy a seat in the nose for better visibility. It also promised a good field of action for a machine gun, and this picture shows the first

such mounting, a pedestal being fitted into the nose to support the gun. The object in view, however, was not aerial combat but ground support; the tests consisted of flying across targets laid out on the ground and firing at them, at which the system proved successful.

The nose-gunner system was applied to a number of fighting aircraft in 1914-15, but as design improved the system died out.

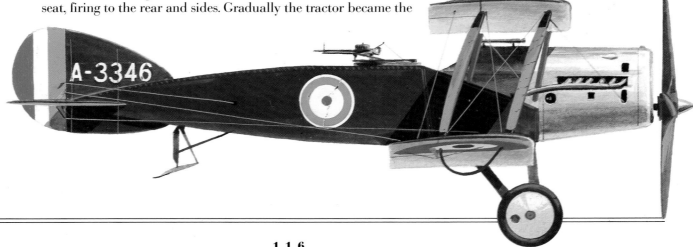

The Fokker triplane
More wing area meant more lift and a faster rate of climb. The idea of a triplane was pioneered in Britain by Sopwith in 1916. It was immediately copied in Germany, and the Fokker Dr.1 triplane became a formidable fighter. Armament was two 7.92-mm Maxim guns firing forward, and the top speed was just over 100mph.

standard even for two-seaters. In this configuration, the gunner covered the more vulnerable rear while one or two fixed guns, built into the aircraft and fired by the pilot, dealt with threats from the front.

DEVELOPMENT OF THE FIGHTER PLANE

The problem with forward-firing guns was the propeller. The first attempted solution was to put the gun on the upper wing of a biplane so that it fired over the propeller disc. But as early guns were magazine-fed, there was a limited amount of firing the pilot could do before having to stand up and change magazines — a fraught procedure in the middle of an aerial battle. Mounting the gun or guns in front of the pilot, where he could easily reach them to clear jams or reload, was a better idea. The French solved the problem by putting steel plates on the propeller blades to divert any hits. Next, the outstanding Dutch aircraft designer Antony Fokker developed a cam-driven device for the German air service which, by means of a cable connected to the trigger, fired the gun only when the propeller was clear of the line of fire. Finally, the Allies developed the Constantinesco Synchronizer, a hydraulic pump that did the same thing but rather more reliably. Once these devices had been perfected, twin guns mounted alongside or on top of the engine became the standard fighter armament. Since there was more space available, they could be belt-fed, for continuous fire without changing magazines.

By the middle of 1915, aerial combat was beginning to take shape. On both sides the armies were demanding more and better reconnaissance, while their opponents were routinely sending up fighter aircraft as a deterrent. Scouting aircraft themselves were increasingly protected by fighters, which came into conflict with enemy fighters, whose numbers increased to deal with the new threat and to attack the scouting aircraft. From a loose free-for-all, formal tactics had been evolved by the middle of 1916. Combat formations developed so as to maximize both all-round protection, with "free" guns in the rear seats, and attacking potential, with "fixed" synchronized guns in the front. Later the observer and rear gun were abandoned and the single-seat fighter emerged. This was a machine designed purely for shooting down other aircraft, relying upon its manoeuvrability and the pilot's skill to avoid being shot down itself.

The Cuffley airship
Lieutenant Leefe Robinson shooting down the Schutt-Lanze airship SL11 over Cuffley, north of London, on 3 September 1916 — the first German airship to be shot down over Britain.

GAS WARFARE

GERMANY, IN 1914, was not prepared for a long war, and, contrary to common belief, did not have inexhaustible stocks of munitions. By the end of that year, the German authorities began casting round to find means of rapidly producing artillery shells. The actual shell bodies could be cast and machined quite quickly in a multitude of engineering shops but filling them was a more specialized task. Increased production of explosives was not something that could be accomplished overnight. The possibility of using non-explosives was examined and a proposal made to use noxious chemicals. The first suggestion was to replace the resin packing around the lead balls in shrapnel shells with an irritant chemical. After a successful test, a batch of these shells was used against British troops at Neuve Chapelle on 27 October, 1914.

However, in the field the idea was a complete failure. The British troops experienced no ill-effects and the plan to use gas was abandoned. Next came a proposal to fill cast-iron shells with xylyl bromide, a tear-provoking gas. Professor Haber, Director of the Kaiser Wilhelm Institute for Physical Chemistry at Dahlem, suggested that a more effective method would be simply to put the gas in cylinders and release it downwind.

Xylyl bromide shells were first used against the Russian Army at Bolimov on 31 January, 1915. Once again, the idea did not work out in practice. This time the cold was so severe that the liquid froze in the shells and did not vaporize. However, the Russians collected some of the shells and, realizing what was being tried, began some low-priority work on devising methods of protection against tear gas. The same type of shells were used against the British at Nieuport in March 1915, but were also ineffective. Interestingly, at this stage neither the British nor the Russians made any public announcement about the use of gas on either of these occasions.

As a result, the popularly held belief is that gas was first used at Ypres on 22 April, 1915, when Professor Haber was given the chance to test his new weapon. The Germans deployed 5,730 cylinders filled with 168 tons of chlorine gas along a 4-mile front.

The small box respirator
This British gas mask was issued in April 1916 as a result of the German use of chloropicrin gas which could defeat existing masks. On the right, in the haversack, is a container with layers of charcoal, soda lime and potassium permanganate. From this a corrugated tube leads to the rubber-cloth face mask. Inside the mask is a mouthpiece and nose-clip to ensure that only air filtered through the canister can be breathed. It remained the standard mask for British and US troops until the war ended.

" *Notwithstanding the remarkable results achieved with chemicals during the World War, the means and methods employed in that conflict appear as crude and feeble beginnings when viewed in the light of our present knowledge and our cooler conceptions of the future. As we draw away from the late war we apprehend more clearly that the potential power of chemicals was then only dimly foreshadowed. Today we realise that all nations are facing new and powerful instrumentalities involving as profound changes in the art and science of war as were brought about by the invention of gunpowder.* "

Chemicals in War: A.M. Prentiss, New York, 1937.

The gas mask in use
Australian troops wearing the small box respirator in September 1917. These men appear to be taking life easy; illustrating a point about chemical warfare: the mere threat of gas, forcing men to don masks and protective clothing, is a valuable weapon. Men in masks and impermeable clothing soon become fatigued, even without strenuous action. Moreover a mask restricts the amount of air a man receives and thus tends to restrict his physical capabilities.

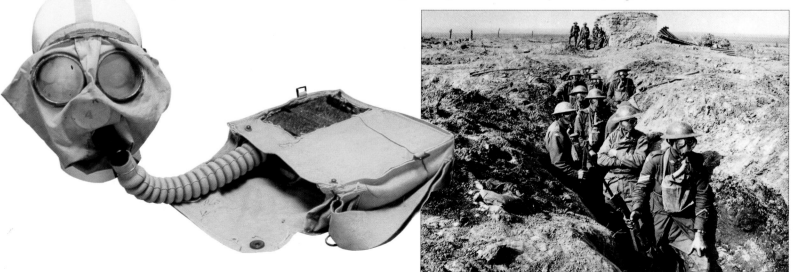

The huge cloud of gas, released at 5.30 pm when the wind conditions were right, cut a 5-mile gap in the Allied lines. But as in so many battles of the First World War, the attackers were not prepared for their success, there were no reserves ready to be thrown in, and the Allies managed to rally and hold their front.

Following the Ypres attack, all the combatants swiftly developed chemical warfare services whose task it was to discover, manufacture, and deliver offensive gases. Over 3,000 substances were tested for their offensive potential during the war, of which some 38 were selected as being capable of use, and of those about a dozen were used in quantity.

Gases used in warfare are classified into five groups: lachrimators (tear gases, such as bromobenzyl cyanide), asphyxiators (lung injurants, such as chlorine), toxic agents (such as phosgene), sternutators (respiratory irritants, such as diphenyl chloroarsine), and vesicants (blister gases, such as dichloroethyl sulphide, known as mustard gas). For tactical purposes they are also divided into two groups: non-persistent (which disperse within 10 minutes) and persistent (which remain active for hours, days, or even months).

The first gases came from the first three classes, since these were already known and relatively easy to manufacture. Chlorine and phosgene were dispensed from pressurized cylinders, while all three classes of gas were used in artillery shells and mortar bombs. For maximum effectiveness, the tactic was to swamp an area with a high concentration of gas so as to disable all enemy combatants. To achieve this, the British devised the Livens Projector. This was a simple mortar-like weapon designed to be sunk into the ground by the hundreds and then fired electrically to launch a salvo of gas cylinders into the target area. It was first used in quantity at Arras, on 9 April, 1917, when 3,827 projectiles released 51 tons of phosgene into the German trenches in one colossal salvo. Over 100 men died instantly while another 500 were hospitalized. A similar device was developed by the Germans after capturing specimens of the Livens Projector.

The Livens Projector
Loading a Livens Projector (ABOVE) with a canister of gas. The canister is fitted with a 30-second time fuze. The range is adjusted by varying the amount of the propelling charge; maximum range was about 1,800 yards. As well as projecting gas, the Livens was used to fire incendiary canisters against inflammable structures and high explosive against field strongpoints.

The P.H. Helmet
The earliest British gas mask, the P.H. Helmet was simply a flannel bag with two eyepieces and a valve to allow carbon dioxide to escape.

Germany, which had a larger and more advanced chemical industry than any other combatant nation, pioneered the use of sternutators and vesicants. Mustard gas was first used on 12 July, 1917, in the Ypres sector. It caused many casualties since it was an unknown substance to the British and had little smell or immediate effect. Some 12 hours later, men who had been in contact with the gas developed severe blistering of the skin and blindness as well as lung damage.

The sternutators, which were not true gases, were introduced at about the same time. They were actually smokes containing tiny solid particles that could penetrate the gas masks worn by the British. Since they were not immediately fatal, sternutators were usually used in combination with a toxic gas. The sternutator forced the victim to remove his mask in order to sneeze or vomit, whereupon he inhaled the toxic agent and died.

Although gas was used frequently from 1915 to the end of the war, fewer than one-third of one percent of battle deaths were attributable to it. British records show that 94 per cent of men gassed were out of hospital and graded fit within nine weeks. Of the postwar disability pensioners, only 2 per cent were disabled by gas. Where these primitive gases succeeded was in swamping hospitals and evacuation services with casualties, which placed a strain upon the whole supply system. Gas was a casualty-producer rather than a killer.

LATER DEVELOPMENTS

During the early 1920s there was research into offensive gases, but in 1925 the League of Nations convened a conference on the supervision of armaments manufacture. From this, the Geneva Gas Protocol emerged, condemning the use of gas and bacteriological weapons and inviting nations to agree to renounce their use. Eventually 40 nations signed the Protocol, but the USA, Japan, and some others refused.

In the 1930s gas was perceived by the public as a major threat. There were forecasts of fleets of bombers dropping gas on cities with terrible results. In response, most European nations made preparations for issuing all their citizens with gas masks. But when war broke out in 1939, the Protocol was respected and gas was not used by any of the belligerents. However, stockpiles were built up and its use was frequently contemplated. When Britain was faced with the possibility of invasion in 1940, gas was considered as a means of defending the beaches. But no nation wanted to be seen as the first to use it, and none was ready to risk retaliation by something worse that the enemy might have in reserve.

At the end of the war it emerged that the Germans did, indeed, have something worse up their sleeves. They had not used it because they believed that the British also had the same type of gas and they had not yet perfected an antidote. This was a new class of offensive gases, called nerve gases because they attack the central nervous system, causing almost instantaneous death.

Nerve gases were discovered in 1936 when Doktor Gebhard Schrader was conducting research into organic phosphorus insecticides and weed-killers. He carried out tests on an efficient insecticide, which proved to be highly lethal to humans as well. Further development followed and it was put into production under the name Tabun at a special factory. The engineering problems of producing this substance in quantity were formidable, so the factory did not attain full production until 1942. Some 15,000 tons were manufactured before the factory was

BIOLOGICAL WEAPONS

BIOLOGICAL WEAPONS can be defined in simple terms as the intentional preparation and dispersion of pathogenic bacteria, fungi, viruses, rickettsia and their toxic products, as well as some chemical compounds, for the purpose of producing death and disease in humans, animals, or crops. Biological agents might include the organisms producing a wide variety of diseases including cholera, typhoid, dysentery, smallpox, diphtheria, influenza, yellow fever, dengue, typhus, tularemia, plague, anthrax, and tetanus. In the 1930s both Germany and Japan were reported to be preparing for biological warfare, as a result of which the British and Americans began studying the subject. Experimental laboratories and test stations were set up and work was done on both aspects — the dissemination of disease and the protection of troops from such attack. The work that was carried out was relatively routine methods of propagating and disseminating diseases, but, most of all, methods of protecting troops against diseases. After the war, it became known that a certain amount of similar research had taken place in Germany and Japan, especially the latter. Japan had established a biological warfare research facility near Harbin, in Manchuria, in 1936; some 2,500 people had been employed there developing artillery and mortar shells loaded with glanders, anthrax, and other disease organisms, and an aerial bomb loaded with bacteria. Work was also done on the dissemination of typhoid, diphtheria, and cholera. Postwar research into biological warfare has continued, but the fact remains that disease is a two-edged sword which can as easily strike those who employ it as their intended victims, and as long as this remains so, soldiers will look very cautiously at any promises biological warfare might make.

Nerve gas shells
An ordnance factory operator, well protected, inserting the sealing plugs into 155-mm shells charged with VX agent. For safety reasons, the shells are charged with gas at one plant, then shipped to another plant to have their explosive bursters fitted.

overrun by the Soviet Army in 1944.

Not satisfied with Tabun, the Germans continued research in this field and discovered Sarin in 1938 and Soman in 1944. These were even more difficult to manufacture and had not emerged from the laboratory by the time the war ended. Some half a million artillery shells and over 100,000 aerial bombs filled with Tabun were found after the war. Taking the German work as their starting point, the victor nations began their own nerve gas programmes almost immediately.

From then on, anything to do with nerve gas was top secret. Even captured German wartime documents relating to nerve gas production are still highly classified. However, it is known that several more advanced nerve agents have been perfected. Most significant among them is the American discovery of binary gases, two harmless liquids that when combined, produce a lethal gas. In the Bigeye bomb and other projectiles, the two liquids are stored in separate canisters. Upon firing or launching, the canisters are breached, allowing the two substances to mix and form a nerve agent which is released upon impact.

Although gas was not used during the Second World War, it has been used occasionally since 1918. It was employed by the Italians against the Abyssinians in 1937, and occasionally by the Japanese against the Chinese in their long conflict between 1930 and 1945. More recently it was used in the Yemen, perhaps in Afghanistan, during the Iran-Iraq war and against civilian Kurds in Iraq. Today there are many nations which have not signed the Geneva Protocol who have the fairly modest resources needed to produce many of the offensive gases. The major nations, while still renouncing the first use of gas, have maintained a watching brief on the subject, and meanwhile train their forces in the use of early-warning devices, counter measures and antidotes.

MONSTER GUNS
BOMBARD
FORTS IN A
STATIC WAR

HEAVY AND SUPER-HEAVY ARTILLERY

AS THE First World War, with its entrenched opposing armies, took on the aspects of a siege, the military on both sides turned to one of the traditional siege weapons — heavy artillery. Before then, the largest mobile artillery piece was of about 9-inch calibre, a limit imposed by the use of horse power. In trials of steam traction it was shown to be slow and conspicuous from its smoke, though steam tractors were used in limited numbers for hauling artillery. Motor traction, in its early days, was unreliable and could not generate sufficient power. But the demands of war accelerated research, guns became lighter, and the internal combustion engine was also improved.

Britain had been developing a 9.2-inch howitzer when war broke out, and this was immediately put into production. Capable of firing a 290-lb shell to a range of 10,000 yards, it was hauled on horse-drawn wagons in three loads totalling over 13 tons. Lightness was achieved mainly by cutting down the weight of the gun carriage. To compensate for the loss of stability caused by the low weight, the unfortunate crew had to shovel 9 tons of soil into an "earth box" on the front of the carriage before opening fire. A 15-inch model, based on the same design, was then developed; this fired a 1,400-lb shell, but as the maximum range was still 10,000 yards it was not considered a success and only 12 were built.

France had placed her faith in the light 75-mm field gun, believing in a war of attack and being therefore willing to sacrifice firepower to mobility. When the war became bogged down, France was forced to strip old heavy guns from fixed fortifications as a stop gap for use on the battlefield. The French started to develop heavier guns and howitzers but it was not until early 1917 that a range of heavy guns from 155-mm to 300-mm began to appear behind the French lines.

The 9.2 inch howitzer

A battery of British 9.2-inch howitzers about to fire, at Guillemont, 4 October 1917. These fired a 290-lb shell to a range of 10,060 yards and were the most common heavy howitzers of the British Army. The NCO on the extreme left has the gun's sight in his hand, having removed it so that the delicate optical instrument will not be damaged by the firing shock. Behind him is a steel box containing nine tons of soil, a counterweight to prevent the gun mounting jumping when fired.

The Paris gun

These remarkable weapons — seven guns and three mountings were built — used the carriage of the 38-cm "Max" railway gun as their base, and then mounted a 21-cm barrel with a smoothbore extension. The breech mechanism of the 38-cm naval gun was used, and the shell was machined with ribs which engaged in the gun's rifling, since the conventional type of rotating band was ineffective at the enormous pressure involved. The barrel lasted for about 60 shots, after which it was removed, lined, and re-bored to a smaller calibre.

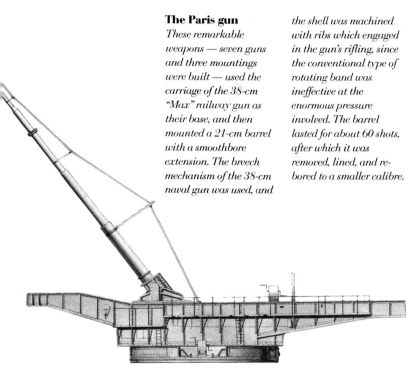

On the other hand, the German Army knew that whichever way it advanced from its own land borders, but particularly along the Meuse and in eastern France, it would meet fortifications designed to stop it. The defeat of these works was of primary importance in the plans of the General Staff. To achieve this, heavy artillery was vital and the forgemasters of the Ruhr were expert at making it.

In 1900, Alfred Krupp had built a 305-mm coastal defence howitzer firing an 800-lb shell to 10,000 yards. In 1908 he decided to build an even bigger version for army use, with the capability of defeating the heaviest fortification. This was a 420-mm weapon firing a 2,100-lb shell to 16,000 yards. As it weighed 175 tons, it was designed to be transported piecemeal by rail and assembled at the firing site. However, the German Army demanded that it be made road-mobile, and a 43-ton version was developed, capable of firing an 1,800-lb shell to 10,250 yards, and of being moved in five loads towed by Daimler-Benz tractors. A battery of two guns was built and during the initial German onslaught of August 1914, they were erected outside the fortress of Liège, on the Meuse in Belgium, where they systematically set about destroying the ring of 12 forts around the city.

"BIG BERTHA" AND THE "PARIS GUN"

The Krupp guns soon became known as Big Bertha, after Krupp's daughter. The Krupp howitzers were augmented by two 305-mm weapons of similar design from the Skoda factory in Bohemia, then part of the Austro-Hungarian Empire. Liège was overrun in four days, and the four monster guns moved on to the nearby fortresses of Namur, also on the Meuse, and Maubeuge. They remained serviceable after that but apart from bombarding the Verdun forts in 1916 they were inactive. However, they justified the effort put into their construction in the first month of the war by opening a way for the German Army to pass through Belgium in the famous Schlieffen Plan, a wheeling advance on Paris.

Professor Rausenberger, Krupp's chief designer, and Captain Becker, the German Army's ballistic expert, now collaborated to design a long-range gun capable of bombarding behind the Allied lines. Rausenberger had amused himself in prewar years by designing a gun that could shoot over the top of the Alps. He now drew upon this theoretical work to design a gun that could bombard Paris from inside the German lines. Known as the Kaiser Wilhelm Geschutz, or more popularly, the Paris Gun, it was a remarkable feat of engineering.

There were, in fact, seven guns. Each one was based on a worn-out 38-cm naval gun, re-barrelled to 21-cm calibre for this application. The 40-m long barrel was braced to prevent it drooping under its own weight, and the mounting was a simple box of steel on a turntable sunk into concrete. The concrete emplacements were built in the Forest of Gobain, between Laon and Soissons, and carefully camouflaged. The 264-lb shell was fired by a 400-lb charge of smokeless powder. In trials carried out in the Baltic, the first gun achieved a range of 82 miles.

The bombardment of Paris commenced on 23 March, 1918, and continued intermittently until 9 August. Only 183 shells landed within the city and 120 outside, killing 256 people and wounding 620. Damage to buildings was relatively light, and as an attempt to undermine the morale of the Parisians the guns were a failure. They were used until they were worn to the point of inaccuracy, whereupon another gun was moved in and the original sent back to Krupp to be re-barrelled to 24-cm calibre and returned with replacement ammunition. Three mountings were erected, but one was destroyed when its gun blew up, and was not replaced. When the Allies started their final unstoppable advance in August 1918, the guns and mountings were rapidly dismantled and spirited away into Germany. Parts of one mounting were captured by US troops near Château Thierry, but the guns and the other mountings were never seen again.

Big Bertha

The howitzer shown here is the 42-cm Krupp "Gamma", the static mounted version of the 42-cm Big Bertha mobile howitzer, undergoing its test firing at the Krupp firing range at Meppen in about 1912.

RAILWAY GUNS

THE GOVERNING factor in determining the size of artillery to accompany a field army was haulage. The railway was the first means of mechanized transport and, if the tracks could be made to go where the guns were needed, artillery could be mobile as never before. The American Civil War saw the first deployment of railway-mounted guns, notably in the siege of Petersburg. However, they were not specially-built, being no more than ordinary field cannon mounted on railway flatcars.

The idea was pursued by some French gunmakers in the later 19th century and one or two countries, particularly Denmark, purchased small railway-mounted guns for use as mobile coastal defence weapons. But it was only during the First World War that the railway gun flourished. Both sides of the trench lines were well provided with railways, and there was ample time to lay tracks to any point on the almost static front. The military demanded heavier guns to reach deep behind enemy lines.

There was a ready-made supply of big guns on hand: old naval guns of up to 14-inch calibre, proven and reliable over many years. These were the main armaments of battleships which had been retained as spares after the ships were de-commissioned. So long as the size of the gun plus its mounting could be kept within the railway loading gauge, there was no limit to what could be carried.

France also had an enormous stock of redundant heavy guns in her land fortresses. They were old, without recoil systems to absorb the shock of firing, but to modernize the guns would have been a lengthy business. Instead, they were directly mounted into simple steel-box structures, carried upon railway bogies. Once the guns had reached the firing site, the bogies were removed and the mountings rested on the track. On firing, the entire recoil force passed into the mounting and drove it backwards a few feet along the track. After a few shots the mounting was put back on its wheels and pushed back to its original position, the gun was lowered, and firing was recommenced.

As these improvised artillery pieces wore out, shaken to pieces by the recoil, they were replaced with properly-engineered mounts and modern guns, notably 270-mm and 380-mm cannon and a 420-mm howitzer.

Three different types of mounting were eventually developed: the turntable mount, which was for light guns, giving them a considerable arc of fire; the sliding mount, which has already been described; and the rolling mount, which stood on its wheels while firing and rolled back along the track to absorb recoil before a locomotive returned the gun to its original position. The heavier weapons had little or no movement on the mount and relied upon being pushed along the curved track until they were aligned with the target.

INNOVATION AND IMPROVISATION

British railway artillery was almost entirely developed by the Armstrong and Vickers factories. The army simply specified heavy guns and the two firms utilized whatever excess naval barrels they had in their factories. They began with 9.2-inch guns, then progressed to 12-inch and 14-inch calibres. Vickers also developed an entirely new 12-inch howitzer mounted on both rail and

A French railway gun
A 194-mm Mle 70/94 gun on the affut-truc tous azimut (all-direction equipment truck). This 64-ton unit carried the gun on a rotating platform so that it could fire in any direction and had a shell magazine and a cartridge magazine at opposite ends of the carriage.

American troops, French gun
A French 340-mm Mle 1912 gun manned by American gunners of the 35th Coast Artillery regiment, firing near Nixeville in September 1918 (RIGHT). *The US Army had virtually no serviceable artillery when it entered the war and relied upon British and French sources until American production could begin.*

The French 340-mm gun fired a 947lb shell to a range of 23 miles. The gun in the photograph obtained hits on targets at a range of nearly 19 miles.

The Boche-Buster
The British 14-inch railway gun "Boche-Buster" about to fire near Arras, France, in June 1918. It was one of the *last two railway guns ever developed for the British Army.*

wheeled mounts. All were widely used in France. Finally, Armstrong's started work on an 18-inch howitzer to fit the same mounting as the 14-inch gun, but this was not completed before the end of the war.

The Germans worked on similar lines to the British, using existing naval gun barrels where possible. The design was left entirely to the Krupp company. They produced a series of guns from 170-mm to 350-mm calibres but no howitzers. The 350-mm "Long Max" was used with good effect against Allied positions around Dunkirk and also during the siege of Verdun. The same mounting, without wheels, formed the basis for the mounting of the Paris Gun.

Curiously, the US Navy developed a unique railway gun, and several were employed in France. By contrast, the US Army had simply followed the French lead and scoured their fortresses and stores for spare naval and coastal defence guns. They adopted the best of the French mounting designs to finish up with a series of 8-, 10- and 12-inch guns and 12-inch howitzers, all rail-mounted. But these took time to design and build, and only a handful were in service before the war ended. The Naval Gun Factory, starting from scratch, designed a mounting to take their 14-inch gun in a matter of three weeks and five guns were built complete with their supporting trains. These went into action in France in September 1918 and in the remaining two months of the war, fired 782 rounds at ranges between 17 and 22 miles.

Railway guns were also built in Austria, Italy, and Russia, but in Russia's case these were used very little. During the postwar years most of the earlier designs were abandoned. Only the later and better ones were retained by Britain, France, and the USA. All the German guns were, of course, scrapped. Between the First and Second World Wars, the Americans developed an excellent 14-inch railway gun, which was primarily intended as a mobile coastal defence weapon. Two were built, one of them being sent to the Panama Canal and the other to the Californian coast in the early 1930s.

ARMOUR AND
GUNS ON
CATERPILLAR
TRACKS
ATTACK WITH
NEW POWER

EVOLUTION OF THE TANK

THE HUSSITE rebels of 15th-century Bohemia were the greatest exponents of fighting from within protected, horse-drawn wagons. However, the full realization of this idea was postponed for many centuries. In 1915, the two opposing enemies on the Western Front faced each other across impenetrable thickets of barbed wire backed up by machine guns. The tactical need to break the deadlock pointed towards a revival of the fighting vehicle.

The caterpillar-tracked tractor had been invented in England by the Hornsby company in 1908; it was demonstrated to the British Army in 1909 and won a £1,000 prize for the best cross-country machine, but failed to win orders from the Army. Hornsby then sold the patents to the Holt Company of the USA, where there was more scope for this sort of machine. In late 1914, Lieutenant-Colonel Ernest Swinton, who was the official (and only) British war-correspondent in France, writing despatches for all the British

The first tank
*"Mother", the first tank, on test in Burton Park, Lincoln, 20 January 1916 (**RIGHT**). The steering wheels at the rear were hydraulically swung to right or left to steer the tank, a system which lasted for about a year before the technique of speeding up or slowing down one track was perfected. The square "turret" housed the tank commander, who also steered the wheels, and the driver, who steered the tracks and changed the primary gear. Two more gear-changers and five gunners manning the two 6-pounders and four machine-guns made up the crew.*

The tank in action
*A Mark 1 tank at Thiepval, 25 September 1916, with infantry using it as a barricade (**LEFT**). The first modification can be seen — a frame of netting to prevent hand grenades blowing in the roof. The steering assembly has been raised from the ground, enabling tighter turns to be made.*

newspapers, recalled a letter that he had received in July of that year. A South African mining engineer had written to him, bringing the Holt tractor to his attention. The tractor, he thought, if fitted with an armoured body and a machine gun, might provide the means of penetrating the wire and achieving a breakthrough.

The idea was taken up by technical experts and the military, and the tank finally appeared in 1916. Built by Fosters of Lincoln, an agricultural engineering firm, it was shaped like an oblong tilted forward so that the sloping track of the front could haul it over and out of trenches. At each side it carried a 6-pounder gun and a machine-gun (if the tank was a "male") or two machine guns (if it was "female"). The 105-hp engine was inside along with the nine-man crew, four of whom shared the task of driving.

The French, who had made a similar assessment of the problem,

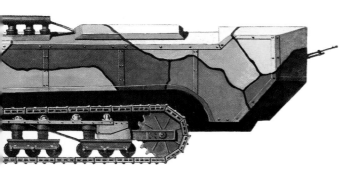

The St Chamond
(ABOVE) *The French St Chamond tank carried a 75-mm gun in its bows and four machine guns,* *and was operated by a nine-man crew. It was first used in April 1917. Propulsion was by a petrol engine driving a* *dynamo which powered electric motors to drive the tracks, and there was a driving position at each end of the tank.*

> " *The tank is new and for the fulfillment of its destiny, it must remain independent. Not desiring or attempting to supplant infantry, cavalry or artillery, it has no appetite to be absorbed by any of them...Absorbed, we become the stepchild of that arm and the incompetent assistant of either of the others...* "
>
> Col. George S. Patton, CO 304th US Tank Brigade, 1919.

The German A7V
This, the only German First World War tank, appeared in September 1917. Using sprung suspension, it was a sound basic design which had good performance, but shortage of vital materials meant that no more than 20 were ever built.

developed their own designs. These appeared as the St Chamond, with a 75-mm gun mounted in its nose, and the Schneider, with a 75-mm mounted on one side of the superstructure. Neither was very successful and the French decided that such ponderous machines did not fit their theory of attack at all costs. Instead they adopted a light two-man design from Renault, armed only with a machine-gun, the intention being to flood the battlefield with these fast and agile machines.

The British fielded the first tanks during the battle of the Somme on 15 September, 1916. Out of a total of 59 tanks then available, only 49 were serviceable and 17 of those broke down on their way to their starting points. The handful that engaged the enemy had a profound effect on the morale of the German infantry, but did not affect the course of the battle. Many British and French officers involved with tanks believed that it would have been better to have kept them secret a little longer until they could have been used in greater numbers to overwhelm the enemy.

Later, British tanks kept to the same overall shape but were gradually improved, with stronger armour, more powerful engines and simpler controls. The French two-man Renault tank proved less useful than had been hoped. The principal difficulty with the early machines was that of operating heavy machinery across soft and muddy ground, which had been cut to pieces by prolonged artillery bombardments. They were also not very reliable. But where the ground was harder, and tactics were modified to take account of the tank's fighting strengths, the results were encouraging, as the battle of Cambrai in November 1917 showed.

THE BATTLE OF CAMBRAI

Cambrai was originally planned as a simple raid, but was turned into a full-scale attack. The country was firm and relatively undamaged, and there was no preparatory artillery bombardment. This was partly to avoid alerting the enemy, and partly to avoid damaging the ground. Instead the advance was accompanied by careful artillery concentrations fired against known German artillery and troop positions, together with smoke screens to mask the movement of the tanks from German observation. The first tank wave consisted of 219 tanks supported by 1,009 guns, followed by another 96 tanks. Among these were 32 "grapnel tanks" whose task

was to haul away the barbed wire to permit the infantry, and possibly the cavalry, to pass through and storm the German lines.

Unfortunately, as with many battles of that period, minor difficulties and mistakes led to major problems. Some infantry commanders who were unused to working with tanks modified their orders and did not achieve their objectives, and the British reserves failed to appear on time. Furthermore, the line of a canal was defiantly held by the Germans and their artillery put up a very tough resistance. As the fighting wore on, the number of tanks was reduced through mechanical breakdown and German gunfire. The advance lost impetus, the battle became bogged down and, as usual, the Germans counter-attacked vigorously. Within a week, the British lines were back where they had been before the battle.

The Germans were slow to adopt the tank. It was so ineffective at first that they considered it not worth pursuing. Then better and more reliable armoured British tanks appeared and the Germans started to take the idea seriously, and to work on a design of their own. The result, the A7V tank, took a long time to perfect but was a sound, though rather large, tank. Armed with a 57-mm gun and six Maxim machine guns, it had a crew of 18 men and was propelled by two 100-hp Daimler-Benz engines. It was not ready until September 1917 and only about 20 were made. The Germans also used a number of captured British tanks.

DOG-FIGHTS

AND

ZEPPELINS:

NEW AIR

FORCES COME

OF AGE

AERIAL WARFARE: 1914-18

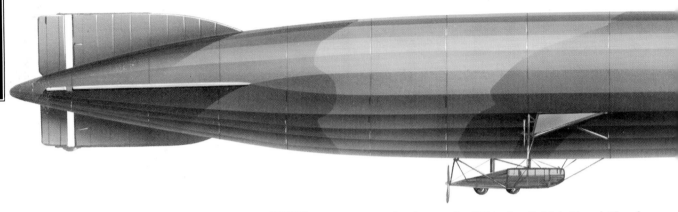

Battle over the Somme

Two German Albatross two-seaters defending themselves against three British Martinsyde Scouts. Although eclipsed by the more famous names of Sopwith and Bristol, the Martinsyde company made a number of excellent small fighters *which were well respected by the Royal Flying Corps. Similarly the Albatross two-seater was usually forgotten in favour of the Fokker and the single-seat Albatross, but it did as much damage to the Allied air forces as they did.*

A S SOON as war broke out in 1914, the British Royal Naval Air Service (RNAS) sent a squadron to Dunkirk and began planning offensive operations. On 8 October, 1914, Lieutenant Marix of the Royal Navy flew a Sopwith Tabloid single-seater biplane from an advanced airstrip near Antwerp to attack the German airship base near Düsseldorf. He achieved two hits with 20-lb bombs on the main airship shed, destroying both the shed and Zeppelin Z-9 inside. The same day Antwerp was evacuated and since Düsseldorf was out of range from Dunkirk, the RNAS moved to a French field near Belfort to attack the Zeppelin factory at Friedrichshafen. From there, three Avro 504 biplanes managed to destroy one Zeppelin and the gas generating plant at the Zeppelin works.

The German air service retaliated with raids against Paris and other French towns within reach of their airfields, prompting the French to mount attacks against German targets. This led to fighter squadrons being withdrawn from the front-line area to defend "the homeland", and to the first use of artillery against aircraft. Since the bombers were vulnerable, they had to be escorted by fighters to protect them. Therefore, like reconnaissance (see Early fighting aircraft, page 116) bombing became a matter of duels between opposing fighters while other fighters attempted to deal with the bombers.

Long-range bombing was, at first, a German affair, since only they had airships capable of making long flights. However, airships were large and expensive machines and were used principally against major targets. The German Navy also operated airships for reconnaissance over the North Sea. The first Zeppelin raid against England took place on 19 January, 1915. Of the three machines that set out, two reached England and dropped a scattering of bombs in East Anglia, before returning safely to base.

This attack was followed, on 31 May, 1915, by the first raid on London, when Zeppelin L-30 dropped 30 high-explosive and 90 incendiary bombs in the eastern suburbs. More raids by German Navy Zeppelins and Army Schutte-Lanze airships followed. The defences of London were strengthened, but since the airships flew high, and the fighters took time to reach them, they were invariably able to escape undamaged.

The first Zeppelin to be destroyed was shot down over Ostend in July, 1915. Sub-Lieutenant Warneford of the RNAS, flying a

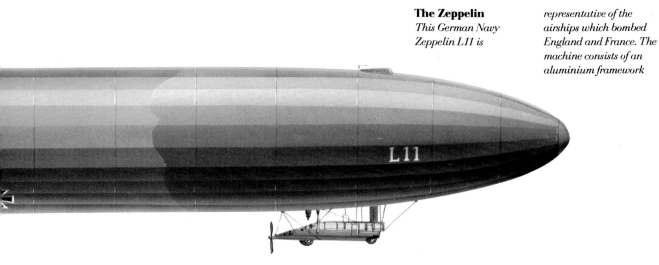

The Zeppelin
This German Navy Zeppelin L11 is representative of the airships which bombed England and France. The machine consists of an aluminium framework covered in fabric and with gasbags filled with hydrogen inside the framework. Four, later six, engines were fitted, giving a speed of 60 to 80 mph. The principal tactical advantage was that the Zeppelin could fly at heights not easily attained by aeroplanes. It was not until late 1916 that aircraft capable of rapid climb became common, after which the Zeppelin's day was over.

Moraine aircraft, managed to get above L-37 and dropped a bomb on it which ignited the hydrogen in the gas-bags. The defenders of London had no success until September 1916, when Lieutenant Leefe Robinson, using the newly-invented Buckingham incendiary bullets, shot down the Schutte-Lanze SL-11 over Hertfordshire. Within a week, two more had been shot down and the bombing role passed to heavier-than-air machines.

Thus on 25 May, 1917, a flight of 26 Gotha bombers — large two-engined biplanes each capable of carrying 400kg of bombs — attacked Kent. Then on 13 June, a flight of 14 Gothas flew up the Thames and delivered a severe attack on various areas of London, killing 162 people and injuring 432 others. This was the beginning of a series of attacks that continued until May 1918, when attrition, improved defences, and the general run-down of the German war effort caused the bombing of England to be abandoned. Raids on targets closer to Germany continued, though at a lower intensity than before.

DEVELOPMENT OF THE WORLD'S AIR FORCES

By this time the Allies had decided to enter the long-range bombing war. By early 1918 there were plenty of aircraft for front-line duty, and surplus aircraft were used in attacks on Germany. These developments strengthened the case for an air force that was not under army or navy control but existed in its own right as a separate branch of the armed forces. A long-range bombing unit had existed since October 1917 when a wing of the Royal Flying Corps was set up to raid German cities, and this was then reinforced by three squadrons of Italian Caproni bombers and a French *Groupe de Bombardement*. A US element was also planned but this never materialized. This force made a number of raids into Germany, dropping 635 tons of bombs with minimal effect, but it pointed the way for the future development of air power.

The Italian Air Force became experts at long-distance strategic bombing. In February 1916, tri-motored Caproni bombers flew from Italy to bomb Ljubljana, then in the Austro-Hungarian Empire, and they later made several attacks into Austria. The Italians also bombed the naval base of Pola and the Fiume torpedo factory, both on the Adriatic Sea, using more than 200 bombers on one raid.

Meanwhile, from early in the war, the use of aircraft as support for ground operations had increased steadily, once the vulnerability of troops on the ground was fully realized. However, early attempts at ground attack were confused. The French, for example, dropped sheaves of arrow-like steel *flechettes* on to marching troops. But the fitting of machine-guns to aircraft soon led to widespread and effective "ground strafing" (from the German *strafen*, "to punish") against troops and transport. This, in turn, led to more fighters being deployed to protect the troops, and gradually the concept of "air superiority" (the deployment of a large enough number of aircraft to deter the enemy from entering one's "air space") emerged.

The Gotha G.Vb bomber
The vulnerability of the Zeppelin in the face of agile fighter aircraft led to its withdrawal from bombing in 1917 and replacement by the Gotha. The G.IV and G.V were those used against Britain.

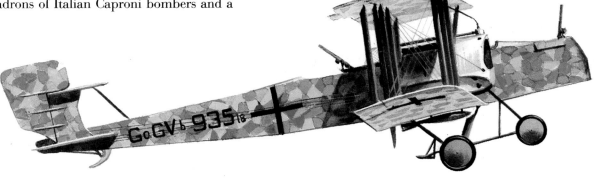

ANTI-AIRCRAFT GUNS

ANTI-AIRCRAFT gunnery can be said to have begun on 13 June, 1794. On that day, the French Army, advancing to the Rhine under Napoleon, deployed a number of tethered balloons for observation purposes, and the Austrians opened fire on them with two 17-pounder howitzers. The bombardment caused the French to haul down their balloons, but they gradually realized that the threat was more apparent than real and continued with aerial activities for the rest of the campaign without losing a balloon.

The next attempt at aerial gunnery was during the Siege of Paris in 1870. The French used balloons to carry messages and important people out of the city, so the German Army commissioned from Alfred Krupp a special 25-mm rifle mounted on a cart. This device made the occasional hit but did little to deter the balloonists.

Specialized anti-aircraft weapons date from 1909. By that time, airships and aeroplanes were appearing in some numbers, and at the Frankfurt International Exhibition of that year, specialist "balloon guns" were on show, made by two German firms — Krupp and Erhardt. These were lightweight, quick-firing guns mounted upon motor car chassis, intended for chasing after aircraft, shooting as they went.

War Departments took note of the rise of the aeroplane, and by the outbreak of the First World War a small number of specialist anti-aircraft guns had been built. The British had developed a 3-inch gun and a Maxim one-pounder "Pom-Pom" automatic. The French fitted their existing 75-mm M1897 field gun to a mounting, which allowed a steep angle of fire and produced a very efficient weapon.

Not surprisingly, the Germans began the war by commandeering the half-dozen Krupp and Erhardt guns that had been exhibited at Frankfurt in 1909. They also adapted numbers

Americans in France
Gunners of Battery B, 1st AA Battalion, 2nd US Division, at Montreuil, 5 June 1918, using the 75-mm "Autocanon", a 75-mm field gun specially mounted on a De Dion truck. Note the jack arm relieving the vehicle springs of the firing shock.

The Motor Balloon Gun
One of the first purpose-built anti-aircraft weapons was this "Motor Balloon Gun" built by Erhardt of Dusseldorf in 1909. It mounted a 75-mm gun in a rotating box and appears to have been a reasonably efficient weapon. The placement of anti-aircraft guns on motor trucks was adopted at this time because aircraft were so slow that it was thought possible to be able to rush guns into their path or even chase them across country. This tactic was soon abandoned, but the truck-mounted gun remained standard for many years.

Action stations
British gunners run to man their 13-pounder 9-cwt guns near Armentières in March 1916. These guns were the standard 18-pounder field gun with the barrel sleeved to 13-pounder calibre (3 inches) so as to fire the 13-pounder shell with an 18-pounder cartridge. This gave better performance than could be obtained from either gun in unmodified form and became the standard British AA gun throughout the war.

of their standard 77-mm field gun to high-angle mountings, and did the same thing with captured high-velocity Russian 3-inch field guns, which they called *Fliegerabwehrkanone* (aircraft defence gun). This word was soon abbreviated to "Flak", which has since become a standard term for anti-aircraft fire.

Apart from the British 3-inch guns, which were specially designed as an air-defence weapon, the other guns were only just adequate to deal with the aircraft of 1914. Under the spur of war, as aircraft began to improve rapidly in their performance, flying faster and higher, better guns and mountings were needed to shoot them down.

PROBLEMS OF TARGETING

Aircraft were a difficult target, capable of moving quickly in three different ways. The shell took time to reach the aircraft, and during that time the aircraft could move up or down, turn left or right, go faster or slower. The gunner's problem was to arrange for the shell and the aircraft to be in the same place when the shell burst. To do this, the gunner had to have an accurate time fuze to burst the shell at the predicted point. But to set the time fuze, he had to determine the height and speed of the target and forecast where it would be several seconds later. Then he had to point the gun precisely at the forecast position where the shell and target were expected to meet. Finally, he had to observe where his shells were bursting, and make corrections to bring shell and target together. All in all, his chances of a direct hit were several thousand to one.

The first attempts to cope with these problems led to extremely complicated sights on the guns, for which half-a-dozen gun layers and sight setters were needed in addition to the normal gun crew. This interfered with the primary task of shooting, so the French Army invented the Central Post system. Here a single sighting instrument in the centre of the battery was used to calculate the firing data, which was then shouted, or telephoned, to the gun crews, who used the information to set their sights and then fired. The system removed the need for the many sight setters and improved the rate of fire, as well as the ratio of shells fired to the number of aircraft brought down.

It soon became clear that early warning of an approaching aircraft was required so that the gunners could be ready as soon as it came within range. Since the sound of the engine travelled much faster than the aircraft itself, sound detectors were quickly developed. These first took the form of large horns, arranged in groups of three and operated by two men who listened and pointed the horns in the direction of the strongest noise. The French improved this by developing a parabolic sound mirror which had a sensitive microphone at the focal point. However, as aircraft speeds increased, the warning time inevitably became shorter.

The fuzing of shells also presented problems. There were many duds as well as erratic bursts. Experiments showed that the common powder-burning time fuzes of the day were unsuited to high altitude because the burning train was extinguished by the lack of oxygen in the atmosphere above 15,000 feet. Once this difficulty was overcome, the guns began to perform reasonably well. By the end of the war British AA (anti-aircraft) guns were bringing down one enemy aircraft for every 1,800 shells fired. The USA bettered this, with one for every 1,005 shots. It was to be a long time before that strike rate was improved (see Advances in air-defence gunnery, page 150).

BIGGER SHIPS

AND BETTER

GUNS IN

THE FIRST

MODERN

NAVIES

NAVAL GUNNERY OF THE FIRST WORLD WAR

B Y 1914 the naval fleets of the industrial world were mainly composed of battleships built to the Royal Navy's Dreadnought pattern, supported by cruisers and destroyers and backed by supply and repair ships, with a handful of submarines. HMS *Dreadnought* was completed in 1906. The main armament consisted of identical 12-, 14-, 15- or 16-inch guns mounted in revolving armoured turrets. Therefore the splashes of a salvo were easily spotted and a single correction applied to all guns. Moreover the heavy calibre of the main armament ensured that damage could be inflicted at the maximum range, before an opponent could get close enough to be dangerous. The secondary armament was principally intended for quick-firing protection against fast and light torpedo-carrying craft.

The British pattern had arisen in response to the growth of the German Navy after 1898, which posed a threat to British naval dominance. The Royal Navy was expanded, and a revolution in gunnery began, which in due course spread round the world. The naval guns of the day had outstripped the methods used to control them. The aiming devices used on big guns in the early 1890s were no better than those on an infantryman's rifle. They used a simple notch-and-post system, so that aiming a gun when the ship

The quick-firing gun
Quick-firing (QF) guns began as small-calibre weapons. Later the metal-cased cartridge had advantages for naval use, notably storage and magazine safety; and the principle was extended upwards to 6-inch (152-mm) calibre. These became the weapon of choice for attacking the unarmoured upperworks of warships and less well-armoured opponents.

HMS Lion
(**ABOVE**) *A British battle-cruiser, Lion was the flagship of Admiral Sir David Beatty at Jutland. Lion was armed with eight 13.5-inch and 15 4-inch guns for close-in defence against torpedo-boats. The main armour* *belt was 9.5 inches thick, with 10-inch armour on the main armament turrets. Lion, launched in 1910, was the first of the "Super Dreadnoughts", a term applied to big gun ships with main armament greater than 12-inch calibre.*

The all-big-gun ship
HMS Dreadnought, *launched in 1906, was the creation of Admiral Sir John Fisher. It introduced the concept of having just two kinds of armament — ten 12-inch guns in five turrets for engaging major warships at long range, and 24 3-inch guns for close-in defence against torpedo-boats. Intermediate calibres such as the 4.7- and 6-inch QF guns were eliminated in the interest of better fire control. The idea was followed by other nations: Germany launched her first big-gun ship (*Nassau) in 1908 and Italy and Japan followed suit in 1910.*

Electric salvo firing had been developed in the early 1890s. This enabled the gunnery officer, high up in his conning tower, to fire all the guns at once and spot the fall of shot. Then, by making corrections in range and azimuth, he could try to bring the shells on to the target. This demanded enormous skill from the gunnery officer, a skill almost impossible to learn without live ammunition and a real target, both of which were scarce in peacetime.

IMPROVING ACCURACY

Gradually, mechanical devices were introduced to aid the gunnery officer. Optical rangefinders grew from 4.5 to 36 feet in a few years. Since they depend upon triangulation, the wider they are, the more accurate the result and the longer ranges they could measure. British rangefinders relied upon aligning two images, one reflected from each end of the rangefinder. German practice was based on stereoscopy, which gives better accuracy but also requires the operator to have exceptional eyesight. Next came instruments to determine the speed and course of the target, measuring the angular movement and comparing it with time elapsed and the range. Finally, there was the problem of compensating for the time taken for the shell to travel to the target. At 10,000 yards, a shell took 18 seconds to reach the target, during which time a ship moving at 15 knots travelled 170 yards. Faster targets and longer ranges were still more difficult. At 20,000 yards, a 25-knot target could travel 500 yards during the flight of the shell. Graphical plotters were used to map the course of the ship and its target on a moving strip of paper, allowing the gunnery officers to identify their relative positions. Later, mechanical plotters such as the Dreyer Table were fed with information from the course plotter, rangefinder, and other instruments, to produce a forward plot of where the shell would fall. It then became possible to adjust the ship's speed and course to make the fall of shot and the target coincide, maximizing the chances of a hit.

Systems of this nature were developed independently by the British, French, German, and US Navies in the 1895–1914 period. None of them were perfect; some excelled at certain aspects and were weak in others, but all were capable, in skilled hands, of placing the shell on target. All that remained was to ensure that the shell had the desired effect. This had become more difficult as the armoured belt and decks on the bigger warships had become thicker. However, the Battle of Tsushima in 1904, in which the Russian Navy was conclusively defeated by the Japanese, showed that much of the damage was not due to the armour-piercing shells but to fragmentation shells fired from medium-calibre secondary armament. These could wreck deck structures, start fires, and disable the damage-control equipment. Armour-piercing shells, on the other hand, often ricocheted when striking at an oblique angle — as they frequently did at the end of a long flight. It was necessary to shorten the range enough to allow shells to plunge down onto the decks and turrets, in search of a weak spot like a hatch.

One lesson that became apparent during the First World War was that the magazines must be isolated from the rest of the ship. Several warships were destroyed by fires that started in the gun turrets and barbettes, and then flashed down the ammunition-supply hoists to cause an explosion in the magazine. Few ships or their crews ever survived such disasters.

was rolling and pitching was more a matter of chance than skill. In a rough sea and at battle speeds, a hit at any range over 1,000 yards was by pure luck. Furthermore there was no method of determining the distance to the target other than by firing a few trial shots. In contrast to the primitiveness of the sights, the big guns of the day were capable of firing to 20,000 yards or more. The question was how to exploit this capability.

Captain Percy Scott RN was a gunnery officer who understood this situation and once he acquired command of his own ship, he set about improving things. His first move was to fit the big guns with simple telescope sights, and then he devised training aids to enable gunners to practise aiming in poor conditions. At the first annual gunnery practice when he was in command, his ship obtained an 80 per cent hit rate, a phenomenal figure for that time, which he repeated in the following year. The Admiralty began to take notice, as did other navies.

Scott's system trained the individual gunner, but did nothing to improve overall fire control. The purpose of identical big guns was to control the salvo — the fall of shot from the big guns — as one unit. However, actual performance was still based on the ability of the individual gunner. The development of optical rangefinders in the late 1890s gave accurate ranges to 4,000 yards, but this could only be communicated to the individual guns. Some form of centralized control was needed.

NAVAL AND

MERCHANT

SHIPS FACE

A THREAT

FROM UNDER

WATER

EARLY SUBMARINES AND UNDERSEA WARFARE

UNSUCCESSFUL ATTEMPTS to make submersible boats can be traced back to the 17th century. The first practical design originated with the Nordenfelt company of Sweden, who, in the 1880s, sold a few submarines to Greece and Turkey. The problem with the Nordenfelt boat was that it only remained submerged when it was moving. Once stationary, it floated back to the surface. This fault was cured by J.D. Holland of the USA who built his first boat in 1898. Holland's financial backer, Isaac Rice, initially attempted to interest the US Navy, without success, so he went to Britain and there entered into an agreement with Vickers which allowed them to use the design.

In 1901, the British Admiralty decided to buy five submarines from Vickers for trial purposes. The Admiralty suggested various improvements to these A class boats, leading to the Vickers B, C, D and E classes. By 1910, 56 boats had been built. Two E class boats sailed to Australia, and another completed 30,000 miles before requiring a refit. This proved their seaworthiness, particularly for such innovative and complex craft. After 1909, Vickers were permitted to sell submarines abroad (though not those of Admiralty design) and by 1912 had sold 18 to the USA, seven each to Russia and Japan, two to Austria, and one to the Netherlands.

The Nordenfeld design was taken to Germany but was not pursued. Instead the armaments firm Krupp set about developing a design of their own. By 1903 they had a working boat, which they sold to Russia, and this same design was the basis for the first "U-Boat" (from *Untersee-boot*) for the German Navy. This was the U-1, launched in 1906. The drawback to the U-1 was that it used a Kortin crude oil engine which advertised its presence with clouds of white smoke. But in 1912 Krupp decided to adopt the diesel engine instead.

The general view of submarines was that they could legitimately attack warships or troop-supply and transport vessels, but that merchant and passenger ships were not proper targets. Many tactical ideas for using submarines as a screen in front of an advancing fleet, or as an ambush force into which an enemy fleet

> **❝** *It is inevitable that when the Germans fully realise the capabilities of this type of submarine — they probably do not do so yet, on account of having had small experience with them at sea (they have but 30 to our 60) — the North Sea and all its ports will be rendered uninhabitable by our big ships — until we have cleaned out their submarines.* **❞**

Admiral Lord Fisher; The Submarine Question, April 1909: Fisher Papers No 4238

British E Class
The British submarine E.14 departing for a patrol in the Sea of Marmora in April 1914. The E Class was the latest type in 1914 and 23 were built. They were armed with four or five torpedo tubes and two 3-inch guns. They could make 16 knots on the surface and 10 knots when submerged. E.14 was sunk by Turkish *gunfire in the Dardanelles in January 1918; her commander, Lt. Cdr. G. S. White was posthumously awarded the Victoria Cross.*

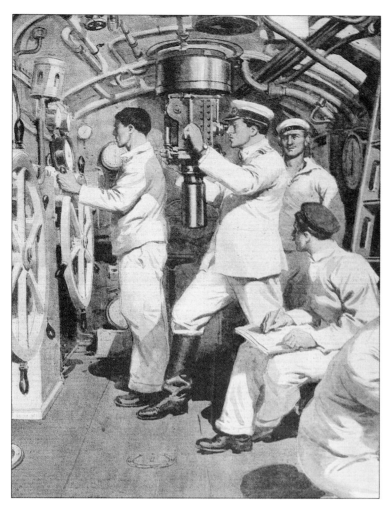

The control room
The command centre of an Italian submarine of 1918 (LEFT). The captain is observing through the periscope, while a seaman watches the depth gauge. A petty officer stands behind him ready to retract the periscope and secure it when the observation is finished, and a writer sits noting down the captain's orders and observations. Out of the picture there would be navigation and torpedo officers.

The U-Boat at war
The German Navy submarine U-29 (ABOVE) waits for the crew to abandon a merchant ship before sinking it with a torpedo. This picture was taken by Captain Lugg of the S.S. Headlands shortly before his ship was sunk in 1915.

might be lured, were put forward. Unfortunately, the early submarines could not keep pace with a surface fleet, so these ideas were abandoned and the submarine began to be considered as a lone patrol boat.

When war broke out in 1914, it was expected that a general engagement would take place between the German and British fleets in the early days of the war. However, both fleets adopted a very cautious approach. A few German raiders were loosed on the oceans but most of them were soon hunted down, and late in August 1914 the British mounted a small naval raid into the Heligoland Bight. After this, the German High Seas Fleet was ordered not to venture into the North Sea and this led to a fall of German naval morale. But if the High Seas Fleet could not stir, other elements could. Thus on 22 September, 1914, the submarine U-9, commanded by Lieutenant Weddingen sank three British armoured cruisers, the *Hogue, Cressey* and *Aboukir*. In the space of an hour 1,459 sailors died.

U-BOATS OF THE FIRST WORLD WAR

As a result of the U-9's exploit, the Germans realized that they had a weapon with which they could strike back at the Allied blockade. In consequence, on 2 February, 1915, the German Navy declared that the seas surrounding Britain were an "area of war". Although of the 20 German submarines in service only four were

ready for immediate use, within a week of the announcement these four had sunk 13 merchant ships. From then on, the submarine became the Germans' prime naval weapon, though the revulsion caused by the sinking of *Lusitania*, torpedoed on 7 May, 1915, with a loss of 1,198 lives, certainly backfired on Germany.

Unrestricted submarine warfare was ended in September of that year in the face of protests from neutral countries and especially the USA. However, the sinking of British merchant ships continued until, by 1916, they were being sunk faster than they could be replaced. In February 1917 the Germans once more began unrestricted submarine warfare.

At that time they had 111 submarines, of which 50 were operational, and within a month had sunk 250 ships. In the next month they increased this to 430 ships. In desperation, the British Admiralty adopted the convoy system, which they believed reduced the chances of the ships being detected and therefore would be safer. Supported by surface warships, many more merchantmen got through and the submarine threat receded.

The principal weapon against the submarine was the depth charge. This was a 300-lb cylinder of high explosive fitted with a depth-sensitive fuze. It could either be dropped from the stern of a ship, or fired from a mortar to about 150 yards range. The object was to form a ring of exploding charges around the submarine, with the fuze set to the estimated depth of the boat. A charge exploding within about 75 yards of a submarine would inflict serious damage on the pressure hull, either sinking the boat or forcing it to surface, whereupon it could be destroyed by gunfire.

Submarine mines were also effective against submarine boats. The British laid extensive deep minefields across the Straits of Dover and the North Channel between Scotland and Norway, forcing German submarines to run the gauntlet before reaching the open ocean. Mines were also laid aggressively, in front of enemy harbours and along likely submarine routes, while fleets of specialist mine-sweeping craft sought to reopen the sea lanes to their own submarines.

FIRST WORLD WAR AMMUNITION

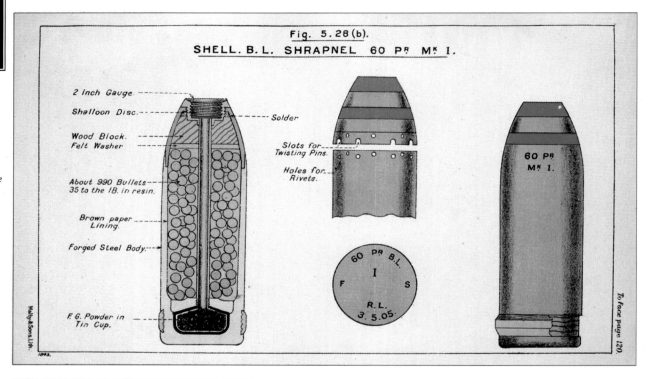

Fig. 5.28 (b).
SHELL. B.L. SHRAPNEL 60 PR. Mᴷ I.

The shrapnel shell

A shrapnel shell for the 60pr heavy field gun. The head is retained by pins and rivets; the body contains lead balls packed in resin, resting on a "pusher plate". A central tube passes from the fuze well to a charge of gunpowder below the pusher plate. When the fuze reaches the set time it sends a flash down the tube to explode the gunpowder.

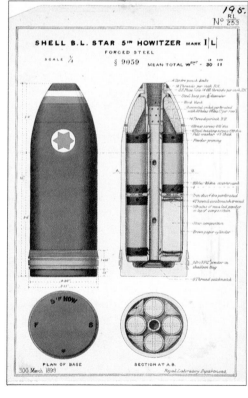

An early star shell

This shell for the 5-inch howitzer worked in a similar manner to shrapnel, using a gunpowder charge and a pusher plate to eject 8 cylindrical stars, which fell to the ground and continued to burn, illuminating the immediate area. They were of more use for signalling than for illuminating.

T HE FIRST World War saw enormous changes in ammunition technology. First there were new types of ammunition to address new tactical problems. Secondly there were enormous changes in production techniques, since the existing government arsenals and factories were unable to cope with the increased demand. Production on the scale demanded had to be contracted to civilian engineering firms with no previous experience in this field.

In 1914, the standard field artillery projectile was the shrapnel shell (see Early artillery, page 64), a murderous weapon against troops out in the open. But once the infantry had dug in, troops only came out into the open during attacks. So the demand for high-explosive shells, to blow open the earthworks, grew enormously. In Britain, this led to the appointment of Lloyd George as Minister of Munitions and to the building of National Factories to expand shell production. In Germany it led to a search for alternative shell fillings and to the development of gas as a war weapon (see Gas warfare, page 118).

New tactical problems created the demand for new types of ammunition. Thus, in the small arms field, the use of steel shields in trench loopholes resulted in the development of the armour-piercing bullet. Equally, the need for aviators to be able to see the trajectory of their machine-gun fire led to tracer bullets which, hollowed out and packed with a pyrotechnic powder, left a trail of smoke and red sparks, from which the firer could adjust his aim. Incendiary bullets were a response to the Zeppelin threat (see Aerial warfare: 1914-18, page 128), as were incendiary shells for anti-aircraft guns, though the standard shrapnel or high explosive shell could do sufficient damage to most types of aircraft.

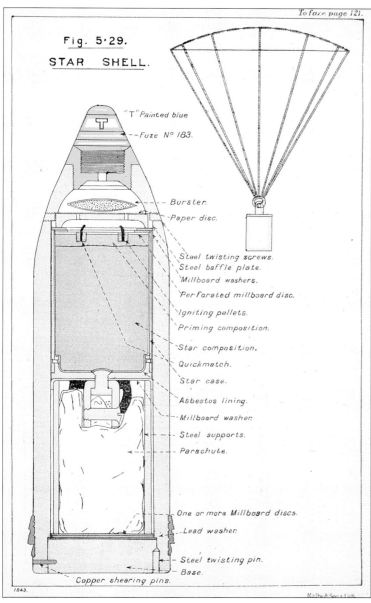

Fig. 5·29.
STAR SHELL.

"T" Painted blue
Fuze Nº 183.

Burster.
Paper disc.

Steel twisting screws.
Steel baffle plate.
Millboard washers.
Perforated millboard disc.
Igniting pellets.
Priming composition.
Star composition.
Quickmatch.
Star case.
Asbestos lining.
Millboard washer.
Steel supports.
Parachute.

One or more Millboard discs.
Lead washer.

Steel twisting pin.
Base.
Copper shearing pins.

A parachute star
A later design of star shell, in which a single star unit is attached to a parachute.

A time fuze
An early time fuze, used with the 5-inch star shell. Spin, causing centrifugal force, made the igniting pellet strike the pin and fire the time ring.

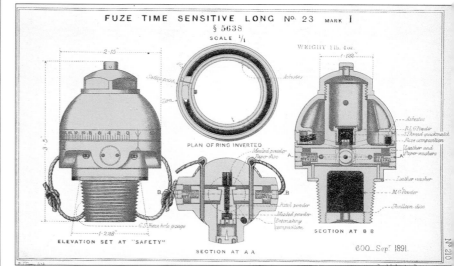

FUZE TIME SENSITIVE LONG Nº 23 MARK I
§ 5638
SCALE ¼

WEIGHT 1 lb. 4 oz.

PLAN OF RING INVERTED

ELEVATION SET AT "SAFETY"

SECTION AT A A

SECTION AT B B

600__Sepʳ 1891.

INVENTION AND IMPROVISATION

One of the few ways to attack entrenched troops was to burst high-explosive shells in the air over them. But this demanded accurate time fuzes (as did shrapnel fire) and, as guns increased their range, conventional fuzes based on a train of burning gunpowder were stretched to their limit. By 1916 the German Army had developed a clockwork time fuze that used a pre-wound spring released by the shock of firing. It could be set very accurately and permitted precise shooting to the longest ranges. When an unexploded fuze was picked up by the British, they and the French set about developing their own versions.

Specialized requirements gave rise to ingenious solutions. To enable the infantry to break through wire entanglements the "pipe charge" or "Bangalore Torpedo" was introduced. This was a 5-foot length of pipe of 1-inch diameter that was packed with explosives. One length of pipe was screwed onto a second length, and then pushed across "no man's land" beneath the enemy wire. Once it was in position, the pushers took cover in their trench and fired the charge, ripping a pathway through the wire. The inventor of this crude but clever device is not known, though it was in the hands of every combatant by 1916. Similarly, when the tank appeared in 1916, it was soon followed by the land mine, a simple pressure-operated charge of explosive that could be buried in likely places and would break the track of any tank which ran across it.

Improvements were also made in naval munitions. Rather than rely solely on contact to detonate undersea mines, pressure-sensitive and magnetic sensors were under development by the time the war ended, and some experimental models had already been used by the British and German Navies.

The proliferation of barbed wire on the Western Front created the need for artillery to destroy it or, at least, to cut gaps in it so as to permit the infantry to get to grips with the enemy. The standard impact fuzes of the day were not sensitive enough for this task, especially in the soft ground of Flanders. More sensitive fuzes, which detonated as soon as they struck the mud, were needed. Despite these, wire-clearing by artillery fire was never very effective as barbed wire was flexible enough to resist the blast. The smoke shell was also developed to screen troops advancing over open ground. This was a shell filled with white phosphorus which ignited when it came into contact with air.

Raids at night were countered, at first, with "star" shells. These had been developed before the war and consisted of bright candles that were released from a shell and fell to the ground, giving local illumination. During the war, parachute-suspended magnesium flares were developed. These could be packed into a shell and, by the action of a time fuze, they ignited and lit up the battlefield.

In the 21 years between the First and Second World Wars science and technology made enormous progress, and this was utilized by the weapons designers after 1939. Consequently, the advances in weaponry that took place in the six years of the war far outstripped anything that had happened in the previous two decades. When the war began most of the weapons were either those left over in 1918 or minor improvements on them. The tank had been the focus of much attention between the wars, but while it had attained some degree of reliability, its proper handling was still a matter of debate. Germany was the first nation to solve these problems and its Panzer divisions stampeded across Europe in 1939–41 in an apparently invincible surge, which led to enormous effort being put into methods of defeating tanks. Similarly, the bomber was the universal threat that worried every nation, and air defence was a major preoccupation with all armies. The need to detect an aerial attack while it was still far enough away to permit some effective defensive action to be taken led to the discovery of radar and to the birth of the electronics industry.

Unlike the 1914–18 war, the Second World War was a highly mobile and widely distributed affair, demanding enormous armies. They, in turn, demanded enormous quantities of arms, so that rapid production of weapons became a matter of importance. This led to the development of mass-produced small arms that could be stamped from sheet steel rather than carefully and slowly milled from solid blocks of steel. It also led to the first "disposable" weapons.

New ballistic principles were explored; the recoilless gun, first attempted in the First World War, became a viable weapon, as did the shaped-charge projectile and the taper-bore gun.

Naval warfare was marked by the end of the battleship era and the arrival of the aircraft carrier as the "capital ship" in its place. The sinking of some of the greatest warships by aerial bombing was a signal that warfare had irreversibly changed.

CHAPTER SEVEN

THE SECOND WORLD WAR

INTERWAR TANKS: 1918-39

T ANK DEVELOPMENT during the interwar years was hampered by low government funding for armies, by doubts about the utility of the tank in battle, by formidable design and engineering problems and, in Germany, by the provisions of the Peace Treaty. The only country building tanks in quantity was the USSR, where some very good models evolved. The other major countries built tanks by the handful to test various designs, at the same time debating whether the tank should fight independently or whether it should accompany the infantry.

It is often suggested that the works of various British military writers — Liddell Hart, Fuller and others — were seminal in guiding various armies to their decisions. The truth appears to be

Panzer III
Backbone of the Panzer divisions in the early part of the war, the Panzer III (**BELOW LEFT**) *was a sound design which had room for upgrading. Originally fitted with a 37-mm gun, the Model J shown here had the long 50-mm gun and appeared in 1941, in time to give British armour a hard time in the Desert.*

Panzer IIB
(**BELOW**) *This light tank dates from 1936 when it was designed as an "interim" tank to accompany the Panzer I until the heavier models arrived. In the event it stayed in service and during the Polish and French campaigns was the most numerous German tank. As late as 1942 there were still 800 in use, though by that time their thin armour and 20-mm gun were well outclassed.*

that while these writers may have stimulated thought, countries made their decisions in the light of their own strategic and tactical doctrines. Certainly the German Army was first to come up with the idea of the Armoured or Panzer Division, a balanced fighting force under one commander with armour, infantry, artillery, engineer, and signal elements all working together. It took much bitter experience before other fighting nations followed this course.

By 1939 there was a wide variety of tanks in service, but their quality and utility varied greatly. Germany and the USSR had opted for a "general purpose" tank, though the Soviets hedged their bets and developed other types as well. Their BT7 ("fast tank 7") used the large-wheeled soft suspension developed by the American Walter Christie which conferred excellent cross-country performance. On the road it had a top speed of 45 mph, and it had sloping 22-mm armour and a 45-mm gun. The Soviet heavy tank, the T-35, was perhaps the last example of a 1930s idea, the multiple-turret tank, and was less successful. While impressive to look at, with five independent turrets, it was impossible for the commander to control the machine effectively.

Germany had the light Pzkw (*Panzerkampfwagen*), which was no more than a training tank armed with a 20-mm gun. It only

The Russian Christie
(BELOW) *The Russian BT-7 fast tank appeared in 1935 and was streets ahead of any other tank in the world. Using the Christie suspension it could run on tracks or wheels, reaching 45mph.*

The French Hotchkiss H-35
Dating from 1936, the Hotchkiss (RIGHT) carried a short 37-mm gun and one machine gun. A heavier version, with a more powerful engine, appeared in 1939.

remained in front-line use because of slow production of later models. The Pzkw II was a 9-ton vehicle with 30-mm armour and a 20-mm gun; the Pzkw III was the mainstay of the Panzer divisions at the beginning of the Second World War. It was an excellent 20-tonner with 30-mm of armour, a 50-mm gun and a top speed of 25 mph. The Pzkw IV was just getting into mass production in 1939 and relatively few were available. This was an exceptional machine, weighing 18 tons, with 30-mm of armour, a useful 75-mm gun and a speed of 18 mph. It was the backbone of the Panzer units in the later years of the war.

HEAVY AND LIGHT TANKS

Britain and France opted for two classes of tank. The heavy "infantry" tank was intended to accompany the infantry assault, while the lighter and faster "cruiser" tank was intended to act as cavalry. The French heavy tank was the Char B1, a 30-tonner with 40-mm of armour, a 75-mm and a 47-mm gun, and a top speed of 17 mph. The cruiser class was composed of Renault and Hotchkiss designs of about 10 tons, with 20-mm of armour, 47-mm guns and a top speed of about 25 mph. The British infantry tank was the Matilda, a two-man 11-ton vehicle of ungainly appearance, with 60-mm of armour, a .50 machine-gun and a maximum speed of 8 mph. The cruisers were the Cruiser Tank Mark III and Mark IV, both of about 14 tons, with Christie suspension and a 2-pounder gun and 30-mm of armour.

Light tanks of 5 to 7 tons were used by the British and French for reconnaissance purposes, but the Spanish Civil War (1936–9) had shown that these were easily defeated by anti-tank weapons.

This lesson was repeated in France in 1940, with the result that, except for some minor use by airborne formations and in the Far East, the light tank was obsolete by 1941.

The US tank force in 1939 consisted of a handful of elderly 1918 designs and various test models developed in the 1930s. A decision was taken to produce the Medium M2 and an order was placed for 15 of them in August 1939, as well as the Light M2, but those decisions were overtaken by events. Rock Island Arsenal, the development centre for American tanks, had done much valuable research and had settled on a volute spring suspension and radial aircraft engine combination. This, in modified form, was to remain their standard formula until 1945. The US Army had watched events in Poland and France very closely, and concluded that the M2, with 25-mm of armour and a 37-mm gun, was inadequate. They therefore set about developing the Medium M3, with 50-mm of armour, a 37-mm gun in the turret and a 75-mm gun in a side sponson. Powered by a 340-hp engine, it could travel at 25 mph, and under the name General Lee was later used by the British Army in the Western Desert. The British Army found it a reliable and effective fighting vehicle unless attacked on the side without the sponson.

By the end of 1940, Germany had standardized the Pzkw III and IV, the pilot model of the American M3 was under construction, and the British had moved on to the Covenanter and Crusader versions of the cruiser tank and the Matilda II infantry tank. In addition an infantry tank, designed by Vickers and called the Valentine, had entered production. All these British tanks were armed with the 40-mm gun, placing them at a disadvantage compared with the German tanks. Moreover the two cruiser designs were grossly unreliable, the Covenanter being so bad that it was relegated to a training role. However, the Matilda II — a 27-ton vehicle with up to 78-mm of armour — was reasonably reliable and a vast improvement on the Mark I. The Valentine, a 17-tonner with 65-mm of armour and a top speed of 15 mph, was produced in greater numbers than any other. Of the 8,275 Valentines built, 1,390 were supplied to the USSR, who described it as "...the best tank we have received from our allies...".

SECOND WORLD WAR TANKS

AS THE Second World War progressed, tanks were fitted with thicker and better armour. They also became more agile and carried larger, more powerful guns. The first major surprise was the Soviet T-34 medium tank, considered by many experts to be the best all-round tank produced during the war. It was so good that the Soviets ceased production of virtually all other designs apart from their new heavy tank, the KV. In the next few years, they turned out 18,000 KVs and over 40,000 T-34s from 42 factories. With a 76-mm gun, cunningly angled 45-mm armour, and a speed of 30 mph, the T-34 weighed 26 tons. It gave the Soviet tank crews superiority over the Germans once production reached full swing.

The Americans soon realized that the side mounting of the 75-mm gun in their tank M3 (the "Lee" to the British) was a drawback and speedily developed the M4 Sherman to replace it. The Sherman became the principal US Army tank. Armed with the same 75-mm gun as the M3 but in a conventional turret, the M4 had 55-mm of armour and a top speed of 25 mph. Like the Soviets, the Americans appreciated the industrial and military logic of settling on one good design and mass-producing it. In pursuit of this policy, they produced over 58,000 M4s before the war ended. However, they failed to back up the Sherman with a good heavy tank, and were uncharacteristically slow to modify the design to correct the long series of faults that were revealed once the Sherman met other tanks on the battlefield. By the end of the war the Sherman was thoroughly outclassed — but there were plenty of them.

The outstanding virtues of the Sherman were its reliability and simplicity of production and maintenance. But the British did not build a reliable tank until the Cromwell in 1944. Armed with a 75-mm gun, protected by 76 mm of armour, and with a speed of 40

The Soviet surprise
(ABOVE) *The Soviet T-34 medium tank was better protected, better armed and faster than any German tank. It led to a crash design programme which produced the Panther and Tiger tanks in record time, and to the* provision of heavier anti-tank guns. The Soviets stayed ahead by increasing the gun calibre from 76mm to 85mm. The T-34 was far enough ahead of its time to give the Americans a hard time in Korea in 1950.

The Sherman
An early production model of the M4A1 Sherman medium tank with cast hull and turret. The infantry clustered behind the turret show a somewhat idealized view of how infantry might accompany tanks, but though this tactic was widely adopted by the Russians, it was rarely seen in British or American formations.

mph, this was the most effective British tank by far at the time of the D-Day invasion in 1944. However, not enough of them were made in time and so the bulk of the British armoured force used the Sherman.

By this time, though, the artificial distinction between infantry and cruiser tanks had been abandoned. The last infantry tank was the Churchill, which was extensively used for special roles such as breaching defences and flame-throwing on D-Day and after. The success of the Cromwell concentrated minds on a "general purpose" design. This led to the Centurion, but not in time for it to be used during the war.

Germany rushed to respond to the T-34, and late in 1942 the Pzkw V Panther appeared. The best German tank of the war, it had 80-mm well-sloped armour, a 75-mm gun, and a speed of 28 mph. However, it was subject to development problems and constant production hitches. A heavier tank was also demanded, and this resulted in the Pzkw VI Tiger, which went into production in August 1942. The heaviest tank in the world at that time, it weighed 56 tons, had armour up to 100 mm in thickness, and was armed with the powerful, 88-mm long-barrelled gun. The final German design was the King Tiger which appeared in November 1944, weighing 70 tons with 150mm of armour, and carrying an even more powerful 88-mm gun. Both Tiger designs were, however, dogged by problems of unreliability.

The Tiger tank
(ABOVE) *The Tiger 1 heavy tank, with an 88-mm high-velocity gun and 100mm thick frontal armour.*

The M26 Pershing
Development of the M26 (BELOW), the USA's answer to the Tiger, was hampered by the Army's failure to recognize the need for a heavy tank. Because of this the first Pershings did not reach Europe until January 1945.

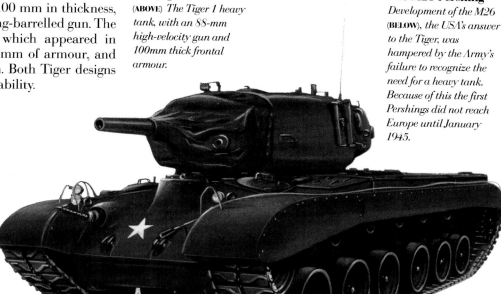

> " *The short-barrelled 75mm gun of the Panzer IV was only effective if the T-34 were attacked from the rear: even then a hit had to be scored on the grating above the engine to knock it out. It required very great skill to manoeuvre into a position from which such a shot was possible.* "

General Heinz Guderian, Panzer Leader.

ARMOUR, MOBILITY, GUN POWER

A good tank design strikes a balance between armour, mobility and gun power. British and US tanks were satisfactory in the first two respects, but were consistently outgunned by German machines. Among the Allies only the Soviets, with the T-34, had the right balance before 1945, and even they decided to beef up the T34's main armaments from 76-mm to 85-mm in 1944.

British tanks started by carrying a 40-mm weapon firing solid armour-piercing (AP) shot. Their German adversaries had 50-mm weapons firing either AP shot or high-explosive shell which was useful against soft-skinned vehicles and as a support to infantry. But the German tanks had also been designed to accept a larger gun in the future, whereas British tanks had not; any increase in armament had to wait for a new tank to be designed.

Even this increased gun calibre was only 57-mm, by which time the Americans and Germans were arming with 75-mm. But the US 75-mm gun was a low-velocity ex-field gun, whereas the German one was a high-velocity weapon purposely designed as a tank and anti-tank gun. Gradually the US 75-mm was improved, and it was crammed into some British tanks. Then the Americans moved to a 76-mm high-velocity gun and the British built their own 76-mm, 17-pounder tank gun. Once more, though, they had to wait for a new generation of tank which had a turret large enough to take it. However, engineers did find a way of fitting the 17-pounder gun into the Sherman turret, creating the Firefly. This was the only tank in northwest Europe in 1944/45 which had any chance at all against the 88-mm of the Panthers and Tigers. The eventual US response was a new heavy tank, the M26 Pershing, which carried a 90-mm gun. But it came too late in the war to have any measurable effect, and only a handful of them reached Europe.

ANTI-TANK WEAPONS: 1920-1945

I N THE 1920s, some thought was given to the design of a light weapon capable of disabling a tank. Most countries settled on a heavy rifle or a light cannon, hoping that it would have the necessary muzzle velocity and weight of shot to penetrate the relatively thin armour of the time and injure the crew inside. Most countries gave these rifles to the infantry, though Britain, for one, manned 2-pounder mobile anti-tank guns with artillerymen. Similar guns between 25 and 45mm in calibre were adopted by France, Germany, the USA, and the USSR, in most cases manned by infantry. Generally, the heavy rifles could pierce 25mm of armour at a range of 100 yards, while the wheeled anti-tank guns could defeat 50mm at 500 yards.

These weapons were adequate against the tanks of the mid-1930s, but as tanks were fitted with longer-range guns and heavier armour, the tank began to outpace its main battlefield opponent. A race between the two began and has continued to this day.

The straightforward solution was to project a steel shot at high velocity and trust that the impact would break the armour. But as velocities increased, it was found that, above a critical "striking velocity" of about 2,800 feet per second, steel shot would break up on impact. The immediate answer was to use a harder material, tungsten carbide. However, tungsten carbide is more dense than steel so a full-calibre projectile would be too heavy to attain the desired velocity. The next idea originated in Germany, where a smaller-than-calibre (sub-calibre) tungsten shot was placed in a softer metal sheath with soft skirts that fitted closely into the breech.

The Krupp PAK 44
This 128-mm gun was developed in 1944 and illustrates the anti-tank dilemma: a gun powerful enough to punish tanks at long range was too heavy to be a practical weapon on the battlefield. It could defeat 173mm of armour at 3,000 yards range, but weighed ten tons.

Discarding sabot shot
A discarding sabot shot for the British 6-pounder (57-mm) anti-tank gun. Top: the shot as loaded, showing the light alloy "sabot" of full calibre diameter. Bottom: one section of the sabot and base has been removed to show the tungsten carbide core inside its steel sheath.

EXPLOSIVE ENERGY ATTACK

Instead of relying upon high velocity and kinetic energy, which led to overweight guns, by 1943 the possibilities of using explosive energy were being explored. Two systems arose, the shaped charge (HEAT — High Explosive Anti-Tank) and the squash-head (HESH) shells. HEAT has a coned metal liner in the face of an explosive charge, and detonates the charge from behind. The detonating wave collapses the cone and "focuses" the explosive energy into a fine, fast-moving jet of gas and metal which punches through the armour. The HESH shell is filled with plastic explosive which sticks to the armour and is detonated by a base fuze to send a shock wave through the steel which breaks off a "scab" of metal weighing several pounds and throws it into the tank at high velocity.

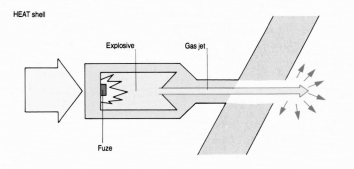

HESH shell
Plastic explosive
Fuze

HEAT shell
Explosive
Gas jet
Fuze

work became known, a tungsten-cored shot was developed. Then came the 17-pounder which, issued late in 1942, became one of the supreme tank-killers of the war. Since it was clear that tank armour would get thicker and thicker as the war went on, work began on a 32-pounder. Pilot models were made, but the war ended before production could begin.

The USA began the war with a 37-mm anti-tank gun copied from the German design, but then adopted the British 57 mm. The Americans began work on a 76-mm gun but there were ammunition problems and they did not pursue it seriously until early 1944. The resulting 3-inch M1 then proved a potent weapon. Work on 90-mm and 105-mm weapons was incomplete when the war ended.

Germany advanced from the 50-mm to 75-mm weapon, but its greatest asset was a misused anti-aircraft gun. In 1940, a German force had been jumped by a number of British Matilda II tanks near Arras in northern France. Matildas were heavily armoured and the standard 37-mm German gun made no impression on them. In desperation the German commander ordered a battery of 88-mm anti-aircraft guns to engage the tanks, which they did with considerable success. From then on the 88-mm flak gun doubled as a second-line anti-tank gun. German designers set about producing a proper 88-mm anti-tank gun, spurred on by the threat of the T-34 Soviet tank. The weapon produced, the 88-mm PAK (*Panzerabwehrkanone*) 43, was an

The anti-tank rifle
This British .55-inch Boys rifle was typical of the anti-tank rifles developed in the late 1930s. Heavy (36 lbs) and with a vicious kick when fired, it could defeat 21 mm of armour at 300 metres range.

outstanding success. Firing steel shot it could defeat 160mm of armour at 2,000-m range and no tank was safe within two miles.

The USSR began with a 45-mm gun copied from the German 37-mm, and then went progressively to 57-, 76-, 85- and 100-mm calibres. The last three were actually anti-aircraft gun calibres. The Soviets simply took the gun barrel and mounted it on a two-wheeled field carriage to produce a useful anti-tank gun.

A PROBLEM OF BALLISTICS

In Britain, the ordnance staff realized that the tungsten-carbide shot posed a ballistic problem. Being light in the bore (compared to steel shot), it did not have sufficient density to maintain its velocity in flight for very long. What was needed was a shot with a low weight/diameter ratio in the bore but a high ratio in flight to retain velocity well down-range. The Armament Research Department finally came up with the "discarding sabot shot". The tungsten core was surrounded by a full-calibre, light alloy sheath with planes of weakness. These gave way when the shot was fired and flew off at the muzzle. All that remained in flight was the tungsten core, which had a very favourable weight/diameter ratio. This was issued for the 57-mm (6-pounder) gun in the summer of 1944 and for the 76-mm (17-pounder) shortly afterwards. With plain steel shot, the 17-pounder gun could defeat 109mm of armour at 1,000 yards. With the new shot it could defeat 231mm.

Another problem was that a gun powerful enough to defeat the latest tanks had to be so big that it was no longer practical as a wheeled field weapon. The answer to this was the "shaped charge" or "hollow charge" (see box).

The gun barrel was bored with a gradual taper, from 28mm at the breech to 21mm at the muzzle. As the shot travelled along the barrel, the soft skirts were squeezed down to the reduced calibre. The gas pressure was then acting upon a reduced base area, and therefore the velocity increased. This "taper-bore" gun could defeat 66mm of armour at a range of about 500 yards, and after this initial success, models in 40/29mm and 75/55mm were developed. But manufacture of both guns and shot was difficult, and by early 1942 there was a grave shortage of tungsten in Germany and it had to be used for machine tools rather than ammunition.

The Germans also developed tungsten-cored projectiles for their standard anti-tank guns of 37-mm and 50-mm calibre, using a sub-calibre core surrounded by an alloy body so that it had less mass than a steel shot and generated very high velocity.

Britain began the war with a 40-mm anti-tank gun, and had a 57-mm version under development, which reached production in late 1940. These guns fired solid steel shot, but after the German

AERIAL WARFARE: 1939-45

T HE AIR forces of the major powers in 1939 had been shaped by the experience of the First World War and postwar theories of air power. Thus the Royal Air Force and the US Army Air Corps adhered to the theory that air forces could win wars by themselves, provided that they had enough bombers. Both forces therefore tended to concentrate on bombers and to limit their fighter strength to defence of the homeland. By contrast, Germany and the USSR viewed aircraft as an adjunct to their ground forces and concentrated on ground-attack fighters and light bombers, with little thought of strategic concepts.

During the opening phase of the Second World War, German air power was an integral part of blitzkrieg tactics, while the British bomber force vainly tried to navigate its way to its targets in Germany. After the fall of France, however, Britain had to rely on its fighters to defeat the German bombing raids and prevent the Germans from establishing air superiority over the English Channel. Without this superiority, Hitler could not launch his planned invasion of Britain.

The British aircraft industry was geared to production of medium bombers, but worked hard to expand fighter production. Germany produced fighters and light bombers but failed to develop effective long-range bombers in time to influence events.

The Long-range P51 Mustang
One of the finest fighter designs ever to come out of America, the North American Aviation Company's Mustang (**BELOW**) *was developed in response to an RAF request in April 1940. Almost 1,000 were delivered to the RAF and it was then adopted by the US Army Air Force. The total production was 15,586. They were capable of carrying two 1,000-lb and four 750-lb bombs in addition to four cannon or machine guns.*

Supermarine Spitfire
Possibly the most famous fighter aircraft of the Second Wrold War, the Spitfire design began in 1934 around the Rolls-Royce Merlin V-12 engine. It was the first all-metal stressed-skin fighter to be built in England and first flew in March 1936. The original Mark I had four .303 Browning machine guns in the wings, but this was soon replaced by the Mark IA (shown here) with eight guns and the familiar bulged canopy. With a top speed of about 350 mph, eight guns were needed to put sufficient bullets into the air to inflict damage during the few seconds of an aerial engagement. Subsequent marks adopted a mix of 20-mm cannon and .303 machine guns.

FIGHTERS AND BOMBERS

By 1939 the biplane fighter was on the way out and the low-wing all-metal monoplane was becoming a standard for first-rate fighter aircraft. The British Hurricane with a top speed of 316 mph and armed with eight .303 machine-guns and the German Messerschmitt Bf109E, which was armed with four 7.92-mm machine-guns and one 20-mm cannon and could fly at 354mph, were fairly evenly matched, and both went through many improved versions. The Spitfire (400mph, eight .303 machine-guns) and the FockeWulf Fw190 (440mph, two 13-mm machine-guns, two 20- or 30-mm cannon) were representative of the mid-war fighter and were joined by the US P-47 Thunderbolt (470mph, eight .50 machine-guns), P-38 Lightning (420mph, one 20-mm cannon, four .50 machine-guns), and P-51 Mustang (440mph, four 20-mm cannon, four .50 machine-guns).

Junkers Ju.87 Stuka
The Stuka (RIGHT) *first flew in late 1935. It saw action in the Spanish Civil War. One 1,800-kg bomb was carried between the wheels, on a launching arm which swung the bomb clear of the propeller, two machine guns were in the wings, and the observer had a third machine gun.*

Other notable fighters were the Soviet Polikarpov 1-16 (325mph, two 7.62-mm machine-guns, two 20-mm cannon) and Yak-9 (375mph, two 12.7-mm machine-guns, one 20-mm cannon) which served well on the Eastern Front, and the Japanese Mitsubishi A6M "Zero" (355mph, two 7.7-mm machine-guns, two 20-mm cannon) which gave the US forces stiff opposition in the Pacific at first.

The most widely used ground attack aircraft in Europe was the Junkers Ju 87 "Stuka" dive-bomber. This provided highly effective flying artillery for the Panzer forces in Poland and the Low Countries, diving with considerable precision to drop a 1,800-kg bomb. It also carried smaller bombs and machine-guns. However, it was later found to be an easy target for fighters and for light air-defence weapons and, for most of the war, was relegated to secondary duties against opposition that was rather less fierce. The Allies adapted their standard fighters for ground attack work as the war went on, using special 40-mm cannon in the Hurricane for tank-killing, for example. Later came heavier specialized machines such as the Hawker Typhoon which, armed with rockets, confined the Panzers to movement at night only, after the D-Day landings in 1944.

The most numerous ground attack machine of the war was the Soviet Ilyushin II-2 "Stormovik". Believed to be the biggest production run of any aircraft in history, over 40,000 of this armoured two-seater were built. Though neither a great aircraft, nor easy to fly, the Ilyushin II-2 devastated the German ground forces on the Eastern Front by sheer numbers. Armed variously with cannon, machine-guns, rockets, and bombs, it was used against troops, tanks, and railways wherever the Soviets fought.

The Luftwaffe started the war using light, twin-engined aircraft such as the Dornier Do 215, Junkers Ju 88, and Heinkel He 111. These carried 1,000–2,000kg of bombs at about 250mph and had an out-and-back range of about 940 miles. Their British counterparts, the Blenheim and the Fairey Battle, failed in combat. So did the medium Hampdens and Whitleys. Of the early British bombers, only the Wellington came up to scratch.

The British and American passion for strategic bombing had led them to design heavy four-engined machines of great range, and these reached production in 1940 in increasing numbers. The principal British heavy bomber proved to be the Avro Lancaster, capable of flying at 290mph for 1,600 miles with a bomb load of 6,350kg. The American long-range bombers were the Boeing B-17 "Flying Fortress", which flew at 180 mph to 1,100 miles with 5,800kg of bombs and was a sitting duck for the German fighters. Later came the Consolidated "Liberator" (190mph to 2,200 miles with 2,300kg), and eventually the Boeing B-29 "Superfortress" (360mph to 3,250 miles with 4,540kg of bombs).

Among the significant technological advances of the period was the gas turbine or jet engine. This concept was originated and pursued independently in both Britain and Germany, and though the Whittle engine was running on the test bed, it was Germany who first put an experimental jet aircraft into the sky, in August 1939. Germany then developed the first jet fighter, the Messerschmitt Me 262, in mid-1942, but it was not put into series production until mid-1944. Once in service, the Me 262 ran rings round every Allied aircraft.

RADAR

THE IDEA of using radio waves to measure distance occurred to different people at more or less the same time. In the 1920s, weather researchers had discovered that they could "bounce" a radio signal off the upper atmosphere and detect its return to earth. From this discovery, scientists began thinking that perhaps signals could be bounced off other things. In 1934 Dr Kuhnhold of the German Navy's Radio Research Establishment began experiments, and by 1936 was sufficiently advanced to be able to persuade the German Navy to place a contract for a range-finding radar for use with naval guns.

US Navy scientists had noticed by 1930 that a radio signal showed distortion when an aircraft passed between transmitter and receiver. In 1933 the US Army's Signal Corps joined in the investigation, and by 1936 both services had produced prototype equipment. The French were also experimenting, aiming to

The H2S system
Although radar began as a detection system it was quickly expanded to provide other vital information. The H2S system shown here was adopted in British bombers in January 1943. Tests of night-fighter radars in 1940 had revealed that centimetric radar could distinguish between built-up areas and

featureless countryside. Since bombing targets were usually in built-up areas, this discovery led to development of a downward-pointing radar which could, effectively, "draw a map" of the ground beneath, with sufficient detail to allow the navigator to correlate the picture with the map and so pinpoint his position.

RADAR

The radar screen around Britain in 1940 consisted of two "chains" of stations. Chain Home was the first, providing cover at high altitude and long range. Chain Home Low came later, giving low altitude cover against raiders flying over the sea. As technology improved, so the boundaries of radar coverage were extended.

- ▨ Limit of low altitude radar
- ☐ Limit of high altitude radar
- △ Chain Home Low stations
- ▲ Chain Home stations

develop an iceberg-finding device for transatlantic liners.

However, only in Britain was the radar principle fully explored and developed. In January 1935, the Committee for the Scientific Study of Air Defence asked Dr Robert Watson-Watt, a radio-physicist, to investigate whether a "death ray" capable of stopping aircraft engines, as discussed in newspapers at the time, was a feasible proposition. He replied that it was not, but there might be other aspects of radio that could be useful. Within a month he submitted a report in which he laid out, in considerable detail, a potential system for detecting aircraft by means of radio waves. The report went further, proposing a defensive system to cover the identification of friendly aircraft, the possibility of counter-measures and much more. The idea was adopted, and by June 1935, aircraft had been detected at a range of 17 miles.

Three years later, Britain had a complete chain of radar stations along the east and south coasts. These were used during the Munich crisis of 1938 and have been operating continuously ever since. But warning of the approach of enemy aircraft by itself is not enough. Working from Watson-Watt's proposals, a complete

Fighter Command
*A temporary operations
room at Fighter
Command, Stanmore, in
1940. Radar provided
information on the
location, speed and
height of an approaching
enemy raid, but this
information had to be
assessed and turned into
instructions to the
defences. Information
from radars, ground
observers, ships, and
other sources was fed to
"filter rooms" controlled
by the RAF where the
different reports were
correlated until a clear
picture of an impending
attack was seen. This
positive information then
went to the operations
room, shown here, to be
plotted on the large map
at floor level.*

communication system between radars and defensive aircraft was set up and was integrated with Air Marshal Hugh Dowding's fighter control system. Incoming raiders were detected, positions were plotted on the control room table, and fighters were "talked" into a suitable position for intercepting the enemy. Without this command and control system, the Battle of Britain might have taken a very different course.

Germany developed a similar system, beginning in 1940 with a handful of "Freya" early warning radar sets borrowed from the German Navy. The Luftwaffe's own design, "Wurzburg", came after and it was the middle of 1941 before a comprehensive warning system was operating.

The USA had a handful of sets operating by 1941. Indeed there was one set covering Pearl Harbor which actually detected the incoming Japanese bombers, but assumed them to be a flight of reinforcement bombers expected from the West Coast of the USA.

SHORTER-WAVE RADAR

These low-powered early sets all operated at a wavelength of about 1m. It was known that if the wavelength were shorter, more power could be generated, giving more range and more precision. However, it was practically impossible to generate such waves using conventional glass valves or tubes. Eventually two young Birmingham physicists devised the "cavity magnetron" which was capable of producing powerful 10-cm waves. Since the wavelength governed the size of the transmitting and receiving antenna, the shorter wavelength made it possible to install more of these effective radar sets inside aircraft.

Airborne installation multiplied the uses of radar. It allowed night fighters to detect bombers, once they had been directed to the general area by the ground radar and controllers. Submarines, risen to the surface at night or in fog, could be detected at long range. Radar allowed a bomber navigator to scan the ground beneath for landmarks and to correct his navigation and also allowed him to detect approaching enemy fighters.

The Germans also had radar, but not the cavity magnetron. Watson-Watt had foreseen this and had proposed countermeasures. Metallic paper strips, cut to half the wavelength of the radar and scattered in the air, could swamp the enemy radar with spurious echoes. This tactic was codenamed "Window". The dilemma over the use of Window was whether the enemy could make better use of it than the Allies. Britain eventually took the plunge in July 1943 to cover the first of the great raids on Hamburg. Window remained effective throughout the war and it was soon joined by other, more sophisticated electronic devices to confuse radar reception.

Probably the earliest successful jamming operation was performed in February 1942, when the German Navy blinded British south-coast radars to conceal the escape of three battleships from Brest harbour. The British returned the compliment in 1944 with a massive radar decoy which kept the Germans guessing about where the Allies would land on D-Day.

ADVANCES IN AIR-DEFENCE GUNNERY

BY 1930, the major powers were all at work developing anti-aircraft "predictors". These were primitive mechanical or electro-mechanical computers that were fed information on the range, speed and height of the target, the velocity of the shell and the weather conditions — wind, and air temperature and density. The predictor would then produce the exact direction — azimuth — for the gun, the elevation and the shell fuze time that would ensure that shell and aircraft would reach the same spot at the same time. Developments took a long time and it was not until the mid-1930s that serviceable and accurate predictors began to appear.

The provision of anti-aircraft (AA) guns was, like that of other military equipment, hampered by financial constraints, so designs were drawn up against the day when production could begin. Britain developed an excellent 3.7-inch (94-mm) weapon, France a 90-mm gun, the USA 90-mm and 105-mm guns. Germany, forbidden to develop guns by the Versailles Treaty, farmed out her gun designers to other countries. One such team posted to the Bofors factory in Sweden worked away quietly on a new 88-mm gun design.

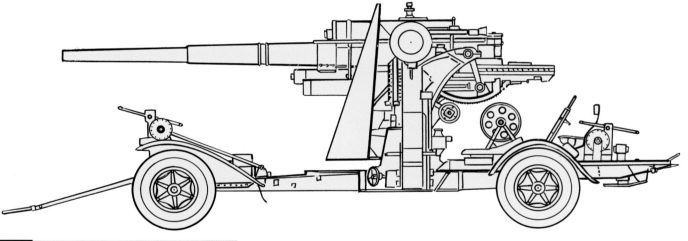

During the three months ending August 1944, German AA fire accounted for no less than 66 percent of the 700 bombers lost and 98 percent of the 13,000 bombers damaged. In 1943, 33 percent of the bombers lost and 66 percent of the damaged were attributed to Flak.

Effects of German AA fire on US 8th
Air Force Bombers; *Air Defense
Review No 6*, SHAEF, January 1945.

The Eighty-Eight
Perhaps the most notorious gun of the Second World War, the German 8.8-cm Flak 18 anti-aircraft gun. The "88" fired a 20-lb explosive shell to 26,000 feet and a well-trained crew could get off 15 rounds a minute. An improved version, the Flak 41, raised the ceiling to 35,000 feet and the rate of fire to 20rpm using the same shell but a more powerful cartridge.

Returning to Germany with it in 1931, they built a prototype and tested it. Then, in 1933, when Hitler assumed power, the gun was put into production. The German "88" built up an extraordinarily high reputation in the Second World War as a field and anti-tank gun. As an air defence weapon, it was not significantly better than those being developed elsewhere.

Exercises in peacetime revealed that there were two types of air-defence targets: the high-flying bomber and the low-flying ground-attack aircraft. One gun could not deal effectively with both. A heavy gun capable of reaching up to the high-flyer could not swing or elevate fast enough to track a low-flying machine. A gun manoeuvrable enough to engage the low-flyer would not have the range to deal with high-flyers. Some countries adopted the Oerlikon or Hispano-Suiza 20-mm cannon as a defence against the low-flyers. Others felt that the 20-mm gun did not have sufficient range or power to damage a modern aircraft. The Bofors company in Sweden studied this problem and in response designed a light 40-mm gun capable of firing 120 shells per minute to an effective ceiling of 5,000 feet. This went on the market in 1931 and soon attracted orders. By

A Soviet 37-mm gun
In use by the Soviet Navy, this twin 37-mm gun (LEFT) is based upon the Bofors 40-mm weapon.

US 120-mm Gun M1
One of the most powerful AA guns of the Second World War, the 120-mm (BELOW) was designed to deal with high-altitude bombers over the USA; none were ever used in action.

Skysweeper
The US 75-mm AA Gun M51 (RIGHT) began development in 1944 but did not reach service until 1951. It was the first "autonomous" anti-aircraft gun, since it carried its own radar, optical tracker and predictor and could thus operate independently of any fire control system. The shell weighed 15 lbs and the ceiling was 30,000 feet.

1939 it was in use in 18 countries. Among the purchasers were Poland, Britain, Germany, and the USA, while the USSR bought a handful and then copied it in 37-mm calibre. The French preferred a 25-mm gun developed by Hotchkiss, while the Italians had a 25-mm designed by Breda.

As the Second World War progressed, aircraft became faster and were built of damage-resistant metal. They also flew higher, stretching the capability of the guns and creating a demand for further development. Germany improved its 88-mm in 1943, lifting its effective ceiling from 26,250 to 35,000 feet and also developed 105-mm (range 31,000 feet) and 128-mm (range 35,000 feet) weapons. Specifications for these had been issued before the war, as had one for a 150-mm magazine-fed gun, but this proved no more effective than the 128-mm weapon. It was abandoned in 1940 and Germany saw the war out with the existing designs.

Britain settled on two options: an improved version of the 3.7-inch gun which lifted the ceiling from 32,000 to 45,000 feet, and a modified naval 5.25-inch gun capable of firing an 80-lb shell to 43,000 feet. Moreover the 3.7-inch guns were fitted with an automatic loader and fuze setter.

When the USA entered the war, its army was still using a 3-inch gun designed in the 1920s. A 90-mm gun was then put into production with automatic loading and fuze setting. This could fire 23-lb shells at a rate of 27 a minute to a ceiling of 39,500 feet. It was supplemented by a limited number of 105-mm guns (32-lb shell to 42,000 feet) and a 120-mm gun (50-lb shell to 47,500 feet), used only in the USA and to defend the Panama Canal.

INCREASED AUTOMATION

The use of radar to detect targets and aim the guns transformed AA gunnery. The arrival of electronic predictors in 1944 made Allied gunnery still more accurate. Another significant improvement was the adoption of power drives for traversing and elevating the guns. They could then be directly controlled by the predictor, leaving the gunners nothing to do but feed ammunition as fast as the gun could fire it.

The most significant advance in air-defence gunnery also came in 1944 when the British and the Americans adopted the proximity fuze. Before this, fuzes were clockwork and were set according to the predictor's forecast of where the aircraft would be. The proximity fuze was a radio device in the shell nose which detected the target and detonated the shell automatically within lethal distance. This converted many near-misses into hits and also speeded up the rate of fire since fuze-setting was no longer required. The combination of radar, electronic prediction, and proximity fuzes was extremely effective when southern England was attacked by the German FZG-1 flying bombs in 1944.

Postwar work was concentrated on making guns more powerful, to reach greater ceilings, and on developing automatic loading systems to allow rapid firing. By 1956 Britain had developed a 3.7-inch gun capable of 70 shots a minute. Just as it was perfected, the ground-to-air missile entered production, and major air-defence artillery development ceased. Light air-defence weapons of 20–35-mm calibre are now integrated into many army formations for defence against ground-attack aircraft.

AIRCRAFT
CARRIERS
EXTEND THE
RANGE OF
NAVIES

NAVAL WARFARE 1939-45

The USS Lexington
Following the loss of the original USS Lexington in the Battle of the Coral Sea, a new Lexington, one of the Essex class of aircraft carriers, was launched in September 1942. This picture (RIGHT) shows aircraft landing and being stowed during Operation Galvanic, the capture of the Gilbert Islands, in November 1943.

THE NAVIES of the major powers in 1939 were still firmly based upon the battleship — the "capital ship" — as their keystone, with cruisers and destroyers as escorts. Submarines were seen as patrol boats and raiders. All had, to some extent, started to build up naval aviation, but in most navies this was largely a reconnaissance force with offensive capability limited to a few torpedo-carrying aircraft.

However, the USA and Japan, locked in increasing rivalry across the Pacific, had spent much thought and energy on naval aviation and the use of aircraft carriers. The European powers had built aircraft carriers but were still unsure of aviation's role and quite oblivious of the threat that aviation posed to the capital ship. Moreover, the British had amalgamated the RNAS (Royal Naval Air Service) into the Royal Air Force in 1918. It was not until the early 1930s that the Royal Navy regained its own aviation

Gneisenau
This German battle-cruiser, sister ship to the Scharnhorst, displaced 31,850 tons, was armed with nine 11-inch guns, 26 of lesser calibre, 26 AA guns and six torpedo tubes, had a top speed of 32 knots and a main armour belt 13 inches thick. Badly damaged by RAF bombing in Kiel in February 1942, she was modified to be re-armed with 15-inch guns. This idea was abandoned in mid-1943 and she was eventually sunk to block Gdynia harbour.

arm. Even then, the design, procurement, and maintenance of naval aircraft was an RAF task. As a result the Fleet Air Arm remained the poor relation of the RAF, a situation which was not remedied until the middle of the Second World War.

The Washington Naval Treaty of 1922 limited the size of battleships to 35,000 tons and they were to be fitted with guns no greater than 40.6-cm calibre. But by 1936, the Japanese refused to ratify a new treaty and in reply, the USA announced that it would build to 45,000 tons. However, most of the battleships built in the interwar period were laid down before the lessons of 1914–18 were fully assimilated. The only exceptions to this were the British battleships *Rodney* and *Nelson*. They were ungainly vessels but were probably the only truly modern battleships afloat in 1939.

Germany, after abrogating the Treaty of Versailles, built *Scharnhorst* and *Gneisenau*, and by 1936 the European building race was on. Britain laid down two King George V class battleships, France the *Richelieu* and *Jean Bart*, and Italy the Littorio class. The only major power without a serious navy was the USSR, which had three battleships left over from the days of the tsar and a handful of smaller ships. Other priorities meant that the Soviet Navy did not begin to build until 1938, when two 59,000-ton battleships were laid down. But they were beyond the capacity of Soviet industry and neither was completed. One was

> **"** *The poor ship rolled nearly over on to her beam ends, and we saw men massing on her upturned side. A minute or two later there came the dull rumble of a terrific explosion as one of her main magazines blew up. The ship became completely hidden in a great cloud of yellowish-black smoke which went wreathing and eddying high up into the sky. When it cleared away the Barham had disappeared. There was nothing but a bubbling oily-looking patch on the calm surface of the sea, dotted with wreckage and the heads of swimmers.* **"**
>
> *Admiral of the Fleet Lord Cunningham*, A Sailor's Odyssey.

A TACTICAL REVOLUTION

The growing importance of naval aviation was demonstrated early in the war by the British carrier-borne raids upon Italian bases in the Mediterranean, and the lesson was driven home by the Japanese raid on Pearl Harbor. Even the Royal Navy, after the successes of its carriers in the Mediterranean, had to suffer the loss of the battleships *Prince of Wales* and *Repulse* to shore-based Japanese bombers and torpedo carriers before the lessons of the revolution in naval tactics sunk in. By May 1942, the US and Japanese Navies were fiercely engaged in the first sea battle to be fought entirely by aircraft, with no warship on either side catching sight of the enemy.

The submarine, particularly in German and US hands, was confirmed as a highly significant weapon during the Second World War. From late 1940, when German U-Boats started to operate from bases in France, the Atlantic Ocean became their domain. They sank merchant shipping by the hundreds of thousands of tons. Gradually, by re-adopting the convoy system of shepherding the freighters across under naval escort (see Early submarines and undersea warfare, page 134), by improved anti-submarine detectors and depth charges, with long-range aircraft patrols, and aided considerably by breaking the German naval codes, the Allies were able to turn the tables on the U-boats.

The U-boat war in the Atlantic tends to overshadow other submarine activities, but there was much happening in other theatres. The British boats in the Mediterranean scored so highly against German and Italian shipping that Germany sent 12 U-boats from the Atlantic to even the score — and lost them all. US submarines became dominant in the Pacific, effectively sealing off Japan from vital overseas supplies. Oil tankers were particular targets. US submarines were also invaluable as reconnaissance and patrol boats, often giving advance warning of Japanese naval movements by setting up mid-ocean picket lines.

stripped to provide steel for the siege of Leningrad, while the other was destroyed by the German Army.

The goal of the Japanese Navy was to defeat anything afloat. To this end, the *Yamato* and her three planned sister ships displaced 64,170 tons and had nine 46-cm guns for main armament, 64cm of armour and a speed of 27 knots. Two were completed in 1940 but were not the war-winning weapons that the Japanese Navy had hoped. The *Musashi* was sunk in the Battle of Leyte Gulf in October 1944 while the *Yamato* was sunk by US carrier aircaft in April 1945 during the invasion of Okinawa.

Even though the war showed up the importance of aviation at sea, the battleship was still a considerable threat and played an important role to the end. Land- or carrier-based aircraft replaced the gun as the long-range naval weapon, but where aviation support was not available, the battleship was still the dominant factor. This was demonstrated in the Mediterranean in 1940 when the Royal Navy engaged the Italian fleet off Calabria. HMS *Warspite* scored a direct hit on Italy's *Giulio Cesare* at a range of 23,775m, a record that still stands. The addition of radar fire control systems also enabled ships to bring accurate fire to bear at long ranges in darkness. At the Battle of Leyte Gulf in October 1944 the US fleet started on the destruction of a Japanese task force at 3 am, using radar-directed gunfire.

The U-Boat
A Type IX U-Boat displaying its armament of 21-inch torpedoes and a 105-mm gun.

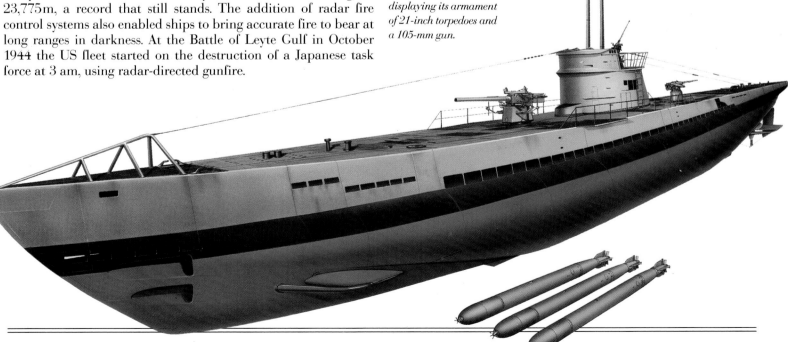

**ADVANCES IN
SMALL-ARMS
GIVE NEW
POWER TO
THE INFANTRY**

AUTOMATIC WEAPONS

THE SEARCH for a serviceable design of automatic rifle was still under way when the Second World War broke out. The advantage of such a weapon is that the infantryman only has to concentrate on his aim — the rifle is automatically reloaded after each shot. By 1939, the Americans had adopted such a weapon as their standard infantry rifle, though only a small portion of the US Army had actually received them. A small number were also being tried by Soviet troops, but the majority of the world's armies were armed with the same rifles that they had carried in 1918, albeit with small changes to simplify mass production.

During the course of the war, the Americans converted entirely to automatic rifles, but the remaining combatants retained their bolt-action weapons. Some made extensive trials with self-loading

The Sten gun
*A soldier of the Free French Army (**RIGHT**) practising with a Sten submachine gun. Notice the correct way of holding this weapon — with the wrist supporting the weight of the magazine. It was risky to use the magazine as a handgrip since the single-column feed was the weakest point of the design and gave rise to jams if twisted. One bonus feature was that the Sten would function in cold and dirty conditions when most other guns gave up.*

The tank riders
*Soviet troops (**ABOVE**) parading with their Degtyarev PPD-40 submachine guns. With a 70-shot drum magazine, these gave the soldier immense firepower and the Soviets armed their "tank rider" battalions with them. These men rode on the rear deck of tanks and leapt off whenever the tank was held up by ground troops.*

or automatic rifles but the German Army, though retaining the 1898 Mauser as their standard, issued several automatic designs in limited numbers and pioneered an entirely new class of weapon. This was the assault rifle.

In the 1930s, a study of First World War action reports led the German Army to question the value of their highly accurate, heavy rifles intended to fire to 1,500m or more. The combat reports showed that men seldom fired at ranges over 400m. A less powerful cartridge would have sufficient performance for this range, and would permit the issue of a smaller, handier, and lighter rifle. Development work on this concept was put in hand, and by 1943 pre-production models were issued to troops on the Eastern Front.

This first version was known as Machine Pistol 43, but it was actually a short rifle capable of single shots or automatic fire, built around the short cartridge. The men in the front line· were enthusiastic about the new weapon and it went into production immediately under the name Sturmgewehr ("assault rifle") 44. It was reliable, accurate, and effective, and because the ammunition was lighter, the infantryman could carry more. Production difficulties caused by material shortages and the Allied bombing campaign hampered production, which was never sufficient to arm more than a small proportion of the German infantry. But enough of the Sturmgewehr 44 were produced to have a considerable influence upon postwar infantry weapons.

Another German innovation was the "general-purpose machine-gun". Experience during the 1914–18 war had led to the development of two distinct types of machine-gun. One was the belt-fed medium weapon, water-cooled and tripod-mounted for sustained defensive fire. The other was a lighter, man-carried, magazine-fed weapon for assault purposes. By developing a fast-firing, lightweight, air-cooled machine-gun, the MG34, the Germans were able to use a single weapon on a tripod for sustained fire or on a bipod for assault work, with belt feed in both cases. The design evolved into the MG42, which incorporated a quick-change system for replacing the barrel when it became hot. This helped eliminate rapid wear due to overheated barrels. The gun, dubbed the "Spandau" by Allied troops, fired at 1,200 rounds per minute.

THE SUBMACHINE-GUN

The universal weapon of the Second World War was the submachine-gun. In 1939 it barely existed — by 1945 there were millions in the hands of every sort of official and unofficial military formation. The submachine-gun is a compact automatic weapon firing pistol ammunition, designed for short-range assault and close-quarter fighting. Its maximum effective range is rarely more than 100m. It was first used by the German Army in 1917–18, equipping small squads of assault troops who infiltrated enemy defences by concentrated firepower, it later found a place in the popular imagination as the "Tommygun", the American Thompson submachine-gun. Though designed as a trench weapon, the Thompson was too late for the First World War, but was enthusiastically adopted by both police and gangsters in the 1920s. This was unfortunate, because professional soldiers tended to look down on it as a "gangster gun" and could not see its tactical possibilities. But in 1939, quantities were bought by Britain and France to arm patrols, and their experience showed that there was ample scope for such a weapon.

The German Army had seen the need rather earlier. Seeking a weapon with which to arm elements of their new Panzer divisions, they recalled the original Bergmann weapon of 1917. One or two similar designs which were still available were tested, and then the Erma company was instructed to come up with a design suitable for mass production. They responded with the Machine Pistol 38, made from stamped metal and plastic, with a folding butt. It is known to history as the "Schmeisser", though Hugo Schmeisser had nothing to do with the design and nobody is sure how his name came to be attached to it.

The Soviet Army also saw advantages in the submachine-gun. It was simple to operate so that raw, even illiterate, recruits could easily be taught how to use it, and it encouraged aggressive action, all of which fitted their situation. Whole divisions were equipped with the PPSh43 and PPS43 submachine-gun by the middle of the war.

Britain, urgently seeking a cheap and effective gun in the dark days of 1940, adopted the Sten Gun, a name derived from the initials of the British designers and the factory in which it was made. Costing no more than £2.50 each, the Sten was produced by the million. As well as arming British troops, it was also distributed to resistance groups throughout Europe.

The US Army liked the Thompson but it was expensive and difficult to make, so the Submachine-gun M3 was developed instead. This was more commonly called the "Grease Gun" from its tubular shape. Like the Sten it was simple but effective, and had the added virtue that it could be converted in a few minutes from the American .45 calibre to the continental 9-mm standard.

THE STEN GUN STRIPPED

A Sten gun reduced to its basic parts. From top to bottom: the receiver (gun body); butt; bolt, lock ring and cocking handle, return spring and end cap; barrel and hand grip. This is the Mark II gun, the most common pattern; other marks had the same component parts.

The German MG42
Designed by Mauser, this was the standard German Army machine gun and was used in both the squad light and company medium roles. Belt-fed, and with a quick-change barrel, it fired at 1,200 rounds per minute, giving an easily-recognized "tearing cloth" noise. The gun was designed to be mass-produced by stamping most of the parts from sheet steel, leaving the minimum of precise machining to be done.

LONG-RANGE ARTILLERY

T HE PARIS gun and Big Bertha (see Heavy and super-heavy artillery, page 122) remained in German memory, and when the Army began to expand again in 1933, long-range guns were on the list of development projects. It was envisaged that any future war would be highly mobile, so heavy weapons would have to be mobile. But this implied the construction of railway artillery, and several German railway guns were designed, of which three were outstanding.

To out-bid the Paris Gun in range, the 21-cm K12(E) — E for *Eisenbahn* ("railway") — was developed by Krupp. This had a barrel 33.3m long, supported on a massive carriage with 36 wheels. The wheels were arranged on four bogies, two beneath a subframe at the front and back of the main mounting. This mounting was separate from the carriage and could slide backwards in recoil across the subframes. The gun barrel could also recoil within the main mounting, so that two independent recoil systems absorbed the firing shock. The barrel was rifled with eight deep grooves and the shell was machined with eight curved ribs which fitted into the grooves. The whole weapon weighed 302 tons and fired its 107-kg shell to a range of 115km. Two sets were built and were stationed on the French coast in 1940, firing shells into Kent in south eastern England. But this effort had no military significance and they saw little use thereafter. Krupp's engineers were of the opinion that as guns, they were a waste of effort. But as ballistic research tools, they were magnificent.

Concurrently with the K12(E), the 28-cm K5(E) was developed as the standard Army railway gun and 25 were eventually built. This had a similar deep-grooved barrel and ribbed shell, and in standard form fired a 255-kg shell to 62-km range. A rocket-boosted shell was then developed, increasing the range to 86.5km. Later a 31-cm smoothbore barrel was built and a special dart-like shell with fins

Leopold

This German 28-cm K5(E) gun was the standard railway super-heavy gun and eventually out-performed everything else. This particular equipment, called "Leopold" by its crew, was known to Allied troops as "Anzio Annie", because it fired into the Anzio beach-head in Italy in 1944. causing considerable damage. The ribbed shell can be seen on the loading platform behind the breech.

The Rocket-assisted shell
(ABOVE) *The high explosive "Ro-Granate 4331" rocket-assisted shell fired by Leopold. The solid-fuel rocket occupies the front half of the shell, with its blast pipe running centrally to the base. The high-explosive payload was around the blast pipe, safely insulated from the heat. The time fuze in the nose ignited the rocket 19 seconds after firing.*

SUPERGUNS

All guns work on the same basic principle: a charge of powder is burned in a tube with a closed end, generating gas which expands and drives a projectile out of the tube. The range reached by the projectile depends entirely upon the velocity at which it leaves the tube. Therefore, in order to increase the range, the velocity must be increased, and there are a number of ways of doing this.

The amount of propelling charge can be increased, or a more powerful substance can be used. Increasing the power of the charge brings problems with barrel wear and may require a redesign of the gun chamber. There is also a considerable increase in operating cost.

Another method of increasing a gun's range is to lengthen the barrel. Increasing the chamber pressure also improves velocity, but this demands a complete redesign of the gun.

A further adaptation that will increase the gun's velocity is to reduce the weight of the projectile. However, the lighter projectile also loses its "carrying power" and although initially faster will actually not reach so far as the original full-weight projectile.

There is, of course, no theoretical reason why these methods of increasing range should not be employed; there is, though, the practical drawback that guns of greater weight and with longer barrels become difficult to manoeuvre and operate, harder to emplace and conceal, expensive to manufacture and maintain. Such problems would have beset the so-called Iraqi "Supergun" for which many claims have been made. This was no more than the huge chamber, long barrel and lightweight projectile combination solution, theoretically sound but, because it had to be built into a hillside, totally impractical. Its maximum range against ground targets, based upon what is known of its charge and barrel length, is likely to have been less than 100 miles, a long way from the world-girdling performance postulated. In fact, it appears that the inventor's prime purpose was to make a simple device for launching satellites; once viewed in this light the proposal makes some degree of sense.

---

designed at the Peenemünde guided-missile establishment. This increased the range to an incredible 151km, so in fact, the "workhorse" outranged the specialized long-range K12(E) by a considerable margin.

The third monster railway gun designed by the Germans during the Second World War were the largest-calibre guns ever built, the 80-cm railway guns "Gustav" and "Dora". They were built by Krupp in response to a request from Hitler for guns capable of destroying the fortifications of the Maginot Line. As it turned out, they were not ready in time, but were used during the sieges of Sebastopol and Leningrad. They were then destroyed. Some parts were found at the end of the war but not enough to assemble a complete gun.

Gustav and Dora had to be taken to pieces in order to fit within the railway loading gauge, and assembled at the firing site. This task took about three weeks. Twin railway tracks were laid down and the bogey assemblies shunted onto them. Then the superstructure was built up, the gun barrel assembled, the breech fitted, and the gun assembled to the recoil system. When completed, the gun weighed 1,350 tons, was 42.9m long, and was operated and guarded by a force of 1,420 men. It fired a 7-ton concrete-piercing shell to 38km or a 4.8-ton high explosive shell to 47km.

THE END OF LONG-RANGE ARTILLERY

In addition to these weapons, which actually became operational, several other projects were discussed. One was an electric solenoid gun firing a 15-cm shell, to be installed in Belgium and fired against London. Another was a multiple-chamber gun, also of 15-cm calibre, with a projected range of 88km. There was also a projected smoothbore version of Gustav firing a finned shell to 160km. Much time and energy was wasted on these projects, all of which came to nothing.

On the Allied side there was only one long-range artillery project, and this was more a test-bed than a weapon. Known as "Bruce", it was a 13.5-inch naval gun with an 8-inch barrel

The US 14-inch M1920
The 14-inch M1920 was a railway gun which could be dismounted and emplaced for coast defence or long range firing, as seen here.

inserted, so that the 8-inch shell was propelled by the 13.5-inch charge, giving a range of 100km. Used for high-altitude research, the gun became unserviceable after firing about 30 shots.

In postwar years, the Americans started the HARP (High Altitude Research Project) which was more or less a continuation of the Bruce idea. A 16-inch US Navy gun, aimed vertically, fired lightweight projectiles into the stratosphere for high-altitude research into rocket and space developments.

However, the use of artillery for extremely long ranges was futile once accurate aerial bombing and ground attack became established on the battlefield. The last of the big guns to see military service was the American 280-mm M65 "Atomic Cannon". This appeared in 1952, firing a 272-kg nuclear shell to a range of 29km. An ingenious design, carried between two tractors, it was a cumbersome weapon to manoeuvre on roads and a sitting target for enemy aircraft. If that was true in the 1950s, it is certainly true today.

SELF-PROPELLED ARTILLERY

SELF-PROPELLED (SP) artillery — field artillery mounted on a tracked or wheeled chassis — falls into two broad groups: self-propelled guns that are used in the same manner as other field artillery but have greater mobility; and guns that are used to give close mobile fire support to the infantry.

Apart from some impractical pre-1914 attempts to mount air-defence guns on motor cars, the first self-propelled guns worthy of the name were designed in France, shortly after the appearance of

Bumble-Bee in Russia
"Hummel" (Bumble-Bee) was the German name for this 15-cm self-propelled howitzer, here in use on the Eastern Front in 1944. It consisted of the standard 15-cm Model 18 field howitzer mounted on a chassis derived from PzKw III and IV tank components. This was the nearest the German Army got to an SP field artillery piece as opposed to a direct-fire assault gun, but by the time they were issued in mid-1944 the war had turned against the Germans and most Hummel were used as assault guns, irrespective of what they had been designed to do.

the tank. If the tracked tank could overcome muddy terrain, then it made sense to apply the same system to guns, since they were often unable to advance fast enough to assist the infantry in an attack. A number of 155-mm guns were mounted on tracked chassis designed by Schneider and St Chamond, but they proved unreliable and the experiments were abandoned. Similar vehicles were built in the USA, notably by Walter Christie who later became famous for his tank designs, but these, too, never got beyond the experimental stage.

The next development occurred in 1926 when the British Army built the "Birch Gun", named after the then Master-General of the Ordnance. This was a Vickers tank chassis fitted with a special mounting for the 18-pounder gun, allowing it to be used either as a field gun or in an anti-aircraft role. Six were built and formed a battery of SP artillery in the Experimental Mechanised Force which lasted from 1926 to 1928. After the disbandment of the Force, the idea was dropped, largely, it seems, because of doubt as to which formation — the Royal Artillery or the Tank Corps — was to operate the guns.

The next move came from the German army who, perhaps considering the likelihood of operations in eastern Europe and the western USSR, demanded an infantry support gun capable of keeping up with the Panzer divisions. The SIG (Schweres Infanterie Geschutz) 33 was designed to meet this specification. This was a 15-cm howitzer mounted in an open superstructure on the light Pzkw I tank chassis. The first batch of these was issued in 1940 and improved versions followed. Altogether, 282 were built before production ceased in 1944. It was followed by "Hummel", a

Soviet heavyweight
The SU-152 assault gun, was developed in 1943 by placing their standard 152-mm field gun on to a hull based on the KV-1 heavy tank; this was changed to the hull of the Josef Stalin (IS) tank, and thus became the ISU-152. A simple weapon, it was designed for short-range direct fire against
obstacles and strongpoints. After 1945 numbers were given to other Communist armies; they remained in use until the early 1970s.

longer 15-cm howitzer mounted on a Pzkw III chassis, of which about 660 were built. Both of these were "pure" SP guns, insofar as they operated like towed artillery, but they were more agile across country.

Most SP guns produced by Germany were assault guns. They used various types of tank chassis, often captured or obsolete, and had a closed superstructure to protect the gun but no turret. Almost as well armoured as tanks, they could head an assault, firing directly at strongpoints and enemy weapons. As the German war in Europe turned to the defensive phase, this type of weapon, which was cheaper and quicker to produce than tanks and often equally effective in defensive positions, gradually outnumbered tanks in the production schedules.

The first British SP to enter service was the "Bishop", a 25-pounder in a large armoured box on top of a Valentine tank chassis. It was used in North Africa in 1942. The box restricted the elevation, and hence the range, but the Bishop was useful and gave some valuable experience in the tactical handling of SP artillery. The British then adopted the American M7, which they called the "Priest". (These two started a tradition of clerical names which has continued ever since.) The Priest mounted the American 105-mm gun but the British Army asked for a version that could carry its own 25-pounder, which had a better range. The Americans were reluctant to produce something that they could not use themselves, so the request was passed to Canada. There a version of the American M4 tank, known as the "Ram", had been developed earlier but had been abandoned as a fighting tank. This was now converted to an SP gun by putting an open

The M7 "Priest"

The American 105-mm Gun Motor Carriage M7 (TOP RIGHT) was the standard 105-mm field howitzer mounted on a hull based on the M3 tank. It was issued in April 1942. Later versions used M4 Sherman bodies. The nickname "Priest", given by the British, arose because of the pulpit-like anti-aircraft machine gun position.

superstructure on the chassis and mounting the 25-pounder. This combination became known as the "Sexton", a highly efficient and popular weapon which remained in service with some armies until the 1980s. The other important British SP was the "Archer", a 17-pounder anti-tank gun mounted on a highly modified Valentine chassis. It proved to be very effective.

US AND SOVIET SP GUNS

The USA, with its enormous automobile industry and penchant for mechanized warfare, embraced the SP idea enthusiastically and scores of designs were put forward. The first model to enter

service was the 75-mm M3 "Gun Motor Carriage", in which the standard 75-mm gun was mounted on a half-track truck and fired over the cab. A handful were used in the Philippines in 1941–2 and some went to North Africa in 1942, but they were not very effective.

A more serious and worthwhile design was the GMC M7 — a standard 105-mm howitzer fitted in an open-topped M3 tank chassis. This was used throughout the war by both the US and British Armies. Next came the 155-mm SP M12, a 155-mm French gun dating from 1917, which was placed on the chassis of a M3 tank. However, the Allied Forces seemed unsure of what to do with a large-calibre SP gun and most of them were stored away until late 1943. A number were then refurbished and were used in the Allied invasion of Europe. Its success confirmed the value of heavy SP artillery and encouraged new designs. The M12 design is noteworthy because it introduced the idea of fitting a bulldozer blade to the rear of the chassis to absorb the recoil shock.

The American contribution to anti-tank SP design was the M10, a modified M3 tank with an open-topped turret, which carried a 3-inch gun. While adequate when introduced in 1942, by 1944 it was falling behind in the gun–tank race, so the British removed the 3-inch gun and replaced it with their own high-velocity 17-pounder, calling it the Achilles.

The Soviets used SP weapons only as assault guns and fitted the biggest-calibre guns the chassis could carry. The first was the SU-76, a 76-mm anti-tank gun mounted on a chassis derived from an earlier light tank and given an open-topped turret. They then moved up to the SU-85, based on the T34 tank chassis with an armoured superstructure that mounted the gun in the front face. Shortly afterwards the T34 was fitted with the 85-mm gun, and the SU85 was upgraded by being given a 100-mm gun. Finally, in 1943, came two really heavy weapons, the ISU-122 and the ISU-152. Both were built on the chassis of the KV-1 heavy tank and mounted a 122-mm and 152-mm gun respectively. These could give massive support and, because of their relatively long range, could also, if necessary, function as indirect-fire artillery.

MORTARS: 1918 TO THE PRESENT

AT THE end of the 1914–18 war, the Stokes mortar had become more or less the accepted standard, since it was simple to make and use and delivered a useful bomb with a reasonable degree of accuracy. Gunmakers began to make slight improvements, notably Edgar Brandt of France, who designed a family of 60-mm and 81-mm mortars which were purchased all over the world and built under licence in many countries. Brandt mortars formed the basis for designs in the USA, Italy, and Japan. Britain adopted the Stokes 3-inch mortar and, after trying various other types, a Spanish 2-inch design in the late 1930s.

The cheapness of mortars meant they could be supplied in considerable numbers. The French Army, for example, had 8,000 81-mm Brandt mortars in service in 1939 and the Germans probably as many of their own version of the 81-mm weapon. Half the world's mortars were based on the Brandt design, with the result that most European medium mortars had the same calibre of 81-mm. When the Second World War came, the various armies found that they could fire the other side's bombs quite safely, though this discovery was more advantageous to the Germans than anybody else since they captured huge stocks in the course of 1939–40.

By 1939, there were the light 50-60-mm mortars, sometimes called "grenade throwers", though they actually fired finned

The US 81-mm M1 mortar
The 81 mm has been the standard US company mortar since 1938. This original M1 is being laid by two men; the man behind the sight lays for direction, while the man in front constantly corrects the elevation as the mortar pivots on its baseplate. The 81-mm M1 fired a 7-lb bomb to 3,290 yards or a 10-lb bomb to 2,560 yards.

> *On this, as on other occasions, we noticed the ability of the German to lie low during the day, but at the same time maintain the most effective watch on our movements. Any carelessness in exposure or movement on our part, by groups of either men or vehicles, drew down the inevitable mortar fire.*
>
> Lt. Col. A.E.C. Bredin, DSO, MC.
> Three Assault Landings.

bombs. The medium 81/82-mm class mortars were the work horses while the heavy 105/120-mm group had a formidable punch. Britain was unique in having a 3-inch (76-mm) as their principal mortar. Its inadequacies were a handicap to British infantry units throughout the war — the bomb was lacking in both lethality and range.

Britain, Germany, and the USA were of the opinion that a future war would involve gas (see Gas warfare, page 118), and they all had specially trained gas troops equipped with heavy mortars. Germany settled on a multiple 105-mm model called the "Nebelwerfer", which also had the role of firing smoke rounds as well as gas. Britain and the USA, quite independently, both settled on 107-mm calibre for their chemical mortars, but as it became clear that gas was unlikely to be used and that useful weapons were standing idle, high explosive 107-mm bombs were developed. Both weapons took their place as infantry support mortars with great success.

Both were rather unusual designs. The British one was eventually provided with a wheeled baseplate and issued to the artillery as a light support weapon, while the American mortar was rifled. Most mortars are smoothbored and drop-fired; the bomb has a percussion cartridge in its tail and, when dropped down the barrel, this strikes the firing pin and fires the bomb. With a rifled mortar, as with rifled muzzle-loading artillery, the problem is to allow the bomb to drop freely but make it engage with the rifling on its way out. This was solved by having a saucer-like copper plate beneath the American bomb (which had no fins) and this expanded under the pressure of the propellant gas and bit into the rifling.

Undoubtedly the best mortar to emerge from the 1939-45 war

was the Soviet 120-mm M1938, which was captured in considerable numbers by the Germans. They were so impressed with it that they copied it as the Granatwerfer 42 and used it by the thousand. Firing a 34-lb bomb to 6,000m at a rate of 15 a minute, it was as effective as light artillery and, with a wheeled trailer mount, a good deal more agile. It was this mortar, and its success in German and Soviet hands, that set the postwar fashion for 120-mm mortars.

There were also advances in mortar ammunition. In 1939, the mortar bomb was a simple cast-iron bomb filled with cheap explosive and fitted with an impact fuze. But as the mortar's potential value was appreciated, the projectile that it fired was changed to a stronger casing with a larger volume of a more efficient explosive with a fully machined surface to reduce skin friction with the air and so improve its range.

One limitation of the mortar bomb was that it could not burst in the air over the target, which was often useful in searching behind cover and into trenches. Time fuzes were not acceptable to the infantry, who preferred to keep their gunnery simple. The Germans found a solution in the guise of the "bouncing bomb" that they developed for the 81-mm mortar. This contained an impact fuze and a loose head carrying a small charge of low explosive. On impact, the fuze set off the first charge, which blew off the head and, in so doing, blew the bomb back up into the air. A delay element detonated it a fraction of a second later when it was a few yards above the ground. The precise effect depended on the ground: if this was too soft it would bury itself before functioning, but it was highly effective on the whole.

After 1945 the mortar was reassessed in the light of its wartime performance. Suddenly the 120-mm mortar became a desirable weapon and it has since been further developed, notably by Hotchkiss-Brandt of France and Tampella of Finland. Several countries have simply copied the Soviet and German wartime model, with just a few modern improvements.

The principal recent advance in mortar design has been the development of more gas-efficient bombs. These were pioneered by the British with their 81-mm mortar, which was developed in the 1960s. The bomb is carefully machined to be a close fit in the barrel of the mortar but leaves just enough "windage" — free play — to allow it to drop freely down the barrel. To compensate for the windage, there is a groove around the body of the bomb containing a carefully-shaped plastic ring. The gas generated by the propellant forces this ring outward, tight against the bore, to make a very efficient gas seal. This simple measure improved the range of the bomb by some 30 per cent, and canting the fins to generate a slight spin improved the accuracy by an equal amount. The mortar is now accepted as a moderately precise weapon, rather than, as previously, an "area saturation" weapon. The design was adopted by the US Army and similar improvements can be seen on bombs developed in other countries in the past 20 years.

Miniature proximity fuzes have also been developed, using solid state electronics. With their introduction, the mortar bomb has now become almost as versatile as an artillery shell, giving the infantry the ability to burst bombs in the air for increased lethal effect against well dug-in opponents.

Another recent advance has been the mounting of mortars inside armoured vehicles and firing out of a hatch. Emplacing a mortar under fire is a dangerous business, since mortars are feared and their operators are a prime target. Carrying the mortar inside an armoured vehicle gives it a "shoot and scoot" capability, highly desirable on the modern battlefield, where a combination of radar and computers is used to locate the enemy mortar positions from the bomb trajectory.

The British 81-mm L16 mortar
This British mortar (RIGHT) *set new standards of accuracy. The ammunition in front of the mortar includes high explosive and illuminating bombs, weighing 9 lbs and ranging to 6,175 yards.*

The computer age
Norwegian troops (LEFT) *firing a British 81-mm mortar and using the "Hugin" fire-control computer. This hand-held computer will calculate firing data, weather corrections and fuze timing.*

HARNESSING FIRE AT SEA, ON LAND, AND IN THE AIR

FLAME WEAPONS

Flamethrower M9
A US Marine, face coated with anti-burn cream, armed with a flamethrower M9 during the battle for Guadalcanal, August 1942. The M9 carried four US gallons of fluid which was ignited by cartridges in the casing around the nozzle. It had a range of about 50 yards.

GREEK FIRE is said to have been invented by Callinicus of Heliopolis in AD 668. According to reports of the time, it could burn under water. The exact composition of Greek Fire is uncertain, but is believed to have been a mixture of sulphur, pitch, naphtha, and quicklime. It was packed in tubes and thrown like a modern grenade and was also discharged from tubes in the bows of galleys. The secret was remarkably well-kept and the terror it inspired lasted for many centuries.

The problem with fire is being able to project it for any useful distance. It fell into disuse when the secret of Greek Fire was lost and was replaced as a long-distance weapon by the siege engine (see Engines, page 30) and, eventually, cannon. Artillerymen attempted to make incendiary projectiles of various sorts and had reasonable success, but these scarcely inspired the sort of terror that the roaring flames of Greek Fire had produced.

Der Flammenwerfer
A German flamethrower in operation on the Western Front in 1918. The relaxed stance of the men suggests that this was a training exercise rather than actual combat. An interesting point is the presence of the NCO holding a long stick with a burning tip, suggesting that the ignition system of the flamethrower was not as reliable as it might have been. This is the "trench" model, in which the tank and nitrogen cylinder were emplaced in a trench and the launcher was at the end of a hose long enough to be brought into the open and used as a defensive weapon against an assault.

The terrifying effect of liquid flames reappeared on the battle-field in 1915 as the flame-thrower. Originally, the Germans might have intended the flame-thrower to act as a blow-torch for cutting through barbed-wire entanglements. However, it was first used as an assault weapon at the Battle of Hooge on 30 July, 1915, and was quickly adopted by the other combatants.

The German machine came in two forms. One had a reservoir of 200 litres of liquid and was fired from the cover of a trench. The other had a 5-litre tank and was carried on a man's back. In both cases, the liquid — a petrol-naphtha mixture — was ejected by a cylinder of pressurized nitrogen. The liquid was fed through a flexible hose into a rigid lance-like tube which had a simple ignition device at its tip to light the fluid as it squirted out. The trench model had a range of about 200 yards while the man-carried version was effective up to 30 yards.

People fear flame, and soldiers are no exception. The result was

that any soldier with a flame-thrower attracted a deluge of gunfire as soon as he appeared, and his life expectancy was short. His only chance of carrying out his assigned role was to give him a "bodyguard" of riflemen and grenadiers to protect him.

THE "MOLOTOV COCKTAIL"

The tanks used during the Spanish Civil War were very crude and the petrol bomb was devised as a response. This was simply a wine bottle filled with petrol, with a burning rag as a stopper. Thrown against the engine cover or hatches of a tank, the bottle broke and the ignited petrol ran into the engine compartment or the interior and set the tank ablaze. Even if the tank was not disabled, the flames and smoke made life difficult for the tank crew and obscured their vision.

The petrol bomb reappeared in the hands of the Finns fighting the Soviet invasion in the Winter War of 1939. At that time, the Soviet Air Force was using an incendiary device consisting of a casing carrying several smaller bombs. Released from the plane as a

Flamethrower M2
The M2 flamethrower, another Second World War US Army weapon, in use in the Pacific theatre in 1944. This view shows the two fuel tanks, holding four US gallons and the pressure tank holding compressed air. The launcher nozzle held five ignition charges, allowing the operator to fire up to five two-second bursts to a range of about 60 yards. This photograph shows the employment of three Browning automatic rifles to protect the two flamethrower operators, a necessary tactic to keep enemy heads down while the flamethrowers exposed themselves. Without such protection the flamethrower men were likely to be killed before they could get off a shot.

single unit, it then split open to shower the area beneath with the small bombs. These were christened "Molotov's Breadbaskets" by the press (after Vyachislav Molotov, who was then Soviet Foreign Minister), and, by extension, the petrol bomb became the "Molotov Cocktail".

While waiting for Hitler in 1940, the British built a number of flame devices as anti-invasion weapons. Experiments were even made with petrol floating on the sea to engulf the invasion barges in flames. This idea turned out to be quite impractical but it made good propaganda. More practical were the various types of inland flame trap to ambush any invading forces. These generally consisted of a primitive mortar, electrically fired, which hurled a 40-gallon drum of petrol and oil mixture into a roadway, or an electrically released drum of fluid which flowed into a roadway, to blaze away there.

The back-pack flame-thrower returned later in the war. It seems to have been used mostly by the US troops in the Far East, and was of particular value in clearing caves and concealed bunkers on the Pacific islands.

The British developed tank-borne flame-projectors and used them to great effect in Normandy in 1944. Among them was the "Crocodile", a Churchill tank towing an armoured trailer full of FTF ("flame-throwing fluid", a thickened petrol mixture) with a powerful projector mounted in the tank hull.

The flame-thrower remains on the inventory of most armies. The pressurized-cylinder type is standard, but one-shot, throw-away devices are also in service. These are small cylinders that can easily be carried by a soldier, and that can emit a short stream of flame sufficient to worry the occupants of a small strongpoint.

NAPALM

Napalm is a granular aluminium soap based on naphthenic and palmitic acids, and is added to gasoline so as to thicken it. In popular usage, the word simply means the resulting thickened gasoline used as an incendiary agent. In 1940 the US Army Air Force tested bombs filled with gasoline as incendiary bombs, but it was found that as soon as the bomb exploded the gasoline vaporized and burned out before it had time to ignite the target. A thickening agent was needed to make the gasoline burn more slowly, and various expedients were tried before napalm was discovered in 1942. Bombs filled with napalm were thereafter used against targets in Europe and the Pacific theatre. In a raid on the Focke-Wulf aircraft factory in Marienburg, East Prussia in October 1943 US Flying Fortresses dropped over 13,000 100-pound napalm bombs which completely destroyed the works. During the Luzon campaign in the Philippines in 1944, air units dropped 1,054,200 gallons of napalm on a variety of targets. Against inflammable targets the 100-pound napalm bomb was found to be 12 times as effective as a 500-pound high explosive bomb.

As a field weapon — as used by American forces in the Vietnam War, for instance — napalm is used to flush defenders out of hiding and thus expose them to more conventional methods of attack such as machine-gun and artillery fire. The effect, against troops in dugouts and foxholes, is to burn up the oxygen and thus cause them to suffocate even when the flame does not actually touch them. (This suffocation theory is frequently disputed by theorists but not by soldiers who have actually experienced napalm in use and seen its results.) Furthermore, the effect of napalm is not localized; it is usually dropped in quantity from a low level, and the combination of height and speed ensures that the flaming napalm rolls forwards and outwards to cover several hundred square yards from the point of impact. The explosion is more severe than might be imagined and the blast can do damage to individuals and structures not hit by the flames. Thus a napalm bomb directed against a legitimate military point target can well have severe effects against civilian life and property in the vicinity. It is for this reason that efforts are being made to restrict or even prohibit the use of napalm and similar incendiary agents.

EXPLOSIVE
POWER
DELIVERED
BY HAND
AND GUN

MODERN GRENADES

MOST OF the hand and rifle grenades of the 1914–18 war were hastily improvised, and as soon as the war was over the armies got rid of them, retaining only the safest and most efficient designs. They then set about designing new types but few designs appeared that were better than the wartime best. The British Mills No. 36, the German stick grenade, the French pineapple became the standards and were in service when war broke out again in 1939.

One drawback with these grenades was that they all used a time fuze. Even with a time as short as four seconds a fizzing grenade could be scooped up by the intended victim and thrown back or, at least, out of harm's way. The solution was to develop a grenade that would detonate on impact.

This was easier said than done. A lobbed grenade can land in any attitude, but impact fuzes were directional — if the projectile did not land nose-first, the fuze would not function. What was needed was an "all-ways" fuze — one that would function on striking in any attitude. Such fuzes were developed before the outbreak of the Second World War. They usually consisted of a steel ball between two conical faces, so that whichever way the ball moved, one face, with a firing pin, was driven onto a detonator. This meant that the firing action had to be delayed until the grenade was in flight. The usual method of achieving this was by a safety pin attached to a long ribbon with a weight. Throwing the grenade caused the ribbon to unwrap, until the weight finally pulled out the pin so that the grenade was "armed".

One such grenade was the Italian "Red Devil", so called from its colour and its habit of not always detonating on impact but lying inert until someone tripped over it. Another was the British No. 69, consisting of a bakelite casing full of explosive. It was intended to shock by blast rather than kill by fragments, so as to allow the attackers to enter a building while the occupants were still dazed.

The grenade was also put forward as an anti-tank device. The early models were bulky, relying entirely upon blast to break tracks or damage the engine cooling system. The invention of the hollow or shaped charge made more handy anti-tank grenades feasible. Perhaps the best was the German Panzerwurfmine, probably first used in combat early in 1942 and consisting of a large conical head with the shaped charge attached to a throwing handle with a canvas streamer; these ensured that the grenade landed nose-first against the tank so that the shaped charge had the best chance of piercing the armour.

Some grenades were less successful, including the British sticky grenade developed early in the Second World War. This was a glass globe filled with blasting gelatine and coated with a strong adhesive. It was fitted with a handle containing a firing lever, a safety pin, and a delay fuze. The globe was protected by two metal hemispheres when in store. To use the grenade, the pin was removed, allowing the metal casing to fall away and expose the adhesive surface. The grenade was then ready to throw at or, better, jam against a tank with the lever released. When the gelatine detonated, the explosion severely damaged the tank. The danger for the user was that he could easily stick the bomb to his trousers. Few sticky grenades were ever used in combat.

The Red Devil
The Italian Breda Model 35 hand grenade was coloured a vivid red and had two safety devices. One, the prominent ribbed tag in the picture, was withdrawn before throwing. The other flew off during flight, leaving the grenade armed and ready to detonate on arrival. However, the fuze was somewhat sensitive to direction and, on soft desert sand, frequently failed to go off. On being disturbed by a careless foot, though, it frequently did go off, which, with its colour, was why British troops called it the "Red Devil".

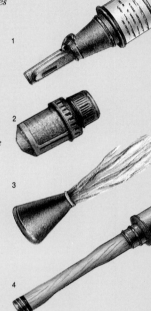
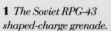

GRENADE TYPES

There are several varieties of grenade, each developed for specific battlefield purposes. Smoke grenades, for instance, can be used as anti-personnel weapons as well as for concealment; anti-tank grenades give infantry the ability to immobilize armour.

1 *The Soviet RPG-43 shaped-charge grenade.*
2 *The British No 77 WP grenade.*
3 *The Japanese Type 3 anti-tank grenade.*
4 *The German Steilhandgranate (stick grenade).*

> **"** *In more recent years we have proceeded more or less according to the theory that since an average American knows how to throw a rock, it is a waste of training time to devote any large amount of attention to grenade technique. In consequence, though approximately 40 percent of American troops have good throwing arms, our grenade tactics are for the most part mediocre, with just here and there an occasional brilliant performance.* **"**

Brigadier General S.L.A. Marshall:
Infantry Operations and Weapons
Usage in Korea, 1952.

Rifle grenades
*Three generations of rifle
grenade (RIGHT).
They are from left
to right: the Energa anti-
tank shaped charge
grenade from 1946; an
FN/Luchaire bullet trap
grenade from the 1970s;
an FN telescoping bullet-
through grenade of 1990.
Beneath the grenades are
their launching
cartridges.*

**A German cup
launcher**
*A German soldier inserts
a rifle grenade into the
"schiessbecher" cup
discharge attached to a
Mauser rifle (LEFT).*

**The telescoping
grenade**
*The telescoping grenade,
seen above right, is shown
(RIGHT) in its extended
form slipped over the
muzzle of an assault rifle.
Once launched it will
contract once more,
arming the fuze.*

RIFLE GRENADES

As well as hand grenades rifle grenades were also designed in quantity. The British stayed with their Mills grenade fitted with a baseplate and fired from a cup on the muzzle of the rifle, a system developed in 1916. In 1940 they also added the No. 68 anti-tank grenade, a finned canister containing a shaped charge, which was moderately effective against lighter tanks. The Germans developed a rifled cup discharger to fit the standard Mauser Gewehr 98 rifle and a wide range of grenades to be fired from it. These had pre-rifled driving bands which, like the old rifled muzzle-loading guns, had to be engaged with the grooves in the cup but which gave very good accuracy when fired. However, the grenade was restricted to the diameter of the cup, which was only 30mm, so that although satisfactory explosive and smoke grenades could be made, a worthwhile shaped charge could not be fitted into the available space. This difficulty was met by making an oversized warhead, which sat outside the rifle cup when loaded, and so could be somewhat larger than the body of the grenade, allowing a more effective shaped charge to be used.

The US Army developed a better method of launching grenades from a rifle. A tubular attachment was made to fit the muzzle of the rifle and then grenades were built with a hollow tail unit which fitted over the launcher tube. As with other rifle-launched grenade types, a special blank cartridge (without a bullet) generated the gas which was needed to drive the grenade from the launcher. Grenades incorporating this system were first used in late 1944.

In postwar years this system has replaced all others and is now so standardized that all modern rifles have muzzles that can act as grenade launchers, with a common diameter of 23 mm. Another innovation has been the development of "bullet trap" grenades, in which a hardened steel trap in the tail unit allows the grenade to be launched by firing a normal ball cartridge in the rifle. The bullet strikes the trap and is arrested, and this blow, together with the propellant gas behind the bullet, launches the grenade. This system is especially useful with modern automatic rifles. It saves the soldier the trouble of having to remove the rifle magazine, empty the chamber, hand-load a blank cartridge, fire the grenade, and then replace the magazine and reload the rifle. In times of stress — as when grenades are being fired — such a lengthy performance can lead to dangerous mistakes and to the soldier being caught with an empty rifle.

BURIED

EXPLOSIVES

AND THE

MEANS TO

COUNTER

THEM

LAND MINES

PART OF the siegecraft of the medieval world involved digging beneath the walls of a fortification to make them collapse. Since this delving in the ground resembled a search for metals, it became known as "mining" and the excavations as "mines". After the invention of gunpowder, the mine no longer relied on gravity and the weight of the wall. Filled with gunpowder, a smallish mine could do the necessary damage. In time, such explosives buried in the ground themselves came to be called "mines" or "land mines".

There are references to explosives as far back as the Seven Years War (1756–62) also being buried in the path of attackers, but it was never a common practice. The difficulty of igniting these charges at the right time was considerable before the percussion cap was invented, and even this was prone to mechanical failure. Land mines were used to a small extent on the Western Front in 1917–18, it was not until the Second World War that the mine really came into its own.

One of the lessons of the First World War was that such devices could be useful against tanks; either to immobilize them, or to allow the threat of mines to shepherd the tanks into ground favourable to the defender, where anti-tank guns were positioned to their best advantage.

Anti-tank mines were simple pieces of equipment: a round metal container with a detonator in the centre of the explosive, and a cover plate, supported by a strong spring and bearing a firing pin. The spring was strong enough to support a man's weight but not that of a tank wheel and track, so that the mine automatically selected the right target. From this simple beginning, refinements were added. A second detonator was placed underneath the mine, coupled to a pull-firing device anchored into the ground as the mine was buried. Anyone digging it up and simply lifting it from its hole would pull the firing switch

Scorpion
The first flailing tank was the "Scorpion", a converted Matilda tank with an external engine

driving the flail. The main defect was that the flail operator had to sit outside the tank.

> ❝ *In the Buthidaung area of the Arakan the enemy made some very powerful anti-tank mines by using about 10 lbs of ammonal, placing on top of it a short piece of board and on top of that an ordinary anti-tank mine with its actuating mechanism downwards, and on top of that again another anti-tank mine with the mechanism upwards.* ❞

Notes from Theatres of War No 19: Burma, 1943/44. *British War Office, May 1945.*

TYPES OF LAND MINE

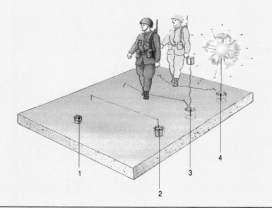

Land mines are laid either to make a physical barrier in front of a defended area or to deny access to an area and thus force an advancing enemy to use a route which can be more easily defended by artillery or other means. Anti-tank mines are the primary barrier; anti-personnel mines are laid to make it more hazardous to remove the anti-tank mines as well as to provide a direct threat to infantry.

Anti-tank mines
1 *Bar mines increase the chance of being struck by a track.*
2 *Pressure mines need to be directly struck.*
3 *Influence mines rely upon noise, vibration or magnetic effects.*
4 *Off-route mines, are also fired by influence or by remote control*

Anti-personnel mines
1 *Stepped on directly.*
2 *Activated by a trip wire to detonate underfoot.*
3 and 4 *Bounding mines are ejected from the ground so as to burst at body height.*

The Sherman Crab
When the Sherman became the standard Allied medium tank, the "Scorpion" principle was adapted to it, with some improvements. The driver now had full command of the flailing system, which could be raised or lowered hydraulically and which had an automatic height control when flailing. Since he could see nothing but dust when flailing he also had a gyro-compass.

and detonate the mine. Then came counting devices: a ratchet mechanism which would allow, say, five vehicles to cross the mine unharmed and detonate under the sixth. This could worry a convoy of vehicles, since it suggested that they were in the middle of a minefield and the first five had been lucky. They would then waste time looking for non-existent mines.

To counter the mine it had to be found and neutralized, and the most difficult part was finding it. In 1938 the Polish Army invented an electronic mine detector that could be carried by one man. As the operator swept it across his path, it emitted an electrical field which became unbalanced by the presence of metal beneath it, causing a note to sound in the operator's headphones. The spot was then marked and someone came along to uncover and defuze the mine. The Polish detector was adopted by the British in 1940 and soon the Germans had a similar device in use.

The Germans then hit upon the idea of making their mines non-metallic. There was no particular reason why a blast mine should be of metal, and it was soon found that plastic, glass, papier-mâché, or even wood were perfectly good materials for anti-tank mines and could not be detected electronically. A wooden mine called the Holzmine 42 was used by the Germans in the North African Desert in mid 1942. Non-metal mines were also used in France in 1944.

The British response to this was not to search for mines but simply to set them off harmlessly. This technique was first explored in North Africa where conditions were ideal for both mining and countermeasures. It involved fitting a tank with heavy rollers in front so that it pushed the roller across the mine and detonated it. The counting device tended to defeat this technique, so the idea was changed to using a rotating drum to which lengths of chain were attached. The drum was revolved by an engine, and the chains thrashed the ground ahead of the tank; since each chain thrashed several times, and chains overlapped each other, counting devices were soon dealt with.

Anti-personnel mines began by being similar to anti-tank mines but smaller and more sensitive. A small tin of explosive with a firing pin was sufficient to blow off the foot or leg of someone who stepped on it, and a wounded man is a greater logistic burden to an army than a dead one. However, it was decided that one mine, one

casualty was not the most economical use of resources. This sort of reasoning led to the development of "bounding" mines, pioneered by the German S-mine.

The S-mine, probably first developed in 1935 and used in the North African Campaign in 1941, was a buried pot containing a small explosive charge and a cylindrical mine filled with explosives and metal. The explosive charge was controlled by a cap which could be fired by direct pressure on the sensitive probe extending above the ground, or by tripping over, or cutting, a tripwire attached to the probe. Once triggered, the charge exploded and blew the cylindrical mine into the air where, at a height of about six feet, it detonated, showering the surrounding area with fragments. There was a good chance that such a mine could strike three or four men instead of just the one who had set it off. It was shortly copied by Britain and the USA, and gradually became one of the most important and dangerous types of anti-personnel mine.

MINES AFTER THE SECOND WORLD WAR

In postwar years the development of mines continued, with plastic components used to prevent detection, and aided by new technology. Anti-tank mines now have shaped charges to blow holes in the bottom of the tank, and are equipped with sensors that react to the noise or vibration of a tank, rather than having to rely on the tank running over the mine. "Off-route" mines are common. These shaped-charge mines are placed alongside a track to strike at the side of a passing tank. They, too, use a variety of sensors, some fitted with counting devices, while others are "self-sterilizing" — that is after a given period of time they destroy themselves so as not to endanger friendly troops who may later be advancing in the area.

The countermeasures in use today include those developed in the 1940s, such as rollers or flailing chains being pushed by tanks. A more recent technique is the use of fuel-air explosives. A fuel, such as oil, is sprayed into the air in aerosol form to make an explosive mixture which is then detonated. The blast spreads across the ground and subjects any mines beneath to a massive pressure which sets them off. This is effective over a wide area.

AUTOMATIC CANNON

FOR A long time the word "cannon" was applied to all artillery, but since the 1930s it has referred especially to automatic weapons of 20- to 30-mm calibre. These now form a separate group of weapons, falling between small arms (up to 15-mm calibre) and artillery (from 35-mm calibre).

Like so many other weapons, the automatic cannon was invented and ignored and then re-invented. It can be said to have begun in about 1895 with Maxim's "Pom-Pom" gun, which was simply a Maxim machine-gun of large calibre — 37-mm was chosen because the St Petersburg Convention on warfare forbade the use of explosive projectiles of smaller calibre. The Pom-Pom was used by both sides in the Boer War, but after that most armies could find no tactical place for it, because it required a clear view over about 3,000 yards, and it was subsequently ignored, except for being used briefly as an air-defence weapon in 1914–15.

In 1914, a German named Becker had begun designing a heavy machine gun of 20-mm calibre for the armament of Zeppelins. The design process took a long time, but in 1917 the

The cannon fighter
A Hurricane Mk II armed with two Vickers "S" 40-mm cannon beneath the wings (BELOW). It also carried two .303-inch Browning machine guns for aerial fighting, since the two Vickers were for attacking ground targets and, in particular, tanks. This model was developed in 1941 and first put to use in North Africa.

The Beaufighter
Once described as "two large engines followed closely by an aeroplane", the Bristol Beaufighter (BOTTOM) delivered devastating firepower. It mounted four .303 Browning guns in the left wing, two in the right wing, and four belt-fed 20-mm Hispano-Suiza cannon underneath the nose.

Becker gun went into production, giving Zeppelins and Gotha bombers explosive firepower to use against Allied fighters. When the First World War ended, Becker sold his patents, drawings, and machinery to a Swiss firm, the Seebach Maschinenfabrik, who continued making the Becker gun under the name Semag. Mounted on a light wheeled carriage, it was promoted with a modicum of success as a potential anti-tank gun. However, in 1924 the Seebach company went bankrupt and the patents were taken over by another Swiss firm, the Oerlikon Machine Tool company. They marketed the Semag as the Oerlikon cannon, and sold it throughout the world, describing it variously as an anti-tank gun, a light anti-aircraft gun, and — in its original concept — an aircraft gun.

Other manufacturers entered this new market. Rheinmetall of Germany, through their Swiss subsidiary Solothurn, promoted a 20-mm cannon which the German Navy adopted as an air-defence gun in 1930; Hispano-Suiza, a Spanish-Swiss company based in France, developed a gun to lie between the banks of cylinders in their new V-12 aero-engine. Breda and Scotti of Italy, Hotchkiss of France, and Madsen of Denmark, all manufactured

their own 20-mm weapons, while Hotchkiss also developed a 25-mm design for the French Army.

The use of 20-mm guns as anti-tank weapons did not last long; they were too heavy to be easily portable, and were soon outclassed by the thicker armour of tanks built during the 1930s. But as an air-defence and aircraft weapon the cannon became invaluable. The fighters of the late 1930s used multiple rifle-calibre machine-guns, but as aircraft were built stronger, it was necessary to score more hits to do severe damage, and this was difficult to achieve within the brief time of an aerial engagement. The explosive power of a cannon projectile overcame this problem. Germany had begun using cannon in its aircraft before the Second World War, as had France — but Britain and the USA maintained their faith in machine-guns until battle conditions in 1939–40 demonstrated the advantages of cannon. The Royal Navy then adopted the Oerlikon gun as a light air-defence weapon, after which the RAF began mounting it in fighters such as the Hurricane and Spitfire. The Americans followed suit, and both nations also used the Hispano-Suiza cannon, which, like the Oerlikon, they manufactured under licence.

FAST-FIRING CANNON

After 1945 the cannon became the sole gun armament for aircraft, but it was abandoned as an air-defence weapon because it was inadequate against ground attack high-speed jet aircraft. To be effective in the air it needed a very high rate of fire, since the higher speeds of fighter aircraft made engagement times even

shorter. Only a fast-firing weapon could put enough shells into the target to do damage in the limited time available. To this end, in 1956 the Americans revived the Gatling multiple-barrel gun, driving it with an electric motor. They achieved a rate of fire of 6,000 rounds per minute with a 20-mm Vulcan gun, which they used to arm fighters in the 1960s. The Gatling principle was also adopted by the Soviet armed forces but in 30-mm calibre.

Meanwhile the Oerlikon company, having absorbed Hispano-Suiza in 1970, became the major maker of cannon. It developed a "revolver" gun, based on an experimental German wartime design. Using a single barrel and a revolving chamber block to speed up extraction and loading, the "revolver gun" gave a satisfactory rate of fire without the complication of the revolving mass of barrels in the Gatling gun.

In the 1970s improvements in sighting and fire control rehabilitated the cannon as a light air-defence weapon. Laser rangefinding, electro-optical and lightweight radar acquisition and tracking systems, and low-light television sights made the

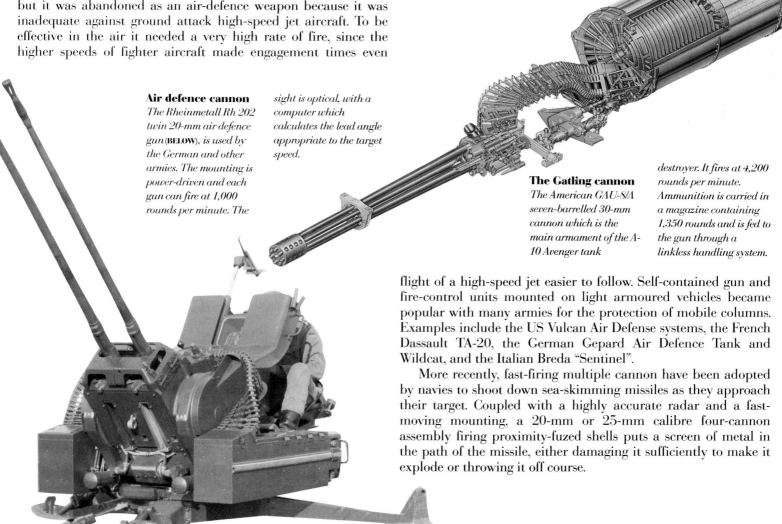

Air defence cannon
The Rheinmetall Rh 202 twin 20-mm air defence gun (BELOW), is used by the German and other armies. The mounting is power-driven and each gun can fire at 1,000 rounds per minute. The

sight is optical, with a computer which calculates the lead angle appropriate to the target speed.

The Gatling cannon
The American GAU-8/A seven-barrelled 30-mm cannon which is the main armament of the A-10 Avenger tank

destroyer. It fires at 4,200 rounds per minute. Ammunition is carried in a magazine containing 1,350 rounds and is fed to the gun through a linkless handling system.

flight of a high-speed jet easier to follow. Self-contained gun and fire-control units mounted on light armoured vehicles became popular with many armies for the protection of mobile columns. Examples include the US Vulcan Air Defense systems, the French Dassault TA-20, the German Gepard Air Defence Tank and Wildcat, and the Italian Breda "Sentinel".

More recently, fast-firing multiple cannon have been adopted by navies to shoot down sea-skimming missiles as they approach their target. Coupled with a highly accurate radar and a fast-moving mounting, a 20-mm or 25-mm calibre four-cannon assembly firing proximity-fuzed shells puts a screen of metal in the path of the missile, either damaging it sufficiently to make it explode or throwing it off course.

BALANCED
RECOIL
FORCES FOR
LIGHTER
ARTILLERY

RECOILLESS GUNS

GENERALLY, THE heaviest part of a conventional gun is the carriage or mounting. To withstand the recoil force from the gun when it fires, a heavy and bulky hydro-pneumatic recoil system is needed, as well as a heavy and robust support to transfer the remaining shock to the ground. If recoil could be eliminated, the system to contain it could be removed and the gun carriage made lighter.

Several inventors tried to achieve this, of whom the first to make a working weapon was Commander Davis of the US Navy in the 1900s. He simply put two gun barrels back to back, with a projectile in one and an equal mass of birdshot and grease in the other. Firing a cartridge in a central chamber blew the two masses out of their respective barrels, and, since the weight and acceleration of both

The German LG1

The 75-mm LG1 was the first recoilless gun to see any extensive use, by the German airborne troops in Crete. It fired the same 13-lb high-explosive shell as the conventional 75-mm field gun, but since most of the propellant gas was ejected from the rear venturi the maximum range was 7,400 yards instead of the 13,450 yards reached by the conventional gun.

was equal, the recoil forces of the two barrels cancelled each other out and the gun remained stationary. A number of these guns, in 57-mm and 76-mm calibre, were purchased by the British Royal Naval Air Service during the First World War as possible anti-submarine weapons. Such guns made it possible to fire a large projectile from a relatively flimsy aircraft but were soon found to inflict damage on the upper wing of the aircraft. Development of the Davis gun was slow and the war ended before it could be used in combat.

During the 1930s the Soviets and the Germans both worked on the idea. Little is known of the Soviet design, though it is said to have been used in Finland in 1940. However, it was probably not very successful since the idea was not pursued during the Second World War. In Germany the firms of Krupp and Rheinmetall co-operated on design, and in 1940 the German paratroops were issued with the 75-mm LG (Light Gun) 1, a simple weapon with a hole in the breech-block leading to a venturi nozzle (that is, a nozzle that first narrows then widens out, thus accelerating the flow of gas). When

Recoilless ammunition

Ammunition for two recoilless guns; left, the British 3.45-inch "Shoulder Gun", right, the American 57-mm M18 recoilless rifle. The British round had a "wallbuster" shell, with plastic filling and base fuze. The cartridge case is pierced with several holes; on firing, the propellant gas passes through and is then channelled to the gun's rear venturi tubes. The American shell is a shaped charge anti-tank shell with a pre-rifled driving band to cut down friction in the bore.

the gun was fired, four-fifths of the propellant gas passed backwards through this nozzle. Since the mass of the gas multiplied by its acceleration equalled the product of mass of the shell and its acceleration, the gun did not recoil. This weapon was used by the German forces in the battle for Crete in May 1941.

The principal defect of the LG1 was that the carriage was too light, and therefore rather flimsy, though later designs in both 75-mm and 105-mm calibre corrected the fault. Crete was the last time German paratroops dropped into battle, and after that the recoilless gun was issued to mountain units and infantry forces.

Britain developed a series of RCL (recoilless) guns based on designs by Sir Dennistoun Burney, an aeronautical engineer. During the Second World War he designed a 20-mm experimental weapon, and the Army encouraged him to produce weapons of 87-mm, 94-mm, and 95-mm calibre. This he did. The 87-mm weapon could be fired from a man's shoulder, while the other two had light wheeled carriages or could be carried in a jeep. The guns were intended for use in the Far East where their light weight would have been of great value, but the war ended before they were ready for service.

The US Army studied the German and British designs and then produced their own. One, for a 105-mm weapon, used the German technique of having a plastic base in the cartridge case which blew out through the breech block venturi nozzle to allow the escape of gas. Two others, 57-mm and 75-mm guns, used Burney's idea of a perforated cartridge case that exhausts into a space around the chamber and from there to the rear by a venturi nozzle. The 105-mm weapon was abandoned, but the 57-mm and 75-mm "Kromuskits" (after their designers, Kroger and Musser) were used with good results in the final phases of the Pacific campaign. They were equipped with high-explosive projectiles for general use and shaped-charge projectiles for dealing with armour.

POSTWAR DEVELOPMENTS

This latter application pointed the way to the future. Conventional anti-tank guns had become too big to be practical (see Anti-tank weapons, page 128), and the lightweight recoilless gun firing a shaped-charge shell looked like it might be the answer. Taking their hasty wartime work as the starting point, Britain and the USA both began development programmes and these resulted in new RCL guns in the 1950s. The USA produced

The 120-mm MOBAT
The BAT gun was gradually improved into the MOBAT — Mobile BAT — which had a much lighter carriage and could, as seen here, be carried in, and fired from, the cargo bed of a Land Rover or similar vehicle. Most countries still employing recoilless guns mount them on light vehicles.

90-mm and 106-mm guns, and Britain the 120-mm BAT (Battalion Anti-Tank) gun. The USSR also went back to first principles and began to manufacture a series of weapons in 73-mm, 82-mm and 107-mm calibres which went into service in the 1960s and were sold around the world.

The disadvantage of the RCL gun is the backblast of flame and hot gas which issues from the venturi behind the gun. This necessitates a clear space at the rear and gives the gun a very recognizable "signature" which advertises its presence. Because of this, today the RCL gun as a major anti-tank defence weapon has largely been supplanted by the light missile.

The recoilless principle was also applied to hand-held weapons. The Germans developed the Panzerfaust in 1942, a simple length of tube with a gunpowder charge which carried a shaped-charge bomb at its front end. The firer tucked it under the arm and fired; the bomb went forwards and the blast went backwards, and the tube was thrown away. Panzerfausts were made by the tens of thousands and were an effective anti-tank weapon at short range. Today a number of simple weapons still use the recoilless principle, such as the Panzerfaust 3, issued to the German Army in 1985. Perhaps the most widespread of these pocket RCL weapons is the Soviet RPG-7, introduced in 1962. This uses a recoilless charge to launch an anti-tank rocket, which ignites and accelerates away.

The 120-mm BAT
The British 120-mm BAT (Battalion Anti-Tank) gun dug into a defensive position. Behind it is the venturi tube through which the recoilless blast will be ejected. This cartridge case had a plastic disc in the base which blew out at a specific pressure, releasing the blast through the venturi.

IMPROVED
PROPELLANTS
BRING
ROCKETS
BACK TO WAR

BATTLEFIELD ROCKETS

The Nebelwerfer
The 15-cm Nebelwerfer (BELOW) was developed in the early 1930s for saturating areas with explosive, gas, or smoke. The rocket was unusual in having the motor in the head, with the exhaust about two-thirds of the way down the body. The launcher consisted of six barrels on a mobile carriage adapted from the 37-mm anti-tank gun. The six rockets were electrically fired over a period of 10 seconds.

A CONSEQUENCE of the First World War was that more research was carried out into gun propellants — smokeless powders. From this came the technique of making large one-piece "grains" of propellant suitable for use as rocket motors. The Germans were the pioneers of the technique, and in the late 1920s they began experimenting with rockets. Their interest is partly explained by the fact that they were forbidden, under the Versailles Treaty, to develop guns, but there was nothing in the Treaty about rockets. They hoped to find a substitute for conventional heavy artillery. By 1931 the German Army was working on a potential anti-aircraft rocket but the research was abandoned in favour of developing a field artillery rocket. The

The British 3-inch AA rocket
A rocket being fired from a 3-inch single projector late in 1940 (ABOVE). It carried a shell of about 20-lbs to a height of 18,000 feet, and was far more dangerous than a gun shell since it had a thinner casing and carried much more explosive. After initial field tests with the single projector shown here, twin and quadruple projectors were put into service. These were grouped as "Z Batteries", each with 128 "barrels" and were used to put up barrages in the path of raiding bombers.

work took up the rest of the decade and it was not until 1940 that the 15-cm Nebelwerfer went into service. It was designed to saturate a target with a salvo of spin-stabilized smoke, explosive, or gas rockets, though in practice it was usually the explosive round that was used. First deployed in North Africa and the USSR in 1941, it had a considerable effect upon the morale of the enemy.

The German Army also went on to develop liquid-propelled rockets (see page 174), and then produced 28- and 32-cm Nebelwerfer rockets using the same motor. The 28-cm warhead was explosive whereas the 32-cm one was incendiary. A 21-cm model followed, which used a similar multi-barrel wheeled launcher to the original 15-cm weapon but had a range of 12,000 yards rather than the 7,500 yards of the early model.

The Soviet armed forces had also been studying rockets as potentially a useful supplement to artillery. When the Germans introduced the 15-cm Nebelwerfer the Soviets countered with the "Katyusha" BM-13 — also known as "Stalin's Organ" from the

Avibras multiple launcher
The SBAT-70 Multiple Rocker Launcher made by Avibras of Brazil. The 36 tubes each carry a 70-mm folding-fin aircraft rocket, to which can be fitted a variety of *warheads including high explosive, shaped charge, white phosphorus smoke, and fragmentation. The rocket weighs 8.5 kg, of which 3.2 kg is the warhead, and has a* *maximum range of about 8,500 metres. The launcher, which weighs only 700 kg when empty, can be towed behind any vehicle.*

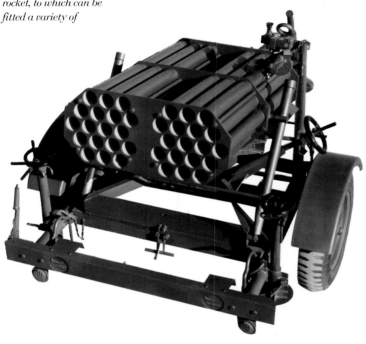

noise it made in flight — a truck-borne launcher firing a bank of forty-eight 13-cm 93-lb rockets to 5,500 yards. They had also developed an effective 82-mm rocket to be fired from aircraft as a ground-attack weapon. First used against the Japanese in Manchuria in 1939, it went on to arm almost all Soviet ground-attack aircraft throughout the war, and was particularly effective against tanks.

Britain began studying rockets in 1934 and by 1936 had designed 2-inch and 3-inch anti-aircraft rockets. These were extensively tested in Jamaica in 1937, but the Army demanded a closed-breech launcher (to avoid problems with backblast) which proved to be impossible. The turbulence of the rocket blast inside a closed launching tube made it unstable and inaccurate, so the rocket was shelved. It was revived in 1939 by the Navy who adopted the 2-inch rocket as an air-defence weapon during the 1941 blitz, firing a cable and parachute into the path of attacking aircraft. To do this they developed a simple frame launcher, and when the German air raids on Britain increased, the Army had second thoughts and adopted a similar open launcher, whereupon the 3-inch rocket showed itself capable of breaking up aerial attacks. The only difficulty was that shortly after a battery had discharged a salvo of 128 rockets into the air, 128 spent rocket motors fell from the sky, so it was vital to site rocket batteries where the debris would do no harm.

A 5-inch rocket was then developed for naval shore bombardment, and was used effectively during the June 1944 invasion of Normandy. The 5-inch warhead, allied to a 3-inch

motor, was adapted by the Canadian Army into a light, wheeled artillery launcher called "Land Mattress", which was used at Walcheren in October/November 1944 and in subsequent battles in northwest Europe. The 3-inch motor, with an improved warhead or with a solid armour-piercing warhead, was also adopted by the RAF as a ground-attack weapon, notably against submarines and tanks.

THE BAZOOKA

In the USA, rocket researchers developed a 4.5-inch spin-stabilized rocket fired from a wheeled multi-barrel launcher, which proved a highly effective bombardment weapon. But the most significant US rocket was undoubtedly the "Bazooka". This stemmed from research done in the 1920s by Robert H. Goddard, a noted rocket scientist. It consisted of a lightweight metal tube held on the shoulder, from which a fin-stabilized rocket could be fired. Once the launching device was developed, the question was what to fire from it. Another US Army establishment had developed a heavy rifle grenade to be fired from the 0.5-inch Browning machine-gun, and when the idea was abandoned, the grenade warhead, attached to a rocket motor, became a shaped-charge projectile for the Bazooka. Introduced in 1942, the bazooka soon became an indispensable anti-tank weapon for the infantry. The first version was of 60-mm calibre, firing a 3.4-lb rocket to a range of 400 yards. Numbers of these were supplied to the USSR where, inevitably, some fell into German hands. In 1943 the Panzerschreck ("tank terror") appeared in the Eastern Front. This was copied from the Bazooka but was of 89-mm calibre firing a 7.3-lb rocket to 165 yards. It was followed in 1944 by Puppchen ("Dolly") which was simply a strengthened launcher on a light two-wheeled carriage. It used a closed-breech launch system and increased the effective range to over 800 yards.

The bazooka
American paratroopers demonstrate how to load the bazooka, Oudja, North Africa, 1943. This is the original 2.36-inch version which had been introduced late in 1942. The loader is holding down the loading latch with one hand while inserting the rocket with the other; later the latch is released to lock into a cut-out in the fins, holding the rocket and making electrical contact for the firing circuit.

V-1 AND V-2 ROCKETS

Enzian

Once the rocket principle had been shown to be practical, many designs were initiated in Germany, of which one of the most promising was "Enzian", a ground-to-air missile. Work began in 1943 and first test flights were made in 1944.

Enzian was a winged missile carrying a 1,000-lb explosive warhead fitted with an acoustic proximity fuze. Launched from a simple frame by four solid fuel boosters, it had a liquid-fuel sustainer motor. Development was slow due to bureaucratic problems and the missile was not perfected in time to be used in the war.

> *" If the Germans had succeeded in perfecting these new weapons six months earlier and putting them into action as opportunity arose, it is probable that our invasion of Europe would have come up against tremendous difficulties, and in certain circumstances might have been impossible. I am certain that after six months of such action 'Operation Overlord', the attack on Europe from England, would have had to be written off. "*

General Eisenhower: Crusade in Europe.

The Diver Belt
V-1 missiles crossing the Kent coast in 1944.

Beneath are the guns of the "Diver Belt", the concentration of air

defence artillery which stretched across the south-east coast.

THE GERMANS began experimenting with rockets as a substitute for artillery from the late 1920s (see Battlefield rockets, page 172). Their work took two directions: one, using solid-fuel rockets, led to the Nebelwerfer; the other, using liquid fuel, was to lead to the A-4 rocket, more commonly called the V-2. this was short for Vergeltungswaffen 2 ("Vengeance Weapon 2"), a title bestowed by Hitler.

The work was begun by General Walter Dornberger and Werner von Braun, at Kummersdorf, near Berlin, in 1931. The first design, A-1, never flew; the A-2 flew successfully over the Baltic in December 1934 and the German Army was sufficiently impressed to finance a missile development station at Peenemunde, on the Baltic coast. Subsequent rockets were developed there. The A-3 was fired in 1938. The A-4 was first proposed in 1936, and some of its technology was tested in the A-3. The A-4 was a liquid-fuelled rocket weighing about 13 tons at launch; the motor burned for about 70 seconds, during which period the rocket was turned on to a ballistic trajectory. Once correctly aligned, a radar signal cut off the motor and thereafter the A-4 coasted to its target. The rocket went into production in 1944 and saw service in the Second World War. About 10,000 were built, of which 1,115 were fired against Britain, 1,341 against Antwerp, and 194 against other targets.

Once the final design of the A-4 was settled, the Peenemunde scientists proceeded to work on even bigger weapons, such as the

A-10, a two-stage rocket intended to bombard the USA, but the war ended before these ideas could be translated into hardware.

Not all development was at Peenemunde; several private companies set about designing guided missiles. Among them was Messerschmitt, who designed Enzian, a radio-guided air-defence rocket with an infrared homing head. Various prototype models were built between 1943 and 1945, of which 38 were fired experimentally. The Rheinmettal company developed Rheintochter, another radio-controlled air-defence missile, and other designers worked on X-5, an air-to-air missile, Wasserfall, an air-defence missile, Rheinbote, a surface-to-surface weapon, Moewe, another air-defence missile, and many more. Of all these projects only Rheinbote achieved success, and some 200 or more were fired at Antwerp in 1945. The war ended before any of the others could be brought into service.

THE "FLYING BOMB"

As the Army laboured with its A-series rockets, so in 1942 the Luftwaffe (German Air Force) began developing the FZG-76, better known as the V-1 "Flying Bomb". The work went smoothly and the first test launch was in December 1942. The V-1 resembled a small aircraft, with a fuselage, wings, and tail and with a ramjet motor mounted above the rear of the fuselage. Launched by catapult, to ensure sufficient airflow through the motor to make it function, it carried 1,870-lb of explosives, flew at about 370 mph and had a range of over 120 miles. Production began in March 1944 and about 35,000 were made; 9,251 were fired against Britain, of which 4,261 were destroyed, and 6,551 against Antwerp, of which 2,455 were destroyed.

As well as being launched from fixed catapult ramps, the V-1 could be slung beneath an aircraft and launched in the air. Flying at speed, the pilot could start the rocket's motor by remote control and release the bomb on its way. Provided that the bomb pointed in the right direction, gyroscopic stabilization ensured that it would fly straight, and its range was governed by the amount of fuel it carried. Once it ran out of fuel it stalled, dived to the ground, and detonated.

Initially, defence against the V-1 was difficult. Although it flew straight and level (ideal for the anti-aircraft gunner), it was a hard target because it flew high and fast and could not be easily tracked by the larger guns. However, with the introduction of the US SCR-504 auto-tracking radar and electronic predictor, targeting became very much easier, and the widespread use of proximity fuzes greatly improved the kill rate. RAF fighter aircraft also played their part, but most V-1s were destroyed by gunfire.

The A-4 rocket was a different matter. It flew faster than the speed of sound, so there was no audible warning of its approach, and it was so fast that even if it was picked up by radar there was not enough time to target it. The only hope was to place a screen of bursting shells in its path on the chance that a fragment might detonate the warhead while it was still well up in its trajectory. Some degree of early warning was achieved by using long-range radar to watch likely launch areas, but since the launching apparatus was mobile, it was pure luck if the radar happened to be looking at the right place at the right time.

Air-to-ground missiles were also used by the Luftwaffe; the Hs-293 gliding bomb was released from an aircraft and steered to

Launching the A-4 rocket
An A-4 rocket about four seconds after being launched from Test Stand VII at Peenemunde Army Experimental Station in the summer of 1943. The flight went to a range of 160 miles and landed within 2.5 miles of its target. A film of this flight was instrumental in converting Hitler to the use of rockets.

its target from the aircraft. It was rocket-propelled and radio-guided and carried a 550-lb warhead. Introduced in 1942, it was used against shipping in the Bay of Biscay and around the Dodecanese Islands, and also at Anzio in 1944, but Allied radio counter-measures were soon developed to jam the control link, and its use was discontinued.

NUCLEAR WEAPONS

A FTER ALBERT Einstein's formulation of the equivalence of mass and energy, the prospect of releasing energy contained within the atom fascinated physicists. Until the 1890s it was assumed that the atom was indivisible and indestructible. Then, in 1903 Ernest Rutherford and Frederick Soddy were the first to discover a sub-atomic particle, the electron. More discoveries followed until, in 1939, Lise Meitner and Otto Frisch split the nuclei of uranium atoms to release a disproportionate amount of energy. This is called nuclear fission. Almost immediately a conference of American physicists was held in Washington, as a result of which a proposal was made to the US President Franklin Roosevelt to develop an atomic bomb using uranium as the explosive. Roosevelt consulted Einstein and then appointed a Uranium Consultative Committee. The first controlled chain reaction, in which a neutron striking a uranium nucleus and releasing energy liberated other neutrons which, in turn, acted on neighbouring atoms, took place in Chicago in 1942.

Similar work had taken place in the UK. The two countries pursued their research independently, Britain forming the "Tube Alloys" committee. Much informal exchange of information took place, but it was not until 1943 that an accord was firmly established on an official basis. By that time Fermi had set the first chain reaction in operation and an enormous constructional effort, codenamed the "Manhattan Engineer District", was set in motion to manufacture the material for a bomb.

Germany had also realized the potential of the atom and had set up a research programme. The German scientists, however, elected to look in the wrong direction, basing their studies on "heavy water". Under British direction Norwegian resistance forces destroyed successive shipments of heavy water from the only plant — in Norway — capable of making it. This action both reinforced the Germans' belief that they were on the right track and also cut off their supplies so that the German effort came to nothing.

At 5.30 am on 16 July, 1945, the first detonation of an atomic bomb occurred in the New Mexico desert, with devastating effect. At that time the invasion of Japan was scheduled for 1 November, 1945, with the possibility of hundreds of thousands of US casualties. President Harry S. Truman decided to bomb the Japanese into

Enola Gay
A B-29 "superfortress" bomber named "Enola Gay" flown by Colonel Paul Tibbets, USAAF, was the aircraft employed to deliver the first nuclear weapon. A special force, the 509 Composite Group of 20th Air Force, was set up in Okinawa solely for the purpose of making the historic attack; without the capture of Okinawa in June 1945 and the availability of the long-range Superfortress, the Hiroshima raid might not have been possible. A similar aircraft was used for the second raid on Nagasaki.

Little Boy
"Little Boy" (or "Thin Man") was the first atomic bomb dropped over Hiroshima (BELOW). It was a uranium fission weapon of about 20 kt power, and carried a core of 137 lbs of Uranium 235. The uranium was in two parts, one fixed, the other in a form of gun. Detonation was achieved by firing the gun half into the fixed half so that the two combined to form a critical mass.

Fat Boy
"Fat Boy" (BOTTOM) was the second atomic bomb. The power, 20 kt, was the same as that of Little Boy. Fat Boy used plutonium fission in which critical mass was achieved by splitting the plutonium into two parts, a central ball and an outer hollow sphere. A conventional explosive was detonated to collapse the sphere and combine it with the ball-like core to produce the critical mass.

submission instead. Hiroshima was bombed on 6 August, 1945, followed by Nagasaki on 9 August. Some 106,000 people died as a result of these attacks. Following the USSR's declaration of war on 9 August, Japan agreed to surrender on 14 August.

The USA assumed it would hold a monopoly on the atomic bomb after 1945, but the Soviets, who began work on one in early 1943, probably knew as much about nuclear technology as the Western allies; not only was their own research far developed but they were greatly helped by their spy network, which informed them of Western developments. Due to the USSR's backward industrial base, it took time, but in 1949 the Soviets were able to detonate their own atomic bomb. The USA went ahead again in 1952, when it exploded the first thermonuclear hydrogen bomb, but less than a year later the USSR detonated its own H-bomb. The

arms race was underway.

Since that time the possession of nuclear weapons has spread from the major powers with high-technology industries to other countries, who have mortgaged much to join the "nuclear club". Treaties and agreements to halt the proliferation of nuclear weapons have been signed, but these are frequently ignored by their signatories. Many countries have built nuclear reactors or nuclear research establishments, and from this stage the production of weapons is a relatively short step. At present, Britain, the USA, France, the former USSR, and China are the only "official" owners of nuclear weapons; but good intelligence suggests that Israel, South Africa, Pakistan, and India might also possess nuclear devices, while countries such as Argentina, Algeria, Libya, and Iraq have taken steps towards a nuclear capability.

THE EFFECTS OF A NUCLEAR EXPLOSION

ALTHOUGH THE explosive content of a nuclear bomb is measured in tons, kilotons, or megatons of TNT, this is merely a rough yardstick of its destructive power as the effect of nuclear detonation is far different from that of a conventional high explosive. The nuclear explosion is not a simple question of blast, but has five interlinked effects: heat, light, blast, fallout and electromagnetic pulse (EMP).

Heat Thirty-five per cent of the bomb's energy is emitted as heat, producing temperatures as great as at the centre of the sun. This heat travels outwards at the speed of light (186,000 miles per second), attenuating as it does so. For a 1-megaton weapon, the heat would vaporize everything within a 3-mile circle of the detonation, would ignite most materials within an 8-mile radius, would severely burn anyone within 11 miles, and would cause first-degree burns up to 20 miles away.

Light The first effect of detonation is an intense flash of light; anyone within 90 miles who happened to be looking in the direction of the detonation would be temporarily blinded.

Blast About 50 per cent of the energy is in the form of a blast wave which travels at about 1 mile in 3 seconds. Broadly speaking, this is a pressure wave some 30–40 times atmospheric normal that lasts 2 or 3 seconds, sweeping outwards and destroying everything in its path until it gradually weakens. Virtually every structure within 4 miles would be flattened. The wave travels faster than sound, so there is no noise warning of its approach.

Fallout The detonation initially causes the emission of an enormous pulse of radiation in the form of neutrons and gamma rays, though the more visible effects of blast and heat tend

to produce such destruction that this radiation scarcely matters. More dangerous, because more insidious, is the secondary radiation caused by the materials vaporized in the detonation condensing back into solid particles of radioactive dust as the fireball of the detonation gradually cools. These particles are then borne by the wind and, depending upon their size, land downwind of the site or may drift in the atmosphere for a long time, coming to earth at great distances from the explosion. The effects of these radioactive particles are not, even now, entirely known and they can constitute a health hazard for hundreds of years to come.

Electromagnetic pulse For a short time the detonation generates an enormous pulse of electromagnetic energy sufficient to cause great damage to communications and electronic equipment over a wide area.

Nagasaki, 9 August 1945
(**ABOVE RIGHT**) *The column of smoke and radioactive dust above Nagasaki after the detonation of Fat Boy.*

Hiroshima, Ground Zero
*This building (**RIGHT**) was directly under the detonation (at 1,850 feet altitude) of Little Boy. The picture was taken in March 1946, after some clearing of damage.*

T he post-1945 period could hardly be called one of peace, with wars in Korea, Vietnam, India, and the Middle East at various times, as well as lesser insurrections. However there was at least no confrontation between the major nations. It differed from previous postwar periods in that the maintenance of armies and the development of weapons did not fall away; indeed it intensified under the pressures of the Cold War.

This period is particularly noteworthy for two major weapon developments: the nuclear device and the guided missile. Once the nuclear bomb had been developed in the USA it was inevitable that knowledge of its construction would be sought by others, though the economic and technological problems of its production ruled it out for all but the largest nations. And once the secret was out, it became a question of constant improvement by each side in order to keep ahead in the race. Thus from tactical guided missiles came intercontinental missiles, and from simple nuclear warheads came the multiple warhead with several individual nuclear devices, as well as decoys and other methods of overcoming defences.

This was also the period in which electronics began to pervade every corner of the battlefield. The computer, originally developed for breaking codes and then for calculating ballistic tables, increased in power and shrank in size until by 1990 it was possible to have a computing sight for an infantryman's rifle. Today's tanks now contain so much electronic equipment that these "black boxes" cost more than the rest of the vehicle.

The Gulf campaign in 1991 provided the first opportunity for many advanced weapons to show whether they would work. In general, they did, though perhaps not quite as well as their advocates claimed. Nevertheless the efficiency of cruise missiles, anti-missile missiles, field-bombardment rockets and aerial attack systems seemed to demonstrate that warfare is now a matter of eliminating specific targets so as to emasculate a country's capacity to wage war rather than of simply throwing armies at each other.

CHAPTER EIGHT

TODAY AND TOMORROW

THE MACHINES WHICH BROUGHT NEW THINKING TO BATTLE

HELICOPTERS

PROBABLY THE most significant addition to military inventories in the past 40 years has been the helicopter, which has completely changed the tactics of battle. The first military use of these machines was in Korea in 1950, principally to evacuate the seriously wounded to field hospitals, but also for limited reconnaissance tasks. After the turboshaft engine (in which the turbine drives a shaft that turns the blades) superseded the turbojet engine (in which the turbine compresses air to generate thrust) in 1955 the power-to-weight ratio improved, and the simultaneous solving of several other problems of helicopter construction led to a very rapid rise in the number of such machines in military use. Since then they have appeared as troop carriers, gunships, tank hunters, cargo carriers, ambulances, and flying cranes.

The deployment of troops by air began with parachute and glider-borne troops during the Second World War. The Soviets had pioneered this technique in the early 1930s, but their biggest paratroop operation against the German Army, the Byrkin bridgehead of September 1943, was by no measure even a qualified success. The Germans enjoyed some success in the 1940 offensive through the Low Countries but the heavy casualties their parachutists suffered in May 1941 on Crete ended their airborne role. British paratroop operations in Normandy in June 1944 achieved much, but this was balanced by the Arnhem fiasco three months later. Today the chance of success of any paratroop action is remote, as the transport aircraft would be unlikely to survive modern anti-aircraft defences. Moreover, paratroops are only lightly armed and need to be relieved by ground troops within a very short time — a demand that has frequently been their undoing, notably at Arnhem.

THE HELICOPTER REVOLUTION

The helicopter has changed the thinking on airborne troop deployment. Instead of taking highly specialized, highly trained troops a long way and parachuting them into battle, the helicopter can take line regiments who have no special training and place them where they are needed. Furthermore they can resupply them, even with heavy weapons. A helicopter-borne artillery battery of 105-mm guns or howitzers can be in action 9 miles away within 30 minutes of leaving its former position, a speed of movement that

Flying artillery
A 105-mm field howitzer of the Portuguese Army about to be lifted by a Super Puma Helicopter of the Royal Air Force during a NATO/AMF exercise. The Allied Mobile Force (AMF) is a multi-national force which deploys on the NATO flanks as a form of "trip-wire", and mobility is its primary strength. The artillery, all armed with 105-mm weapons, is entirely air-portable and can be moved around the battlefield at high speed.

Huey the workhorse
One of the most popular and prolific of military helicopters, the Bell Model 204 "Iroquois" will always be better-known as the "Huey" from its US Army designation UH-1 (RIGHT). Since its introduction in the late 1950s it has moved steadily onward through a succession of improved models, though the basic shape has remained the same. The US Army plans to keep these versatile machines in service until well into the 21st century.

The helicopter gunship
A machine-gunner in an American helicopter over Vietnam watching for targets below, while another gunship flies in the distance. Notice that the waist gunner uses a "flexible" machine gun, one which he can direct at targets from his position in the door, and beyond him can be seen two "fixed" guns mounted on the side of the machine and controlled by the pilot. Two more fixed guns were fitted to the other side of the machine as well as a further flexible gun. These gunships proved invaluable in Vietnam, not only as independent attack weapons but as escorts for medical evacuation flights, supply missions and infantry deployments .

The tank hunter
A McDonnel-Douglas 530MG "Defender" helicopter (**BELOW**) *carrying anti-tank guided missiles in pods and with a mast-mounted sight above the rotor.*

gives an entirely new degree of mobility to artillery. The fact that a wounded man can be picked up by helicopter and speedily borne away to skilled medical attention is also a big morale-booster.

But it is the assault role of the helicopter that is now coming to the fore. Soviet strategists have described the helicopter as a lightly armoured tank that is not constrained by considerations of terrain. There is some truth in this. A helicopter armed with anti-tank missiles is a grave threat to any tank today, so much so that some armies, including those of the USA, Germany, France, and Britain, are devoting thought to specialized anti-anti-tank helicopter weapons to accompany armoured formations. The helicopter can be an exceedingly difficult target; it can manoeuvre at treetop height, dodging in and out of sight, and using a masthead sight above its rotor it can see its targets but is effectively invisible to them. Moreover, the spinning rotor has been found to do peculiar things to radar echoes and radio-operated proximity fuzes so that some conventional air-defence weapons are useless against them.

Technology has significantly increased the range, accuracy, and lethality of modern weapon systems. Modern field surveillance systems enable a commander to know where significant enemy forces are all the time. But these advances in technology and efficiency have had to be paid for in increased weapon costs, so that the future battlefield will be one with fewer, more effective, more expensive weapons. At the same time, economic conditions are slimming down the size of armies.

With fewer men and fewer weapons, future battles will revolve around operations by small, highly skilled, well-equipped forces that are widely dispersed. The old rule of "march dispersed, fight concentrated" still holds good, but instead of marching to the concentration of forces, and thus advertising one's intentions for days in advance, the soldier will now be carried to the concentration area by helicopter, a move that can be accomplished in an hour or two and be completed before an enemy can organize a countermove.

Moreover, that concentration area, where the troops form up, will no longer necessarily be behind the soldiers' own lines, as it always had to be in the past. With the mobility bestowed by the helicopter, the forming-up area can be inside enemy territory. At the same time, unoccupied enemy sectors will be detected by surveillance systems and exploited by air-mobile forces.

This rapid deployment will be supported by massed artillery fire and ground-attack aircraft. The most recent concept of the AirLand Maneuver Battle (in US Army-jargon) visualizes four phases of combat: detect, fire, manoeuvre, and reconstitute. A force commander will first disperse his forces and then detect the enemy and assess its positions and strengths before massing his artillery fire and ground support aircraft strikes to do the maximum damage. He will then manoeuvre and land his air-mobile forces to fight the ground battle, and then disperse, reconstitute his forces, and begin the detection phase again. The whole concept relies upon the commander taking the initiative and fighting a pro-active, rather than a reactive, battle.

These tactics can be discerned in the action in the Gulf campaign of 1991. Although the scale was enormous, the concepts outlined above can be distinguished in the various phases of the war. Moreover, study of that campaign also shows the associated problems of logistics and supply, which frequently tend to be overlooked by amateur strategists and tacticians. Unless troops and equipment can be taken to the theatre of war and maintained there, there is little point having them there in the first place. The success of this operation depends largely on air mobility.

SPECIALIZED AIRCRAFT FOR HIGH-TECH MODERN WAR

TACTICAL SUPPORT AIRCRAFT

ONE OF the lessons that should have been learned after 1945 was the importance of dedicated ground-support aircraft, but in fact the lesson took several years to sink in. In the immediate postwar years, the fighter aircraft doubled as a ground-attack machine, as it had done in wartime, sometimes with the addition of specialized weapons such as rockets. This was largely a question of economics: few air forces were sufficiently convinced of the priority of the ground-attack role to spend money on dedicated aircraft. It was cheaper to adopt a fighter that could be adapted to the role. Consequently, the fighter/ground-attack machine has remained a standard item — aircraft such as the McDonnell Douglas F/A-18, the Dassault Mirage F1EQ, the Soviet MiG-27 "Flogger F", and the Anglo-French Jaguar. These aircraft carry gun or cannon armament and air-to-air missiles in their fighter role, but can also carry bombs or ground-attack missiles in their close support role.

Gradually, it was appreciated that for some tasks a dedicated aircraft could be more cost-effective, and the most important of these tasks was attacking tanks. Wartime experience appeared to show that aircraft could master tanks, although postwar analysis showed that the wartime airborne weapons were less effective than had been thought at the time. But improved weapons made it probable that a heavily-armed and armoured aircraft would be able to deal more powerful blows and also be more likely to survive above the modern battlefield.

The Mirage F1

A Mirage F1 fighter of the French Air Force firing a Matra Super 300 air-to-air interception missile. Although first developed as an all-weather interceptor, the Mirage F1 has since been adapted to the ground attack role, carrying a variety of weapons on external underwing mounts up to a maximum load of 6,300 kg. Up to 14 250-kg bombs can be carried, or 30 anti-runway bombs, or 144 rockets.

Fairchild A-10A Avenger

Familiarly called the "Warthog", the Avenger is the ultimate purpose-built ground-attack machine, developed because the US had fought in Korea and Vietnam with aircraft designed for European air combat. Development took almost ten years but the result was worth the waiting. Highly manoeuvrable and capable of carrying any available bomb, the Avenger showed its worth in the Gulf.

GROUND-SUPPORT AIRCRAFT

A good example of this type of aircraft is the USAF A-10 Thunderbolt II, introduced in 1974. Its primary armament is the 30-mm GAU-8/A seven-barrelled Gatling gun with a rate of fire of 4,200 rounds per minute — 70 rounds a second. Using armour-piercing ammunition, this cannon can destroy a main battle tank in seconds and is even more devastating to lighter armour. The aircraft can also carry up to 16,000lbs of bombs, missiles, or rockets on underwing pylons and the engines (twin turbofans) are mounted above the rear fuselage to give the smallest possible infrared signature. The pilot is surrounded by titanium armour, and such aids as laser designators and electronic countermeasures are also available. With a full load of munitions it can fly at 440mph but it can also "loiter" over the battlefield, picking out targets at will.

The Harrier GR-3
(**LEFT**) *Development of vertical take-off and landing (VTOL) machines began in the 1950s, the first vertical flight of a test-bed taking place in 1960 and the first Harrier prototype in 1964.*

The AV-8B
*The Harrier GR-1 version (**BELOW**) was adopted by the US Marine Corps as the AV-8A and given beach assault and defensive tasks. The AV-8B shown here is an improved model, due to collaboration between the US and British manufacturers.*

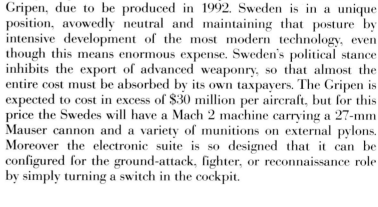

The nearest British equivalent is a very different machine, the Hawker Harrier GR Mk3. The principal claim to fame of this aircraft is its ability to take off and land vertically, so it requires no airstrip. Armed with twin 30-mm cannon, it can carry up to 5,000lbs of external munitions of any sort, and can be employed in a close support, bombing, or reconnaissance role. With a top speed of around 760 mph it is more versatile than the A-10 but less effective in the pure ground-support role.

Several NATO air forces employ the Panavia Tornado, which was developed jointly by Britain, Germany, and Italy. This can be configured as either an air-superiority fighter or as a close-support strike machine, and in the latter role it can carry almost 16,000lbs of munitions in addition to its standard twin 27-mm Mauser cannon. It is a two-man machine, the observer taking charge of the various munitions while the pilot flies the machine and controls the cannon and other "personal" armament. Capable of flying at over Mach 2 (twice the speed of sound) it has an operational range of 1,000 miles, without resort to external fuel pods.

The Soviets had concentrated upon air-superiority fighters, with de-rated versions armed for ground support, but more recently, before the break-up of the USSR, they began to consider the multi-role aircraft. This has considerable economic advantages, though there is always the argument that a multi-role machine does all jobs moderately well and none excellently. Nevertheless the MiG-29 "Fulcrum" was their latest choice for ground support; it was originally built as a fighter, but had scope for adaptation to the ground-support role.

The multi-role concept has been adopted in other countries, and perhaps the most recent example is the Swedish JAS-39 Gripen, due to be produced in 1992. Sweden is in a unique position, avowedly neutral and maintaining that posture by intensive development of the most modern technology, even though this means enormous expense. Sweden's political stance inhibits the export of advanced weaponry, so that almost the entire cost must be absorbed by its own taxpayers. The Gripen is expected to cost in excess of $30 million per aircraft, but for this price the Swedes will have a Mach 2 machine carrying a 27-mm Mauser cannon and a variety of munitions on external pylons. Moreover the electronic suite is so designed that it can be configured for the ground-attack, fighter, or reconnaissance role by simply turning a switch in the cockpit.

The MiG 29 "Fulcrum"
"Fulcrum" has been in service since 1985 and is primarily an air-to-air fighter, but it has a full dual-role ground attack capability as well.

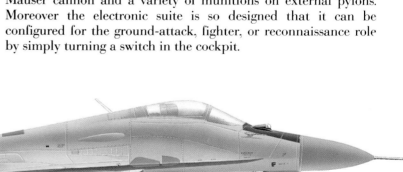

ROCKETS BECOME MISSILES, AND THE SPACE RACE STARTS

STRATEGIC MISSILES

THE STRATEGIC missile has completely revolutionized the theory of warfare by its ability to girdle the globe and land on a target 10,000 miles away with an accuracy measured in feet. When the first missiles appeared in 1957 they were hailed as the "ultimate deterrent", and this appears to have been correct; they eventually became so accurate and so powerful that they neutralized themselves.

The first strategic missiles were the FZG-76 and A-4 weapons used by Germany against Britain and other targets in 1944-5, and Germany had plans for a transatlantic missile when the war ended (see V1 and V2 rockets, page 174). In the aftermath of the war the USA and USSR gathered up most of the German rocket scientists and put them to work on missile designs. Strangely, the Americans were slow to begin work on long-range missiles, spending most of their effort on tactical weapons, but the Soviets had their SS-3 missile in service by 1955. This was really little more than an improved A-4 with a range of about 750 miles, but by 1960 the SS-4 appeared carrying a 1-megaton nuclear

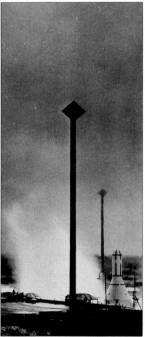

warhead and with a range of 1,120 miles. SS-5 followed, but various lines of research had been moving in parallel, and the more advanced SS-6 appeared in 1957. Known to NATO as "Sapwood", this was an enormous weapon using 32 rocket motors to lift a massive 5-megaton thermonuclear warhead to a range of over 6,000 miles. It was virtually obsolete as soon as it appeared, however, and was used principally as a vehicle for putting various space capsules into orbit, including Sputnik 1 and Yuri Gagarin's manned flight in 1961.

Subsequently a stream of Inter-Continental Ballistic Missiles (ICBMs) appeared in the Soviet inventory, culminating in the late 1980s with the SS-26. Of all this series, the SS-18 was probably

Launching the Titan
A series of pictures (ABOVE) *showing the launch of the Titan I missile from the first silo, built at Vandenberg Air Force Base, in May 1961; a launch which proved that the underground silo concept was practical. Development of this missile began in 1955; Titan I became operational in October 1962, but by 1966 it had been replaced by Titan II, with improved motors and double the payload/range. More important, the improved fuels meant that the weapon could be readied for launch in less than one minute, rather than the half hour of Titan I.*

Minuteman III taking off

Minuteman III (LEFT) is the latest of a series of missiles which began development in 1957. All have been three-stage rockets powered by solid fuel motors, and the third version is fitted with a MIRV head which is virtually a fourth stage, with its own manoeuvering engines. This contains three independently targetable 330 kt nuclear warheads together with a variety of deception devices.

At the target end

A remarkable photograph (RIGHT) showing six independently targeted MIRV warheads from a Minuteman III trial shot approaching their targets near Kwajalien Atoll in the Pacific Ocean in July 1979. Close to the apex of the triangle of paths can be seen a decoy shedding a load of "chaff" to blind radar sets, one of the many countermeasures incorporated inside these multiple warheads.

the most formidable; a huge weapon, weighing 110 tons, it was propelled by two liquid-fuel rockets and could carry various types of warhead including a 25-megaton thermonuclear bomb, to a range of 10,000 miles. It was "cold-launched" from an underground silo, that is, ejected from the silo by compressed gas before the rocket ignited, allowing the silo to be reloaded and used again. Alternatively it could be carried on a launcher-transporter and launched from any location. Approximately 300 of these weapons were stationed in the USSR and their prime purpose appears to have been to attack US ICBM installations.

The USA actually began developing an ICBM immediately after the Second World War with Snark, but it was given a low priority and development was slow. Snark did not enter service until 1957. A winged vehicle like an aircraft, it was rocket-launched, and sustained by a turbojet engine. Snark carried a warhead of 5 megatons, which was later raised to 20 megatons, and had a range of about 6,000 miles. Like almost all ICBMs it used inertial guidance.

Once begun, the US programmes produced ICBMs at a rapid rate; Jupiter appeared in 1954 but was shuffled between services before coming to rest with the US Air Force and entering service in 1958. This was classified as an IRBM — Intermediate-Range Ballistic Missile — since it had a range of just over 1,800 miles. Thor (1956) had a similar range and numbers of them were sited in Britain at US Air Force bases until 1965.

The first ICBM in missile form (rather than aircraft form) was Atlas, which flew in 1957 and was perfected for service in 1959. Atlas missiles were originally emplaced on the surface, but when the size of the Soviet ICBM programme became known, many were resited in underground silos. The Atlas was an enormous weapon, weighing 115 tons at launch, standing 75 feet high, and with a range of 12,000 miles. It was withdrawn from military service in 1966 and many were later used as space launch vehicles.

In 1955 the US Navy developed a solid-fuel missile. This led the US Air Force to examine this system since their current missiles were all liquid-fuelled and needed one hour's warning before they could be launched, unlike a solid-fuel weapon which could be launched at any time. The Air Force developed

Minuteman, which carries a 2-megaton thermonuclear warhead and has a range of over 8,000 miles.

The most recent US missile is Peacekeeper. It has a range in excess of 5,000 miles and a multiple warhead. Peacekeeper supplements Minuteman, whose silos are being modified to take the new weapon.

Britain made one attempt to develop an ICBM in 1955. Known as Blue Streak, it was based on Atlas technology imported from the USA, used a Rolls-Royce liquid-fuel rocket motor and inertial guidance, and weighed about 90 tons when armed with a nuclear warhead. It was abandoned in 1960. Since then Britain has relied entirely upon the products of the USA for missiles. France developed the SSBS (Sol-Sol Ballistique Stratégique) in the 1960s, and installed it in 18 silos in the south of France; it carries a 150-kiloton warhead and has a range in excess of 2,000 miles.

MULTIPLE-WARHEAD MISSILES

The prospect of being bombarded with missiles led, of course, to thoughts of how to defeat them. The general view that emerged was "fire one at the incoming missile" and hope to destroy the warhead by a nuclear blast in the stratosphere. To counter this strategy, the Multiple Warhead was devised. On returning to the atmosphere, it would open to deploy a number of smaller warheads, one or two of which would be nuclear, and the rest dummy, leaving the defender in doubt as to which warhead posed the real threat. The reasoning was carried a stage further with the MIRV — Multiple Independently-targeted Re-entry Vehicle. This was a multiple warhead containing a number of small missiles, each with its own warhead and each programmed to set a fresh course from its release point towards a specific target. A MIRV containing 10 warheads would thus threaten 10 targets, which could be several hundred miles apart. The distance between them depends upon the altitude at which the individual units were released, for they do not carry any propulsion but rely entirely on their remaining velocity and on gravity. MIRVs might also contain electronic decoys capable of countering radar tracking of incoming missiles or of drawing radar to themselves instead of to the actual warheads; the possibilities are endless.

TACTICAL MISSILES

MISSILES USED by armies on the battlefield are called tactical missiles. Compared with other missiles, their range is short and their warheads are small. Many countries have tactical missiles which are much simpler and cheaper than strategic weapons and so can be manufactured without access to the highest levels of technology.

The idea of a flying bomb (which is, essentially, a tactical missile) was an early one (see V1 and V2 rockets, page 174). Britain, the USA, and Germany all worked on pilotless radio-controlled aircraft carrying explosives during the First World War; they all flew successfully but the war ended before they reached service. Britain continued working after the war and produced the Larynx in 1926; this carried a 200-lb bomb and some were used in Iraq in 1929. The idea re-appeared during the Second World War, culminating in the "Weary Willies", old B-17 Flying Fortress bombers loaded with explosives and flown off the ground by a crew who then parachuted out, leaving the aircraft on autopilot and aimed generally at Germany. The idea was dropped when one blew up before the crew had got clear. The Japanese, however, utilized the principle of the piloted bomb in the kamikaze squadrons.

The first "proper" missile came from Germany; this was Rheinbote (see Battlefield rockets, page 172), a 90-lb warhead with a range of 135 miles.

The Soviets had experimented with pilotless aircraft in the 1930s but had shelved the idea, under pressure of war, to develop the Katyusha field rocket. After 1945, they resumed the research and, armed with knowledge of German work, rapidly began to develop free-flight rockets. Their first model went into service in

the early 1950s and was dubbed "Frog" (for Free-flying Rocket Over Ground) by NATO. This cumbersome weapon, mounted on a JS-3 tank chassis, weighed about 3 tons, carried a nuclear warhead, and had a range of just over 20 miles. It was the first of a series which extended to Frog-7 (1967), but by that time the design had been refined, the weight reduced to 2.5 tons, and the range almost doubled.

Frog was followed by "Scud", which in terms of its construction was more or less an improved German A-4. Scud-A used similar liquid fuel, radio fuel cut-off, and gyro-stabilized flight to the A-4. It carried a nuclear or conventional warhead and had a 90-mile range. Scud-B appeared in 1962 and was later seen on a new eight-wheeled carrier-launcher that gave it better deployment speed. It carried the same warheads but the range had increased to 170 miles. Scud-B used inertial guidance, making a long preparation time necessary before firing. Scud-C was reported in 1978; surprisingly little is known about it, other than its range of 280 miles, since, unlike the -A and -B models it was never exported outside the former Soviet Union.

Frog and Scud missiles were liberally distributed in field armies — the Scud was one of Iraq's chief weapons in the Gulf War, for instance. However, in 1967 came "Scaleboard", a much improved weapon which is thought to resemble Scud. Scaleboard uses liquid fuel, has inertial guidance, carries a nuclear warhead and has a range estimated at 560 miles.

Corporal

A Corporal missile stands ready during an exercise on Salisbury Plain in the early 1960s.

SS-1C SCUD-B

Scud (BELOW) was first thought to be a better version of Frog, but it was then discovered to have a primitive form of inertial guidance which had been gradually improved through its life. Scud-B had a range of up to 175 miles and could carry nuclear or conventional warheads. Scud-C is reported to have a range of about 280 miles but with a lower accuracy. It is carried into action on an eight-wheeled transporter.

MLRS

The American Multiple Launch Rocket System, now deployed by NATO and used with good effect in the Gulf campaign. The autonomous vehicle can register its own location and, given target information, computes firing data, aligns the launcher pod, and fires automatically. The two pods carry six missiles each, and each missile carries sub-munitions which smother the target area in anti-personnel/anti-armour bomblets.

Frog-7 was replaced in the middle 1970s by the SS-21 "Spider". This uses solid propellant, carries a nuclear warhead, has a range of 75 miles and is said to be far more accurate than Frog. Similarly, Scaleboard has been largely replaced by SS-22; little information is available about this weapon other than its range of 560 miles.

The US Army's equivalent of the German A-4 was the "Corporal", which appeared in 1953 and was later adopted by the British. Liquid-fuelled, it used similar guidance to A-4 and Frog, had nuclear or conventional warheads, and a range of up to 90 miles. A cumbersome and slow weapon to deploy, it remained in service until 1966. Corporal was followed by "Sergeant", which was shorter, fatter, was driven by solid fuel, and was far more mobile and faster into action. It became operational in 1961 and remained in service until 1978.

For a faster and cheaper response, the US Army also developed "Honest John", a simple free-flight rocket mounted on a six-wheel truck. With a nuclear or conventional warhead and a range of about 25 miles, this entered service in the early 1950s and was supplied to most NATO armies. It has now largely been replaced by "Lance", which also replaced Sergeant. Lance is inertially guided. A simple, lightweight system, it can be helicopter-lifted if necessary. The warhead can be nuclear or can be a cluster of sub-munitions, and the maximum range is about 80 miles.

FREE-FLIGHT ROCKETS

Among other countries with tactical missiles, France has the "Pluton", which has a 25-kiloton warhead and a range of 80 miles. It is currently being replaced by "Hades", which uses the same warhead and has a 220-mile range. Taiwan has the "Ching Fen", which bears a distinct similarity to Lance. Egypt produced a number of small missiles in the 1960s but apparently no longer does so. By far the most prolific of this class of missile in smaller countries is the free-flight rocket. Argentina, Brazil, China, Egypt, Israel, Italy, Japan, South Africa, and Spain all produce lightweight battlefield-support rocket systems with ranges between about 15 and 25 miles; all are transportable on wheeled vehicles, and many of them are sold to other countries.

Perhaps the ultimate in free-flight rocket systems is the American MLRS — Multiple Launch Rocket System — currently in use by the US, British, French, German, and Italian Armies. This self-propelled system fires a solid-fuel rocket to a range in excess of 18 miles; 12 are carried in the launcher unit and all can be fired in less than one minute. The warhead is loaded with sub-munitions — dual purpose anti-personnel/anti-tank mines — which are dispersed in the air over the target. A volley of 12 rockets can dump 8,000 sub-munitions into a 67-acre area. Each sub-munition has the fragmenting ability of a hand grenade and a shaped charge to allow it to penetrate armour. Other warheads include anti-tank mine dispensers and guided anti-tank sub-missiles. MLRS was used to good effect in the 1991 Gulf conflict.

NAVAL MISSILES

ALTHOUGH LAND-service missiles could probably also serve for naval use, navies have preferred to specify their own versions of weapons. Indeed, the mountings of naval weapons have always had to be more complex than those for land weapons, largely to compensate for the movement of the ship.

Naval missiles therefore take a slightly different form from their land equivalents, and tend towards greater specialization. They can be subdivided into strategic and tactical groups, but naval tactical weapons tend to subdivide further according to the target.

Sea strategic weapons are a result of the dispersion theory advanced in the 1950s: scatter your ballistic missiles about the globe so that they cannot easily be located and thus cannot be neutralized by an enemy first strike. The US Navy developed the "Regulus" missiles in the 1950s; these were winged and jet-propelled, and carried nuclear warheads to ranges betwen 500 and 1,000 miles. Regulus was carried in submarines and surface ships, and was first radio-controlled and then had inertial guidance. But even while these missiles were still entering service, a significant step forward was taken with the "Polaris" missile, a rocket that could be launched from a submerged submarine to a range of over 3,000 miles.

Polaris was a solid-propellant rocket which could be ejected from a vertical launch tube in the submarine by a gas discharger

Standard missile
The US Navy's "Standard" missile being launched from USS Bunker Hill *in May 1986, using the Mark 41 Vertical Launching System. Standard was originally a surface-to-air weapon, was then adapted as an air-launched anti-radar missile, and finally further adapted to the surface-to-surface role.*

system. As it broke the surface of the sea, the rocket was ignited and the launch completed. Polaris used inertial guidance and was always fitted with nuclear warheads. The first submarine armed with Polaris, the SSBN598 *George Washington*, was operational on 15 November, 1960, since when the US Navy has maintained a fleet of 41 Fleet Ballistic Missile submarines. Polaris was superseded in US service by "Poseidon" and "Trident," but the British Royal Navy still operates four submarines armed with the Polaris system, though these are due for replacement by Trident.

Poseidon was similar in concept to Polaris but much larger; the Polaris missile was located in its wide launch tube by piston rings riding in a glass-fibre liner. By removing the liner and doing away with the rings, Poseidon could be made some 20 inches larger in diameter, giving it a greater payload and allowing the fitting of a multiple re-entry vehicle warhead with ten 50-kiloton independently-targeted sub-warheads as well as a number of decoys. The maximum range remained about 3,000 miles, but it was also possible to have a 14 MIRV warhead for shorter ranges. Poseidon went into service in March 1971 and some are still in use.

Trident is basically Poseidon 3 with a third-stage rocket motor added, which increased the range to 4,600 miles. The later Trident 2 increased the range still further, to 6,500 nautical miles (7,400 miles). Trident 2 will be adopted by the British Royal Navy in the mid-1990s to replace Polaris but will carry a British warhead.

The Soviets were early starters in the submarine missile race. By about 1953 they had produced a missile that could be launched from a submarine on the surface, and by the mid-1960s they had achieved submarine launching. A succession of improved designs have followed, and the current SS-NX-23 has a range of 5,200 miles carrying a 10-warhead payload. China and France have also produced submarine-launched missiles.

Ship-launched Exocet
An AS40 Exocet missile of the French Navy clearing its shipboard launcher. Although it came into public prominence during the Falklands campaign in 1982, Exocet has been in service with many navies since 1972. The curved plates falling away are the "sabots" or shoes which support the missile in its launch tube. The warhead contains 364 lbs of Hexogen and a steel plate which is driven through the target at high velocity and creates enormous damage.

Air-launched Exocet
The AS39, air-to-surface version of the Exocet anti-ship missile (ABOVE), here being launched from a French Navy Super Puma helicopter.

Underwater-launched Harpoon
Harpoon (RIGHT) is the US Navy's surface-to-surface missile which can be launched from submarines, surface ships, or aircraft. Here it has been launched from a submarine.

ANTI-SHIP TACTICAL MISSILES

Tactical shipboard missiles fall into two groups: anti-ship missiles and anti-submarine types (for a discussion of the latter, see Undersea weapons since 1945, page 206). The anti-ship missiles form a mixed array, ranging from converted anti-tank missiles to cruising missiles with ranges of 150 miles or more. The French Navy deployed SS-11 and SS-12 anti-tank missiles on their fast patrol boats in the 1960s, using stabilized sights, and demonstrated impressive accuracy at a 3-mile range. But perhaps the best-known sea missile (due to its performance in the Falklands campaign in 1982) is the French "Exocet", developed in 1972 and since adopted by the French, British, Greek, and other navies. Exocet is fired from a box-like launcher/container which can be fitted to almost any ship; it is fed with the target coordinates prior to launch and its mid-course guidance is inertial, the missile remaining about 8 feet above the surface of the sea. Some 9 miles from the target a radar seeks out the target and homes the missile in to impact. It has a maximum range of about 45 miles.

A similar weapon of Italian origin is "Otomat", which has been widely sold to smaller navies around the world. Otomat uses radio guidance and its flight can be corrected by a hovering helicopter or other airborne platform. It has a range of over 60 miles.

The Soviet "Styx" missile is another widely distributed design, which came to prominence in 1967 when an Egyptian patrol boat used it to sink the Israeli destroyer *Eilat* while in harbour. Like most early Soviet ship missiles it was a rocket-propelled winged device, was radio-guided into the general area of the target, and used radar homing.

The US Navy developed the submarine-fired tactical missile "Harpoon", which has been adopted by a number of navies. With a range of over 80 miles it is an anti-ship weapon with inertial guidance, and is programmed with its target coordinates before launch. It skims the surface of the sea and, when close to the target, uses radar homing to lock on. It then performs a sudden swoop upwards and dives onto the target from above, to attack the lighter armour of the deck and upperworks rather than the heavy side armour.

As well as being submarine-fired, Harpoon can quite easily be fitted on surface ships and this application is widely used throughout NATO navies.

The most recent US Navy system is "Deadeye", a guided missile that is launched from the standard 5-inch naval gun. Much of the technology has been derived from the Copperhead artillery projectile (see Smart bombs, page 210), and Deadeye uses a similar laser homing system, the target being illuminated from an aircraft. Deadeye's range is claimed to be in excess of 15 miles.

AIR-DEFENCE MISSILES

THE PROGRESSION from the free-flight air-defence rocket to the guided air-defence missile is fairly logical, given the advances in electronics that took place between 1939 and 1945. It is therefore hardly surprising that by 1942 both Britain and Germany were attempting to develop such weapons. Neither managed to put a weapon of this kind into service before the Second World War ended, but their wartime research encouraged further development in this field when the postwar peace turned into the Cold War.

Beginning in 1949, Britain developed "Thunderbird" for the Army and "Bloodhound" for the RAF. Bloodhound entered service in 1957 and Thunderbird in 1959. Both were large missiles with external boost rockets for the launch, but Thunderbird also used a liquid-fuel sustainer motor, to maintain the impulse until the missile reached its maximum speed. Bloodhound was driven by two ramjet motors — a form of jet-propulsion engine. Both missiles used semi-active radar homing, in which a ground-based "illuminating radar" locks on to the target and the missile detects the reflected radar energy and steers towards it.

In 1960 the first Soviet surface-to-air missile was put on show for the first time, though experts believe that it had been in service since 1954. Known as the SA-1 or Guild in NATO code, it appears to have been a liquid-fuel rocket with active radar homing, having its own radar system in the nose, but little is known of the details. It was replaced by better designs in the 1960s. Since the SA-1's first

Roland
Roland was developed by a French-German consortium in the 1960s and went into service in 1977 with the French and German armies. It was later adopted by the USA and other countries. It is a totally self-contained system mounted on an armoured vehicle — here a US M109 SP gun vehicle suitably adapted with launchers alongside the turret and with surveillance and fire control radars on the turret.

Nike Hercules
Nike Hercules was an improved missile grafted on to the existing Nike defensive system in order to avoid making previous expenditure obsolete. Although an expensive way of doing things, the Hercules missile was worth the trouble, as it
could provide Mach 3.65 speed to an altitude of 150,000 feet and effectively spoiled any chance of an enemy avoiding the missile by flying high.

appearance, an enormous variety of Soviet air-defence missiles have been seen; some, such as the SA-2 Guideline were exported to other countries, and in time most of their details became known. Others, such as the SA-5 Gammon, were never seen outside the USSR and much less is known of them, though Gammon is believed to be fitted with a nuclear warhead.

The USA threw a great deal of money and effort into the air-defence missile field and produced a number of weapons whose names became well known. Their pioneer missile, "Nike Ajax", went into service in December 1953 with the US Army and was the first air-defence guided missile to enter service anywhere in the world. By modern standards it was a big, cumbersome system, using permanent emplacements of considerable complexity. It employed a solid-fuel boost motor for the launch and a liquid-fuel sustainer motor. The guidance system was complicated. One radar tracked the target and another tracked the missile while a computer analysed both tracks, calculated how to bring target and missile together, and then commanded the missile accordingly. As well as being deployed in the USA, Nike was sold to several NATO countries and to Japan. Over 3,000 launch units were eventually placed in service.

One drawback of Nike Ajax was that it made an extremely expensive air-defence system to replace. Its successor, "Nike Hercules", had to accommodate much of the earlier equipment so that it was simply a more powerful missile grafted on to the same control system. The improvement can be judged by its range, which was 87 miles, as compared with the 26 miles of Nike Ajax. Finally, in 1964 came "Nike Zeus", a three-stage rocket with a thermonuclear warhead and a range of 250 miles.

The US Air Force also deployed air-defence missiles and adopted Bomarc in the middle 1950s. This was an aircraft-like winged missile driven by two ramjet engines, capable of a speed of Mach 4; it was vertically launched, using a solid-fuel booster, and had a maximum range of 435 miles. Used as a long-range interceptor for the defence of the USA, it was guided towards the target area by radar from ground control, after which it used its own on-board active radar to lock on and steer to impact.

DEVELOPMENTS WORLDWIDE

As the electronics industry spread throughout the world in postwar years, so the development of missiles spread with it. In 1968 France produced "Crotale", a four-tube launcher on an armoured vehicle firing a Mach 2.5 missile with radar guidance and infrared homing, that is, locking onto the target by pursuing the heat emitted from it. Crotale was followed in the late 1970s by "Shahine", an improved version using a six-tube launcher. These were all sold abroad; France itself relied upon the Roland system, developed jointly with Germany in the 1960s. This is an entirely self-contained system within a single armoured vehicle, which includes surveillance radar, electro-optical tracking, and two firing rails each of which is fed by a four-missile magazine. As well as being adopted by France and Germany, Roland has been purchased by the US Army.

Almost all these missiles depended on getting within lethal distance of the target and then, having sensed the target by means of a proximity fuze, detonating a powerful warhead to wreck the target by blast and fragment. But heavy and powerful warheads mean heavy missiles, making some of these systems barely mobile and scarcely capable of accompanying a field army. Both Britain and the USA realized this and in the 1960s the Americans began developing "Mauler", which would be a self-contained system on a tracked vehicle with surveillance and tracking radars, and a 12-round automatic launcher firing a missile to a 5-mile range. However, after much time and money had been expended, this system collapsed because it tried to do too much with the technology available. The Americans then produced "Chaparral", which was little more than an existing air-to-air missile with infrared homing allied to a mobile launcher with optical tracking. The British developed "Rapier", which entered service early in 1967. This was the first "hittile", a missile intended to achieve a direct hit, so that it could be smaller and lighter than those that relied on proximity blast to defeat their targets. Rapier uses a solid-fuel motor of high thrust and is controlled by optical tracking of the target. The missile, which is also in the line of sight, compares its trajectory with the sight line of the target and corrects by radar as necessary. Rapier has achieved hits on targets as small as 8 inches in diameter and has a maximum range of 5 miles; it was deployed in the Falklands campaign of 1982 and is in use by several countries as well as Britain.

The miniaturization of electronic components enabled missiles to be made much smaller; there are now several types that can be fired off the shoulder. In 1967, the US Army pioneered this concept with "Redeye", an infrared homing missile which locks onto the target before being fired. The following year, the British adopted "Blowpipe", which was controlled in flight by the firer,

Stinger
Stinger(ABOVE) entered service as a man-portable system, as seen here, and it has been adapted to pods which can be carried on helicopters and light aircraft.

Tracked Rapier
The British Army's Tracked Rapier(RIGHT) carries eight ready-to-fire missiles on the vehicle.

who also steered it to the target. This was replaced by "Javelin" (1985), which uses a system similar to that of Rapier in which the operator keeps his sight on the target and the missile is automatically corrected. The Americans replaced Redeye with "Stinger" in 1989. Redeye had a defect, common to all early infrared homers, that it chased the hot jet efflux rather than the aircraft; Stinger has correction circuits which cause it to compensate and hit the aircraft; it also has an IFF (Identification of Friend or Foe) system which simplifies the problem of identifying targets.

Other countries followed these leads. The USSR developed "Grail", which was more or less a copy of Redeye, Bofors of Sweden produced the RBS-70, and France the Eryx. In 1990 the British announced that they would be adopting "Starfire", an updated version of Javelin, which launches a single missile that closes with the target and then discharges three independent warheads to ensure a successful contact.

TANKS SINCE 1945

AS THE war in Europe ended in May 1945, the British were about to bring into service the 40-ton Centurion tank with its 76-mm gun. The Americans had just introduced the M26 Pershing tank, also weighing 40 tons, with a 90-mm gun. At the Victory Parade held in Berlin the Western allies were surprised to see a new Soviet tank, the Joseph Stalin (JS) 3. It mounted a 122-mm gun, weighed 46 tons and was not only heavier and better armed than Western tanks, but its sleek shape and curved surfaces gave it a better chance of survival in battle. Its apparent advantages worried western designers, especially as the Cold War between the former allies developed in the late 1940s.

The Centurion and Pershing served in the Korean War (1950–3) where they encountered the Soviet-made T34/85, the up-gunned version of the tank that had vanquished the German Panzers. British and US tanks showed themselves to be superior, but given that the Soviet design was much older, this should have been no surprise. Meanwhile British, US, and Soviet tank designers were striving to get ahead of each other. Initially the move was towards heavy tanks, resulting in the US M103 (1953) and British Conqueror (1954). However, these were soon seen as logistic nightmares, demanding as they did strengthened bridges, special transporters, and expensive support and maintenance facilities. They were dropped in favour of the class that has since come to be called MBT (Main Battle Tanks).

Britain developed the Centurion through 17 variants over the years. The main armament was gradually improved from 76 mm to 84 mm and finally to an excellent 105-mm gun, which was adopted by the USA and then by most NATO countries. Similarly, the Americans took the M26 Pershing as their model and developed from it the M48 and M60, for which the British 105-mm gun was

The S-Tank

The Swedish S-Tank uses no turret; instead it has its 105-mm gun mounted rigidly into the body of the tank, and in order to point the gun it is necessary to point the tank. Elevation is provided by an adjustable hydraulic suspension that raises and lowers the front of the tank and hence the angle of the gun. Direction is given by swivelling the tank bodily on its tracks. Surprisingly, the controls are fine enough to permit accurate shooting.

Leopard II

Built in Germany for the German Army, the Leopard II has also been adopted by the Dutch Army (this picture) and Switzerland. It is armed with a 120-mm smooth-bore gun which fires fin-stabilized APDS and HEAT projectiles at high velocity. Operated by a four-man crew, Leopard II is provided with night-vision equipment, electronic fire control, laser rangefinding and electronic navigational aids. The engine is a 1,500-hp turbo-charged 12-cylinder diesel with automatic transmission, giving a maximum speed of 72 km/hr.

adopted in 1958. The Soviets used the T-44 (a successor to the T-34 produced only in small numbers) as their starting point and improved it into the T-54/55 and then the T-62. The T-62 introduced a new concept in tank warfare, with a 115-mm smoothbore gun as its main armament. The gun was expressly designed to fire fin-stabilized discarding sabot (see Anti-tank weapons, page 144), and shaped-charge ammunition. The performance of a shaped charge is weakened by spinning, which would be caused by rifling in the gun barrel (see Rifling, page 72). Similarly, the performance of discarding sabot shot is improved by the absence of rifling, as this reduces friction and allows a higher velocity to be achieved. The development caused a great deal of upset in the NATO camp, where designers hurriedly worked on armour-piercing, fin-stabilized, discarding-sabot (APFSDS) ammunition which had to be adapted to fire from existing rifled guns, at the same time as they began to develop smoothbore weapons. In fact, though they did not know it for several years, the Soviet 115-mm gun was not a success, having to be withdrawn and partially rifled before it could be considered sufficiently accurate for service. But for NATO's reaction the Soviets might well have abandoned the idea; as it was they persisted and eventually developed a much better 125-mm smoothbore weapon with which to arm their next tank, the T-72.

The M1A1 Abrams
The American Abrams tank is armed with the same 120-mm smooth-bore gun as the Leopard II, and driven by a 1,500-hp gas turbine engine. In the Gulf War, seven were hit by shots from Iraqi T-72 tanks, but none sustained any damage. The thermal sight allows crews to fire through oil smoke and in total darkness.

Although the British developed fin-stabilized ammunition for its 105-mm gun, they remained unconvinced that a smoothbore was the complete answer. A rifled gun allows a wider choice of ammunition types, and the British were inclined to trust their own invention, the high-explosive squash-head (HESH) shell, more than they trusted the shaped charge. The HESH shell contains plastic explosive which is spread on the surface of the target on impact and then detonates. This sets up an intense shock wave in the armour, which detaches the inner face of the plate to whirl off inside the tank, seriously injuring the crew. This type of shell works better in a rifled gun. Britain had adopted a 120-mm rifled gun in the new Chieftain tank, which could fire a HESH shell as well as spin-stabilized sabot ammunition.

Meanwhile other countries had begun to build their own tanks. Among the most remarkable of these was the Swedish S-Tank. This vehicle, introduced in 1966, was intended to improve "survivability" by having a very low silhouette; simplify manufacture and maintenance by having no turret; and reduce the number of trained men required, by using a three-man crew and an automatic loading mechanism for the gun. There were two engines, a diesel for ordinary running and a gas turbine to give a boost for cross-country manoeuvring. The gun was rigidly fixed in the hull, and aimed by swinging the whole tank, using the adjustable suspension to lift or lower the rear of the tank to find the range. Built by Bofors, it was a technical masterpiece, but whether it would have survived in war is an unanswered question. Nevertheless, it gave tank designers some new ideas and it remains an influential vehicle.

Germany began rebuilding its army in the 1950s and was initially equipped with American M48 tanks, but soon set about designing its own. The Leopard 1, which appeared in 1965, was a conventional turreted tank using the British 105-mm gun. It was an excellent design, and some 6,000 were built, of which many were exported. Leopard 2 followed in 1979.

In the 1970s the British had developed Chobham Armour, a laminated armour using steel, ceramics, and titanium, which, it was claimed, could withstand any form of shaped-charge attack then known. This claim is no longer true, but even so, this laminated armour is extremely resistant. It was first adopted by the Germans in Leopard 2, together with a 120-mm smoothbore gun of great power and accuracy.

Leopard 2 came about because of the failure of a joint US-German programme to develop a new MBT. Germany went ahead with Leopard 2 and the Americans went on to develop the M1 Abrams. By the late 1970s the electronic revolution had transformed the tank from a simple piece of machinery into a vehicle bursting with computerized black boxes. This new technology included a laser rangefinder, thermal imaging (infrared) sights for night shooting, a fire-control computer to apply corrections for temperature, wind, tilt, and many other factors, and stabilization of the gun so that once laid on a target it would remain there irrespective of later manoeuvres.

The day of the million-dollar tank arrived with the Abrams. It was armed initially with a 105-mm gun, but later up-gunned to take the German 120-mm smoothbore weapon; it also had a powerful gas turbine engine which gave it great agility at the cost of very high fuel consumption.

Britain's equivalent was the Challenger, which entered service in the 1980s; Challenger uses a new rifled 120-mm gun and a conventional engine, but has the latest fire-control and electronic equipment. Both Challenger and Abrams proved their effectiveness in the brief Gulf campaign of 1991.

LIGHT ANTI-TANK WEAPONS

THE END of the Second World War found the infantry of the countries involved holding an odd assortment of light anti-tank weapons. The Soviets alone clung to the anti-tank rifle, since their 14.5-mm model was quite potent against lighter armour, and they had enough artillery to deal with the heavier armour. The Americans had the 2.36-inch Bazooka, and

LAW-80
The British Army's LAW-80 is a 94-mm rocket carried in a reinforced plastic launching tube. As well as a sight, the tube contains an aiming rifle loaded with bullets which create a flash and smoke when they strike.

The firer therefore has simply to fire the rifle until he sees a strike, then, holding the same aim, fire the rocket.

The RPG-7
The Soviet RPG-7 launches a rocket by means of a recoilless charge (LEFT).

the Germans the Panzerschreck and Panzerfaust. The British had the PIAT (Projector, Infantry, Anti-Tank), a peculiar weapon which launched a shaped-charge bomb from a steel rod, the cartridge being inside the bomb's tail. The Americans also had on the drawing board a new 3.5-inch Super Bazooka.

The Korean War (1950–3) brought the Super Bazooka off the shelf and into production and the British adopted it in place of the obsolete PIAT. The larger warhead of the 3.5-inch model gave good results for both the British and US Armies. The Soviet bloc, however, was in need of a new anti-tank weapon. Having been impressed by the German Panzerfaust, Soviet designers took this as their starting point and developed the RPG-2 launcher. This was a simple tube with a pistol grip and trigger; the projectile was a thin rocket motor with flexible fins wrapped around it so that it could be slid into the tube, and a larger-calibre shaped charge warhead which protruded from the front of the tube. On firing, the rocket was ignited and went to a range of about 200 yards; the

warhead could defeat about 7 inches of armour. The design was copied by, among others, the Czechs, who called it Pancerovka, and the Chinese, to whom it was Type 56.

Other countries copied the Bazooka, including the Belgians who produced the 83-mm Blindicide in about 1953. This had a highly efficient motor and a rocket with spring-out fins giving better accuracy than the American model, and an effective range of over 500 yards. The French developed LRAC (Lance-Roquette Anti-Char), which introduced a novel two-part system: the rocket launcher was the usual tube and pistol grip, with a bayonet joint at the rear end. The rocket was packed inside a short sealed tube which was attached to the launcher by the bayonet joint. After firing, the short tube was discarded and a fresh loaded tube attached. The system was quicker than manually feeding a rocket into a tube and clipping on the firing contacts (as in the Bazooka), it also kept the rocket clean and dry until the moment of firing. Meanwhile Germany dusted off the wartime Panzerfaust, gave it a

Folgore
The Italian Army's standard anti-tank weapon is "Folgore", an 80-mm recoilless gun whch fires a rocket projectile to a range of 4,500 metres, though its maximum anti-tank range is 1,000 metres. It can be tripod-mounted or, as seen here, fired from the shoulder, since it weighs only 18 kg.

The M72 LAW
The M72 is a "disposable" weapon; as can be seen here, the launcher is a telescoping tube pre-loaded with a rocket, and when extended can be fired from the shoulder by a simple press-trigger on the top surface. Extending the launch tube automatically cocks the weapon and erects the simple sights, and once fired, the empty tube is simply thrown away. the rocket has a range of about 300 metres against tanks and up to 1,000 metres against other targets. The shaped charge warhead will defeat over 300 mm of armour plate.

new warhead, and called the weapon Lanze.

All these weapons had two defects: they were generally long and cumbersome for the infantryman to carry; and they gave off considerable backblast when fired. This made the selection of a good firing position vital; they were difficult to site in street fighting, for example.

The Americans tackled the length problem and developed the M72 LAW (Light Anti-tank Weapon) in the 1960s. This consisted of two tubes, one sliding inside the other, the smaller tube pre-loaded with a 66-mm shaped-charge rocket. With the inner tube pushed inside the outer, the whole thing was only 24 inches long. To fire the weapon, the soldier first pulled out the inner tube until it locked in place, making the weapon 35 inches long. This action erected the sight and cocked the trigger. The soldier then laid the tube on his shoulder, took aim, and squeezed the trigger once, the rocket was fired, the empty tube was thrown away. It was the first "expendable munition", cheaper to discard than return and reload. Against tanks the M72 had an effective range of about 300 yards, but could be used up to 1,000 yards against soft targets.

The success of this weapon led to many armies dropping the Bazooka, and the American idea was soon copied by the Soviets. In fact, they already had one of the most effective short-range weapons, after transforming their RPG-2 into the considerably improved RPG-7. This was very similar to the early model but with two important differences. First, the rocket was ejected from the launcher by a small recoilless charge. After about 10 yards of flight the rocket motor fired and the rocket accelerated away to an effective range of about 500 yards. The peculiar trajectory was compensated for in the sight and the weapon was quite accurate. Secondly the warhead used a piezoelectric fuze. The effect of the warhead touching the target crushed a crystal in the nose which

generated an electric impulse, firing the shaped charge much faster than any mechanical fuze could, to give a more efficient penetrative jet. The RPG-7 has since been copied in China and has sold throughout the world.

The problem of the backblast was solved in Germany by the Armbrust launcher. The Armbrust reverted to the recoilless (see Recoilless guns, page 170) principle of the Panzerfaust, but instead of ejecting gas like other recoilless weapons, it ejected a mass of about 5,000 flakes of plastic, The gas was entirely trapped between two piston heads, one of which drove the projectile from the front of the weapon, the other driving the plastic flakes out of the rear. Since the flakes were light they soon lost momentum, making Armbrust safe to fire inside a building or with a wall close behind, and hence ideal for street fighting.

As tank designs continued to improve, (see Tanks since 1945, page 192), the 66-mm LAW was no longer the complete answer to the MBT, if, indeed, it ever had been. In the early 1980s many countries began looking for a newer and more powerful LAW. Britain introduced the LAW80, an 94-mm rocket with a powerful shaped-charge warhead. The USA has tested almost every weapon available, but has retained the M72. The replacement for it, currently in the development stage, is a man-portable missile. France has introduced the Apilas (1990), a man-portable missile guided by an infrared beam, while Italy has developed Folgore (1988), a recoilless launched rocket. Germany has improved the original Lanze into Panzerfaust 3 (1990), using a similar plastic ejection mass to Armbrust and with a high-efficiency shaped-charge warhead that is larger than the calibre of the firing tube. All these weapons have warheads in the 85–110-mm calibre range and can, it is claimed, defeat the frontal-armour of any current main battle tank.

ANTI-TANK MISSILES

IN THE immediate postwar years the major armies of the world tended to adopt the recoilless gun (see Recoilless guns, page 170) as the prime anti-tank weapon, using shaped-charge or HESH shells (see Tanks since 1945, page 192) as projectiles. However, experience soon showed that the recoilless gun had its drawbacks, including a voracious appetite for propellant, a vicious backblast that gave away its position as soon as it fired, and a relatively restricted range. It was also a low-velocity weapon, which therefore fired in a looping trajectory, leading to problems of accuracy in estimating the range. A slight misjudgement of range that would be of little or no consequence in a high-velocity, flat-trajectory gun could make a recoilless gun miss the target altogether. Nevertheless, given adequate rangefinding and a short field of fire the recoilless gun still has its uses.

In the 1950s missile designers turned from the inter-continental strategic giants (see Strategic missiles, page 184) and began studying the anti-tank problem. As a solution, they proposed a rocket-propelled missile, armed with a suitable shaped-charge (HEAT) or HESH warhead, which could be guided by an observer, using a joystick type of control. The guidance instructions were relayed down a wire reeled out by the missile as

Vigilant
Vickers began to develop an anti-tank missile in 1956 (LEFT). It was first fired in 1958, was christened "Vigilant", and by the mid-1960s was in service with Britain, Finland, and several Middle Eastern countries. A first-generation missile, it had to be steered to impact, a somewhat demanding task, but was highly effective with a skilled operator.

> *We were advancing and in the distance I saw specks dotted on the sand dunes...As we got closer I thought they looked like tree stumps. I asked the tanks ahead what they made of it. One of the tank commanders radioed back 'My God, they're not tree stumps, they're men!' For a moment I couldn't understand. What were men doing out there when we were advancing in tanks toward them? Suddenly all hell broke loose. A barrage of missiles was being fired at us, many of our tanks were hit. We had never come up against anything like this before...*

An Israeli armoured commander, quoted in Blitzkrieg, *by Charles Messenger; Ian Allen, London, 1976.*

TOW
TOW (BELOW) went into service in 1970 and has been adopted by over 40 countries. A second-generation missile, TOW is guided automatically. A sensor in the sight detects a flare in the base of the missile, compares its position with the axis of the sight, and sends flight corrections to make the missile's course match the sight line.

it flew. Unfortunately, what appeared easy on a testbed proved less so in the smoke and heat of battle, against a target moving rapidly across rough country. The first generation anti-tank missiles, such as the British Vigilant, Australian Malkara, German Cobra, French SS-10, and Soviet Snapper, were not so easy to control in real life. Arab operators of Soviet Snapper missiles, in the Arab-Israeli conflict of 1967, were frequently put off their aim by enemy machine-gun fire.

By then, however, the second-generation anti-tank missiles were beginning to take shape. These are more properly called SACLOS (Semi-Automatic Command to Line of Sight) and they involve a degree of automation. With SACLOS, the operator only has to keep the sight directed at the target, and can ignore the missile. In its tail the missile carries an infrared flare, which is detected by a sensor in the sight unit, and the position of the missile relative to the centre of the sight (and hence the line to the target) is analysed by a computer. The computer calculates the correction needed to bring the missile to the sight line and transmits this information down the trailing wire to the missile. Inevitably, the missile over-corrects and the sight brings it back in decreasing loops until it settles down and flies to the target.

Among the earliest second-generation missiles were Milan, HOT, and TOW. Milan (Missile d'Infanterie Léger Anti-Char) and HOT (Haut-subsonique Optiquement Téléguide) are both joint developments between France and Germany, HOT was intended for mounting on vehicles and helicopters, and Milan for infantry use and on the turrets of light armoured vehicles. HOT had a 165-mm shaped-charge warhead and a range of about 5,000 yards, Milan a 105-mm warhead and a range of about 2,750 yards. Both have been gradually improved since their introduction in the late 1970s. The current version of HOT has a 150-mm warhead capable of defeating over 40 inches of armour, that of Milan a 115-mm warhead capable of defeating 39 inches of armour.

TOW (Tube-launched, Optically-tracked, Wire-guided) is an American missile which has been adopted by over 40 countries and has been constantly improved since its introduction in 1970. In its original form Basic TOW had a 127-mm warhead and a range of 4,000 yards. ITOW (Improved TWO) had the same size warhead, but with a much improved shaped charge inside. A long, extensible probe on the nose detonated the warhead before it reached the armour, giving the penetrative jet space in which to attain optimum shape and velocity. TOW 2 has a 152-mm warhead and improved guidance circuitry, TOW 2A uses a tandem warhead (described below), while TOW 2B is designed for "top attack".

The tandem warhead, as used on TOW 2A, is simply two shaped charges, one behind the other. On striking the target the first charge detonates the reactive armour. Microseconds later the main charge detonates and has a clear path to the steel armour, now devoid of its explosive protection.

"Top attack" is a new approach to destroying the tank. The side and front armour has become progressively thicker, and the development of Chobham laminated armour has made the tank a harder target. As a result, in the 1980s Bofors of Sweden began to explore the feasibility of attacking the top surfaces of the tank, which are much thinner than the sides. They produced the BILL (Bofors, Infantry, Light and Lethal) missile, which is programmed to fly one yard above the sight line, so that aiming at the tank turret causes the missile to fly above it. A proximity fuze detects the turret of the tank, and a specially-adapted shaped charge fires obliquely downwards into the turret roof. Once Bofors had shown that this could work, other manufacturers took up the challenge.

The anti-tank war is one of constant change as each side develops new weapons or countermeasures. One such countermeasure, first seen during the Israeli invasion of Lebanon in 1982, was reactive explosive armour. This consists of metal boxes filled with high explosive and shaped to form an outer layer to those areas most likely to be attacked — the tank turret and parts of its hull. The idea is that any projectile or shaped-charge jet striking this layer will detonate the box of explosive. This will not affect the tank, but the detonation will either disrupt the shaped-charge jet, or shatter a tungsten core, or deflect a projectile, and so prevent penetration of the main steel armour.

Bofors Bill
A Swedish soldier about to launch a "Bill" missile (**RIGHT**) *in its sealed transit/launch tube alongside the day-and-night sight. Wire-guided, it has a range of about 3 km. The Bill is a "top attack" weapon* (**BELOW**); *the firer aims at the tank turret and the missile flies 750 mm above the sight line.*

This, added to laminated armour, was touted as the ultimate protection for tanks in the late 1980s, but within a couple of years the ammunition makers had found a solution.

THIRD-GENERATION MISSILES

Current development efforts are being directed to the third generation of missiles, popularly called "fire-and-forget" weapons. As the term implies, the intention is a self-guiding missile. With the first and second generations the firer is tied to the sight until the missile strikes, which in some cases may be up to 20 seconds, a long time to remain exposed on the battlefield. With the fire-and-forget system once the missile is launched the firer should be able to take cover or turn to another target, sure in the knowledge that the missile has homed. Achieving this makes considerable demands on the guidance system. An air-defence missile has a discrete target against a clear background, but a ground missile has a target that is liable to merge with its background. Radar transmitting on millimetre waves is currently favoured as the most likely method of guidance, with thermal imaging another contender. In any case, it will not be until the late 1990s that the first types are in operation.

THE COLD
WAR GIVES
AN OLD
WEAPON NEW
IMPORTANCE

LAND MINES SINCE 1945

THE COLD war raised the possibility of NATO having to contend with the Soviet Army in Europe. In particular, the Soviet doctrine of offensive large-scale tank warfare worried NATO members and revived an interest in land mines. Mines can be used either to damage directly tanks and personnel, or simply to force them into routes and areas that are more easily defended. Both these applications were attractive to NATO, which always lagged behind the Warsaw Pact in terms of its armour and anti-armour defences.

The laying of a minefield is a labour-intensive operation, so one of the first design requirements for NATO, which had fewer members of the armed forces than the Warsaw Pact, was to develop mines that could be laid mechanically at high speed. The next requirement was to obtain the maximum effect from the minimum number of mines. If the width of the tracks of an enemy tank is known, the positioning of the mines to give the best chance of encountering a tank can be calculated. An important factor in the calculation is, of course, the size of the mine. Moreover, if the mine can be made to detonate by some means other than direct pressure from the tank track, then the strike rate will improve considerably.

The British solved some of these problems by developing the Barmine, which entered service in 1970. Unlike the wartime round mine, the Barmine, was, as its name suggests, in the shape of a bar about 3 feet long and 6 inches wide. Laid across an enemy's course, it could be expected to multiply the chances of being driven over. Furthermore, because of its shape it could be

The spoils of war

An Israeli ordnance technician examines captured mines after the 1973 Yom Kippur war. The mines, taken from Arab minefields, are actually of Italian manufacture; they are of plastic, and thus hard to detect, and contain 5.5 kg of an RDX/TNT mixture. Pressure greater than about 180 kg on top of the mine will depress the top pressure plate against the striker until a retaining collar breaks, releasing the striker to fire the mine.

The Bar mine

*The British Bar mine (**ABOVE**) was introduced in the late 1960s and was specifically designed for rapid mechanical laying. It is plastic, with only a few tiny metal components, and is loaded with 7.2 kg of explosive. Its long shape doubles its chances of being activated by a tank and reduces the number of mines needed to make an effective barrier.*

The Bar mine layer

*The other part of the Bar mine system is this mechanical layer (**RIGHT**), capable of being towed behind most vehicles. A simple machine, it ploughs out a groove, arms the mine fuze, drops the mine into the groove, and then covers it over. The depth of the mine and the interval between them can be easily adjusted to suit the particular tactical needs. With a three-man crew feeding the mines into the layer, some 700 mines can be laid in an hour.*

> " Among the lessons the Vietnam War offers us is the proof that we still need to find better ways of dealing with land mines. Because of the nature of the war the enemy was able to do great damage with random mines, some of which were relatively simple. Historically, anti-armour land mines have been a persistent and vexing problem for which no really satisfactory solution has ever been found. Our failure to solve the problem of mines laid in patterns has been aggravated by our similar failure to cope with random mining tactics. "

General Donn A. Starry; Armoured Combat in Vietnam: Blandford Press, 1981.

rapidly laid by a special plough towed behind a suitable vehicle, such as an armoured personnel carrier. The crew of the towing vehicle fed the mines down a chute on the two-wheeled plough. As the mines slid down, the fuze was automatically armed. The mine fell off into a furrow cut by the plough, and was immediately covered over. Little trace was left on the ground, and up to 700 mines an hour could be laid by a single vehicle.

To increase the mine's effective radius, the tilt fuze was developed. This was attached to the mine in addition to the normal contact fuze and left a thin antenna sticking up above the ground. Should the tracks of a vehicle straddle the mine, the body would strike this antenna and detonate the mine. Use of the tilt fuze considerably increased the probability of stopping a vehicle.

Another tactic was to position a mine to one side of the tank's expected route in order to strike from further away. The tactic had been tried by the German Army in 1944, using a special type of shaped charge to blast a heavy steel plate at the tank, but the concept was still being developed when the war ended. After the war, the idea was taken up by the French who, instead of the steel

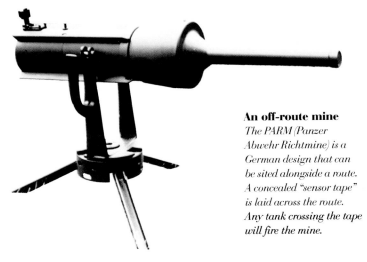

An off-route mine
The PARM (Panzer Abwehr Richtmine) is a German design that can be sited alongside a route. A concealed "sensor tape" is laid across the route. Any tank crossing the tape will fire the mine.

plate, used a massive shaped charge with a piercing jet that reached out across several yards with sufficient force to penetrate armour. The problem remaining was to detect the passage of the tank. Initially, simple pressure switches in the ground were connected to the mine, but with improvements in electronic technology in the 1970s more sophisticated sensors became available to make the "off-route" mine far more effective.

First, an acoustic sensor alerts the mine to the approach of a tank. The mine then uses video or thermal imaging, or laser sensors, to detect the tank as it enters the line of fire. A computer calculates the tank's speed and fires the mine precisely at the right moment to direct the explosive jet into the most sensitive spot. Alternatively, the acoustic sensor can alert a human operator located at a distance from the mine.

MINELAYING SYSTEMS

Anti-personnel mines are likely to need to be laid quickly, and various high-speed methods of dispersion have been devised. The Ranger system used by the British Army from 1974 involves mounting a rack containing the mines on top of a vehicle. The rack is loaded with 72 disposable tubes, each holding 18 small mines. Once the vehicle reaches its destination, where the mines are to be laid, the Ranger rack is activated, firing one tube per second until the rack is empty. As each tube fires, the 18 mines are flung at random to a range of up to 100 yards. Twenty seconds after being fired, the mine arms itself. When the rack is empty it can easily be reloaded within a few minutes to scatter further mines if required.

The US Army developed FASCAM — the "Family of Scatterable Mines" — a similar system to Ranger. However, FASCAM can also be carried by helicopter to permit even faster laying over a wider area. The helicopter flies low over the chosen area and the system scatters the mines across the ground below. These scatterable mines, British, American and others, are plastic, and a little over 2 inches in diameter. They are coloured to match the ground and are difficult to detect and neutralize. In mobile warfare there is always the danger that today's minefield in defence might be tomorrow's obstacle to an advance. To deal with this problem, the "self-sterilizing" mine has been developed. After a specific period of time, this will either blow itself up or simply lock the fuze and make itself inert, enabling friendly troops to pass over the area safely.

At the end of the Second World War, the use of nuclear land mines was proposed for last-ditch use in Germany to close certain natural routes of advance in the event of a Soviet invasion. But no one has so far developed this idea further. Many of the bridges in Europe have been built with chambers in the structure into which explosives can be placed should it ever become necessary to demolish the bridge in the face of an attack. In similar vein, visitors to Switzerland and other European countries will often see plates in the roads at borders, evidence that these roads have been prepared for rapid cratering in time of war.

The latest advance in mining is the remote delivery of mines by means of artillery and rockets (see Smart bombs, page 210). The neutralizing of mines still relies largely upon the techniques described under land mines, page 166.

MODERN-DAY ARTILLERY

FROM THE end of the war in 1945 until the mid-1960s there was little development in artillery technology. Clearly, the mass-destructive power of atomic weapons far surpassed anything that artillery would be likely to achieve. Gradually, however, it became apparent that the nuclear weapon was often not a feasible option, and that nuclear missiles would be grossly expensive and never sufficient. Moreover, air forces were little better at accurate delivery than they had been in the Second World War. A second reason for the initial lack of interest in new artillery lay in the question of control. So long as artillery targets could be seen by an observer with the forward infantry there was no incentive to develop long-ranging guns that could not accurately pinpoint their targets. A further effect of the nuclear pre-occupation was that air forces were emphasizing the strategic role and neglecting their close-support responsibilities, including that of artillery observation.

Britain was forced into artillery re-equipment in 1955 by NATO's insistence on 105-mm and 155-mm calibres as standard; neither had ever been used by Britain, and therefore new weapons had to be produced. The quick solution was to purchase a 105-mm howitzer from Italy (the M56) and a 155-mm weapon from the USA (the SP M44) and then set about designing an SP (self-propelled) 105-mm gun, since the Italian weapon — and most other available 105-mm howitzers — used the standard American ammunition. The result was the "Abbot", a mobile gun which fired a new family of ammunition to 18,600 yards range. The gun was carried in the turret of a tracked vehicle, which proved agile and efficient. To provide a lighter weapon for airborne and helicopter-borne use, the Light Gun was developed, firing the same ammunition to the same range.

The Americans developed a string of self-propelled weapons in various calibres, all mounting wartime guns and howitzers. The principal aim was to produce equipment that could survive on the atomic battlefield. Eventually the Americans settled on the 155-mm M109 as their standard support weapon, and this was adopted by Britain and several other NATO states.

In the early 1960s more attention was devoted to artillery target acquisition. This led to the adoption of drones — radio-controlled pilotless aircraft carrying cameras. The early drones were vulnerable to jamming, and were superseded in the 1970s by autonomous ones that flew pre-programmed courses. Pre-programming made them immune to electronic interference. Television links passed information on in "real time". These new drones enabled the artillery to see deep into enemy territory, which encouraged the development of weapons to take advantage of this.

105-mm light gun
British airborne artillerymen (ABOVE) firing the 105-mm light gun.

NEW DESIGNS

In 1966, Bofors of Sweden unveiled the Bandkanon, a remarkable SP 155-mm gun which automatically reloaded from a clip of 14 rounds. Firing a 48-kg shell to nearly 28,000 yards range, it was a technological feat, but was found to be somewhat slow and cumbersome. It weighed almost 60 tons and had a top speed of only 18mph.

66 *The battlefield has expanded away from the (front line) so that the targets of greatest, if not most immediate, importance lie at longer ranges but still within the range of field artillery...This will cast artillery as an offensive arm fighting in its own right, rather than merely in a supporting role.* **99**

Major J.B.A Bailey; Field Artillery and Firepower; *Military Press, Oxford, 1989.*

At much the same time Britain, Germany, and Italy began cooperative development of the 155-mm FH70 (Field Howitzer of the 70s). This was a towed weapon with a 39-calibre barrel, much longer than hitherto considered suitable for a howitzer. Moreover the carriage, basically a two-wheeled split-trail type, had an "auxiliary propulsion" package — a Volkswagen engine which drove the main wheels. The trail ends were carried on two small steerable wheels, so the gun could be motored into and out of its firing position. This allowed it to be rapidly moved after firing, without having to call up its towing vehicle, which reduced the risk of being hit by retaliatory fire.

A new family of ammunition produced for FH70 went into service in 1978, firing a 43.5-kg shell to 15.5 miles. With new improved shells the range is increased to nearly 20 miles.

Following the appearance of FH70, Bofors produced FH77, a very similar design with a 38-mm calibre barrel, a range of 13.5 miles and with a similar auxiliary propulsion system. Since then comparable designs have appeared from France, South Africa, Spain, and Singapore.

In the late 1970s France also produced a self-propelled howitzer that broke new ground. The GCT155 has a fully automated loading system contained in its large turret; only two soldiers are required to operate the weapon, the gunlayer and the loader. The loader has only to push buttons to select the type and number of rounds, whereupon the gun loads and fires. The layer has a fully computerized sight which takes account of weather conditions, and some experimental models have been fitted with inertial platform navigational aids so as to allow the gun to operate independently of any fire control centre.

In the late 1960s the Space Research Corporation of Canada, a private concern, began developing a 155-mm howitzer that used a shell with stub wings on its forward taper. This ERFB (Extended Range Full Bore) shell gave increased range because of the aerodynamic assistance given by the wings. The gun reached a range of 18.6 miles. The company then went on to develop a system known as "base bleed", in which a form of gunpowder was burned in a recess in the shell base. The gas produced flowed into the vacuum left behind the shell as it cut through the air and lessened the base drag — something that is always detrimental to the flight of any projectile. The "base bleed" shell increased the range to 24 miles, an astounding distance for a 155-mm howitzer.

The Canadian gun was also built in Austria as the GC45, and some of the principles were used by the South Africans in their G5 howitzer, for which they developed their own base-bleed shell and tested it in combat in Angola. The successors of the Canadian firm then worked with China and Spain and probably other countries, but in 1990 the murder of Gerald Bull, the driving spirit behind the designs, put an end to their activities.

The 175-mm M107 SP gun
Developed in the late 1950s as a heavy and long-range gun that was still light enough to be airlifted in heavy transport aircraft, the 175 mm (ABOVE) fired a 148-lb shell to a range of 32,700 metres and was operated by a 13-man crew.

155-mm GCT SP howitzer
The standard French SP weapon, the GCT (RIGHT) can be operated by two men, the gunlayer and the loader.

CRUISE MISSILES

THE WEAPON now known as the cruise missile began life in the late 1940s as the "stand-off bomb", which well described its function. The problem facing the US Air Force in the event of war with the USSR, was that their heavy bombers stood a poor chance of penetrating Soviet air defences far enough to reach significant targets. This gave rise to the idea of a self-propelled bomb. An aircraft would carry it to some point close to the target and then release it to continue on its own, allowing the bomber to turn back before it ran into trouble. The bomb would be so small that it would be difficult to pick up on radar and would, in any case, be so fast that it would be an extremely difficult target to counter.

Work on the idea began in 1946 but the first such device, the American "Rascal", did not enter service until 1957. It was propelled by a liquid-fuel rocket system and used inertial guidance, being pre-programmed with the location of the target. Once released from the carrier aircraft, it flew at Mach 1.6 and three types of warhead, including two nuclear, were available.

Precision guided munitions are essential to mission accomplishment with minimum collateral damage. It takes fewer sorties to destroy the target. This also reduces exposure and, therefore, reduces the potential for aircraft losses.

Lt. Gen. Charles A. Horner, US Air Force; Desert Storm: The Air Campaign; *Military Review, 9/1991.*

Tomahawk on test
A series of high-speed photographs showing a live warhead test of a Tomahawk cruise missile against a reinforced concrete structure. The missile was launched from a submerged submarine some 400 miles away and used Terrain Contour Matching (TERCOM) to reach the target area and Digital Scene Matching to zero the missile on to the target. From left to right: the Tomahawk missile approaching the target; impact with the target, and the nose of the missile pierces the structure; detonation of the 1,000-lb warhead; fireball from the warhead detonation; light debris being flung into the air; and finally heavy debris, including concrete blocks from the building, being scattered hundreds of feet into the air. The structure, representing a hardened command bunker, was totally destroyed.

Rascal was followed by "Hound Dog" in 1961. This had been designed to suit the B-52G bomber, which went into service at the same time. Advanced bomb technology allowed it to be two-thirds the weight of Rascal even though it carried a more powerful, thermonuclear warhead. Driven at Mach 2 by a turbojet engine, Hound Dog had a range of over 700 miles, allowing the delivery aircraft to stay well clear of enemy defences. Improved methods of guidance were used as better technology became available. Hound Dog was the first stand-off weapon to adopt Tercom (Terrain Contour Matching) guidance, a system that gave the missile a detailed plan of its flight path. The missile constantly compared this with the ground over which it was passing, correcting as necessary to keep to the prescribed route.

In 1957, the Soviets produced their stand-off bomb, known in NATO code as "Kennel", which resembled a small aircraft. It appears to have been guided by simply being released in the right direction under autopilot control, and then having its flight corrected by radio from a small and fast observer aircraft until it was close enough to use its own radar to lock on to the target. Kennel was soon replaced by more sophisticated designs until finally Kingfish appeared in the early 1970s with full inertial guidance. Development then slowed down, but in recent years the AS-13, with a speed of Mach 3.5 and range of 500 miles, and the AS-15, with a range of 1,860 miles carrying a 200-kiloton nuclear warhead, were placed in service.

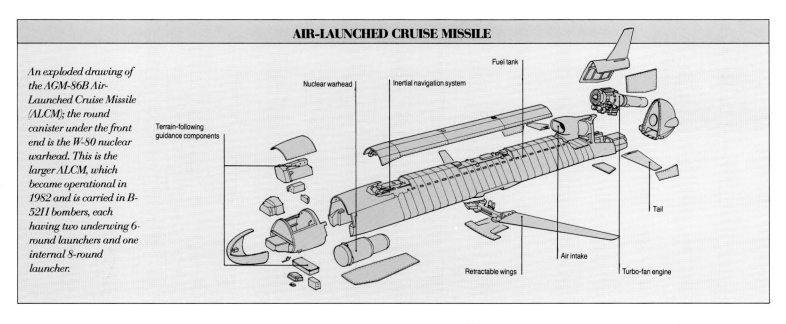

AIR-LAUNCHED CRUISE MISSILE

An exploded drawing of the AGM-86B Air-Launched Cruise Missile (ALCM); the round canister under the front end is the W-80 nuclear warhead. This is the larger ALCM, which became operational in 1982 and is carried in B-52H bombers, each having two underwing 6-round launchers and one internal 8-round launcher.

Terrain-following guidance components

Nuclear warhead

Inertial navigation system

Fuel tank

Tail

Air intake

Retractable wings

Turbo-fan engine

The Americans continued with the process of miniaturizing nuclear warheads, and by the early 1960s it seemed probable that a cruise missile small enough to go under a fighter aircraft would become feasible. This became SRAM (Short-Range Attack Missile), but instead of being used by fighters it became the armament of B-52 bombers, which used a rotary launching device in the bomb bay which was capable of carrying eight missiles. SRAM is 16.5 feet long, weighs 2,230lbs and has a range of up to 105 miles carrying a 200-kiloton warhead. It is inertially guided and rocket-propelled, flies at Mach 3, and is said to have a radar signature "no bigger than a bullet". SRAM went into service in 1972 and a total of 1,500 were manufactured. It is still in service, though it is due to be replaced with an improved model in the mid-1990s.

DECOY MISSILES

SRAM was accompanied in the developmental stages by a device called SCAD (Subsonic Cruise Armed Decoy), which was intended to be launched at the same time. SCAD was to carry radar-jamming equipment and other electronic measures to decoy air defences away from SRAM. SCAD itelf was also supposed to be capable of carrying a nuclear warhead. The idea was that the defences would not have time to decide which was the decoy and would have to shoot down everything, revealing the whole defensive organization to electronic watchers. However, the project ran into political opposition on financial grounds. The US Air Force astutely recast it under a new name — ALCM, for Air Launched Cruise Missile — in 1972. It was interchangeable with SRAM in the same rotary launcher but was a considerable advance on SCAD. A new inertial guidance system, periodically updated by a Tercom system, was incorporated. However, ALCM turned out so well that commonality with SRAM was forgotten, and a new, larger ALCM was developed along with a new rotary launcher. The present version, AGM-86M, uses a turbofan engine, the same combination of inertial and Tercom guidance and carries a 200-kiloton nuclear warhead.

At much the same time as the US Air Force developed ALCM, the US Navy developed its own version, called "Tomahawk", as an anti-ship missile. Sensibly, a number of common components and concepts were used in the two projects, enabling the Air Force to use either ALCM or Tomahawk according to what may be available. But the Navy took things a step further and developed Tomahawk as a ship- or submarine-mounted cruise missile, so that it could be used against other ships or for the attack of land targets. The results of this development were seen in 1991 when the Tomahawk was used in considerable numbers by the US Navy in the war against Iraq. Tomahawk missiles were seen on the world's TV screens flying along Baghdad's streets.

Tomahawk
A Tomahawk BGM-109 Sea-Launched Cruise Missile (SLCM) being launched from the USS New Jersey during trials off California in May 1983. Tomahawk can perform ship-to-ship or ship-to-shore missions, the latter being demonstrated during the Gulf campaign in 1991. The land-attack version has a range of 1,550 miles and can carry an HE or nuclear warhead; for ship attack the range is reduced to 280 miles and only an HE warhead is available. The cruising speed is 530 mph.

TARGET ACQUISITION

U NTIL 1915 the only methods of targeting were with the human eye or the inspired use of a map; an observer could either see a target or look at a map and guess where the target was likely to be. From the late 18th century balloons were used occasionally to try to give the eye a higher viewpoint, but a balloon is itself a very obvious target and it soon came under fire.

Ground surveillance radar

(RIGHT) *The French "Rasit" ground surveillance radar can detect moving targets to 40 km range. Targets are indicated by a cathode ray tube display which indicates their position.*

Night observation device

(BELOW) *The NOD AN/ TAS-6 is a complete observation post in one unit; it includes an infra-red (thermal imaging) long-range telescope (the central lens) with a binocular viewer (on the right as seen in the picture) and a laser rangefinder (on the left).*

An observation balloon

A battery of Royal Artillery, accompanied by an observation balloon, during the advance towards Johannesburg, South Africa, in 1900. Balloons to assist in the observation of artillery fire had been used since Napoleon's campaigns, and most notably during the American Civil War.

In late 1914 a French officer, Charles Nordmann, suggested that it might be possible to detect the noise of guns firing at a distance and determine their position. From this inspiration the art of sound ranging developed. It was used by the French from February 1915, and then considerably improved by the British under Lieutenant (later Sir) Lawrence Bragg. In its final form it consisted of a number of specialized microphones placed across about one mile of the front line and connected to a recorder, which drew the sound waves for each microphone on a moving strip of paper. By measuring the time interval between the sound as it struck pairs of microphones it was possible to plot directional rays which intersected at the position of the gun. An accuracy of 30 yards was normal, though this depended on weather conditions. The system was used during the Second World War in essentially this form, with some improvements on the recording and plotting systems.

Another system — flash spotting — was developed in 1917. This system, which relied on visual observation of gun flash by three or more widely dispersed observers, could locate an enemy gun to within 10 yards. It, too, continued in use until 1945, and was the system used to detect the launch of A-4 missiles (see V1 and V2 rockets, page 174) in 1944-5.

Remotely piloted vehicles
The "Ranger" Mini-RPV, developed by an international consortium led by Contraves of Switzerland, is typical of the light type of drone. Driven by a propeller, the aircraft can be flown manually by observation or programmed to follow a particular course.

After 1945, both systems declined: flash spotting because of the increasing use of flashless propellants; sound ranging because of the slowness of deploying a microphone base and linking the microphones, observers, and recorders with miles of wire — an operation ill-suited to open warfare.

In the 1970s, however, a method of linking the sound-ranging system by radio was perfected, and this rekindled interest in this system. Moreover, modern thermal-imaging technology has shown that flash spotting, using infrared-sensitive instruments, is also still a viable system. The German Army is on the point of introducing a modern IR flash-spotting system into service.

Aerial observation, relying upon the eye, was adopted in 1915 and was then extended by the use of cameras. These allowed stereoscopic examination to defeat camouflage and make comparisons with previous pictures to detect new movement. At the same time, aerial observers were able to range guns deeper into enemy territory, again simply by elevating the position of the eye in order to be able to see further. In the Second World War aerial observation of fire became an artillery function. British, German, and US artillery units all had light aircraft manned by artillerymen at their disposal.

PILOTLESS AIRCRAFT AND LASER BEAMS

In the 1960s, the use of RPVs (Remote Piloted Vehicles — ie pilotless aircraft) was introduced (see Modern-day artillery, page 200). First with cameras, then with "real time" television or thermal-imaging links, these could be pre-programmed to fly over specified areas to detect targets or to study the effect of previous shooting. As the range of these vehicles increased, so they were adopted by services other than artillery. Air forces could use them to check on targets and for post-strike assessment; armoured forces for examination of potential obstacles and approach routes to an objective. Using thermal imaging, RPVs can operate equally well in daylight or darkness.

The development of the laser brought another tool to target acquisition. Using a laser designator, a forward observer could direct a laser beam at a target. Some of the laser energy would be reflected off the target and they could then be detected by an approaching missile or projectile equipped with a suitable sensor. The missile would then home on to the source of the reflection to obtain a direct hit on the target. The laser designator could easily be used by a foot soldier, or by an RPV, or from a piloted aircraft or helicoper. The directional beam of the laser ensured that it would not be detected by the sensor, which would only "see" the reflections from the target.

With improvements in electronics, allowing smaller and cheaper components, it became possible to fit television cameras and laser projectors into the nose of missiles, linking these with the operator, who might be on the ground or in an aircraft. The operator could then watch as the missile approached its target and either correct the flight, guiding the weapon to impact, or, at worst, determine by how much it has missed and then correct the guidance settings for a subsequent missile.

The ultimate method of target acquisition, with a variety of possible sensors, is the satellite. A properly positioned satellite can undertake continuous observation of the battlefield, using radar, video, thermal imaging or a combination of these systems to maintain a watch on any movement. It can deliver its digital image to a ground computer which can store the image at a given moment. The computer compares the latest image with earlier images of the same area to highlight any discrepancy. This can then be viewed on a screen for checking by a human analyst. If the difference is important, information on the precise position can be extracted and sent to various agencies — air, artillery, naval gunfire — for appropriate action to be taken.

SONAR LEADS THE WAY TO DEFEAT SUBMARINES

UNDERSEA WEAPONS SINCE 1945

UNDERSEA WARFARE (USW) can include many things, but the term is generally taken to mean one — the detection and destruction of submarines. It is also a misleading term, since the destruction of submarines inevitably often takes place on the surface.

The key to USW is successful detection. Once submerged the boat is beyond the grasp of visual or radar detection and only two methods of detection remain: sound and the magnetic signature of the boat. Sound detection was pioneered by the British in the 1914–18 war, calling the apparatus ASDIC (after the Admiralty Submarine Detection Investigation Committee who developed the system). ASDIC involves sending out a pulse of sound which is reflected back by the submarine and then picked up by the sounding vessel. Knowledge of the speed of sound in water allows the distance to be calculated, and by making the transmitter directional the azimuth of the target can be determined.

Unfortunately, the propagation of sound in water is affected by its salinity, temperature, and various other physical properties, so that what appears simple is, in fact, very complex. It has taken many years of research to determine the effect of those variables and work out ways of compensating for them. In fact, by now, the receiving apparatus has been so refined that "passive" methods of detection can be used — merely listening for the noise made by the submarine's engines, pumps, and propellers, and even its movement through the water. The name has also changed; under American influence it is now sonar, the sound analogue to radar.

Sonar is used in three ways: first by sinking receivers in relatively constricted sea areas where the target submarine is expected to pass on its way to the open oceans; second by dropping or lowering sonobuoys from aircraft or helicopters to listen for submarines; and, third, by employing sonar in submarines and surface vessels to detect targets. Given a reasonable distribution of sonobuoys or sonar-equipped vessels, cross-fixes can be obtained that will locate the submarine with a high degree of accuracy.

The alternative system is known as MAD (Magnetic Anomaly Detection). The earth's normal magnetic field will be affected by the passage of several hundred tons of metal across it, and with

The heliborne torpedo
A French Navy "Lynx" helicopter launching a Mark 46 torpedo. As part of an anti-submarine force, the helicopter will be guided to a suitable position by sonobuoys or other sensor-derived information. Once it is within striking distance, the torpedo is launched. The Mark 46 is an American torpedo, widely used by other countries, and is a deep-diving, high-speed model with an active/passive acoustic homing system designed for use against submarines.

Air-launched depth charge
The British Mark II Mod 3 depth charge has been designed specifically for dropping from helicopters and maritime patrol aircraft, having been strengthened to withstand the harsh vibration of helicopters. On entering the water the tail unit is broken off and the 145-kg weapon sinks. Water pressure acting on the fuze (seen centrally inside the weapon in this sectioned view) causes it to operate at a specified depth, thus detonating the 80-kg charge of high explosive.

suitable sensors this anomaly can be detected. The earliest of these systems, used in the First and Second World Wars, involved laying huge loops of cable on the seabed in such places as the English Channel or the Straits of Gibraltar, so that the passage of a submarine over the loop would be detected. Today the method more usually employed is to place a sensitive detector in an aircraft and to fly across the suspect area. Once a submarine is detected, a sonobuoy can place its position more accurately.

The traditional weapon with which to attack a submarine once it has been located is the depth charge. This is still used, but the dropped depth charge has the drawback that as the dropping ship passes across the position of the submarine to fire the charges, it loses sonar contact. An astute submarine captain can evade the depth charges by a sudden change of direction and often break sonar contact as well.

MODERN METHODS

During the Second World War the British addressed this problem by developing "ahead-throwing" projectors and mortars, which fired a depth charge to some considerable distance ahead of the ship. These devices fired multiple charges that were designed to fall in a pattern that corresponded roughly to the shape of a submarine, giving a high probability that at least one charge would do some damage. Mortars and projectors are widely used today, some of which can throw their charges over 2,000 yards ahead of the ship.

Nuclear depth charges have been developed for the more certain destruction of large submarines, but the obvious defect here is that the ship must be well out of the area when the nuclear charge detonates. The Soviet FRAS-1 and the US Navy Subroc, Asroc, and Sea Lance systems all use rockets to deliver nuclear depth charges of about 1 kiloton to ranges up to about 40 miles.

Another method of attack is to turn the submarine's own weapon, the torpedo, against it. Torpedoes are normally assumed to travel at a pre-set depth so as to strike a surface ship. However specialized ASW (Anti-Submarine Warfare) torpedoes can dive and then use sensing devices to detect the noise or magnetic signature of the submarine and home in upon it. Torpedoes can also be launched by missiles. If an aircraft or helicopter detects a submarine some considerable distance from its parent ship, the ship can launch a missile that will fly to the locality and drop an acoustic or seeking torpedo into the water. The torpedo will then circle until it locks on to the target.

Finally, of course, submarines can fight submarines; it is an art rather than a science, since all that the captains have is their sonar, together with acoustic or wire-guided torpedoes. Some submarines, however, carry missiles that can be launched from a torpedo tube, swim to the surface, ignite a rocket motor, fly through the air, return to the water, and then release a depth charge or torpedo. The US Subroc and Sea Lance and the Soviet SS-N-15 weapons are of this type.

Launching Asroc
Asroc is the American anti-submarine rocket system that uses a solid-fuel rocket to carry either a Mark 46 torpedo or a nuclear depth charge. It is fired from an eight-cell launcher, seen here on the destroyer USS Paul F. Foster.

Mines can also be deployed against submarines, but like static sonar and magnetic loops they need to be located in some choke point through which a submarine must pass en route to its patrol waters. Such mines are generally pressure-, magnetic-, or acoustic-sensitive, otherwise to ensure that boats at various depths would be caught by a simple contact mine would be enormously expensive in mines and laying time. In very restricted waters it is possible to use electronic detection methods to obtain an accurate fix on the submarine and then detonate a nearby mine by remote control from shore.

Launching SubRoc
The American SubRoc missile is a submarine-launched device which follows an underwater trajectory for a short time before surfacing and then flying through the air for the major part of its task. It then dives back into the water and releases a 1-kiloton nuclear depth charge.

STRATEGIC BOMBERS

LONG-RANGE AIRCRAFT CARRYING VAST BOMB LOADS

I N 1945 the strategic bomber appeared to be the ultimate weapon, having justified all the faith of its advocates. It had been responsible for dropping atomic bombs on the Japanese cities Hiroshima and Nagasaki (see Nuclear weapons, page 176) and had, on the face of it, so devastated German industry as to bring the war to an end. In fact, German war production had increased under Allied bombing, rather than decreased, but by the time this was known, the building of postwar strategic bombers had got into its stride. The strategic bomber emerged as the most threatening weapon before the adoption of intercontinental ballistic missiles (see Strategic missiles, page 184) and even for some time after that.

The USA, with its wealth of experience from wartime bomber development programmes and its enormous factories and resources, produced some formidable machines. The Boeing company, which built the Flying Fortress and B-29 Superfortress during the war, followed them in 1947 with the B-50 Superfortress, an improved version of the B-29. Then, in 1950, came the B-47 Stratojet, from a design begun in 1943. This was a swept-wing six-engined aircraft capable of carrying a 22,000-lb bomb load to 3,600 miles at 550 mph. During the 1950s the Stratojet equipped 28 bombing wings of the US Strategic Air Force, each with 45 aircraft, and a fully-armed squadron was always in flight, acting as the nuclear deterrent for the USA.

As aircraft performance improved, new designs appeared, such as the Boeing B-52 Stratofortress, the biggest, heaviest, and most powerful bomber ever built, which was unveiled in 1955. Weighing almost 230 tons, it carried 27,000 lbs of bombs inside and up to 70,000 lbs under the wings to a range of 12,500 miles at 650 mph. The B-52 was the last of the big Boeings.

During the war other manufacturers had also begun producing designs that attracted the attention of the US Air Force. One of these was the Convair B-36, which went into service in 1947. Originally designed to bomb Germany from the USA in case Britain was

The Stratofortress
The Boeing B-52 Stratofortress, last of the big Boeings, ran to several models. The principal role was that of strategic bombing, carrying nuclear bombs and stand-off missiles, but in Vietnam the B-52 D to F models carried up to 70,000 pounds of gravity bombs to disrupt the Ho Chi Minh Trail. It was also used as an electronic counter-measures platform, with jamming equipment and anti-radar missiles carried on underwing pods.

The Vulcan
Almost a perfect triangle, the Vulcan had fighter-like maneuverability in spite of its size (111-feet wing span). Originally intended as a strategic bomber to carry the Blue Steel stand-off missile, by 1966 it had been re-cast as a low-level tactical bomber armed with gravity bombs. It maintained this role until it was made obsolete in 1984.

mph to a range of 4,500 miles. Introduced in 1954, it was used during the Suez campaign of 1956. Next came the Handley-Page Victor in 1957, a swept-wing four-engined aircraft carrying 35,000 lbs of bombs at 650 mph to a range of 4,600 miles. However, development had been so retarded that the Victor was incapable of evading the newer fighters and missiles and the cost was enormous; most were converted to reconnaissance or refuelling roles. The third of the British bombers was the Avro Vulcan, a delta-winged machine of fighter-like manoeuverability. This could carry 21,000 lbs of bombs at 650 mph to a range of 4,600 miles. Entering service in 1958 it did not see action until the Falklands campaign of 1982, by which time it was obsolescent and was scrapped two years later.

"STEALTH" BOMBERS

One serious defect of bombers has been their vulnerability to air defence systems; they can easily be detected by radar and then attacked by missiles or interceptor fighters. In a bid to overcome this the US Air Force began investigating "stealth technology" in the 1970s. Radar detection and radar guidance of missiles depends upon the reflection of radar energy by the target. Using carefully selected synthetic materials with low reflectivity, and a shape that reduces the area of reflecting surfaces, an aircraft can be designed with a very low "radar signature" — that is, it remains invisible to radar at ranges where other aircraft would be detected. Similarly, by careful design and selection of materials, an aircraft's infrared signature can also be reduced considerably.

The first "stealth" aircraft was the Lockheed F-117A, officially described as a fighter but actually a fighter-bomber. It was used with success in the Gulf war of 1991, when it carried "Paveway" laser-guided bombs and successfully evaded all Iraqi air defences. A new, larger machine, the Lockheed B-2 stealth bomber, has appeared in prototype form, but with the ending of the Cold War its future remains in doubt.

invaded, it carried 84,000 lbs of bombs and was driven by six conventional radial engines with pusher propellers. However, with a maximum speed of barely 400 mph it was obviously falling behind in the developmental race and most B-36s were converted into reconnaissance machines. In 1959 Convair produced the B-58 Hustler, the first supersonic bomber, which could fly at Mach 2 (1,385 mph) for 5,125 miles carrying almost 20,000 lbs of bombs.

Heavy bombers formed the strategic deterrent for the USA until the early 1970s, by which time much of their role had been taken over by missiles. Nevertheless, it was decided that there was still a role for the bomber, and in response the Rockwell International B-1 bomber appeared in 1979. This was a swept-wing aircraft of great complexity. It was also very costly, and there was considerable debate before it was finally taken into service in the early 1980s. Capable of Mach 1.6 at high altitudes, it has a range of over 6,000 miles carrying some 75,000 lbs of bombs or SRAM cruise missiles.

Other nations besides the USA developed bombers in the postwar period. The Soviets had been able to study American technology when three Boeing B-36 bombers made forced landings in the USSR in 1945. From this came the Tupolev Tu-4, a virtual copy of the B-36. The Tupolev design bureau went on to develop, in 1952, the Tu-16 "Badger", a jet aircraft capable of carrying 20,000 lbs of bombs at 600 mph to a range of 4,500 miles. It was succeeded, in 1956, by the Tu-20 "Bear". Essentially, this was an improved Tu-16 but with four turboprop engines instead of two turbojets and a larger wingspan. It could lift 25,000 lbs of bombs a distance of 7,800 miles and had a top speed of 550 mph. Finally, in 1960 came the Tu-22 "Blinder", a supersonic aircraft carrying 20,000 lbs of bombs at Mach 1.4 to a range of 1,400 miles.

In the 1950s Britain developed three strategic bombers based on designs produced in 1946. The first was the Vickers Valiant, a four-engined machine capable of carrying 21,000 lbs of bombs at 560

The stealth bomber
The Lockheed F117 stealth aircraft has been designed with concealment in mind. The shape is calculated to reflect radar energy in directions other than back to the radar, while the materials used in its construction are of the lowest possible reflectivity. The engine emissions are masked so as to present only a small infra-red signature.

SMART BOMBS AND GUIDABLE SHELLS

THE TERM "smart" munition appeared in the early 1980s, but has never been formally defined. It can be best explained as a munition that, prior to the application of electronics, was "dumb". For example, a dumb anti-tank mine sat in the ground doing nothing until a tank ran over it, whereupon it exploded; a smart anti-tank mine uses sensors to detect a nearby tank, assesses whether it is within lethal range, and if so it explodes. A dumb artillery shell fired from a gun did nothing but follow a preordained trajectory; a smart artillery shell can deviate from its trajectory, hunt for targets, analyse them, and then take appropriate action.

The move to this type of munition began with smart bombs for aircraft. The old "iron" bombs merely dropped on a curving trajectory, their accuracy depending on a complex bombsight and a good operator. During the Second World War the Americans began developing bombs that could be steered during their drop: Azon (Azimuth Only) could be steered from side to side; Razon (Range and Azimuth only) could also be directed up or down to give more or less range. They were standard 1,000-lb bombs with steerable tails and radio control. Azon was used in Italy, France, and Burma with some good results, notably against bridges.

Merlin
Merlin is a terminally guided bomb for the British 81-mm mortar. Loaded and fired like any other mortar bomb, it carries a millimetric wave radar seeker which, during the downward flight of the bomb, searches first for moving and then for stationary targets.

SADARM
SADARM (Seek And Destroy Armour) (RIGHT) is an artillery shell containing three or four anti-armour sub-munitions. These are ejected over the target area and descend by parachute.

Razon was perfected too late for wartime service but an improved version, Tarzon, weighing 12,000lb was used with considerable success in the Korean War (1950-3).

Until the early 1960s, American efforts at munitions development went almost entirely towards missiles. Then a programme called Paveway was begun, whose aim was to improve the accuracy of tactical air-to-ground weapons. Many systems stemmed from this, covering navigation, night vision, and other aspects, but most notably a series of add-on guidance systems that could be attached to standard bombs to make them into guided bombs. Guidance was by means of a laser sensor giving orders to fins mounted on the add-on unit fitted to the nose of the bomb. The sensor locked on to laser energy reflected from the target, which had been "illuminated" by a laser source from the bombing aircraft, or another aircraft, or a ground observer. The Paveway 1 bombs showed such remarkable accuracy on test that, by 1968, they were in use in Vietnam. They have since been followed by Paveway 2 and 3 versions, the principal differences being the addition of extensible fins to the basic bomb and rather more advanced electronics.

The accuracy shown by the laser system led to other applications being examined, and from this came "Copperhead," the first guidable artillery shell, which went into service in 1983. Shells are a difficult subject for guidance, largely because, unlike bombs, they suffer a colossal acceleration when fired, which subjects any electronics and control systems to enormous stresses. Advances in electronics such as solid-state modules, printed circuits, and microchips have made it possible to develop circuitry that is resistant to this firing stress. Copperhead, like Paveway, depends on the target being illuminated with a pulse-coded laser beam. This coding is programmed into the projectile before loading, so that it will only respond to the specific beam illuminating its own target. Copperhead is then loaded and fired from a 155-mm howitzer just like any other shell, the gunners aiming to place it within a half-mile circle of the designated target. Firing energizes Copperhead's internal batteries, starting a gyroscope to stabilize the projectile. As it leaves the muzzle of the howitzer, fins extend to provide stability and control surfaces. The laser detector in the nose is activated and seeks its special signal. Once this is detected Copperhead homes in on the reflecting target. It carries a heavy shaped-charge warhead which can destroy armour.

ANTI-TANK WEAPONS

The principal target of most smart munitions is tanks. They present a small target, which demands high precision. The use of smart munitions allows field artillery to engage tanks when they are too far away to be seen and, very often, when they are so far behind their own lines that they are not expecting attack, are bunched together, and have their hatches open.

SADARM (Seek and Destroy Armour) is an artillery projectile designed for this type of target. A 155-mm or 203-mm dumb shell, it contains three or four sub-munitions. These are canisters containing a millimetric-wave radar seeker, a "self-forming" fragment charge, and a parachute. When the shell ejects its sub-munitions over the target, the parachutes open and the canisters descend. The parachute is so designed to spin the canister in a circle so that it scans the ground beneath. Once the canister gets within 80 yards of the ground it will detect any tank within its scan area and, having detected one, fires the armour-piercing fragment at the weaker top surface of the tank. The self-forming fragment is a development of the shaped charge. It uses a curved face to the charge and fires off a heavy metal plate that is deformed by the blast into a slug capable of penetrating armour.

STAFF (Smart Top Attack Fire and Forget) represents another approach. It uses a 155-mm shell with a microwave sensor mounted in its side, so that as the shell spins, the sensor scans a patch of earth beneath. The sensor is programmed to recognize the "signature" of various types of target — tanks, armoured personnel carriers, parked aircraft, and so forth — whereupon it will fire a self-forming fragment downward at it.

Germany has developed a similar projectile, called ZEPL, and also EPHRAM, which is a 155-mm shell carrying a spin braking system that slows down its speed of descent over the target area. At an altitude of about 2,600 feet a microsensor head begins scanning the target area ahead of the shell. Like STAFF, it has been "told" the various parameters of targets, and as soon as it recognizes a suitable target it locks on and fires lateral thrust rockets to steer the shell on to the target; on impact, a shaped charge detonates.

Copperhead CLGP M712
*High-speed photographs showing (**TOP**) a Copperhead CLGP (Cannon-Launched Guided Projectile) round approaching a tank target and (**BELOW**) impact and detonation on the tank's turret. Copperhead is fired from a 155-mm howitzer and contains a powerful shaped charge warhead together with a laser detector.*

REMOTE-CONTROLLED MUNITIONS

Robotic Ranger
Developed by Grumman in the USA, Robotic Ranger is a small wheeled vehicle carrying three rocket launchers and a video camera. The operator "sees" via the video camera and drives the vehicle by radio control. The camera incorporates a sighting system by which the rockets can be fired when suitable targets present themselves.

T HE APPLICATION of electronics to dumb munitions (see Smart bombs, page 210) is only one way to produce "smartness"; another way is to place an otherwise dumb munition under remote control. This idea was first pursued in the USA and Britain in the mid-1980s with the development of robotics. It seems to have originated in reconnaissance with the placing of an expendable television camera at some point where it could observe an enemy area, while being able to view the picture and control the camera's movements from a distance. The video picture could also be re-transmitted by line or radio to headquarters, so that an army commander could, if he so wished, witness the situation on his front line as it developed. Next, the camera was given more flexibility by mounting it upon a small tracked vehicle, which was also remote-controlled. This enabled the camera to be concealed, trundled out to look at whatever was going on, and trundled back into concealment; or it could be driven to some other viewpoint.

The next step was to make the robotic vehicle more aggressive. Instead of merely reporting that a tank was within its purview, why not do something more active? This led to the Robotic Ranger, a light tracked chassis carrying three loaded anti-tank rocket launchers and a video camera, which first appeared in 1984. It could drive from cover, take aim at a tank, fire a rocket, and drive back into cover to await the next tank — all operations remotely controlled from a safe location. Once the third rocket had been fired, the Ranger could be driven back into some safe haven where it could be reloaded, or, if this was not feasible, simply abandoned.

Similar devices were proposed by a number of manufacturers in Britain and the USA, but the idea seems to have come to a standstill. Currently, the US Congress has authorized development funds solely for a reconnaissance robot.

In what might seem a retrograde step, the German manufacturer Dynamit-Nobel has developed a robotic anti-tank device that is static. Called "Fire Salamander", it comprises four anti-tank rocket launchers clustered on a field tripod, together with a video camera. The device can be planted in cover, overlooking some likely tank route, while a remote operator with a video screen keeps watch. In fact, using a sensor to alert the operator to the approach of tanks makes a constant watch unnecessary. Once targets appear, the mounting can be swung and aligned for firing a rocket. When all four rockets have been launched, the unit is considered expendable.

Larger robotic devices are also being developed, including, in the USA, the Robotic Wiesel, a German 3-ton light reconnaissance tank fitted with video and thermal imaging cameras, computers, and communications equipment. A troop of four Wiesels will be controlled from a Robotic Command Centre (RCC) using stereoscopic and conventional cameras to permit driving by remote control, plus a "panoramic reconnaissance platform" with thermal-imaging and colour video cameras to perform reconnaissance missions and make night driving possible. Direction will be controlled by the remote operator, using a stereoscopic image on a display screen. A computer translates the operator's instructions into commands for the vehicle.

Panzerfaust in waiting
A Panzerfaust anti-tank launcher set up in hiding and controlled by an infra-red sensor. A similar device, the Fire Salamander, mounts four such launchers and controls them remotely through a radio link and video camera, allowing the distant operator to seek out targets and engage them.

Ajax/Apilas ambush
A combination of the British "Ajax" sensor system and the French "Apilas" anti-tank rocket, this can be planted in some suitable spot and will detect and fire at a tank. It can be remotely programmed to switch on and off or report movement.

A ROBOTIC TANK

If all this proves feasible, it may be possible even to add armaments to produce a robotic tank. With automatic loading available for the weapons, there seems to be no reason why such a vehicle should not be able to perform routine patrols. In fact, something close to this has already been produced in France. In late 1991 the Thomson Company demonstrated a remotely controlled light utility vehicle fitted with cameras and other sensors that could be used to patrol the perimeter of, say, an airfield or an oil refinery. Operated from a central control point, it allows inspection to take place by day or night, and any indication of something amiss can be followed up by dispatching a manned vehicle. Perimeter guarding of oil rigs and similar sensitive installations has been done by static remote-controlled equipment for some years. The Belgian company Fabrique Nationale developed a video camera system which carried machine-guns in the camera mounts. Situated at intervals around the defended area, these cameras constantly scanned the scene and compared the picture with a "control" picture; any change in the picture, such as an intruder, caused an alarm to sound, whereupon the central control could use audio equipment to challenge the intruder or, if that had no effect, open fire with the machine-guns.

THE STRATEGIC DEFENCE INITIATIVE

THE STRATEGIC Defence Initiative (SDI) — or Star Wars to the sceptics — was primarily intended as a defensive system to protect the USA from attack by strategic nuclear missiles (see Strategic missiles, page 184). Promoted in the early 1980s by President Reagan, it had, in fact, really begun long before that. As early as 1954 the US Air Force began the Wizard project for an anti-missile missile intended to intercept incoming ballistic rockets at a 1,000 mile distance. Although Wizard never reached the hardware stage, much of its control equipment was adapted for the Nike air-defence system (see Air-defence missiles, page 190). Nike Zeus was an air-defence system which, it was hoped, could double as an anti-ICBM system as well, but by the early 1960s it was obvious that this would not work. The speed and trajectory of missiles was now so varied that huge fast-reacting radars and computers would be needed to control a strategic-defence system. Moreover, only a fast-accelerating missile would be able to react quickly enough to destroy any enemy nuclear missile before it was within lethal distance of friendly territory.

As a result of this reasoning, Nike-X was developed between 1965 and 1970, incorporating the necessary radars and the Sprint exo-atmospheric missile. Sprint could reach a target 25 miles away in a few seconds, destroying it with a low-yield nuclear warhead. But no sooner was this system working than the first SALT (Strategic Arms Limitation Talks) agreement between the USA and the USSR limited the USA to two such installations. The first of these, guarding the Minuteman ICBM silos in North Dakota, was declared operational on 1 October, 1975, but on the following day the US Congress ordered the system to be de-activated — and that brought an end to it.

The Soviets developed Galosh by the early 1970s and installed this system around Moscow. It was very similar to the US Sprint system, though the radar control equipment was more massive. Under the SALT treaty the Soviets were allowed more installations than the Americans and they appear to have continued developing and building them.

The drawback to these systems was the enormous cost, both in developing the highly specialized radars and computers, and in installing and maintaining the systems. It was this, as much as anything else, that closed the Sprint system down. But in the 1980s the US took the bull by the horns and resolved to develop an entirely new defensive system in space. Very likely, this was a deliberate ploy by the USA, who reasoned that they could afford to do it while the USSR could not and would bankrupt themselves in the attempt. Subsequent political developments suggest that there may have been some truth in this reasoning.

The US effort began with the Homing Overlay Experiment in 1983. This used a combination of spacecraft-, aircraft-, and ground-based sensors to determine the nature and trajectory of the approaching missile; computers to calculate the interception data; and a combination of missiles to effect destruction of the threat. Suggested missiles included an exo-atmospheric conventional warhead weapon; an updated Spartan missile with a thermonuclear warhead; the endo-atmospheric Sentry missile

Launching ASAT

A test launch of the ASAT Anti-Satellite Missile from an F-15 "Eagle" aircraft in September 1985. ASAT is 5.18 metres long and consists of an SRAM missile first-stage motor, a second-stage motor from a "Scout" space rocket, and a miniature homing vehicle warhead. In order to achieve escape velocity and break out of the earth's atmosphere the ASAT is carried to a high altitude and launched at high speed, giving it considerable velocity even before the rockets are fired and also the advantages of a much thinner atmosphere.

with conventional warhead; and, the SRHit missile with conventional warhead. Having three levels of sensor and four levels of missile was designed to ensure sufficient overlap in all areas to prevent any threat slipping through the net.

One of the sensor platforms was, of course, a satellite; it was known that the Soviets were working on a similar satellite-based system, and so the next task for the Americans was to develop an anti-satellite capability. The Soviets were believed to have had a primitive anti-satellite weapon operational by the early 1970s. From 1975 or earlier, the Americans worked on their own anti-satellite weapon ASAT. The current device is a three-stage missile that can be carried by an F-15 fighter aircraft to high altitude and from there launched into space.

DIRECTED-ENERGY WEAPONS

The next component of SDI development was in the field of directed-energy weapons — those using laser beams and charged-particle beams as kinetic energy devices. To make a destructive laser beam with a worthwhile range takes an enormous amount of power, so nuclear power would be required. This meant placing the power source as well as the weapon in space. Lasers capable of shooting

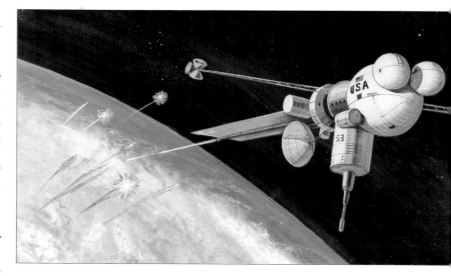

Homing overlay experiment
An artist's concept of the HOE missile performing its test flight of September 1984.

The railgun concept
The railgun in space is the artilleryman's dream: there is no gravity and no atmosphere to distort the trajectory, so the

projectile will fly in a straight line without losing velocity.

down light aircraft under controlled trial conditions have been developed, but there is a great deal of difference between this and destroying a high-speed missile at a range of several thousand miles. There is a lot of work still to do before directed-energy weapons will be a practical proposition.

Positioning weapons in zero-gravity space has the advantage that they can be large and cumbersome without the problems of weight and distortion that would affect such structures in the earth's gravity. This has led to suggestions for enormous electromagnetic guns capable of launching projectiles by use of magnetic fields or pulses. The attraction of such weapons is that in space these projectiles could attain very high velocities and their trajectory would be a straight line. This would considerably reduce problems of aiming over an immense distance. Again, these devices need huge amounts of power, which only a nuclear supply in space could provide.

Ideas such as these are not new. They were first put forward at the turn of the century and have been revived periodically as electrical engineering has improved. However, the power demand has always ensured that any working weapons were little more than laboratory experiments. One such "electric gun", proposed as an air-defence weapon by Germany in 1944, sounded so promising that Britain and the USA continued the investigation after the war. It ended when it was discovered that to put a 40-mm projectile into the air with a reasonable chance of success would demand a power station capable of supplying a small city.

At present, work on SDI is proceeding, but the urgency appears to have declined in proportion to the disintegration of the USSR. But with the former Soviet Union now a Confederation of Independent States, some of them unstable, and the remains of the Soviet nuclear arsenal no longer under central control, any decision to scrap research into anti-missile defence might be premature.

INDEX

Reference numbers in *italics* indicate the inclusion of captions and illustrations.

FURTHER READING

The Rocket: D. Baker, London, 1978
The Automated Battlefield: F. Barnaby, Oxford, 1987
Arms and Armour: Howard L. Blackmore, London, 1965
Hunting Weapons: Howard L. Blackmore, London, 1971
European and American Arms, 1100-1850: Claude Blair, London, 1962
European Armour: Claude Blair, London, 1972
Tanks of the World: P. Chamberlain and G. Ellis, London, 1972
The Nuclear War File: C. Chant and I.V. Hogg, London, 1983
Arms & Equipment of the Civil War: Jack Coggins, New York, 1962
European Armour in the Tower of London: Arthur Duffy, London, 1968
European Swords & Daggers: Arthur Duffy, London, 1974
Submarine Design and Development: N. Friedman, London, 1984
Carrier Power: N. Friedman, London, 1981
Romische Paraderustungen: J. Garbsch, Munich, 1978
Biological and Toxic Weapons Today: E. Geissier, Oxford, 1986
The Devil's Device: E. Gray, London, 1975
The Hidden Menace: M. Griffiths, London, 1981
Elements of Ordnance: T.J. Hayes, London, 1938
Military Small Arms of the 20th Century: I.V. Hogg and J. Weeks, London, 1992
Artillery 2000: I.V. Hogg, London, 1990
A History of Artillery: I.V. Hogg, London, 1974
Weapons and Tactics of the Soviet Army: D. Isby, London, 1981
Soviet Military Strategy in Space: L.N. Johnson, London, 1987
Tank Warfare: K. Macksey, London, 1971
Greek and Roman Artillery: E.W. Marsden, Oxford, 1969
North American Bows, Arrows & Quivers: Otis Mason, New York, 1972
The Archaeology of Weapons: R. Ewart Oakeshott, London, 1960
The Sword in the Age of Chivalry: R. Ewart Oakeshott, London, 1964
The Crossbow: Sir R. Payne-Gallway, Rep. London, 1958
Daggers & Fighting Knives of the Western World: Harold L. Peterson, London, 1968
Chemicals in War: A.M. Prentiss, London, 1937
Instruments of Darkness: Alfred Price, London, 1977
The Indian Sword: Philip Rawson, London, 1968
Italian Armour: H. Russell Robinson, London, 1959
Oriental Armour: H. Russell Robinson, London, 1967
The Armour of Imperial Rome: H. Russell Robinson, London, 1976
Chemical and Biological Warfare: S. Rose. London, 1968
Weapon Technology: Rust & Brassey, London, 1978
Les Armes Blanches Modernes: Christian Henry Tavard, Paris, 1971
The Roman Soldier: G.R. Watson, London, 1969
The Roman Army: G. Webster, London, 1958
Edged Weapons: F. Wilkinson, London, 1970
Soviet Air Defence Missiles: S. Zaloga, London, 1989

CREDITS

All photographs from the author's collection except for the following:

Abbreviations: Newark — Peter Newark's Western Americana;
Mars — Military Archive and Research Services;
Salamander — Salamander Books Ltd;
TRH — TRH Pictures;

a — above; **b** — below; **c** — centre; **l** — left; **r** — right

8 Salamander	**41 (a)** Bridgeman Art
8-9 Mars	Library
9 ETarchive	**41 (b)** ETarchive
10 (a) ETarchive	**42** ETarchive
10 (bl) Newark	**42 (inset)** Octopus Books
10 (br) ETarchive	Picture Library
11 (l) ETarchive	**43** ETarchive
11 (r) Newark	**44** ETarchive
12 ETarchive	**45** Mansell Collection
13 Wallace Collection	**46 (l)** Newark
14 ETarchive	**47** Salamander
16 Christies	**48 (a)** Octopus Books
17 Christies	Picture Library
18 York Archeological	**48 (b)** Newark
Trust	**49** Octopus Books
19 (a) Dave Longley	Picture Library
19 (b) The British Museum	**50 (b)** Bridgeman Art
20 ETarchive	Library
21 (a) Newark	**51** ETarchive
21 (b) ETarchive	**52** C M Dixon
22 (l) ETarchive	**54 (l)** Mars
22 (r) Newark	**54 (r)** ETarchive
23 ETarchive	**55 (r)** Octopus Books
24 ETarchive	Picture Library
25 Newark	**56** Newark
26 (a) ETarchive	**57** Mars
26 (b) Newark	**58 (l)** Mars
27 Giravdon	**58 (r)** ETarchive
27 (b) C M Dixon	**59 (b)** Octopus Books
27 (r) Newark	Picture Library
28 ETarchive	**60 (b)** Newark
29 ETarchive	**61** Newark
30 ETarchive	**62 (a)** ETarchive
31 (bl) ETarchive	**62 (b)** Newark
32 ETarchive	**63** Newark
33 Newark	**67 (r)** ETarchive
34 (l) Wallace Collection	**68** National Army
34 (c) ETarchive	Museum
34 (r) Wallace Collection	**70 (c)** Mary Evans Picture
35 (l) Wallace	Library
35 (r) Quarto	**72 (l)** Newark
36 ETarchive	**73** Christies
37 (a) ETarchive	**74** HMS Warrior
38 (l) ETarchive	**74 (inset)** Newark
38 (r) Newark	**76** Octopus Books
39 (l) Newark	Picture Library
40 ETarchive	**77** Newark

78 ETarchive	**158-9** Salamander
79 Mars	**162 (l)** Salamander
80 Mars	**162 (r)** Newark
84 Newark	**163** Newark
85 (a) Salamander	**168 (a)** ETarchive
85 (b) Newark	**169 (r)** Salamander
87 Octopus Books	**174 (b)** Mars
Picture Library	**175** Mars
89 Newark	**176 (a)** Salamander
90-1 Octopus Books	**176 (b)** Mars
Picture Library	**177 (a)** Newark
91 Newark	**177 (b)** ETarchive
93 (bl) Newark	**178** Mars
94 TRH	**178 (inset)** Salamander
94-5 HMS Warrior	**179** Salamander
96 (b) ETarchive	**180 (r)** Mars
106 ETarchive	**182** Salamander
107 National Army	**184 (a)** Salamander
Museum	**185** Salamander
109 Salamander	**189-192** Salamander
111 Mars	**195** Salamander
112-3 Salamander	**196 (l)** Salamander
113 Newark	**198 (r)** Salamander
114 Newark	**202** Salamander
115 Newark	**202-3 (l)** Mars
117 Newark	**203** Salamander
118 TRH	**206 (r)** TRH
119 (b) TRH	**207 (b)** Salamander
120 Salamander	**210 (r)** Salamander
125 (b) Salamander	**212 (a)** TRH
128 Mars	**214-5** Salamander
131 Salamander	
132-3 ETarchive	
133 (r) Salamander	
134 Salamander	
135 (l) ETarchive	
135 (r) Salamander	
138 ETarchive	
139 ETarchive	
141 (l) Salamander	
146-9 ETarchive	
150-1 Salamander	
152 Salamander	
153 ETarchive	
154 (r) Salamander	
155 ETarchive	
158 Salamander	